Outposts of Empire
Korea, Vietnam, and the Origins of the Cold War in Asia,
1949–1954

Following World War II the United States, determined to prevent an extension of the influence of the Soviet Union and Communist China, took the lead in organizing the defence of Western interests in Asia. Steven Lee explores the foreign policy objectives of the United States, Canada, and Great Britain and examines the role that economic and military aid played in their attempts to establish pro-Western, anticommunist governments on the periphery of communist East Asia.

Drawing on a wide range of recently declassified documents, Lee outlines the regional and international context of American diplomatic history in Korea and Vietnam and analyses the relationship between containment, the bipolar international system, and European and American concepts of empire at the beginning of the era of decolonization. He argues that although policy makers in Canada and the United Kingdom adopted a more defensive containment policy towards Communist China than the United States did, they generally supported American attempts to promote pro-Western élites in Korea and Vietnam.

This is an important book for anyone interested in American foreign policy, Anglo-American relations, Asia and the international system, and Canadian foreign policy.

STEVEN HUGH LEE is assistant professor of history, University of British Columbia.

Outposts of Empire

Korea, Vietnam, and the Origins of the Cold War in Asia, 1949–1954

STEVEN HUGH LEE

McGill-Queen's University Press
Montreal & Kingston • London • Buffalo

© McGill-Queen's University Press 1995
ISBN 0-7735-1326-4 (cloth)

Legal deposit fourth quarter 1995
Bibliothèque nationale du Québec

Printed in Canada on acid-free paper

Published simultaneously in the European Union by
Liverpool University Press.

This book has been published with the help of a grant from the Social
Science Federation of Canada, using funds provided by the Social Sciences
and Humanities Research Council of Canada.

McGill-Queen's University Press is grateful to the Canada Council for
support of its publishing programs.

Canadian Cataloguing in Publication Data

Lee, Steven Hugh, 1962–
    Outposts of empire: Korea, Vietnam and the origins of the Cold War
in Asia, 1949–1954
    Includes bibliographical references and index
    ISBN 0-7735-1326-4
    1. United States – Foreign relations – Asia. 2. Asia – Foreign relations –
United States. 3. Canada – Foreign relations – Asia. 4. Asia – Foreign
relations – Canada. 5. Great Britain – Foreign relations – Asia.
6. Asia – Foreign relations – Great Britain. 7. Cold War. I. Title.
    DS35.2L44 1995   327.7305'09645   C95-900363-0

This book was typeset by Typo Litho Composition Inc.
in 10/12 Baskerville.

For my parents

Contents

Tables

Abbreviations

ANZUS Australia, New Zealand, and the United States
CRO Commonwealth Relations Office
DEA Department of External Affairs
DBPO *Documents on British Policy Overseas*
ECA Economic Cooperation Administration
EDC European Defence Community
ESC Economic Stabilization Committee
FEOC Far Eastern Official Committee
FRUS *Foreign Relations of the United States*
JCS Joint Chiefs of Staff
KMAG Korean Military Advisory Group
MAAG Military Assistance and Advisory Group
NA National Archives (U.S.)
NAC National Archives of Canada
NSC National Security Council
PRC People's Republic of China
PRO Public Record Office
PUSC Permanent Under-Secretary's Committee
ROK Republic of Korea
SSEA Secretary of State for External Affairs
UNC United Nations Command

Acknowledgments

This work could not have been completed without the assistance, scholarship, and generosity of many people. In Montreal, I would like to thank Professor Carman Miller of McGill University for his continued support. His encouraging words and wisdom have been greatly appreciated. At Oxford, Dr Anita Inder Singh provided invaluable tutorials and advice. Professor Robert O'Neill gave generously of his time and shared his broad expertise on Asia's cold wars. Professor Stockwin and his seminar classes on East Asia in the International System were also a very important source of inspiration. Dr Rosemary Foot made useful comments, and Professor Geoffrey Warner looked at my ideas about informal empire with a critical eye. At the Department of External Affairs, I have relied on the expertise and generosity of Dr Hector Mackenzie. I would also like to express my appreciation to Dr John Hilliker and Professors David Marr, Tom Naylor, Al Riggs, and John Herd Thompson. My editor at McGill-Queen's, Mr Peter Blaney, has given intelligent advice and criticism, and Carlotta Lemieux copyedited the manuscript with a delicate, judicious, and meticulous eye. Many thanks also go to Joan McGilvray. Most of all, Dr Avi Shlaim, my supervisor at Oxford, provided sage advice, pointed out omissions, and was most generous with his time. His personal kindness made it a pleasure to work with him. He was a model supervisor.

Financial support from British and Canadian sources has been instrumental to this project. My work has benefited from an Overseas Research Scholarship, a St Peter's College Graduate Award, a scholarship from the administrators of the Beit Fund, and an Arnold, Bryce, and

Read travel grant to Washington. The University of British Columbia provided a UBC New Faculty grant for a research trip to the Truman and Eisenhower presidential libraries. The Social Sciences and Humanities Research Council supported the publication of this work through its Grants to Scholarly Publications Program.

In Ottawa, I would especially like to thank the family of Mr Ken Kim for their hospitality and kindness while I worked in the National Archives of Canada. Mr and Mrs Guy Marcoux were also very generous in offering a warm room in the cold Canadian winter. Douglas Lee and his family in Virginia provided comfortable lodgings and family hospitality during a second trip to Washington in 1992. Jamie, Paul, Rhonda, Danielle, Barbara, Maurice, Gillian, Arif, Stuart, Maristela, Hiro, Sit, Steve, Sarah, Myoung-Soon, and Nik were all supportive. I would like to thank my two anonymous readers as well as Stephen Keck, Josephine Chan, and Joanne Poon for their comments on the manuscript. At the National Archives of Canada, Janet Murray, "the two Gilles," Paulette Dozois, Lori Baker, and all the photocopy staff worked hard and efficiently. In Independence and Abilene, Randy Sowell, David Haight, and the staff of the Truman and Eisenhower libraries were most helpful. Thanks also go to the staff of the National Archives, Rhodes House Library, and the Public Record Office. To my Korean language professors, Mrs Hizung Kim-Matsuura and In-Sun Lee, I would also like to express my appreciation. This work owes more than can be expressed to my parents. Their love, support, and encouragement sustained me and was my greatest source of inspiration. Without their love this work could not have been attempted.

Outposts of Empire

1 Introduction: The New Empire

The American and allied victory in the Pacific War did not bring peace to Asia. The return of European powers to Southeast Asia ignited colonial anticommunist wars in Vietnam and Malaya. In China the Nationalists and Communists fought each other in civil war. In the northeast, Japanese colonial rule in Korea was replaced by occupation forces from the United States and the Soviet Union, and by 1950 the two Korean political systems were at war with each other.

In spite of the continuity in conflict, the context of Great Power diplomacy in Asia was in the process of being radically altered. The war had erased Japan as a power of regional import, and both Britain and France were too preoccupied with the European peace settlement and with economic difficulties at home to act as stabilizing powers against the regional communist threat. Determined to prevent an extension of the influence of the Soviet Union and Communist China, the United States began to take the lead in organizing the defence of the West in Asia, and in the two areas most directly threatened by communist movements after 1949 – South Korea and Vietnam – it provided military and economic aid to contain the danger. For the first time in its history, the United States was the preponderant Western power in the Far East.

A central theme of this work is how American diplomats wielded their newly acquired power and status in the half-decade following the rise to power of the Chinese Communist Party. While most of the historiography on American-East Asian relations has concentrated on the bilateral aspects of U.S. diplomacy at the expense of more synthetic methodologies, the regional and comparative framework adopted in this study underlines both the continuities and the distinctiveness about American foreign policy in Asia. An examination of the policies of America's allies, especially its two closest Atlantic partners, Britain and Canada, contributes to recent trends in historiography moving away from an American–centric view of the Cold War. The object is to enhance our knowledge of the regional and international context of American diplomatic history in the postwar era and to broaden our understanding of how other Western states responded to the Cold War in Asia.

In the last decade, historians John Lewis Gaddis and Geir Lundestad have made significant contributions to the study of the American "empire."[1] Both historians agree that this empire was global in scope but that it was based on defensive strategic motives. Gaddis pointed out that "this was expansion with limitations; it was an empire operated, at least initially, along defensive lines, and with some sense of restraint." The major theme to emerge from their work is the concept of "empire by invitation." According to this theory, the American empire was an informal one in the sense that Americans found themselves being invited by other states that recognized the communist threat. "It seems beyond argument," writes Gaddis, "that there was an American empire, and that a surprising number of governments around the world wanted to be associated with it, given the alternative."[2] Empire by invitation thus arose out of the global threat of the Cold War to democratically oriented governments.

The idea of empire by invitation is a valuable one, but the formulation is centred on the developed First World. As Lundestad admits, "the invitational aspect was nowhere as consistent as in Western Europe."[3] The relationship between empire and containment in the Third World is only tangentially dealt with, and the theory works less well in Third World areas where political structures were less developed or where they were subservient to colonial control. The concept needs to be recast when speaking of American policies towards the periphery of continental East Asia in the early postwar era. Although "empire by invitation" was an important aspect of American diplomacy towards the region, the American "empire" in Korea and Vietnam was neither as monolithic nor as passive as the Gaddis and Lundestad formulation suggests.

The concept of informal empire is not new. It has been used by historians for several decades.[4] What is novel is its application to the postwar world of international diplomacy. Lundestad makes the linkage between the British and American empires, arguing that after the Second World War the United States "was so strong that it could exert its influence more indirectly. Here the parallel to British informal rule in the 1840s–70s is clear."[5] Although the bipolar nature of international relations after 1945 meant that Gallagher and Robinson's framework for British imperialism in the nineteenth century cannot be applied rigidly to the postwar context, America's attempts to create informal empire in East Asia retained some similarity with Robinson and Gallagher's concept insofar as American diplomacy attempted to influence the political and economic orientation of Korea and Vietnam through informal mechanisms rather than through formal colonial control. Economic factors fuelled America's new empire but the immediate objectives were political. Informal empire in Korea and Vietnam at the height of the Cold War was characterized by attempts to foster indigenous, pro-Western, anticommunist allies through the provision of political advice, economic support, and military aid.

A second definitional distinction should be made between the concepts of hegemony and empire. The Lundestad and Gaddis definition of empire in some ways resembles that of hegemony. However, a more rigorous definition of informal empire would deal with the differences between influencing a nation's external relations and influencing both its foreign and domestic policies.[6] Between 1945 and 1954 the United States played the predominant role in directing and influencing the internal economic and political orientation of South Korea. In Vietnam, the processes whereby the United States attempted to influence the domestic programs were more complex because of the presence of French colonialism, but the origins of America's empire in Vietnam in the 1960s can be traced to U.S. support for the indigenous nationalist grouping under Bao Dai.

CONTAINMENT AND COLLABORATION IN THE COLD WAR

An examination of American policy on the East Asian periphery forces a reconsideration of the Gaddis-Lundestad thesis in two important ways. The first, as we have seen, is how the concept of informal empire can be understood with respect to the Third World, in particular continental East Asia. The second issue that this work will address is how other Western nations reacted to American containment policies in a region in which they had relatively peripheral interest.

Western countries formed a comparatively united and cohesive block against the Soviet threat. NATO was the key structure of the Western alliance, and the bipolar international system was the major distinguishing feature of the Cold War. What tended to solidify the NATO countries was a perceived need to prevent the further spread of communist movements. The danger of communism undermining the sources of allied economic and political power was the common denominator of North Atlantic diplomacy in this period. Furthermore, while the bipolar nature of the system was new, the realities of power in the postwar world often corresponded to older patterns of international behaviour. The United States designed strategies within a historical context in which traditional Great Powers such as France and Britain had established spheres of influence in Third World areas. In view of limited American resources, strategic necessities, and the communist threat, the United States developed a policy of relying on British and French power to maintain Western spheres of influence in the Third World. This was the case, for example, in Southeast Asia.

Yet the international system after 1945 brought out contradictory impulses in American diplomacy. The polarized international system held dangers for a long-term reliance on the influence of the older Great Powers. In developing areas, American policymakers wanted to reinforce the political position of moderate nationalists, for they feared that disillusioned colonial nationalists would turn to "communism" as a solution to their ills. This would upset the West's favourable balance of power *vis-à-vis* the Soviet empire and might possibly overturn it. These considerations fuelled traditional American suspicions about formal empire. In the Cold War context, colonialism was recognized as a potentially dangerous and retrograde system of government. Thus, the United States' short-term support of its Western allies in developing areas was combined with goals for the long-term development of moderate and pro-Western indigenous nationalists. These distinctions between short- and long-term objectives must be held in mind in evaluating U.S. diplomacy towards the Third World.

These objectives were presented in formal terms to a meeting of the National Security Council on 30 December 1948. According to the CIA "Review of the World Situation," it appeared "inevitable that the authority of European colonial powers" would "undergo further decline." Although the "rate of disintegration" between the Middle East and Southeast Asia would vary, the long-term result would be the emergence of "a belt of comparatively powerless states." This would invite the Soviet Union to "champion the ambitions of indigenous peoples." The origins of the domino theory lay in the perceived weakness of traditional European formal rule and informal influence. The most satisfactory solution would be for the Europeans to work out a "new relationship with their colonial and semi-colonial peoples more

quickly than the USSR could exploit the breakdown of previous authority." The memo foreshadowed the broad outlines of American policy
in Vietnam between 1949 and 1954. Ideally, formal colonial rule
would be replaced by improved relations between moderate nationalists and the French. However, the strength of the communist movement and the reluctance of France to undertake colonial reform
undermined this possibility, and by 1954 the United States was posed
to replace France as the new informal imperial power in the region.
This process had been envisaged in the 1948 memo. If the Europeans
failed to engage the moderate nationalists, the memo stated, the only
alternative would be "a positive U.S. effort to replace the authority of
the Western colonial powers with U.S. influence and thus to fill the developing power vacuum."[7]

Although the United States and its allies agreed on the broad outlines of containment strategy, a comparative analysis of Western states'
diplomacy demonstrates that the West cannot be treated as a monolith; historians should be sensitive to the regional priorities of America's allies and to the subtle competition for spheres of influence that
often underlined their diplomacy towards the Third World. Britain
and Canada emphasized the centrality of preserving Western Europe
against the Soviet menace, and both nations adopted a more defensive
containment posture *vis-à-vis* East Asia than the United States did.
France, though generally welcoming of American aid, viewed American diplomacy towards Vietnam as a potential threat to the integrity of
its overseas empire.[8]

The United States recognized the imperatives of working with the
French and British to defeat communism in Asia, but the heart of its
containment policy for the East Asian periphery was to foster indigenous proxy governments capable of holding back the borders of the
regional communist threat. The United States in the immediate postwar era did not act as a traditional imperial power. On the other hand,
the major impetus for American involvement in Vietnam and Korea
was not an "invitation." To counter the Soviet empire, U.S. officials created an informal system of their own; American anticommunist strategies were tailored to mirror those of its enemy. The ultimate goal was
the build-up of indigenous military forces and the creation of viable
political systems that would be capable of running economies independent of long-term American aid. The economic imperative of scarcity
thus shaped informal empire, for although the United States was para-
mount within the West, it did not possess enough power to counter the
communist threat unilaterally on an international scale. Ultimately,
American strategy was designed to cause a reduction in the commu-

nists' power base, not only in Asia but at the core of the communist empire – the Soviet Union. To this extent, informal empire became an integral part of America's global strategy of containment.

It is significant, in exploring the historical roots of informal empire in Asia, that the historiography on American empire in Asia is dominated by U.S.-Philippine relations. The United States' experience in the Philippines provided a crucial starting point for the evolution of its political strategies in Asia after the Second World War, and there are significant parallels between American policies towards the Philippines and those pursued towards Korea and Vietnam. H.W. Brands has argued that the "imperatives of power that shaped American treatment of the Philippines were, mutandis mutandis, the same imperatives that conditioned American responses to the revolutionary developments of the twentieth century throughout Asia and the world."[9] However, the American "empire" in Korea and Vietnam after 1945 was not simply a product of U.S. experience in the Philippines; the Cold War provided the international context and the urgency for the perceived need to expand American power globally and to create and nurture pro-Western governments in areas considered important for reasons of prestige and global strategy.

THE UNITED STATES AND CONTAINMENT IN EAST ASIA

The guiding principle of American containment strategies on the Chinese periphery after 1949 was the perceived need to undermine the bases of Soviet power. The thread that linked American policies towards Europe and Asia was the idea of competition for power with the Soviet Union. It is within this framework of global rivalry with the Soviet Union that American containment policies for East Asia in the period 1949–54 must be placed.

To understand the objectives of the United States towards East Asia in the five-year period following the rise to power of the Chinese communists, it is important briefly to outline the emergence of the containment doctrine in the years leading up to 1949. In *Strategies of Containment*, John Lewis Gaddis describes the piecemeal nature of America's attempts to block Soviet diplomatic initiatives in the Middle East, Germany, and Northeast Asia in the 1945–47 period. He portrays American policy towards the Soviet Union in these years as one of "patience and firmness."[10]

An important turning point in America's strategy to prevent the extension of Soviet influence was the decision taken in the spring of 1947 to underwrite Britain's commitments in Greece and Turkey. Gaddis argues that historians have tended to exaggerate the extent to which the United States globalized its containment doctrine as a result of this decision by the Truman administration. Compared with America's undertakings for international security that emerged in light of the National Security Council policy paper NSC 68 and the Korean War, this is certainly true. American strategy in 1947 was geared towards consolidating anti-Soviet governments in grey areas that were threatened by internal communist movements. The Marshall Plan was designed in part to combat the threat of communism in Western Europe, particularly in France and Italy. Less comprehensive strategies were also emerging for Greece and Turkey, and for Korea south of the 38th parallel. Containment had not yet developed into a confrontation based on military build-up and limited war with Soviet "satellites."

Nevertheless, the Truman Doctrine laid down a framework for further action against what was coming to be viewed as the Soviet Union's desire for global supremacy. As one expert on Soviet affairs in the State Department, Charles Bohlen, wrote, there were now "two worlds instead of one."[11] The emerging perception of a dual world order with only one possible victor had tremendous implications for American foreign policy.

It was in the context of a perceived need to counter the increasing global threat of the Soviet empire that the author of containment, George Kennan, developed his ideas. Kennan argued that there were five basic power bases in the world. These were the United States, Great Britain, the Soviet Union, the Rhine Valley, and Japan. Only one area was under Soviet control. According to Kennan, the "main task of containment" was to ensure that "none of the remaining ones fell under such control." The Soviet Union was seen as a rival "core" whose power needed to be separated from other potential core states. Thinking in terms of a global balance of power, Kennan noted, "Any world balance of power means first and foremost a balance on the Eurasian land mass. That balance is unthinkable as long as Germany and Japan remain power vacuums."[12]

The Marshall Plan was designed to fill these gaps and to reconstruct the world economy in the context of reduced trade barriers and greater access to raw resources, making it easier for the world to purchase American goods and lowering American costs of production. It was envisaged that the plan would create three regional integrated economies: the United States (in the centre), Western Europe, and Japan. Michael Schaller has remarked: "The creation of these integrated regional economies, with access to low-cost raw materials would alleviate demands for American aid and reduce the strain of dollar imports on Europe and Japan. It would also forge a matrix of anti-communist states linked to America."[13] It is within these broader economic and political constraints that the Cold War in Asia must be explored.

Kennan's thinking on Japan helped lay the groundwork for America's containment policies on Japan, but on China his ideas were less influential. The limits to using Kennan's conception of holding back Soviet expansionism in Asia as a means of explaining American actions in the region after 1948 stem from his conception of the role of Communist China in postwar Asia. Because China did not possess much of an industrial base, and because he viewed any possibility of Sino-Soviet cooperation with scepticism, Kennan called for American disengagement from continental intrigues. It was not that he accepted the Communist regime in Peking;[14] in 1948 he wrote about his "wish to see the [Chinese] Communists defeated and replaced." However, America was without sufficient influence to affect the situation. Although American secretaries of state in the postwar era realized, as did Kennan, that any attempt to oust the Chinese Communists with military force would overextend American resources for correspondingly little gain, the United States adopted a more belligerent containment policy towards continental East Asia than Kennan had recommended. President Truman's views on Communist China tended to be more instinctually aggressive than Dean Acheson's, and after China's intervention in the Korean War such ideas moved closer to the forefront of U.S. policy. Officials such as John Foster Dulles, who believed that a China aligned with the Soviet Union represented a threat to the global balance of power, took the lead in formulating a more provocative containment policy towards the People's Republic of China.[15]

INFORMAL EMPIRE AND CONTAINMENT BY PROXY ON THE ASIAN PERIPHERY

The combined power potential of China and the Soviet Union was a critical factor in the formulation of U.S. policy. America's determination to foster pro-Western governments on China's East Asian perimeter was a product of its attempts to contain the global extension of Sino-Soviet influence. It was not only how much Japan meant to the West in economic terms but also what Communist China meant to the accretion of Soviet might. The National Security Council paper NSC 48/1, dated 23 December 1949, which analysed "The Position of the United States with Respect to Asia," argued that "Communist domination of China is significant to the USSR because it enhances USSR capabilities for obtaining Soviet objectives in Asia."[16] America's nation-building strategies for Korea and Vietnam emerged as part of a larger framework designed to preserve Western influence in Asia and limit the potential power of the Soviet core. Once local governing elites affiliated themselves with anticommunist ideals, their armies could act as proxy power bases for these broader American containment goals. As NSC 48/1 noted, "To the degree that Asian indigenous forces develop opposition to the expansion of USSR influence, they would assist the U.S. in containing Soviet control and influence in the area, possibly reducing the drain on the United States economy. The indigenous forces of Asia, including manpower reserves, would also be a valuable asset, if available for ... the United States in the event of a war."[17] This reliance on the development of indigenous power is a fundamental feature of America's informal empire and one that distinguishes it from previous Japanese and European imperialism in Asia.

The NSC 48 series reflected the American distaste for formal empire. Sentences in NSC 48/1 refer to the dangers of charges of American imperialism, Asian suspicions of colonialism, and the need to develop "truly independent" states in Asia.[18] John Lewis Gaddis takes up this last theme, arguing that the "ultimate objective" of Kennan's containment strategy was to "build an international order made up of independent centres of power, in which nations subject to Soviet pressure would have both the means and the will to resist it themselves."[19] Kennan's ideas about containment, however, as Gaddis himself notes, were somewhat distorted in their implementation in the post-1947 period. The goal of American policy was to create interdependent centres of power, not independent ones. In Asia this included South Korea and, later, Vietnam.

For American officials, the corollary of "truly independent" was anticommunist and pro-Western. It was in the process of forging this interdependent relationship between East and West to contain the Soviets that the United States constructed an informal empire on China's periphery. Like the European and Japanese empires in Asia before it, the American empire was neither static nor monolithic. But whereas formal colonialism had sought the centralization of power for the benefit of the metropole, the United States concept of "empire" was a decentralized one, based on the development of relatively independent local actors on the communist perimeter which were capable of holding back communist advances without direct American involvement or expenditure of resources. In this way, the theory underpinning the United States' empire differed significantly from the previous era of Great Power imperialism.

THE ORIGINS OF INFORMAL EMPIRE IN KOREA

For South Korea, the transition from being a formal Japanese colony to coming under the more flexible control of the United States took place in the immediate postwar years. Korea was not a formal participant in the war, yet it was the only nonbelligerent to undergo a military occupation. This anomaly is explained by Soviet-American competition in Northeast Asia following the end of formal hostilities. American occupation policies in South Korea in the immediate postwar years were designed to limit Soviet influence to the North and to secure an American sphere of influence in the South. In some ways it is misleading to describe the occupation as "informal empire." However, it was during these years that the transferral of power to indigenous pro-Western elites took place. Until the outbreak of the Korean War, the containment of Soviet-backed force in North Korea entailed the destruction of local communists in the South and the strengthening of indigenous moderate leaders hostile to Communism. As the leading American historian of the occupation has written, by late 1945 occupation policies had established "national" defence forces for the South, put former Korean collaborators into positions of power, and taken initial steps towards creating a separate government that would "merge selected exile nationalists (Syngman Rhee and Kim Ku, mainly) with the colonial bureaucracy."[20] After failing to come to an agreement with the Soviets on a policy for the unification of the two Koreas, in 1947 the United States took the Korean issue to the United Nations. Under U.N. auspices, elections were held in the South in May 1948 which brought Syngman Rhee and his conservative Korean Democratic Party to power.

The American occupation created the context for the emergence of a pro-Western South Korean government, but the task was complex. Syngman Rhee recognized the importance of working with the Americans in the bipolar world, but he also had his own strategies for unification. He was determined to do whatever it took to unify the peninsula, even if that meant criticizing U.S. policies. Furthermore, the political goals of the United States required both economic stability and military security, both of which were conspicuously absent for many years after the war. Between 1945 and 1948, many American officials were sceptical about the possibility of southern Korea sustaining itself economically. In early 1948, John Allison of the Division of Northeast Asian Affairs and J.E. Jacobs, the political adviser to the commanding general, John Hodge, expressed their concern about the ability of the Korean economy to move past what Jacobs described as the "ox cart" stage.[21] In December 1948 a CIA intelligence estimate reported that the South Korean government was reducing the effectiveness of American economic aid through its "short-sighted ineptness." It had adopted "oppressive and terroristic" security measures, and inefficiency in administration was "threatening to undermine the chances of building up a viable economy."[22] Nevertheless, officials were determined to make their proxy partners viable on U.S. terms. The American army estimated in 1948 that to help counter the communist force in the North and communist activists in the South, South Korea would require a Korean military force of about 100,000 men. According to Allison, "the Koreans would have to be assisted both in the training of such a force and in the acquisition of arms and ammunition, and ... the United States is the most logical source of such assistance." Korea was an important symbol of American prestige in the Cold War. Allison told the Canadian representative on the United Nations Temporary Commission on Korea, George Patterson, that strategically Korea was unimportant but the United States had to hold on: "If the United States were to allow Russia to make further encroachments in Korea, United States prestige in Japan and China and throughout the Far East, would be seriously undermined."[23]

The United States' strategy towards Korea was closely linked to its regional and global strategies designed to replenish Japan as a regional actor in Asia. Hopeful of restoring Korea's traditional role as a supplier of food to Japan and of alleviating the rising costs of U.S. food exports to Japan, the Americans provided the South Koreans with fertilizer to grow surplus rice for export to Japan. Dean Acheson became a strong proponent of this policy.[24] The strengthening of South Korea's economy would benefit Japan, would tie these two countries closer to the West, and would help prevent further Soviet penetration in the area. The difficulty was that Korean officials, particularly Syngman Rhee, were reluctant to cooperate fully with the State Department's strategy for integrating Korea and Japan into a Northeast Asian political economy tied to the United States.

The United States had successfully nurtured anticommunist South Koreans into positions of national power, but important differences existed between American and Korean containment strategies. American policy was much more global in outlook than Syngman Rhee's perceptions, and Rhee's fundamental objective as president of the newly constituted Republic of Korea (ROK) was the unification of the country. Although many U.S. State and Defense Department officials also advocated unification of the country, American global strategic interests prevented them from adopting a rollback containment strategy against the Democratic People's Republic of Korea. Whereas Rhee consistently advocated the use of force to cross the artificial boundary, the United States on the whole preferred to use diplomatic means to achieve its objectives.

The interplay between Korean and American officials is crucial to understanding the evolution of America's informal empire strategies in Korea. Despite numerous protests, Rhee realized that if his goal of unifying the country was to succeed, Korea would have to work within the context of official U.S. policy. In late 1948 Rhee dismissed his foreign minister, Chang T'aek-sang, after the U.S. ambassador, John Muccio, told Rhee that Chang's public advocacy of recovering "lost" territory from northern Korea contradicted America's peaceful reunification strategy.[25] In the 1949–54 period, the president often acted as a thorn in the side of the allies, threatening to use unilateral military force against the communists and to provoke global war. The decentralized nature of America's empire in Korea after 1945 allowed for some local manoeuvrability. The potential costs of informal empire were very high, but the United States maintained the balance of power *vis-à-vis* Rhee's regime. As we shall see, successive administrations were able to influence the economic development of the country, direct the military build-up of the ROK armed forces, and constrain Rhee from initiating unilateral military action to reunify the peninsula.

THE UNITED STATES AND VIETNAM

Prior to 1950, American policymakers did not assign much importance to Vietnam: the major regions of United States diplomacy lay in Western Europe, the Middle East, and, finally, Northeast Asia. Nevertheless, American concern with Europe required a consideration of European colonial objectives in Asia. U.S. officials realized that the two were closely related: Great Britain, Holland, and France depended on Southeast Asia as an important source of raw materials, foreign exchange, and investment. Southeast Asia was perceived as a region through which West European reconstruction could be accelerated and national prestige rebuilt.

Before the end of the war, U.S. officials recognized the tension in their policy goals for Western Europe and Southeast Asia. A paper prepared in the State Department in June 1945 noted: "A problem for the United States is to harmonize, as far as possible, its policies in regard to the two objectives: increased freedom for the Far East and the maintenance of unity of the leading United Nations."[26] Although the United States supported its European colonial allies, in order not to alienate the moderate Asians it initially pursued a cautious policy in Southeast Asia: transportation was not made easily accessible for the return of Dutch and French colonial power in Indonesia and Indochina, and the Americans demanded that the "USA" emblem be removed from lend-lease materials used in Southeast Asia.[27]

By late 1946 and 1947, American concern about communism and the possible consequences of repressive colonial policies caused the

United States to become more directly involved in events in Southeast Asia. Worried that the use of military force would bolster anti-Western sentiment, American diplomats began to put diplomatic pressure on the Dutch and French to work towards a political settlement with Asian moderate nationalists. Although officials had already rejected Ho Chi Minh as a political alternative to French rule in Vietnam, in late 1946 the State Department instructed the U.S. ambassador to France, Jefferson Caffery, to tell the French that their Indochina policy should avoid anything that "Vietnamese irreconcilables and extremists might be in [a] position [to] make capital of." The Americans hoped to avoid a long colonial war and pressed the French for greater concessions. Caffrey was to warn the French not to implement policies that might turn the Vietnamese "irrevocably against [the] West and toward ideologies and affiliations hostile" to democracy, since this could lead to "perpetual foment" in Indochina with consequences for all Southeast Asia.[28]

By mid-1948 the United States was more desperate for a diplomatic solution to problems in Indochina. French military operations since December 1946 against the Vietnamese communists had been inadequate because they had not been backed by a policy supporting the moderate nationalists. French colonialism clashed with the emerging concept of an informal and decentralized empire based on collaboration between local politicians and the West. A State Department policy memo of September 1948 pointed out that the conflict in this colonial area was "detrimental not only to our own long-term interests which require as a minimum a stable Southeast Asia but also detrimental to the interests of France, since the hatred engendered by continuing hostilities may render impossible peaceful collaboration and cooperation of the French and the Vietnamese peoples." Only the Soviet Union benefited from the anti-Western feeling engendered as a result of the hatred between the colonial French and the indigenous population. A solution had to be found that would "strike a balance between the aspirations of the peoples of Indochina and the interests of the French."[29] Underlying American thinking was a belief that a stable Southeast Asia required a change in the nature of the colonial policies pursued by the French.

Although the Americans found French political strategies frustrating, they recognized that a political settlement would not be forthcoming as long as the communists remained a powerful force in Vietnam. By 1948 it was becoming apparent that a negotiated settlement could occur only after the destruction of the Viet Minh. Although the United States was not yet directly involved in the war, one prerequisite for American direct involvement already existed: the association of Vietnamese communism with Soviet communism. In July 1948, Secretary of State George Marshall wrote to the American embassy in China that Ho Chi Minh was a communist, though he noted that there was no direct evidence of a Soviet-Vietnamese conspiracy: the communist goal of global domination was taken as an article of faith.[30]

In the period of Dean Acheson's secretaryship, and especially after the French ratified the Elysée Agreements recognizing Vietnam as an independent entity within the French Union, the United States relied more heavily on the French military presence as a means of holding back the communist advance. Acheson basically pursued a policy of supporting France's military commitment; as a corollary to this, he emphasized the need to develop the power of indigenous military forces. However, he understood the limits of pursuing a purely military strategy. As Acheson told the French ambassador in Washington, M. Bonnet, in July 1949, the basic problem was to "convert nationalist sentiment from pro-Communism to anti-Communism." This would require farsightedness and a willingness of France "to be liberal in the powers it gave [the Bao Dai] government."[31] Secretary Dulles was less willing than Acheson to support the French presence in Southeast Asia, and looked towards greater Asian participation in containing communism in the region. Dulles pursued a more "dynamic" containment policy in Asia than Acheson did, and his "United Action" strategy was designed to sustain a short-term French presence in the region, deter the Chinese, and defeat the Viet Minh.

In South Korea the Americans had successfully helped a pro-Western indigenous political elite come to power. In Vietnam the inability of the Americans and French to foster such a political base plagued American administrations until 1975. The subordination of a political solution to the use of military force reflected the failure of U.S. attempts to implement informal empire strategies in Vietnam.

CONTAINMENT AND COLONIALISM IN MALAYA AND HONG KONG

From an historiographical point of view, the role of economic factors in shaping Western containment policies towards Asia has tended to be neglected. However, Britain's economic difficulties after the Second World War had important implications for its containment strategy in Asia. The crucial postwar economic variable was the imbalance of American dollars in the international balance of payments and trade. In the first postwar decade, Great Britain's foreign economic policies were largely geared towards solving these dollar shortages.

The United Kingdom's major interests in the Far East in this period were its colonies in Malaya and Hong Kong. Malaya's rubber and tin exports to the United States made critical contributions to Great Britain's foreign exchange position and provided an important reserve of scarce dollars. As one Foreign Office paper put it, "Malaya is of the utmost importance strategically and economically to the United Kingdom and is the major dollar earner of the sterling area." Malaya was by far Britain's single largest earner of dollars, but in 1947–48 British power was threatened by Malayan communists, a group largely consisting of Chinese Malayans who had been active in the resistance against the Japanese during the Second World War. The communists were anticolonial and anti-British, and they felt politically threatened by the majority Malay ethnic group, who had collaborated with the British. The communists controlled large numbers of unionized workers, and they organized strikes that hurt the productive capacity of the Malayan economy. On 5 April 1948 the Labour government's colonial secretary, Arthur Creech Jones, noted, "There is at present a widespread feeling in Malaya ... that His Majesty's Government, by controlling the price of tin, has hitherto denied to the Malayan Governments and producers the benefits which should rightly be theirs." Although somewhat sympathetic to these complaints, he warned that "we have here the germ of a powerful and dangerous secession movement in Malaya, which is the bulwark of our whole position in S.E. Asia and indeed in the whole of the Far East."[32]

In response to the internal communist threat, the colonial authorities declared a state of emergency against the Malayan communists in June 1948. Soon afterwards, the Commonwealth Relations Office reported, "The plain fact is that Malaya is the only place where we are actively fighting against Communism, and moreover it is a territory for which we are responsible. Clearly we cannot afford to lose Malaya to Communism."[33]

The successes of the Chinese communists in the second half of 1948 resulted in increased concern about the implications of a communist-dominated China for both Malaya and Hong Kong. It was in the light of its colonial interests and economic difficulties that Britain defined its response to the Chinese revolution. In December 1948 the Foreign Office produced a position paper which remained British strategy for the remainder of the postwar era. The policy was described as "keeping a foot in the door." Entitled "The Situation in China," the paper argued that "provided there is not actual danger to life, we should endeavour to stay where we are, to have de facto relations with the Chinese communists insofar as these are unavoidable, and to investigate the possibilities of continued trade in China." More important than the prospects for trade with China was the need to maintain a hold on Hong Kong. At the end of May 1949, Prime Minister Clement Attlee told his cabinet that a failure to meet the threat to the security of Hong Kong "would damage very seriously British prestige throughout the Far East and South-East Asia. Moreover, the whole common front against communism in Siam, Burma and Malaya was likely to crumble unless the peoples of those countries were convinced of our determination and ability to resist this threat to Hong Kong."[34]

The foreign secretary himself considered Hong Kong as "the Berlin of the East." In September 1949, Esler Dening stated that the British cabinet had authorized Foreign Secretary Ernest Bevin to tell Acheson that Hong Kong was the "right wing bastion of the Southeast Asian front." If Hong Kong were to be lost to the communists "the whole front might go." The United Kingdom regarded its colony in the same way as it regarded Berlin, noted Dening, and it would "disregard the extent of military commitment necessary to hold Hong Kong."[35]

Several historians, notably D.C. Watt and Ritchie Ovendale, argue that for Britain the Asian Cold War began with the declaration of the emergency in Malaya.[36] However, Great Britain was not involved in a crusade against communism as an end in itself; rather, it defined its anticommunist goals in the light of specific threats to its power and prestige. The British never developed as grand a strategy for the containment of communism as the Americans did. Great Britain's containment strategies for Asia as they evolved after 1945 stemmed in large part from considerations regarding its colonial empire in Southeast Asia. It was important to contain the Chinese revolution within its borders and to hinder the export of its revolutionary ideals into Southeast Asia, where substantial Chinese communities existed. These Chinese were regarded by suspicious Foreign Office officials as "potential agents of their Government whatever its political complexion."[37] Communism threatened national interests, but in the postwar era there were limits of British power and therefore threats to that power as well. British anticommunism in this period was less global in scope than its American counterpart; consequently, to speak of "global containment" from the British perspective is somewhat misleading.

THE UNITED KINGDOM'S DEFENSIVE CONTAINMENT STRATEGY FOR ASIA

The emergence of Communist China exacerbated the problem of dealing with the internal threat to colonial control, but British policymakers maintained a defensive posture towards the new communist state. Britain's willingness to maintain ties with the new regime did not mean that it saw Chinese and Soviet communism as fundamentally opposed; Foreign Office officials did believe, however, that they could ex-

acerbate tensions between the two regimes. In July 1949 the Foreign
Office sent the United States a memo which pointed out that the Chinese communists were orthodox and that their pro-Soviet stance hurt
Western interests in Southeast Asia and China. Economic aid might
help convince the Chinese of "the natural incompatibility of Soviet imperialism with Chinese national interests."[38]

Britain's "defensive" containment strategy towards China and its determination to defend its colonies in Asia had important consequences
for its policy *vis-à-vis* the United States. As a general rule, it meant that
the United Kingdom was suspicious and wary about American initiatives that might anger or provoke the Chinese. This was particularly
the case when the Chinese intervened in the Korean War, during the
negotiations to end the Korean War, and during the negotiations at
the Geneva Conference on Indochina in 1954. Discussions with American officials regarding a possible naval blockade of the China coast
were looked on with dismay by British officials, who were worried
about the impact that such a blockade would have on trade between
Hong Kong and the mainland. These concerns were felt by all three
British foreign secretaries in the period.

India also had an important role in Britain's defensive containment
strategy in Asia. In 1949 the permanent under-secretary of the Foreign
Office, William Strang, became convinced that India could be a useful
ally in containing communist activities in East Asia generally and in
Southeast Asia specifically. Strang concluded that India could play a vital role in Britain's attempts to stabilize the region and persuade
Southeast Asians to align with the West against Soviet communism. In
his memoirs he recalled: "India, I was sure, had a primordial part to
play in peripheral politics, as a Great Asian Power, as a member of the
Commonwealth, as a country with whom the United Kingdom had
now an opportunity to develop relations on a new basis, and as a country with political, cultural and economic interests in South-East Asia,
which we should try to carry with us in the framing of policies and the
development of action in that region." Strang was successful in convincing Foreign Secretary Bevin that, as a Commonwealth member, India could be an important diplomatic tool against the spread of
Communism in Asia.[39]

British officials – including Bevin and the chairman of the Far Eastern Official Committee (FEOC), Esler Dening – argued that Britain
had to take the lead in any regional program involving the Commonwealth and Southeast Asia. Unilateral action by India might hurt British prestige. In Malaya, for example, it was to the British that the
Malays looked to solve their problems. Unless the Indians were carefully guided, Indian anticolonial sentiments might undermine British

power and influence. Yet Dening was enthusiastic about the possibilities for an Indian role. In a Foreign Office minute of April 1949, he wrote: "If we can achieve a degree of regional cooperation in which the United Kingdom is a full partner, then the time may come when we can convince Pandit Nehru that South East Asia has need of the West and that India should maintain a close association, not only with us but also with other Powers including the Dutch and the French."[40] Such a course appealed to Dening, who was critical of American policy towards Asia. Although British policy in the Far East would benefit from American support of the Commonwealth, India was a potential asset independent of the Americans which would help assert British power in world affairs.

In the period after 1949 the United Kingdom attempted to follow up on this strategy, but it met with little success. In many cases the attempt to use Indian influence in Asia conflicted with Britain's broader goals connected with the Anglo-American partnership. This was demonstrated during the Korean War. When forced to make a decision between aligning itself with American policy or supporting India, British official policy invariably supported America's more belligerent stance. Two concrete examples of this were British support for the 1 February 1951 United Nations resolution condemning China, and the United Kingdom's alignment with the United States' negotiating position in May 1953. Korean officials themselves were suspicious of Indian diplomats, and this too served to weaken Britain's strategy for a regional Indian role in Cold War diplomacy. Finally, Nehru's perception of the Vietnam War as a colonial struggle and his suspicion of American intentions undermined British hopes for Indian support in Southeast Asia.

ERNEST BEVIN, ANTHONY EDEN, AND THE ANGLO-AMERICAN "SPECIAL RELATIONSHIP"

Although there were many elements of continuity in foreign policy towards the United States and the Far East between the Attlee and Churchill governments, there were important differences in emphasis between the foreign secretaries Ernest Bevin and Anthony Eden. As David Reynolds has written about Bevin, "behind the enlightened rhetoric, the determination to maintain Britain's world role remained positively Churchillian." Bevin's policies essentially were designed to uphold the power of the British Empire. Peter Weiler has pointed out that "Bevin and other British policymakers assumed that the British

Empire was a 'beneficent force' in world affairs. They saw it as 'natural' that Britain should be the dominant power in the Middle East or in parts of Asia, including countries that bordered on the Soviet Union." Bevin's perception of Hong Kong as the right-wing bastion of the anti-communist front supports this evaluation. However, Attlee's support of Bevin on this issue indicates that his conception of deficit areas in the Cold War did not extend to the empire.[41] Unlike his attitude to the Middle East, where he was prepared to limit British involvement, he was not prepared to bargain away or lose without a fight parts of the empire.

Bevin was essentially an inductive thinker, one who disliked theoretical constructs. His pragmatic empirical approach to international relations showed itself in his support for the Colombo Plan and technical aid program. This program was promoted under his guidance as a means of containing communism and integrating peripheral Third World regions into the anticommunist core.

Bevin's conception of Anglo-American relations emerged from an attempt to preserve British world power in the context of limited resources. From this perspective it was a pragmatic strategy, based on an understanding of the possible uses of the Anglo-American alliance in global affairs. In the Middle East, he welcomed American aid under the Truman Doctrine. American support in Greece and Turkey had demonstrated the importance of getting the United States to counter communism where it threatened British and Western interests. It illustrated the benefits of a close Anglo-American partnership in the postwar world.

In Southeast Asia between 1949 and 1951, British officials attempted to get a greater American commitment to the area. They tried to define this commitment in terms of an Anglo-American partnership. What Bevin underestimated, however, was the possibility for competition within the alliance and the fact that American actions in the international arena often superseded the narrow interests of an Anglo-American special relationship. Thus, once the United States began to commit itself to Southeast Asia after 1950, British officials began to worry that American strategy was too belligerent for the safe preservation of British interests in the region. Nevertheless, the Foreign Office agreed with the broad tenets of American policy in Vietnam. Like the Americans, British officials were concerned about France's determination to maintain central control over the associated states (Vietnam, Laos, and Cambodia). The British backed American attempts to devolve power onto the moderate nationalists and supported attempts to sustain an informal empire in Vietnam to contain communist expansion.

In general, the Dutch and French experience in Southeast Asia was looked on with suspicion. In August 1949 a memorandum of the Permanent Under-Secretary's Committee (PUSC), entitled "Regional Cooperation in South-East Asia and the Far East," argued that the French and Dutch had been "slower to appreciate the inevitable march of events in Asia." The danger was that their reluctance to agree to devolve power onto the indigenous moderates "would drive the nationalists ... into the arms of the Communists [and] discredit the West with all national movements – a discredit in which Great Britain, despite her own more generous policy, would share."[42]

Like Bevin, Anthony Eden was a believer in the righteousness of the British Empire. But unlike Bevin, he was not a strong proponent of the Anglo-American relationship. Underlying Eden's attitude towards the United States was a lingering suspicion and dislike of things American. Eden understood the competitive nature of Anglo-American relations, but he failed to design a strategy that could achieve his goal of preserving the international influence of Great Britain. His tactical approach and his failure to think in broad terms and in the long term meant that he was ill-equipped to realize the nature and extent of Britain's overcommitment in international affairs.[43]

More so than Churchill, Eden was an enthusiast of the "Old Commonwealth and Empire," but even here these links only serve to demonstrate the basic weakness of Britain's strategy. Thus, although Eden took a liking to the Canadian secretary of state for external affairs, Lester Pearson, there were limits to the power and influence of Canada and other members of the Old Commonwealth in international affairs.

Strategic considerations also went beyond individual personalities where decision making was concerned. It is unlikely, for example, that the United Kingdom's decision in June and July 1950 would have been different had another government been in power. The war in Korea is a good example of how Britain and America compromised and employed diplomatic strategies to reach a relatively unified position. The compromises that resulted in agreed Anglo-American positions on the passing of the aggressor resolution in 1951 and the methods of achieving an armistice in Korea in 1953 were hard won, but these U.S. initiatives were supported by the United Kingdom. It is difficult to evaluate these compromises as demonstrating the value of the "special relationship" because of the animosity that was engendered in the process. What the actions of the United States, Britain, and others in the Korean War do demonstrate, however, is the importance which the Western-led anticommunist alliance placed on mobilizing public opinion in favour of rearmament and containing and deterring not only Asian communism but also Soviet power and prestige.

CANADA AND THE ANGLO-AMERICAN RELATIONSHIP

Canadian foreign policy has thus far been treated only tangentially by non-Canadian historians, who are more interested in the role of the Great Powers. The historiography of Canadian diplomacy in the Cold War is slim in comparison to its British and American counterparts, and it has been dominated by Canadian historians. In the 1960s, Canadian "revisionists" focused on the nature of Canada's relationship with the American empire, and the emphasis on the Canadian-American relationship carried on into the 1970s and 1980s.

One consequence of this has been a comparative neglect of Anglo-Canadian relations in the postwar era and an underestimation of the influence that the perceptions of British policymakers had on the formulation of Canadian foreign policy, especially in the period before Suez. This is a gap in the literature that has only recently started to be filled by the appearance of Denis Smith's monograph, *Diplomacy of Fear*.[44]

Traditionally, Canada's foreign policy has been closest to that of Britain's at times when the existence of the United Kingdom has been threatened. Thus, the two world wars began for Canadians in 1914 and 1939, respectively. Canadian officials in the interwar period however, tended to be suspicious of defending the periphery of the United Kingdom's empire. Canada's noninvolvement in the Chanak Crisis was one example of this. But in the bipolar international system, peripheral areas of the globe were seen in a very different light; in the Cold War, threats to the American or the British perimeter were seen as potential threats to Canada as well.

The influence of Great Britain on Canada's foreign policy stemmed from shared cultural values and Canada's evolution as a parliamentary democracy within the British Empire and Commonwealth. Many Canadian politicians of this period had a British education, and the list includes Canada's secretary of state for external affairs after 1948, Lester B. Pearson. Like Britain's foreign policy, the strategic centre of Canadian foreign policy lay in Western Europe. A Department of External Affairs memo written in 1948 pointed out that "Canada's interest in the security and prosperity of Western Europe has long been a basic factor in Canadian political and economic calculations." Canada's "way of life," said this memorandum, was closer to Western Europe than "all or most of the other American nations and the Canadian people have always been quick to respond when their way of life was menaced in Western Europe ... Such is the case today, when the danger is Soviet Communism."[45]

Like British officials, Canadians feared that the United States might turn once again towards isolationism, leaving Europe to work out its own defence against a surging Soviet Union. They wanted the Americans involved in international affairs. In late 1947, Canada's ambassador in Washington, Hume Wrong, wrote that "a very significant point in U.S.–U.S.S.R. relations is the question of the ability of the United States to support a long term policy of reviving the world economy and of containing the Soviet Union patiently and firmly." Although Wrong lauded the "admirable general purposes" of American diplomacy and admired Kennan's defensive conception of containment, there were important qualifications to Canada's "invitation" to the United States to participate in containing the Soviet Union. Wrong echoed British concerns when he noted that American diplomacy had too much of a tendency towards bluster and emotionalism. The fear that American containment strategy might provoke the Soviets into war was a widely held belief among Canadian policymakers in the Cold War period. Many sympathized with the sentiment underlying the minister of agriculture's remarks to Louis St Laurent in 1948 that too much reliance was being placed on American power in the postwar world. World peace depended on the "re-establishment of a strong British Commonwealth in lasting friendship with the United States." A key player in that future was Canada, "the most important dominion in the British Commonwealth."[46]

But Britain was no longer the pre-eminent power in world affairs and there were limits to Canada's willingness to underwrite British prestige and power. In the Cold War context, Canadians generally accepted, with some reservations, that the future of the West would rest on the foundations of U.S. power. The benefits of American prosperity were demonstrated in 1947, when Canada, like Britain, faced a financial crisis based on dwindling reserves of American dollars. Marshall Plan aid served to help alleviate this shortage by providing dollars for the purchase of Canadian wheat and other goods destined for Western Europe. As Lester Pearson told the Canadian high commissioner in London, Norman Robertson, "If we are forced to chose some closer economic and financial alignment, and I hope we won't be, it will have to be with Washington rather than with London." Pearson's words contained overtones of disappointment, and he warned Robertson that it would be best for the Commonwealth if Bevin and others did not make grand declarations about the common defence of the empire.[47]

Canadian politicians were not passive actors in the emerging Cold War, however. Their allegiance to the West was demonstrated in the context of the Berlin crisis when the then secretary of state for external affairs, Louis St Laurent, said that "Canada would necessarily be involved if war were to arise from the present crisis."[48] What emerged in Canada was a hybrid containment strategy, one that was more dependent on the Foreign Office than on the State Department for its strategic conceptions, yet one that recognized the need to maintain good relations with the United States and preserve Canada's "special relationship."

When St Laurent became prime minister, he based his government's foreign policies on maintaining the special relationship. Satisfied with the existing Commonwealth framework, he too criticized attempts to centralize strategic planning for the defence of the empire. Canada would only defend British interests where there was Anglo-American agreement. It was, he said, "quite clear that Canada's foreign policy, particularly her relations with the United States must be at all times under the sole control of the Canadian government." Canada could not be part of any Commonwealth bureaucracy "which would affect our ability to deal directly with the United States." It was, he said, "quite unrealistic for Canada to participate in military planning which did not include the United States."[49]

A lawyer by profession, St Laurent was a convinced internationalist. The disagreements he had with Mackenzie King when he was Canada's secretary of state for external affairs bear this out. When King was reluctant to agree to Canadian participation in the United Nations Temporary Commission on Korea in 1947, St Laurent offered his resignation. There was some continuity between the King and St Laurent premierships: although the domestic sources of traditional Canadian caution in external relations had been largely eliminated by the onset of the Cold War, St Laurent remained concerned that foreign policy should not undermine domestic unity. A committed anticommunist, his sympathy for anticolonial and anticommunist nationalists in the Third World paralleled to some degree the perceptions of American policymakers. Much more than King, he was willing to take on an activist foreign policy.

CANADA AND CONTAINMENT IN ASIA

Canada's involvement in Asia in the immediate postwar period was limited, but the momentum of the Cold War accelerated its interest and participation in Far Eastern diplomacy. Although the Chinese civil war was peripheral to Canadian concerns between 1945 and 1948, Canada extended credits and a loan to the Nationalist regime. The implications of communist victory in China alarmed Canadian policymakers, but Britain's defensive containment strategy was attractive to officials who recognized the limits of Canadian power on the continent and who believed that the revolution did not necessarily mean a long-term alliance with the Soviet Union. Lester Pearson can be described as an anglophile where his policies towards China are concerned. He supported recognition of the new regime until the outbreak of the Korean War and consistently advocated policies designed to accept the legitimacy of communist power.[50]

Canadian strategic interests in Western Europe precluded any military commitment to the mainland. Yet there was a growing awareness among Canadian officials of the importance of maintaining a containment line in Asia. A memo prepared for Prime Minister St Laurent's visit to Washington in early 1949 pointed out that "the need for working out common solutions to the more acute problems raised by the Communist menace in East Asia is an over-riding one."[51] In Korea the government acknowledged the necessity of supporting America's containment objectives. In view of the economic weakness and military vulnerability of the Rhee government, a cabinet memorandum on recognition of the Republic of Korea argued, it was desirable to provide moral support to the South Koreans, "especially so in view of [Korea's] location on the fringe of Communist-dominated territory." A commentary prepared for guidance of the Canadian delegation to the United Nations pointed out that it was "in the Canadian interest for continued military and economic support to be given to the new South Korean Government by the United States."[52] The Canadian government supported the broad outlines of America's containment in Korea; but despite this confluence of interest, the Canadians remained wary about American methods for containing communism in Asia. After China intervened in the Korean War, departmental officials echoed their British counterparts' concern that American policies might lead to a global war with the Soviet Union. Thus, Canadian diplomats used diplomatic initiatives to try to contain what they perceived to be American enthusiasm for self-destruction and undisciplined containment strategies.

Denis Stairs has extensively explored the Canadian policies that were designed to constrain the more belligerent American initiatives in Korea. But American pressures, the importance of the special relationship, and the strategic need to maintain a united front towards the Soviet Union resulted in allied compromises that tended to back the United States' more aggressive initiatives towards China. Canada, like Britain, France, Australia, and other allies, supported America's condemnation of the Chinese in the United Nations in early 1951, and it gave public support to the risk-filled U.S. strategy to end the fighting in Korea. Although both Britain and Canada were wary of provoking the wrath of the Chinese communists, they supported the parameters of America's informal empire in Korea and Vietnam.

Canada's lack of direct interests in Southeast Asia, its hopes not to antagonize the People's Republic, and St Laurent's suspicion of European colonialism led to a policy that diverged somewhat from that of the British and Americans. It was not until 1952 that the Canadian government extended recognition to the Bao Dai government, thus bringing itself into a closer association with the Anglo-American-French partnership in Southeast Asia. Yet Canada's adherence to the moderate nationalists in Indochina was inextricably tied to its agreement with the West's global anticommunist initiatives. Canadian support of the Bao Dai and Syngman Rhee regimes – qualified as it was – reflected a recognition of the need to sustain indigenous centres of pro-Western influence in the Far East. Alliance with the United States and the West in the Cold War involved undertaking increasing responsibilities in peripheral areas of the globe.

In sum, the minimum aim of Western containment strategies in this period was to prevent the expansion of communist influence in Asia. American containment policies on the Chinese periphery related to a broad range of considerations, including the need to sustain Japan and to reverse adverse trends in the balance of power caused by the Chinese revolution. In the process of implementing their policies, American policymakers tended to move away from Kennan's conception of containment. In order to limit Soviet influence in East Asia, they developed a strategy of supporting the emergence of indigenous governments linked politically and economically to the West. Informal empire required greater U.S. commitment to the mainland periphery than Kennan wanted.

Although British and Canadian containment strategies towards East Asia were defensive in orientation, both countries supported the basic framework of America's policies for East Asia. Differences within the alliance centred mainly on Communist China. Britain and Canada backed American initiatives during the Korean War, and their support of the Bao Dai "solution" reflected the common interests of the North Atlantic triangle in the Far East. A strategy of meeting the communist threat in the Third World by devolving power onto indigenous elites was accepted by both Canadian and British policymakers. In the context of the bipolar postwar world, they accepted the need for a Western informal empire on the Asian periphery.

2 Informal Empire and Continental East Asia, January–June 1950

The success of the Chinese revolution resulted in increased American concern about the expansion of communism in East Asia. In light of the recommendations of the National Security Council's NSC 48 series, the United States began to implement policies designed to shore up the strength of countries on China's East Asian borders. In South Korea, it continued to press for American military and economic aid to stabilize and strengthen that country's ability to meet both internal and external communist threats. The maintenance of Rhee's government was perceived as a means of securing a sphere of pro-Western influence and containing the extension of the Soviet core in Asia.

In Southeast Asia, an area of perceived Western prestige and power, the United States was in the process of formulating a policy to secure moderate pro-Western governments and stabilize the region against the threat of communism. It tried to enlist the cooperation of the French and moderate nationalists represented by Bao Dai, but this was an uneasy trilateral relationship. While American officials recognized the importance of the French military presence in Indochina, they also wanted the French to delegate more political responsibility to the anticommunist Vietnamese.

The United States wanted the French to work towards an informal empire in Vietnam, but American strategy was dictated to a large degree by the French colonial presence and by the inability of Bao Dai to attract popular support. Vietnam was different from Korea in that the

United States faced more obstacles in implementing its containment policies there. U.S. support of France's military presence in Vietnam impeded the evolution of an informal empire. American recommendations regarding the future of the French colony were looked on with some suspicion by French policymakers. Yet French officials understood the importance of American aid, and the maintenance of good Franco-American relations was a critical factor in the emergence of the "Bao Dai solution."

The British were more willing to work within America's framework for containing communism. In early 1950, Bevin was determined to engage American resources in South and Southeast Asia. His goals were to create a stable external environment for the internal security measures undertaken in Malaya and to undercut the possibilities for further unrest in the region. Communism in Indochina posed a threat to British colonial power in Southeast Asia, and British policymakers hoped that American military and economic aid would provide a more secure setting for their own strategies for Malaya. The military destruction of the communists and support for Bao Dai represented a move in this direction.

To understand British diplomacy fully, we must also explore Britain's conception of the Anglo-American special relationship in the postwar era. The crucial factor in determining British strategy towards the United States after the Second World War was Britain's weakened power. Foreign Secretary Ernest Bevin was very keen on utilizing the Anglo-American relationship to enhance Britain's imperial and foreign policy objectives. Attempts to secure American aid to support British policy sparked debate and disagreement. Bevin's efforts to get the United States to accept his regional defensive containment strategy in Asia contributed to tensions in the alliance. Although the United Kingdom was supportive of piecemeal containment initiatives in Vietnam and Korea, it was not pleased when American diplomacy *vis-à-vis* these countries threatened to undermine the United Kingdom's broader objectives for China. There existed subtle levels of competition for power and distribution of resources within the Anglo-American partnership.

The Colombo Plan represented one attempt by the United Kingdom and Commonwealth to engage American resources in Asia. The plan was designed in part to foster U.S. economic aid to countries in South and Southeast Asia that were threatened by communism. But the Colombo Plan was more than a regional containment strategy. It was also an effort by the British to get the United States to subsidize Britain's collective commitments to the sterling area: American developmental aid to South Asia would help underwrite the sterling area and decelerate the flow of sterling that Britain was paying out. Under Bevin's conception of the Anglo-American partnership, American dollars would support Britain's global power. The United States was to be Britain's proxy partner in the postwar international order. To this degree, the British wanted the special relationship to extend beyond the bounds of America's self-interested containment strategies.

Andrew Rotter has pointed out that British diplomats were successful in bringing an increased American commitment to Southeast Asia. He notes that by the spring of 1950 "the British could claim they had strongly influenced American policy towards Southeast Asia during the previous nine months."[1] There were limitations, however, on the extent to which the United States was willing to back Britain's regional Asian policies. It was reluctant to underwrite the sterling area, it took a cautious approach to the Colombo Plan, and it was unwilling to support the United Kingdom's initiative to seat the new Communist China government in the United Nations. But these practical limits to the Anglo-American "partnership" in Asia did not deter Bevin. He remained enthusiastic and optimistic about the possibilities for the special relationship until his death early in 1951.

As members of the Commonwealth and as enthusiastic supporters of anticommunist measures designed to uphold Western power against the Soviet empire, Canadian policymakers in the Department of External Affairs were generally willing to support the broad goals of Britain's postwar international objectives. Canada was a participant in the Colombo discussions and contributed resources to the plan as part of a collective bid to engage American prestige in South and Southeast Asia. Canadian officials also supported Britain's defensive containment strategy in East Asia: Canada moved towards recognition of the People's Republic of China in the first six months of 1950.

But there existed a tension in Canadian policy, a tension that reflected broader Anglo-American differences in Asia. Prime Minister St Laurent and several of his cabinet were wary about moving too quickly on the recognition issue, fearful of hurting the Canadian-American special relationship. Only the conflict in Korea prevented strains in Commonwealth-American relations that threatened to emerge over issues connected with Chinese representation in the United Nations. The outbreak of the Korean War provided a context in which differences between the United States and its two closest postwar allies were submerged within broader alliance objectives.

TOWARDS INFORMAL EMPIRE: U.S. MILITARY AND ECONOMIC AID TO SOUTH KOREA

American policy towards the Republic of Korea in 1949–50 was designed to stabilize the South Korean economy and uphold the ability of the republic to protect itself from internal and external military threats. The achievement of these objectives would provide the United States with the strategic flexibility to disengage from the peninsula. Policymakers did not want the United States to become entangled in a long-term and costly commitment to Korea. Instead, the American presence would be replaced by increased Korean responsibilities; the anticommunist orientation of the Rhee government would ensure a sense of shared outlook between the two countries. American diplomacy in Korea aimed at creating an interdependent political relationship based on common political, economic, and strategic objectives.

The basic strategic objective of the United States prior to the outbreak of the Korean War was the withdrawal of its troops from South Korea without endangering the stability of the Korean regime. The National Security Council policy paper NSC/8, which was approved in 1948, called for the earliest possible withdrawal of American troops and argued that the creation of the South Korean government would facilitate the "liquidation of the U.S. commitment of men and money with the minimum of bad effects."[2] NSC 8/2 was given presidential approval in March 1949 and, like its predecessor, called for a decentralized American role in the Republic of Korea (ROK). The withdrawal of U.S. troops did not represent a diminution of American support for the South Korean government but rather "another step toward the regularization by the U.S. of its relations with that Government."[3]

America's containment policy towards the Northeast Asian continental periphery was essentially defensive in nature. Yet the United States accepted an implicit responsibility to defend Korea from any external communist attack. According to NSC 8/2, an abrupt disengagement from the republic would hurt American prestige and "would be interpreted as a betrayal by the U.S. of its friends and allies in the Far East and might contribute substantially to a fundamental realignment of forces in favour of the USSR throughout that part of the world."[4] A top-secret memo, which emerged from a series of high-level meetings in the Department of State, noted, "Since Korea is another area in which United States influence should show results in the social and economic life of the country, it is important that we not let the Republic fail."[5] An American military response to a communist attack was thus an implicit policy assumption in the event that South Korea was attacked.

The United States continued to provide military aid to the republic while its forces were being withdrawn. This was one aspect of U.S. – South Korean relations in which the transition from formal occupation to informal empire was being worked out. NSC 8/2 pointed out that the United States could maintain its influence in South Korea and ensure the continued orientation of the pro-Western regime without the presence of American troops if it continued to train, equip, and supply South Korea's security forces in 1949 and in the fiscal year 1950. The object was "to ensure that such forces are capable of serving effectively as a deterrent to external aggression and a guarantor of internal order in South Korea."[6] In this way, South Korea was to serve as a proxy containment power, assisting American objectives and working within America's framework of containment for Northeast Asia.

To implement the recommendations of NSC 8/2, the Utited States decided to establish an initial force ceiling for the ROK army at 65,000. In July 1949, when Korean officials complained that these force levels were too low, U.S. State Department representatives responded that they were the maximum force levels consistent with scales of economy and strategic requirements.[7] When the remaining American occupation troops left Korea on 30 June, a Korean Military Advisory Group (KMAG) of 500 men was established to continue the U.S. training of Korean soldiers in modern American warfare techniques. Although NSC 8/2 had recommended the establishment of a military force able to defend itself against external attack, the priority of the U.S. government lay in shoring up the internal security of the ROK. For the most part, tanks, heavy guns, and aircraft were withheld. As Walter Hermes pointed out, "despite expansion of the ROKA to 100,000 men in 1950, its arms and equipment were more suitable to a police force than to an army. KMAG decided to train the South Koreans in individual arms first." Although the military aid was woefully inadequate to defend against the North Korean attack in June 1950, the significance of the American attempt to establish the beginnings of a modern army in Korea should not be underestimated. An NSC progress report in February 1950 pointed out that the transferral of $56 million in equipment for the Korean army, coast guard, and police had substantially been completed by the fall of 1949. On 6 October 1949, President Truman signed the Mutual Defense Assistance Act and earmarked an additional $10.2 million for the ROK. In the first quarter of 1950, additional equipment for a force of 15,000 men was transferred. At the end of April 1950, Ambassador Muccio told his American colleagues that the KMAG was effective and was doing a "heartening" job. The Korean army had "kept pace with the aggressive [border] actions of the north" and had been "successful in controlling the constant flow of saboteurs and special agents from North Korea."[8] Despite bottlenecks, limited resources, and major strategic concerns beyond Korea at this time, the United States was making progress in implementing its containment goals for Korea, prior to the Korean War. Between 1945 and 1950, not including the costs of occupation, almost a half billion dollars in military aid was provided to the ROK (see table 1).

The process of creating a viable state to contain Soviet power in Northeast Asia was arduous and American intentions and actions did not al-

Table 1
U.S. Aid to the Republic of Korea, 1945–1950

Office of the Foreign Liquidation Commissioner (surplus military property)	$141,000,000
Department of the Army (government and relief in occupied areas – GARIOA)	$301,000,000
Economic Cooperation Administration (shipments through 31 May 1950)	$53,700,000

Source: Harry Truman Library, John Ohly Papers, box 115, Korea, pt 1.

ways bring about the desired consequences. President Rhee often made it difficult for American policymakers to carry out their strategy. Korean-American differences in the period stemmed from Rhee's greater commitment to rollback containment strategies *vis-à-vis* both North Korea and the Sino-Soviet alliance. Worried about the consequences of U.S. disengagement, Rhee's government lobbied forcefully for U.S. backing for a military solution to the division of the peninsula. In the spring of 1949, the Korean prime minister, Lee Bum Suk, told the American ambassador in Seoul, John Muccio, that the United States should keep South Korea "within its Pacific line of defense as a bridgehead on the continent for the impending war with the U.S.S.R."[9] On 20 August 1949, Rhee sent a letter to President Truman requesting more military aid from the United States. This was needed, Rhee proclaimed, to counter an attack from North Korea, to defeat the North Koreans and "hurl them back, but also to attack their retreating forces and in so doing to liberate our enslaved fellow countrymen in the north."[10]

At this level, Rhee's "invitation" to America posed a distinct threat to U.S. containment objectives as enunciated in NSC policy papers. In the course of the late 1940s and 1950s, American officials came to believe that if no controls were placed on Rhee's objectives, the United States America might be drawn into a conflict that would endanger its global strategies of containment. South Korea was a strategic liability, and American policy towards East Asia was based on the "defensive perimeter," a concept that recognized the futility of committing U.S. troops to fight Chinese communist armies on the mainland. There was to be no formal military commitment to the Northeast Asian mainland, and American officials refused to support Rhee's rollback strategies for the peninsula. President Truman wrote to Rhee on 26 September 1949, saying that the United States government felt that "the security of the Republic of Korea can best be served by the development of an efficient, compact Korean force rather than by amassing large military forces which would be an insupportable burden on the economy of the country."[11]

The development of the ROK's internal military power was one element of a three-pronged strategy of nation building in South Korea. The other two elements were economic aid to enhance the ROK's economic viability, and political support of the ROK within the U.N. framework.[12] U.N. support was meant as a deterrent to communist attack and as a means of imparting legitimacy to the newly formed government. It also formed part of America's political response to the continued division of the peninsula, acting as a means of diverting Rhee from adopting military solutions to the problem of the two Koreas.

The role that economic aid to South Korea played has been a much less examined aspect of American containment policy. U.S. programs to stabilize the Korean economy were seen as complementary to military aid. Together, both types of assistance would serve to consolidate a pro-Western anticommunist government in the ROK. Ideally, South Korea would become a mirror reflection of American strategic and global goals. The United States attempted to develop the ROK's economy in ways consistent with America's strategic and economic aims for the region.

As in the military field, American aid was making a positive impact on the Korean economy. In late January 1950, the chief of the Economic Cooperation Administration (ECA) Mission to Korea, Dr Arthur Bunce, noted that "much progress had been made in the past year, especially in the field of production." The major shortcoming, however, was in the area of inflation. To stabilize the Korean economy, the ECA was determined to reduce the level of inflation in Korea. The problem was exacerbated by government spending policies, particularly on defence. By keeping defence spending and inflation under control, U.S. policymakers also hoped to prevent Rhee from undertaking a military solution to the Korean situation. But President Rhee had different ideas. U.S. economic aid policies were subject to problems that were a consequence of his different approach to the unification issue.

On 15 March 1950, representatives of the Department of State and the ECA discussed the internal Korean economic situation. They were frustrated by several aspects of the ROK's domestic economic policies and were concerned about Rhee's reliability as an ally. Dr Arthur Bunce pointed out that the Joint Korean-American Economic Stabilization Committee (ESC), a body established to deal with issues relating to the Korean economy, "was receiving a gratifying degree of cooperation from all branches of the Korean Government except the defense and police authorities who, despite the efforts of KMAG, continued to expend government funds excessively and irresponsibly within their respective bailiwicks."[13] Niles Bond, a State Department official in the Northeast Asian office, noted that Rhee's strongest weapon was "his knowledge that the U.S. could not let the Republic of Korea fall without incurring the gravest political repercussions." The officer in charge of economic affairs, Edward W. Doherty, replied curtly that "if the present trend continued very long, the time might come when the lesser of two evils would be to cut loose and run the risk of incurring such consequences."[14]

In the event, the United States used diplomatic means to press the South Korean government into making the necessary adjustments in its economic program. On 23 March the ECA director, Paul Hoffman, sent a letter to the Korean prime minister complaining about the inflation rate. In the letter, Hoffman said it was his "duty" to remind the prime minister that the ROK "must take such measures as will satisfy the ECA Mission in Korea and will satisfy me that the inflationary problem is being dealt with effectively." He warned Lee that in the present circumstances it would be difficult to justify the U.S. aid program, and he said that unless the government took action to convince him that "a forthright, immediate effort will be made to control inflation," less money would be available for the ROK in the current and subsequent fiscal years. One week later Muccio warned the U.S. government of the situation, noting that progress was being made in certain areas of joint policy. "We have all pushed Korean counterparts as strongly as possible," he wrote, "and almost to breaking point at times." He argued that recent U.S. successes included a food and cereals agreement, land reform measures, aid pricing, and an agreement for a balanced ROK budget in 1950–51. The Americans, he said, should not publicly do anything that might undermine the position of the Korean members of the ESC, "who have gone along with us at times under tremendous opposition."[15] But the inflation issue was too important to drop.

On 3 April, Acheson sent a further note to the Korean government, warning that unless its economic policies were changed, American aid to Korea might be seriously jeopardized. The Hoffman-Acheson duet had an impact in Korea. The vice-chairman of the Korean National Assembly, Yun Chi Yung, told an American embassy official that after these letters had been received, "no one had the courage to do more than discuss the budget in a cursory manner." Yun said he "thoroughly recognized, as did all members of the Assembly, that although Korea was nominally an independent country it was actually dependent upon the United States for its very existence." Without further U.S. aid, "the Republic of Korea would collapse." The issue was not one of conforming to American policy demands but of "saving face as a supposedly independent legislative body of an independent government."[16] At the end of April 1950, Ambassador Muccio told a group of American Far Eastern analysts that American pressure had "jolted the Koreans and recently every recommendation of the Joint Commission on Economic Stabilization has been accepted."[17]

This is a good example of the relationship between America's hegemonic goals and its informal empire. Intervention in the domestic affairs of the ROK in this case was a consequence of attempts to stabilize the Korean economy. Economic stabilization also would have the effect of restraining Rhee's unification objectives. Ironically, the rhetoric and actions of the Rhee government resulted in greater American influence over his government's domestic and foreign policies. Informal empire was required not only to contain the Soviet Union but to restrain Rhee as well. The major motivation for sustaining the South Korean regime, however, stemmed from the dangers of the competitive bipolar international system. The political motivation for informal empire was summed up in 1949 by Dean Rusk when, speaking of Korea and other countries, he said: "We must support against aggressive pressure from the outside even states which we regard unfavourably. We must preserve them merely as states."[18]

American policies towards Korea confronted congressional reservations as well. On 19 January 1950, Congress voted down the administration's request for economic aid by a vote of 193–191. Disturbed by the decision, Secretary Acheson immediately warned President Truman of the potential "far-reaching adverse" consequences of this decision. "We have not only given the Republic of Korea independence," he informed Truman; since 1945, "we have provided the economic, military, technical and other assistance necessary to its continued existence." If Congress withheld current aid, the United States' efforts would end in mid-course. Without further aid, the chance for the ROK's survival could be lost and all of America's previous efforts could prove to have been in vain.[19] To get more money for the ROK, Acheson reduced the original amount of aid, and after this bill passed, he quickly organized another $100 million to be appropriated for fiscal 1951. In February 1950 a memo on U.S. aid to the ROK declared that "the Korean economy will for the foreseeable future continue to be dependent upon economic assistance from the U.S, as will, therefore, the support of its armed forces."[20]

Economic aid was combined with political pressure. Together they were intended to help stabilize the Korean economy and political system in early 1950. Military and economic aid to the ROK also promoted America's objective of realigning trade between Japan and Korea, and establishing a regional interdependence between the two countries. In 1950 the ROK was expected to import $49 million of Japanese goods, and in the long term Korea was seen as essential to Japanese recovery.[21] Korea had became an essential part of America's overall regional containment strategy for Northeast Asia.

The ROK-American relationship after 1948 was not an equal one: the United States held the balance of power. American policymakers recognized this asymmetry, yet the degree of the asymmetry was diminishing, a consequence of U.S. strategies for developing the internal strength of the ROK. For many Koreans, however, the cost of increasing Korea's strength was a loss of essential sovereignty over domestic decision making. There were limits to which the ROK could exercise its newly found power, and the transition in South Korea towards interdependent status within an American-led anticommunist core was making advances in the period before the Korean War. The war disrupted this process and once again required American intervention to secure a Western sphere of influence in the peninsula.

FORGING THE ANGLO-AMERICAN PARTNERSHIP: JANUARY–JUNE 1950

The United Kingdom accepted the United States' dominance in Korean affairs, but British policymakers were determined to bring a greater American commitment to Southeast Asia. Increased U.S. support of pro-Western regimes in South and Southeast Asia was seen by British officials as one means of consolidating an Anglo-American partnership in the postwar world. These were regions in which that partnership could produce advantages to Britain's global position. The special relationship in Southeast Asia was to be built on British prestige and influence and American resources. As a British memorandum prepared in the spring of 1950 for bipartite discussions with the Americans noted, "It is only we who have the knowledge of South East Asia and the respect of the inhabitants."[22]

Britain's attempts to involve the United States in the region went beyond pure containment considerations and involved the larger issue of American support of British power and prestige globally. The six months leading up to the outbreak of the Korean War represented a period of relatively high optimism on the part of British diplomats anxious to consolidate the Anglo-American alliance. Southeast Asia was only one region in the world where the partnership could operate to the perceived benefit of both Britons and Americans. "We are already on the road to regaining strength," the spring memo declared. "It is our determined aim to develop that strength and to maintain our position as a World Power ... The American attitude may largely depend on their estimate of our confidence in our own future."[23]

An Anglo-American partnership was perceived as the best means of effecting British recovery and maintaining Britain's world-power status. A top-secret memorandum entitled "A Third World Power or Western Consolidation" (PUSC 22), prepared initially by William Strang's

Permanent Under-Secretary's Committee, argued that the United Kingdom could not operate in international affairs as a viable third world power. Outside the Soviet Union and the United States, there was no alliance structure that could promote Britain's foreign policy objectives. The Commonwealth option was discarded because of Britain's economic and military weakness: "An attempt to turn the Commonwealth into a Third World Power would only confront its members with a direct choice between London and Washington, and though sentiment might point one way interest would certainly lead the other." The same would happen if Britain aligned itself with Western Europe and the Commonwealth. This also was rejected because of its weakness against Soviet power. The paper concluded that only a close association with the United States would promote British objectives, contain the Soviet threat, and preserve Commonwealth and West European solidarity.

The framework within which the United Kingdom was to operate was called "Western consolidation." The possibility of increased British influence within that "system" was foreseen: "The United Kingdom in particular, by virtue of her leading position both in Western Europe and in the Commonwealth, ought to play a larger part in a Western system." Faced with the option between two "core" world powers, Britain chose an alignment with the Western anti-Soviet core of powers led by American power and resources.

The North Atlantic Pact was perceived as the key to the consolidation of this Western power. It is a weakness of the policy paper, however, that it did not deal in any depth with the Third World or with East Asia. The paper merely noted that "it may prove to be the case that the consolidation of the West in a passive sense will not prove to be enough, and that the only final hope for a settled world will be that the ideas it represents and the system which incorporates these ideas should spread eastwards."[24] This argument was flawed, since it was based on a greater projection of British power in the underdeveloped world than was possible. The document also failed to evaluate the negative implications for Britain's "Western system" of the worldwide expansion of American power after the outbreak of the Korean War.

Perhaps the reason why the impact of Anglo-American differences in the Third World was not discussed was Bevin's caution about exacerbating tensions in the partnership over Far Eastern issues. Or perhaps it was because he thought that an Anglo-American partnership in the Far East could be forged. In early 1950 he was actively working towards such a possibility. However, the United States had reservations about working within Britain's "Western system" containment strategy. The Asian crises after 1950 demonstrated to American policymakers the difficulties of relying on a purely Western framework to achieve their policy goals in East Asia. Bevin's strategy for developing a global Anglo-American partnership was to fail in the Third World, but in early 1950 the limits of the strategy were not yet evident, and British policymakers maintained a rather optimistic belief in the possibilities of enhancing their country's position as a world power.

THE COLOMBO PLAN AND ECONOMIC CONTAINMENT IN SOUTH AND SOUTHEAST ASIA

An important source of British official optimism in this period lay in the fact that by early 1950 Britain's balance-of-payments situation was beginning to improve. Although its economic position was still perceived as somewhat precarious, British dollar reserves were growing. The chancellor of the exchequer, Sir Stafford Cripps, told the cabinet that ministers could look forward to an improving economic situation. The sterling area was still in a weak state, however, and pounds were scarce for sterling area countries such as India, which looked to the United Kingdom for development funds. In this economic context, Britain devised a strategy that related American resources to two inter-related themes: the weakened position of the sterling area and the threat posed to Western interests in Asia by indigenous communist movements.

Lacking the capital itself to finance development in Asia, the British government turned to the Commonwealth to subsidize common objectives, with the additional belief that a Commonwealth project combining the twin objectives of anticommunism and development would induce the United States to participate. In early 1950 the British presented a memo to American authorities which pointed out that Britain simply could not afford to pay out the sterling balances requested by the South Asian and antipodean Commonwealth. If withdrawals were reduced to a level which the United Kingdom could afford, the South Asian Commonwealth would be "unable to maintain, far less increase, their present rate of development," the memo stated. There could be "no prospect of a satisfactory settlement of the sterling balance problem consistent with a continuous economic development … unless new money can be found for development (or for settlement of the sterling balances) from outside the Sterling Area. On any realistic assessment this can only mean dollars."[25] These problems became more acute by the spring, when concern began to mount about the impact of the end of Marshall Plan aid to the United Kingdom. In late April the Commonwealth Relations Office (CRO) stated, "We must recognize that

[the] sterling area already faces economic problems of great gravity." It pointed out that the "economic structure of almost every sterling area country is dependent upon Marshall Aid"; and since that aid would end by 1952, the first task of the sterling countries "must be to balance its dollar accounts and to restore the reserves to a level at which it can hope to weather future world depressions." The CRO's "main conclusion" was that the development problem could not "be solved on Commonwealth basis alone." For effective progress to be made, it argued, "we shall have to enlist co-operation of United States of America as well as of other non-Commonwealth countries in the area."[26]

Canadian policymakers also were concerned with the economic development of South and Southeast Asia, and like British, Australian, and American officials they wanted to alleviate the social conditions that might give rise to protest movements and communism. Canadian participation in the Commonwealth economic program, which emerged from the initial conference at Colombo in January 1950, demonstrated Canada's affinity with British and Commonwealth strategic global goals in the context of the Cold War. The conclusions of PUSC 22 were consistent with Canada's perceived need to consolidate Western power within the framework of NATO. Canadian officials were also keen on encouraging a greater American commitment in South and Southeast Asia and hoped that American aid to the South Asian Commonwealth would be forthcoming. On this level, Canada was willing to pursue a policy of supporting the strength of sterling in the international arena. A memo by the Interdepartmental Committee on External Trade Policy, dated 2 March 1950, was hopeful that the creation of a consultative committee for South and South-East Asia would "make it easier for the United States to participate later in some kind of economic assistance plan for Asia." American aid would strengthen the economies of the region, help them combat the spread of Communism, and also supply the sterling area "as a whole with a flow of dollars which might be expected to continue after the end of the European Recovery Programme." A context could be created "in which attempts to scale down the sterling accumulations, or at least severely restrict drawings on them, would have a greater chance of success."[27]

The cabinet memo outlining the instructions to the Canadian representatives at the follow-up Sydney Conference in May was more cautious about Canadian support of the Commonwealth plan. These instructions reflected the dominant concern of Canadian politicians about not undertaking policies that might have a negative effect on Canadian-American relations. The memo expressed the need for a cautious approach to the plan, for a close examination of the problem, and the importance of self-help and "*maximum utilization of local re-*

sources." Emphasis was also placed on working within already existing United Nations programs for development. The United Nations approach would have the practical benefit of American participation and money, which Canada believed was vital to the success of such aid programs. Like American officials, Canadian policymakers preferred modest aid programs designed to lay the foundations for greater private investment in underdeveloped countries, and they discouraged broad regional programs in Asia based on the Marshall Plan precedent.[28] Canadian support for the Colombo Plan was thus based on a sympathetic understanding of Britain's economic needs, a genuine interest in the South Asian Commonwealth, and the perceived need to work within a broader American framework. In economic terms, Canada would benefit from American participation in technical aid programs because these would help establish the foundations for additional American private capital investment in the Third World. If the United States substantially increased its international investment in the developing world, "the resulting circulation of United States exchange should be to the advantage of Canada."[29]

THE UNITED STATES AND THE DOLLAR GAP

For the United States, the postwar period represented a great boom for its exports – so large in fact that it had to subsidize its exports through loans and economic programs such as the Marshall Plan. The crucial economic problem that American policymakers faced in this period was the "dollar gap." This meant essentially that countries were importing more goods from the United States than their reserves could afford. Such was the case with Britain. But this was a global problem, and American policymakers wanted a worldwide solution that would not require continued American economic aid. The difficulty lay not so much in finding new markets for products as in how to maintain current levels of exports in the context of the shortage of world dollars. Broadly speaking, the American executive branch proposed a double-edged strategy to solve the problem: increased imports, and greater capital investment in the underdeveloped world.

The problem of the dollar weighed heavily on the minds of American policymakers early in 1950. In a memo to President Truman on 16 February 1950, Secretary of State Dean Acheson argued that the "time is rapidly approaching when the Government and the people of the United States must make critical and far-reaching decisions of policy affecting our economic relationships with the rest of the world." He went on to define the problem: Marshall Plan aid would end in two years and unless the United States formulated a strategy to deal with this contingency, the domestic economy would come under increasing strain. American exports, "including the key commodities on which our most efficient agricultural and manufacturing industries are heavily dependent, will be sharply reduced, with serious repercussions" for both the United States and its allies. "European countries, and friendly areas in the Far East and elsewhere, will be unable to obtain basic necessities which we now supply, to an extent that will threaten their political stability."[30]

The solution to the dollar gap reinforced the need for America's empire to be an informal one. A formal empire would have meant an expenditure of funds beyond the bounds of limited economic assistance plans. It would have tied down American prestige and power in areas of peripheral strategic concern. The emergence of pro-Western anticommunist governments in the Third World became critical in the context of America's global competition with the Soviet Union, its economic strategy to reorient world trade, and its attempts to eliminate the dollar gap. A failure to solve the economic problems of the free world could have disastrous implications for the West's favourable global balance of power *vis-à-vis* the Soviet empire.

Multilateral free trade in most sectors of the free world economy remained an important American policy objective. The Anglo-American alliance was also a very important aspect of the United States' postwar international strategy, and officials realized that a weak Britain would hurt American policy objectives in Western Europe and elsewhere. To help further these complementary postwar objectives, American foreign economic policy towards the United Kingdom was designed to promote the convertibility of sterling. But the United States needed to ensure that convertibility would not gravely weaken the British pound or the sterling area. This meant finding extra sources of dollar supply for the area. As a Department of State working group reported in the fall of 1950, "While there is a greater likelihood of the sterling area being in balance with the dollar area in 1953 than there is of Germany and Japan being in balance, it will still be necessary to provide additional opportunities for the sterling area to earn dollars if exchange restrictions are to be sufficiently relaxed to approach convertibility of the pound sterling."[31] Here was one basis of Anglo-American cooperation in financial matters after the Second World War.

As Andrew Rotter has pointed out, American officials recognized the weakness of Britain's external position and took steps to shore up Britain's financial position.[32] Yet the U.S. government approached the problem of global economic stability from a somewhat different angle than the British, for there were important reservations underlying America's support of British power in the postwar world.

The limits to this cooperation, and therefore also the Anglo-American partnership, were not always well understood by the British. With regard to the sterling balances in South and Southeast Asia, American policymakers argued that the provision of American dollars would have only a limited impact on Britain's sterling balances problem. Although direct American aid to the holders of sterling balances might make them more willing to reduce or fund their balances, American aid "would not cause a reduction in those balances unless aid was made with that specific proviso."[33]

American policymakers initially looked on the Colombo scheme with a certain amount of scepticism. They were particularly concerned about appearing to Asians to be underwriting British colonial power in the region. Although Commonwealth aid was welcome insofar as it promoted stability, the United States was wary about backing a purely Commonwealth scheme. In March the assistant secretary of state, W. Walton Butterworth, told Dening that the United States "welcomed" the Colombo initiative; but, recognizing Britain's economic weakness, he was "a little anxious" that further Commonwealth discussions "might reveal an extensive gap between the requirements of the 'have not' Commonwealth countries on the one hand and the ability of the 'haves' on the other to satisfy those requirements." The United States faced a major obstacle in Europe in the coming years, noted Butterworth, and he hoped that "there would be no question of working on the principle of 'one good gap deserves another.'" The United States preferred to work in "backward areas" through Point Four, the United Nations, the World Bank, and the International Monetary Fund. The assistant secretary of state for economic affairs, Willard Thorp, later told Sir Leslie Rowan that the United States "could not consider what we might do in this area as related to the sterling balances. If whatever we were able to do had the effect of helping the British in the solution of their separate problem, we would be very glad."[34]

VIETNAM, ANGLO-AMERICAN RELATIONS, AND THE BAO DAI "SOLUTION"

One reason why the British wanted a greater U.S. commitment to Southeast Asia was that the insurgency in Vietnam was a potential threat to British colonial power in Malaya. In late December 1949, Malcolm MacDonald, the British commissioner general in Southeast Asia, warned: "If Indo-China is lost, then Siam and Burma will probably go the same way shortly afterwards. That will bring the power of international Communism to the border of Malaya."[35] His conclusions were confirmed later that week by British officials attending a conference at Bukit Serene. A cabinet memo on the meeting noted that a French withdrawal from Vietnam would have "disastrous" effects on the United Kingdom's position in Southeast Asia, and the participants recommended that as much assistance as possible be given "to the French in their attempt to rally and consolidate the Vietnamese national movement round Bao Dai."[36]

The United States recognized the important role the region played in British power, and it also recognized the advantages of coordinating its containment strategy with the British. Britain might be able to influence the French to adopt more "liberal" policies towards Indochina, and its prestige and influence among Asian governments might secure Asian support for Western containment strategies. One conclusion of the National Security Council's policy paper NSC 51 – "U.S. Policy toward Southeast Asia," dated 1 July 1949 – was the need to work with the British to influence the French to devolve sovereignty onto a native Vietnamese regime.[37] The United Kingdom could thus work with the United States to lobby for a more decentralized French empire in Indochina.

While British diplomats helped convince the Americans of the importance of preserving Southeast Asia from communism, there were also many other reasons why American policies were becoming more concerned with the conflict in Vietnam. For the United States, a successful solution to the conflict would not only contain the spread of communism but would demonstrate to the world that the West could create a partnership with indigenous nationalists. There were also important economic objectives associated with containing Ho Chi Minh's power, and these were indirectly related to America's dollar gap strategy. The elimination of communist power in Indochina would preserve Southeast Asia's strategic and economic value as a source of Western and Japanese raw materials. However, although the preservation of British colonial power in Southeast Asia was compatible with these other American objectives, the United States did not formulate its policies towards Indochina primarily in the light of British advice and interest.

The overriding U.S. policy considerations towards Vietnam were political and strategic in nature: the establishment of a viable political alternative to communism. Like the British, the Americans supported Bao Dai. The creation of an anticommunist government with close relations with the West was the ultimate goal of America's strategy in Vietnam. According to NSC 51, French imperialism was simply playing into the hands of Stalin. If French colonialism was eliminated in favour of a policy of yielding sovereignty to the nationalists, civil war would likely break out between the "true" nationalists and the communists. It would then be necessary for the United States, "working through a screen of anti-communist Asiatics, to ensure, however long it takes, the triumph of Indochinese nationalism over Red imperialism."[38] The Truman administration set the basic policy objectives that led to America's long-term involvement in Vietnam. The attempts to sustain anticommunists in Korea were largely successful, but in Vietnam the strength of the communists and the frailty of the anticommunist nationalists effectively undermined U.S. efforts to devolve political power onto selected indigenous politicians.

Neither Dean Acheson nor Ernest Bevin wanted his government's support for France to appear as a condonation of Western imperialism in Asia, and both men tried hard to persuade other Asian states to recognize the Bao Dai regime. Both also emphasized the need for the French to ratify the 9 March 1949 accords defining areas of responsibility for France and the Associated State of Vietnam. In early January 1950, Bevin was given assurances by the French government that the accords would be passed by the French parliament around 12 January. The French were anxious that Britain not recognize the new Chinese government before recognizing Bao Dai. Bevin was sympathetic to French objections and delayed British recognition of China for several days to give the French parliament more time to ratify the accords.[39]

It is in this context that Bevin's diplomatic manoeuvring at the Colombo Conference must be understood. He went to Colombo hoping that French ratification would give him the necessary diplomatic leverage to convince Commonwealth representatives, and particularly the South Asian ones, to recognize the new fledgling Vietnamese government. Commonwealth support would help achieve several diplomatic objectives. It might provide an impetus for increased American aid to Vietnam and Southeast Asia. U.S. aid would stabilize the region against the communist threat and would strengthen Britain's colonial position in Southeast Asia. Support for the French position in Indochina would also allow the French to conserve resources it badly needed at home, to shore up its economy, and to strengthen its defence. In general, pusc 22's hopes that the Western system would be consolidated in the Eastern areas of the globe would be one step closer to fruition. The fact that it was a Commonwealth meeting that would accomplish these goals would give prestige to Britain's leadership role and would emphasize to the Americans the advantages of supporting the sterling area. Bevin's determination to implement this strategy is reflected in the fact that he undertook the long boat journey to Ceylon despite being very ill and weak.

His plans were frustrated, however, when the French National Assembly failed to ratify the accords. On 17 January, Bevin cabled the

Foreign Office with disappointing news: the majority of the Common-wealth were sceptical about French policy in Indochina and were suspicious of France's good faith in transferring power to Bao Dai. India, in particular, took a very critical line. "I cannot pretend that we had any noticeable influence upon the attitude of Pandit Nehru," Bevin wrote.[40]

Bevin encouraged Australia and New Zealand to recognize the new associated state, but it fact they were already moving in that direction. Australia's foreign secretary, Percy Spender, was worried about the possibility of Vietnam falling to the communists and was prepared to give his diplomatic support to the French strategy. During the conference, he said that the French were "genuinely working towards a goal of complete independence for Indo-China," and although he considered that there were several unhappy elements to French policy, he would recommend de facto recognition of the Bao Dai government. The Australians had a strong regional interest in Southeast Asia, and at Colombo Spender often referred to the need to provide economic aid to Indonesia. But the communist threat was perceived in regional terms as well. "South and Southeast Asia is gravely threatened by Communist pressure," the Australians claimed. Immediate economic measures, designed to "stabilise Governments and promote production are the primary means at our disposal to meet this urgent threat." By contrast, the South Asian Commonwealth remained critical of the French and were sceptical of accepting the associated states into the Colombo Plan. Nehru "expressed doubts" about the strength of Bao Dai, maintaining that the French transfer of power had fallen "far short of complete independence" and that France's approach to India for recognition had "confirmed the impression that the Bao Dai government was a puppet government acting under French control."[41]

The Americans encountered similar criticism from Thailand and the Philippines. Thus, both the United States and Great Britain realized that there was substantial Asian resistance to their plans to devolve power onto Bao Dai. These Asian reactions underlined the Great Power objectives of Anglo-America's Southeast Asian containment strategies prior to the outbreak of the Korean War. Telegrams sent by Acheson to American embassies in the Philippines, Indonesia, and Thailand requested U.S. representatives to find out the attitude of these Southeast Asian governments to Bao Dai: "You should emphasize," Acheson wrote to his ambassador in Manila, that the Bao Dai regime is the "only apparent present alternative to Commie domination of Indochina"; if Indochina fell, the Philippine government would find itself "facing dangerous forces on [the] Asiatic mainland."[42] Although Acheson hoped that diplomatic pressure would convince

Southeast Asian countries of the necessity of recognizing Bao Dai, he was disappointed with the negative responses. While some Asian leaders such as Mohammed Hatta of Indonesia expressed concern about the implications of communist power in Indochina, none was initially prepared to recognize the ex-emperor.

General Carlos Romulo of the Philippines had refused to recognize Bao Dai on the grounds that Bao "was and is regarded throughout Asia as a French puppet." Only the Thai government changed its mind on the recognition issue. However, Thai support for the new Vietnamese government came at the expense of an internal cabinet crisis and the resignation of the Thai foreign minister, Pote Sarasin.[43] Despite concern about alienating Asian opinion, in practice both the United States and Britain were prepared to recognize a state towards which Asian governments expressed strong reservations. Cold War considerations predominated in America's decision to recognize Bao Dai.

Bao Dai was in a weak position as head of state of Vietnam, partly because he was forced to work within a constitutional framework that provided France with substantial means of controlling the country. The Elysée Agreements, which the British and Americans were pushing the French to ratify, provided only limited powers to the Vietnamese. Foreign affairs, military operations, and most economic issues were still under French sovereignty. Bao Dai's "nationalism" was hampered by French unwillingness to grant him powers of any substance.

Nevertheless, like Syngman Rhee, the Vietnamese leader was not a simple puppet or pawn of Western imperialism. He had specific objectives and worried about how he would consolidate his legitimacy. To acquire greater respect in the eyes of Vietnamese nationalists, he believed that France would have to give his government more responsibility and independence. On 8 June 1950 he told Edmund Gullion, the American chargé at Saigon, that he had returned to Vietnam "only because he had assurances from the French that seemed [to] promise independence for Vietnam." Angry at France's failure to live up to its promises, he continued: "This independence, what is it? Where is it? Do you see it? Is a government independent without a budget? When it has to beg 20,000,000 piastres a month for its existence?"[44] Bao Dai hoped that the United States would be more successful in convincing the French to make important political concessions.

American officials were sympathetic to Bao Dai's protests. Gullion believed the United States should see the issue as an "Asiatic and Vietnamese problem and one of our own security." The United States might yet have to send troops to Indochina. The French had blackmailed Americans into giving their support to French policies. They would not withdraw their troops from Vietnam, not only because of their interests in Indochina but because it would mean an end to the French Union and the falling away of the African colonies. "We had fallen for blackmail and not put one single condition on aid to French nor pressed any of our requests," Gullion complained.[45]

Vietnamese officials also complained to the British about French colonial policies. On 11 May, Nguyen Dac Khe, the assistant to Vietnamese representative Buu Loc in Paris, told a diplomat from the British embassy that the French were "doing everything possible to prevent Viet Nam from attaining a real degree of independence." The Vietnamese had looked at the Commonwealth as a model for French policies, but he pointed out that the British "were gradually being eclipsed by the Americans, whose assistance – both military and economic – was badly needed." To support Vietnamese sovereignty, Khe asked the United Kingdom to provide Vietnam with token assistance, just to prove that it was regarded as a sovereign and independent state. When it was pointed out that direct assistance to the Vietnamese would contravene the accords of 8 March, Khe argued that "it was only by asserting its independence in matters of this sort that the Bao Dai regime could obtain a more liberal treatment from the French."[46]

Bao Dai's government was overly optimistic about the success it might have in gaining concessions from the Western powers. Despite Gullion's protests, the State Department qualified its willingness to work for greater autonomy for Vietnam. The American government pursued a policy of gradual independence for Bao Dai, but one that was circumscribed by the need to work with the French and by the inability of Bao Dai's government to attract wide support. The weakness of the indigenous anticommunist nationalists in Vietnam undermined America's attempt to implement its containment strategies. There is an irony here in that French colonialism and American support of the French military presence contributed to the political problem. In a message to the American embassy in Paris at the end of March 1950, Acheson told Ambassador David Bruce that the State Department had "predicated its course of action in Indochina since Feb 2 this year on assumption that fundamental objectives of U.S. and France in Indochina are in substantial coincidence." Bruce would "surely understand," said Acheson, that the department did not believe that the present situation called for "further substantive concessions ... *at this time* ... Bao Dai and company [are] barely able to discharge responsibilities they are now facing."[47]

Military considerations were an important factor leading to diminished pressure on the French for concessions to Bao Dai. Acceptance of France's military role in Indochina led to some legitimization of its political role. The dangers of American pressure resulting in French military withdrawal were too great. Vietnam lay outside the American defensive perimeter in East Asia, and the French could be relied on to contain and roll back communism in Indochina. In the short term, the collective interests of the West were being served by the French military presence in the region. In the absence of a direct American commitment, and until more Vietnamese troops could be raised, French troops would serve American interests. To this extent, the United States supported France's formal presence in Indochina. The demise of formal French colonialism might have to await the outcome of French military operations.

Although American military planners were concerned with the political ramifications of aiding French colonialism in Asia, they believed that military aid was needed to prevent a possible total collapse of the Western sphere of influence in Southeast Asia. In a memo to the State Department in the spring of 1950, the Joint Chiefs of Staff pointed out that there would be no political alternative if the French withdrew. Without the French military presence, the chiefs argued, the Vietnamese regime would probably not last the year, even with U.S. aid. U.S. insistence on a phased withdrawal might help the political situation, but what was required was an increase in American military and economic aid. The provision of military aid was "psychologically overriding" and should be provided at the "earliest practicable date."[48]

The memo underlined the weakness of Bao Dai as a viable political alternative to the Viet Minh. It also emphasized Bao Dai's dependence on Western aid for his government's survival. Though not a pawn, he was in a dependent position *vis-à-vis* French and American power, and to that extent was a creation of Western policy. To a much greater degree than President Rhee, his freedom to consolidate his internal power base was constrained by the actions of external governments.

American policy was designed to overcome some of France's reluctance to devolve more power on his regime. As Acheson told the acting assistant secretary of state for Far Eastern affairs in February 1950, the Vietnamese should be encouraged to work within the French Union, but "they should be in a position where they could in fact, if they so elected, walk out of the French Union at any time."[49] But Acheson saw this as a long-term process. In the short term, U.S. policymakers felt constrained to accept France's interpretation of the constitution of the French Union. There was a clash of imperial strategies between the French and Americans over Indochina, but it was submerged under the pressing need to contain the communists. The French wanted to develop and maintain an empire based on a predominance of French control within the rubric of the French Union. Both British and American diplomats conceived of empire after 1945 in more decentralized terms. To the extent that the United States disagreed with France's conception of colonial policy towards Indochina, there existed a subtle competition for spheres of influence between the United States and France in the region. The competition underlying the broader pattern of Franco-American cooperation can be seen in terms of America's preference for informal over colonial empire.

U.S. officials wanted the French to operate an informal empire of their own in Vietnam in a manner comparable to the American experience in South Korea. In the minds of Americans imbued with Cold War ideology, U.S. state building in the Republic of Korea was a worthy experiment. But France's inability to resolve the military deadlock with the Viet Minh and its general reluctance to decentralize its empire according to American wishes resulted in increased direct American responsibilities in Vietnam. This was done in order to do what the Americans criticized the French for failing to do – to devolve political power on indigenous elites and provide them with the technical capacity for maintaining their own state apparatus. Under American "guidance" – and, when necessary, with direct U.S. involvement in Vietnamese internal affairs – Vietnam would emerge as a pro-Western state with all the appearances of legal sovereignty. The Vietnam War was fought to establish the security needs of a new "state" that never materialized.

The implications for the United States of a prolonged French failure in Vietnam were understood by American officials in early 1950. A CIA memo entitled "The Crisis in Indochina" published in February warned that if present trends continued, "France can do no more than maintain a temporary stalemate with the Vietnamese resistance." Tragically, even as the United States was moving to rally other governments to recognize Bao Dai, the CIA predicted that the experiment would ultimately fail: "It is unlikely that Bao Dai will be able to win the political support of any appreciable fraction of the resistance movement." The French objective of "direct military conquest" had not achieved any notable successes, noted the memo. The French had committed a total of 150,500 troops to Vietnam and "only a relatively small area of Vietnam is under French control." The implications for American policy were clear before the Korean War: increased direct American involvement in the nation-building experiment and, if necessary, the gradual displacement of France as the controlling power in the region. As the CIA knew, "French progress toward both political and military objectives has been substantially less than is necessary to eliminate the threat posed by the vigorous resistance forces." Unless the French and Bao Dai received "substantial outside assistance," the combined political and military pressure of the Viet Minh might "accelerate a French withdrawal from all or most of Indochina."[50]

The Americans still hoped that they could influence the French to adopt containment strategies that were consistent with U.S. interests, but the difficulties were tremendous. To get the French to accept its concept of informal empire, the United States had to obtain the cooperation of both the French and the Bao Dai group. The successful implementation of American aid depended on the ability of Vietnam and France to coordinate their policies. Richard Bissell, the acting administrator of the Economic Cooperation Administration (and later CIA head), wrote on 6 May 1950 that American aid was "premised on [the] understanding that political relations between Indochinese Govts and France will rest firmly upon mutual consent ... Only if this decisive factor of consent is present can we assure that Indochinese people will have the will to resist external pressure, and make aid a worthwhile gamble."[51] Given the tensions between France and Bao Dai's government, this was a difficult thing to achieve. On all levels of policy implementation the United States was faced with competing and conflicting claims on the part of the French and the Vietnamese anticommunists.

In the summer of 1950 the Vietnamese threatened not to attend the Pau Conference. The conference had been called to discuss the distribution of economic power between France and the associated states. On 29 March, Acheson told Gullion in Saigon that while the United States was prepared to interpret Franco-Vietnamese agreements in a liberal manner, he also expected the three states and Bao Dai in particular to discharge their responsibilities under the 8 March accords, especially in matters affecting defence.[52]

The British tended to be a little more sympathetic to France, in part because the United Kingdom was also a colonial power. But like U.S. policy, the British strategy was designed to devolve central power into the hands of pro-Western local regimes that were willing to fight communism. Thus, when it came to the French empire, British policymakers hoped that the French Union would eventually evolve into a framework like the British Commonwealth. As early as June 1948, the secretary of state for Commonwealth relations, Philip Noel Baker, wrote that the Vietnamese nationalists were "pressing for diplomatic and military concessions which would amount to the grant of Dominion status." Although the French were "extremely reluctant to surrender their power to this extent," a gesture of this sort would be required, he said, "if the new government is to win the less extreme Nationalist elements from the Viet Minh."[53] In 1949 the British agreed with the United States that recognition of Bao Dai would depend on the French ratification of the 8 March accords. Like the Americans, they also pressed for Indochinese affairs to be moved from the Ministry of Overseas France to the Quai d'Orsay. This would provide some perceived legitimacy to the fiction of Indochinese sovereignty. It would also serve as a symbol of France's willingness to treat Indochina as a separate and independent state.

When asked to compare British and French colonial policy, British policymakers stressed the more "liberal" nature of their approach. To a degree this was true. Bevin's comment in January that he wanted the French to demonstrate materially that "the Colonial period has come to an end" contrasted sharply with Minister for Overseas France Jean Letourneau's pronouncement that "France was determined to maintain her civilising influence in Indo-China."[54] In Britain, "liberal" was associated with a decentralized empire. On this level, Britain gave diplomatic support to America's concept of informal empire. At the Colombo Conference, While Bevin emphasized to Nehru that he had urged the French for three and a half years "to adopt a similar policy to that which the United Kingdom Government followed in India, Pakistan and Ceylon." While Bevin recognized that the French situation was not analogous to Britain's in 1947–48 and that "a too hasty surrender of power might plunge Indo-China into administrative and economic chaos of which the Communists would take advantage," he nevertheless belived that recognition of Bao Dai would give impetus to a more far-sighted policy: "We should be helping to bring peace and stability to Indo-China."[55]

Britain's ideas regarding decentralized empire and commonwealth were an important underlying basis for the Anglo-American special relationship after the Second World War. American and U.K. policymakers could agree within certain bounds on the need for informal empire in the Cold War context. A secret British draft memo entitled "The Colonial Empire Today" argued, "We are engaged in a worldwide experiment in nation-building." The British aim was to "create independence – independence within the Commonwealth – not to suppress it." The challenge was to direct colonial nationalism in a manner consistent with the interests of Britain and the West: "Nationalism is an emotion requiring to be harnessed for constructive purposes if it is not to become extremist, destructive and the instrument of Communist incitement." Moderate nationalism was seen as a key to continued Great Power status for Britain. Despite this convergence of views between the United States and Britain, caution should be exercised in describing British colonial policy or American foreign policy as more liberal than the French. The British were not less reluctant than the French to use military force to achieve their Great Power objectives. The United States did react differently to the maintenance of British colonial rule in Malaya, but this had more to do with the internal dynamics of Malayan society than with any specific aspect of England's colonial policy.

In Malaya, as in Vietnam, Cold War issues kept the United Kingdom from implementing its "liberal" colonial policies. As Foreign Secretary Ernest Bevin told Dean Acheson on 13 September 1949, the Malayan "terrorists made it difficult to make any further progress in the way of constitutional development." British containment policies in Malaya were exceptional only because the Malay majority were willing to work peacefully with the British for their independence. The peasant communist uprising posed a danger to British colonial power, but it was weaker than the Vietnamese movement, and the Chinese ethnicity of the communists prevented the uprising from co-opting the predominantly Malay society. Bevin's memo of his meeting with Acheson recorded: "There was general agreement on the American side that the situation in Malaya was quite different from that prevailing in Indo-China since the Malays looked to the British for protection against the Chinese, and were not at present seeking any further degree of independence."[56]

Britain was prepared to support the broad outlines of American diplomacy towards Indochina, but it lacked the resources to affect French policy. In March 1950, J.L. Lloyd of the South East Asia Department told Commonwealth representatives that French officials had asked British military authorities for spare military equipment and parts, including small arms, mortars, and aircraft. However, Britain "held out very little hope that military assistance would be forthcoming in view of existing commitments in Malaya, Hong Kong and elsewhere." When the French foreign minister, Robert Schuman, referred to the US$75 million available for the general area of China, during a conversation with Bevin on 7 March, the foreign secretary made no commitments and simply noted that "France was a good candidate for United States aid in Indo-China."[57]

On the issue of colonialism generally, the United Kingdom did feel some solidarity with the French. In a cabinet memo dated 19 May 1950, the foreign secretary noted that he had recently taken "the opportunity of stressing to Mr. Acheson how important it was that the Americans should not undermine our position in the Colonial field. Britain was making a big contribution to the common cause and it would be fatal if this contribution were lessened by the loss of Colonies by the Western European Powers, since they were an essential part of the foundation of European economic existence."[58] The statement was made largely with Europe's African colonies in mind, but it had important implications for Asia as well. Britain wanted to support the principle that colonial policies were ultimately the domain of the mother country. After the tripartite meetings in London in May 1950, Bevin was reassured about America's basic support on colonial issues:

"It was satisfactory that in the tripartite meetings the Americans again reaffirmed their readiness to try and meet us and the French more fully than in the past over the Colonial question."[59]

Beyond this issue, no Western nation seemed to question the nature of its ideological commitment to a noncommunist power in Indochina. Prevalent in U.S. State Department summaries of the situation in Vietnam, for example, was the idea that the communists led by Ho Chi Minh were, a priori, illegitimate. They were considered illegitimate because American policymakers assumed that the communists were working for Soviet imperialism and therefore did not have the interest of the Vietnamese people at heart. "Nationalists" who aligned themselves with communism were not nationalists at all but were cynical pawns of Soviet power politics.

The Viet Minh were communists who aligned themselves with the Sino-Soviet bloc, but the nature of their nationalism was misunderstood. The Americans tended to disregard the genuine anticolonial basis of Vietnamese communism. American fears about the spread of Soviet communism in East Asia were largely of a hypothetical nature. Fear of the Soviet core expanding over East and Southeast Asia seemed to blind Western policymakers. Thus, one reason given for the American recognition of the Associated State of Vietnam was "a demonstration of displeasure with Communist tactics which are obviously aimed at eventual domination of Asia, working under the guise of indigenous nationalism."[60]

British perceptions of communism in Indochina were similar to the American, but the Britons and Canadians tended to view the conflict in terms of competition for nationalist sentiment, not one of illegitimate nationalism versus legitimate nationalism. On 7 February 1950, Bevin noted that "of the two nationalist movements in Viet Nam that led by Ho Chi Minh was being exploited by the Communists."[61] These different perceptions of the common threat illustrate the emotive tone of American anticommunist rhetoric as well as America's stronger dedication to eliminating the perceived Soviet threat entirely. American rhetoric was symbolic of the global scale on which the United States was preparing itself to fight the communist core in early 1950. To the extent that the U.S. goal in Indochina was designed to contain the global threat of communism, the interests of the Vietnamese people were a secondary policy consideration.

CANADA AND VIETNAM

Memos produced in the Canadian Department of External Affairs (DEA) during this period suggest that Canada's interest in Indochina stemmed from its broad goals of containing communist movements in Asia and supporting the policies of its major Western allies. On 31 August 1949 the Canadian government was officially informed by French authorities of the establishment of the Government of Vietnam. This was acknowledged in a noncommittal note to the French government on 10 October. In passing the note to French Ambassador Guerin, Under-Secretary of State Arnold Heeney said that "as a Pacific power [Canada] is interested in the re-establishment of peaceful conditions in the whole Pacific basin." A settlement of the differences between the moderate Vietnamese nationalists and the French in Vietnam would "prevent possible Communist domination of all East Asia"; it would also promote conditions for peaceful commerce, facilitate the activities of Canadian missionaries in the region, and help France in meeting the drain on its resources. Canada, stated Heeney, officially approved of "the efforts of the French government" to meet the "legitimate aspirations of the annamese Nationalists for self-government." However, Canada could not recognize the full formal sovereignty of this government and therefore it was "doubtful if we could give support at this time to an application by Viet Nam for United Nations membership."[62]

There was substantial official support in Canada for the British and American position on Vietnam. Canadian officials believed that France could play an important role in the region if it could be made to understand the negative implications of formal colonial rule. Heeney believed that France "might still make a considerable contribution for the reconstruction and development of Indochina." The idea of decentralizing the French empire and creating moderate anticommunist elites was appealing, but like the British and Americans, the Canadians argued that in the short term, only French military actions could prevent the Indochinese communists from coming to power. The Canadian ambassador in France, Georges Vanier, wrote to Pearson in November 1949 saying, although "the Bao Dai experiment has not obtained much success thus far I am inclined to endorse the efforts of the French Government to establish some prestige for the Bao Dai Government. The French assertion that there is no suitable alternative policy at the present seems to be true." Canadian attitudes were summed up by the chief of the general staff, Lieutenant-General G.G. Simonds. He believed that the French empire in Inchochina had been misguided and that only something approaching the Commonwealth model would be successful in Vietnam. In August 1950 he told a meeting of the Canadian Chiefs of Staff Committee that "France was still very colonial-minded in its attitude towards the Bao Dai government which, as a result, was not giving its fullest support to the French authorities." Nevertheless, French power was required in Vietnam because if Indochina fell, "the rest of the Far East would also probably succumb to communist domination."[63] By 1950, most of official Ottawa accepted the premises of the domino theory.

Unlike Britain and America, however, Canada did not accord recognition to the Vietnamese in early 1950. This decision was based in part on arguments which the British themselves had put forth about the associated states – that they did not meet the basic requirements of national sovereignty. France retained substantial control over Vietnam's internal affairs, and territorially Bao Dai's government controlled perhaps less than a quarter of the country. The rest was in the hands of the communists under Ho Chi Minh. Historians James Eayrs and Douglas Ross have argued that Nehru's opinions held strong force with Prime Minister St Laurent and were a major reason for Canada's decision not to recognize the associated states at this time. According to Eayrs, "L.S. St Laurent set great store by Pandit Nehru's opinions; he had not much use for Bao Dai; and he suspected the French government of having neo-colonialist, if not colonialist, designs upon Indochina."[64] St Laurent was reluctant to aid the older Great Powers in their colonial wars, and he was critical of formal colonialism. He refused to provide direct military aid to the British in Malaya, and he held that Canadian military aid for France under the mutual aid program should not be earmarked for Indochina, though ultimately France decided where its aid should go. Lester Pearson also had been influenced by Pandit Nehru at the Colombo Conference, and he was concerned about the implications that recognition of the associated states would have for the Commonwealth and for Asian nationalism. A DEA memo in early 1950 noted with alarm the possibility of creating an "undesirable 'white versus Asiatic' alignment within the Commonwealth on this issue."[65]

Canadian policy towards Indochina at this stage was ambiguous – Canada did not want to alienate the Asian Commonwealth, yet it was concerned about the Western position in Indochina. The importance of Nehru should not be exaggerated, though. India had recognized the People's Republic of China, something that Pearson also advocated in the Canadian cabinet, yet St Laurent delayed the Canadian recognition until the Korean War made it an impossibility. Ultimately, the importance of the Canadian-American special relationship outweighed sympathies for Nehru's views.

Officials were genuinely worried about the power of the communist movement in Vietnam, and Pearson's basic desire to accord support to Western objectives was revealed in a speech to the Canadian House of

Commons on 22 February 1950. Pearson said that the French government's policies in Indochina "deserve our gratitude." Bao Dai was wished "every success." Only under the "autonomous government of Bao Dai has Vietnam at this time the opportunity to acquire freedom and unity and stability," stated Pearson.[66]

There is evidence that the Anglo-American decision to recognize Bao Dai in February 1950 influenced Canada's position on Vietnam. Canada was coordinating its strategy for recognizing Vietnam with its policies on China. On 9 June, Heeney wrote to Pearson mentioning that "the possibility was discussed of our recognizing the Bao Dai government in Viet Nam and the two other Associate States of Cambodia and Laos a week or so before we take steps to recognize the Peking Government in China." Heeney thought this procedure might complicate ongoing discussions with the Chinese and recommended recognizing the two states simultaneously: "This would, I think, satisfy the French, who are primarily concerned that we do not recognize Peking *before* Bao Dai." Heeney suggested that the British formula of qualified recognition be used. The Canadian government would recognize "Viet Nam as an Associate State within the French Union" and Bao Dai as "the government of that state." Despite a reluctance to provide military aid to Indochina, Canada acknowledgeded its NATO interests in the issue and seemed to be on the verge of recognizing the Vietnamese government in 1950. However, the Korean War prevented further consideration of this topic largely because Pearson did not want to exacerbate Western relations with China by recognizing the Bao Dai regime. On 12 July he told the cabinet that "in view of the present tense situation and the uncertainty of developments in the near future, it would be wise to hold up recognition for a short period."[67] The "short period" was extended after the Chinese intervention in the late fall of 1950. Although formal recognition of the associated states did not occur until 1952, Canada's support for the new Vietnamese leader reflected its underlying sympathy for the Anglo-American containment strategy in Vietnam. The emergence of a pro-Western state headed by Bao Dai was a common goal of British, American, and Canadian governments in this period.

THE NORTH ATLANTIC TRIANGLE AND CHINA: JANUARY–JUNE 1950

Although there was substantial Anglo-American agreement on the strategy on Vietnam, an examination of Anglo-American relations over the Peoples Republic of China (PRC) illustrates some of the broader disagreements within the partnership. Whereas Britain adopted a defensive containment policy towards China, the United States' reluctance to work out a *modus vivendi* with the PRC stemmed in part from its more forceful containment strategies towards the Soviet Union. In the United Nations for example, American policymakers (and Dean Acheson in particular) associated Communist China's membership with appeasement of the USSR. Despite British diplomatic efforts, the Americans steadfastly refused to adopt the United Kingdom's defensive containment strategy towards China.

The picture that emerges from British Foreign Office and cabinet records for the first half of 1950 is that Britain's policy towards the PRC was not governed primarily by hopes or expectations of economic advantage arising out of the PRC itself; the protection and preservation of British financial and industrial interests in China was not the major reason for according recognition to the new regime. A cabinet memo of 20 April 1950 pointed out that Britain expected the Chinese to continue to attack Western "imperialism." There was no suggestion that recognition would lead to any substantial economic advantage for the United Kingdom. The British government did not vigorously push for the interests of British economic concerns on the mainland; indeed, the policy reflected a certain complacency in this matter. There was some optimism for the interests of British traders, but as the cabinet memo argued, "It must be accepted that the Communists are indifferent to the fate of British interests and it may even be that by a simple policy of inaction they are conniving at their liquidation."[68]

The United Kingdom's policy towards the PRC was based on two fundamental concerns: the threat of Soviet expansionism into Asia, and Britain's colonial possessions in Southeast Asia. The real danger was that the PRC would become a pawn of Soviet expansionism and would threaten the area around China's borders. Britain's "Titoist" strategy towards China emerged from its concern about the potential threat of a Sino-Soviet partnership to British and Western economic and political power in East Asia. Although Chinese communism was "repugnant" to the West, a boycott of the regime would simply strengthen Sino-Soviet bonds. Only by maintaining links with the West could China be weaned away from Kremlin influence. This policy promised no material benefit, but the only other alternative was "to write China off as irretrievably lost to Western democracy and to invite her open hostility."[69]

The British government was thus not motivated by traditional considerations associated with Western hopes of gaining access to the vast Chinese market. British containment strategy towards China was defensive and was designed to limit the influence of the Soviet Union. It was a diplomatic strategy which hoped to avoid the exhaustion of re-

sources that a confrontation with China, acting under Soviet conniv-
ance, would entail.

Canadian thinking on China was heavily influenced by the British
framework. Like the United Kingdom, Canada's national security lay
in an alliance with the United States and Western Europe. There was a
consensus in Canada on the need to consolidate Western power on the
basis of the North Atlantic Western "system." This entailed adopting a
defensive containment strategy towards continental East Asia and preventing the Western alliance from unnecessarily expending valuable
resources in a peripheral region.

In essence, Canada's Department of External Affairs adopted Britain's policy of preventing a consolidation of Chinese and Soviet power.
A key policy memo prepared for Prime Minister Louis St Laurent in
November 1949 pointed out that "China must now be regarded as a
potential enemy state and would probably side with Russia in the event
of a general war." The rise of communist power on the mainland "confronted the Atlantic Pact powers with considerable strategic and political problems." In Japan, argued the memo, the U.S. position was
threatened by a potentially hostile power in China; the usefulness of
Korea and Taiwan as military bases would be undermined, and in
Southeast Asia, "the source of vital raw materials," Western interests
were menaced by the impetus the Chinese revolution gave to communist movements. The beneficiary of these developments would be the
Soviet Union. Its prestige would increase throughout Asia, and it
might be tempted to divide and distract the West "from their work for
the political and economic restoration of Western Europe." A list of
recommended counter-measures included internal surveillance of
overseas Chinese, both in Canada and abroad, the institution of export controls on strategic goods going to the PRC, and a policy of preventing a full integration of Sino-Soviet interests. The latter objective
could be achieved through recognition of the PRC government and by
"keeping China dependent upon imports from the West for her economic wellbeing [*sic*] and progress." While Canada needed to consult
with Britain and the United States, Commonwealth considerations
seemed to be predominant, and Canada should be prepared to consider recognizing the Chinese government soon after Britain and
India did so.[70]

The revolution provided extra impetus for Canada to support the
state-building initiatives of its Atlantic allies in Asia. In late December a
high-level memo surveying the international strategic situation from
the Canadian perspective pointed out that the objectives of the Commonwealth and North Atlantic powers should be to support moderate
indigenous governments in East Asia and encourage "legitimate na-

tionalism" in order to "enlist the aid of nationalism in the area against the spread of communism." In the economic sphere, the West should make every effort to maintain continued access to the region's strategic raw materials such as tin and rubber. It should assist in the economic reconstruction of Asia and should endeavour to "raise the standard of living as a means of achieving political stability." Militarily, it was now important to "build up the forces of the democratically inclined native governments" through the sale of arms and equipment and the provision of training facilities and military advisory groups."[71] The Canadian government accepted the basic premise of creating proxy allies in the Asian Cold War.

After the Colombo Conference, Lester Pearson recommended that Canada implement some of the recommendations of these memos. At a cabinet meeting on 23 February 1950, he stated that after "serious consideration," he favoured Canadian recognition of the PRC "at an early date"; recognition of the regime was inevitable, and "from the Canadian as well as the international point of view there seemed to be every advantage in granting recognition as soon as possible."[72] Unlike the Americans, many officials in the Canadian government accepted the legality and legitimacy of the communist regime by the standards of international law. Recognition would increase China's bargaining power with the Soviet Union, and the continued presence of missionaries and traders would sustain Western influence. In sum, stated Pearson, the "democratic powers would apparently stand to gain more if this policy were successful and China were kept from full integration with the Soviet Union than they would lose if it failed."[73] Here was Canada's agreement with British strategic objectives towards the Sino-Soviet alliance.

There was also an important economic consideration affecting Pearson's judgment, for the Chinese Nationalist government had defaulted on its payments of a Sino-Canadian loan of $60 million: "If any part of this outstanding is to be paid back, it can only be as the result of re-negotiation with the Communist Government." Strategic and political considerations outweighed economic ones, however, and Canadian recognition was seen as a means of getting the United States to adopt more conciliatory policies. Although Hume Wrong had written Pearson from Washington in early February that Canadian recognition might stir up the American public, Pearson suggested to cabinet that "Canadian recognition would probably make it easier for the United States Government to follow suit in due course, which it inevitably must do."[74] Pearson thus hoped to align U.S. policy towards China with British and Canadian objectives. He was attempting to realize his broader vision of a North Atlantic diplomatic strategy centred firmly on Western Europe.

The Department of External Affairs' strategic thinking on China paralleled Foreign Office perceptions. Yet the Canadian government did not actively pursue the department's recommendations. Prime Minister St Laurent refused to heed his minister's request to grant early recognition, because he was concerned about the impact it would have on Canada's special relationship with the United States. On 10 March 1950, St Laurent told cabinet that "no country in the Western Hemisphere had as yet granted recognition to the Communist Government." He recognized the difficulties the British were experiencing and viewed their strategy as problematic for Canada's special relationship. Backed by other influential cabinet ministers – the powerful minister of trade and commerce, Clarence Decatur Howe, the minister of national health and welfare, Paul Martin, and the agriculture minister James Gardiner – St Laurent noted that although recognition might be inevitable, "it seemed undesirable for Canada to take the lead in breaking the stalemate that had developed since the first group of countries had recognized the Communist Government," and he stated that "Canadian action should wait on the progress of events."[75] There was to be no open break with American policy.

The preservation of Canada's close ties with the United States was the prime minister's primary policy objective. It was not that he disagreed with the importance of consolidating Western power on the basis of NATO. Rather, it was that where Anglo-Canadian strategic concepts conflicted with American policy, he was wary about causing tensions within the Canadian-American relationship.

By the spring of 1950, however, the British and Canadians were very concerned about the impact the Soviet Union's refusal to participate in the Security Council would have on the United Nations. The Soviets had walked out of the Security Council in January and had refused to participate in U.N. bodies until China was admitted. In a telegram to the secretary of state for external affairs dated 17 March, the British secretary of state for Commonwealth relations reported that his government had decided to seek the "speediest possible decision" on the Security Council in favour of a change in Chinese representation. The present situation was "unsatisfactory," he said, and the Soviet bloc boycott brought the agency into public "disrepute" and impaired its usefulness.[76] In Canada, the deputy under-secretary of state, Escott Reid, argued that public opinion in the United States and Canada was such "that it seems necessary to take some initiative towards re-opening negotiations with the Soviet Union." The Soviet peace campaign was influencing Western public opinion, and it was desirable to counter this with action in the United Nations. Even before the Soviet campaign, a Canadian poll in June 1949 had indicated that only 30 per cent of Canadians were satisfied with the progress made to date in the United Nations. In Britain the same poll in January 1949 had found that 22 per cent were satisfied and 55 per cent were dissatisfied. In the United States 63 per cent of the population in May 1949 had approved of top-level discussions with the Soviets. Reid argued that Canada should recognize the PRC in the hope that this action "would be followed by other governments and would result before many weeks in a change of Chinese representation in the United Nations."[77] This would placate Western public opinion, achieve Anglo-Canadian goals for Communist China, and result in the return of the Soviet Union to the Security Council.

At this time, Pearson was also recommending a respite from the Kennan conception of containment. On 24 March he wrote Wrong that on the subject of renewed negotiations with the Russians, "I do not think our public will be content for long merely with the achievements of the Kennan policy of containment, on no matter how wide a front that policy may be successfully applied." A certain level of strength had been achieved and Pearson was now prepared for discussions: the effects of Kennan's policies "are, or should be, a greater sense of confidence in the strength of our own position and we should therefore be prepared to make a renewed effort at settlement with a much greater feeling of assurance that, at least, we can come out of the process in a good light so far as our own public is concerned." Not all the old Commonwealth agreed, however. As on many Far Eastern issues, the Australians were a little bit closer to the American position than the British or Canadians were. On 2 March 1950, Percy Spender wrote to the Canadian foreign minister that the Australian parliament was currently enacting anticommunist legislation. Recognition and this legislation "would be related in the minds of people in Australia and it is desirable to postpone recognition until after that legislation is past all stages."[78]

Commonwealth arguments about reducing tensions had little impact on the Americans. U.S. officials were sceptical of their allies' more accommodating approach to the PRC, in part because their own policies towards the communist bloc were hardening in 1950. In the United States, public opinion could be used against the recognition and seating of the Chinese. The Canadian public was divided on the issue, and in December 1949, 45 per cent of the United Kingdom's population were against recognition; only 29 per cent were in favour. In the United States, of those who had an opinion on the subject, twice as many were opposed as were in favour of recognition. The percentages were 42–20 in November 1949.[79] "It appears that the United States Government is not in a position to do anything about recognition at the present time," Pearson complained on 1 March, and he

added that neither the public nor the U.S. Congress would be prepared for such a move for "some time to come." Opinion had hard-
ened because of what was "considered to be the anti–United States
attitude of the Chinese Communists, culminating in the seizure of
United States Consular property in Peiping and the consequent withdrawal of United States representation in China."[80]

The relationship between U.S. strategies for containing the Sino-
Soviet alliance and the U.S. policy on China has been neglected by historians, who have tended to concentrate on American Far Eastern
strategy too much, in isolation from broader trends in American foreign policy. In a recent article, Nancy Bernkopf Tucker has made a
strong case that Acheson's foreign policy in 1949 was more accommodating than some previous American historiography has admitted. On
issues of trade and Taiwan, the secretary of state adopted a relatively
moderate containment policy.[81] However, by February-March 1950, a
period not treated in depth in Tucker's article, Acheson's disposition
towards China was superseded by a perceived need to make no concessions to the Soviets on any issues, including China. Acheson's European strategies of containment, described correctly by Tucker as
vigilant and potent, came to dominate his more moderate policy towards China.

Far from appeasing the Soviet Union at this time, the United States
was setting a context for developing its military strength. This had a
significant impact on its China policies. In January 1950, Truman had
given the go-ahead to develop the hydrogen bomb, and that in the
winter the first drafts of NSC 68 were formulated. Domestically, the administration was being attacked for harbouring communists. Any concession to the Soviet Union or China at this time would only serve to
undermine the administration's larger goal of getting public backing
for an *increased* commitment to containing the threat of communism.
At a dinner in early March with the British ambassador, Sir Oliver
Franks, Acheson revealed his concern about the trend in international
relations over the previous six months. Franks reported that Acheson
"feels that there has been a deterioration in our common position and
a corresponding increase of strength to the Russians. He is therefore
searching for major new policies to reverse this trend." Acheson's fears
about China had surfaced in an earlier conversation with Bonnet, the
French ambassador in Washington. According to Massigli, the French
ambassador in London, the United States was "very touchy at any suggestion of recognition." When Bonnet mentioned the possibility of
French recognition, "Mr. Acheson reacted very badly."[82]

North Atlantic concerns were at the centre of Acheson's fears. On
15 March, when Hume Wrong pressed Dean Rusk about reopening

negotiations with the Soviets on some of the main outstanding issues, Rusk urged the ambassador to tell Pearson "the grave apprehension felt by the State Department about the risks involved in undertaking a negotiation of this sort." Rusk was in a serious mood. A Western peace initiative could plausibly be presented to the public as pacific, "whereas in fact the prospects were that it would greatly increase the dangers of early war." Examples of the Soviets' intransigence in Europe included their refusal to work on the Austrian peace treaty, their policies of dividing Germany and making satellites of Eastern European countries, and their bad treatment of Western diplomats. But the Americans were concerned with more than Soviet policy. Significantly, Rusk referred to "the defeatist spirit in Western Europe," which might increase with high-level negotiations with the Soviets. This could result "if there were a showdown, in a very powerful wave of popular sentiment in favour of attempted neutrality involving a repudiation of the obligations undertaken in the North Atlantic Treaty." The Americans would not have to wait much longer for a reason to consolidate the alliance, and the Korean War provided the justification for a tougher policy which the United States had been searching for since early in the year.

Until the outbreak of the war, State Department officials continued to discourage any negotiations. The theme was picked up again in mid-April, when Pearson spoke with Rusk and Phillip Jessup, the U.S. ambassador-at-large, who had recently returned from a survey trip in Asia. The discussions focused on general relations with Russia and on policy towards the United Nations. With respect to recognizing China, "Jessup and Rusk made it clear that the United States had no immediate intention of altering its attitude. If anything, American policy in this regard had become more firm." Jessup himself was hopeful that the PRC's difficulty in establishing authority in South China might result in the "emergence of two Chinese governments on the mainland." The situation in Southeast Asia had also influenced U.S. policy, and the Americans were "anxious to use all possible means for encouraging the anti-Communist forces on which their policy depends." On the whole, the Americans had nothing "very useful to suggest in regard to the question of Chinese representation in the United Nations." Unlike other governments, they did not believe the Soviet boycott had done permanent harm to the United Nations Organization.[83]

There were other indicators of a hardening in American policy towards the Sino-Soviet bloc. In the months leading to the Korean War there were growing British and American difficulties over China. Tensions within the Anglo-American alliance were exacerbated by a dispute between the PRC and the U.S.-backed Nationalists over the rightful ownership of some seventy civilian aircraft in Hong Kong. In November 1949, after the general managers, staff, and eleven of the aircraft had defected to the PRC, the Chinese foreign minister, Chou En-lai, proclaimed that the remaining planes in Hong Kong were the property of the PRC. The New China News Agency described the story as the "Uprising of the 4000." In early December 1949, however, the Nationalist Chinese announced the transferral of the majority shares of the planes to the CIA-backed Civil Air Transport (CAT) company, operated by Clare Chennault. Both Communist China and the Americans now claimed ownership of the planes. An initial appeal to the Hong Kong courts resulted in a decision favourable to the communist claims, and on 23 February 1950 the Hong Kong court rejected CAT's application for the appointment of a receiver for the assets. The legal point made by the judge was that the defections had made the property immune from judicial procedures. The suit filed by CAT was outside the jurisdiction of the Hong Kong court, and the injunction preventing the removal of further equipment by the communist employees was dissolved.

At this point, considerable American pressure was brought to bear on the British not to allow these planes to be handed over to the communists. In Chennault's estimation, the planes would make the difference in any Chinese invasion of Taiwan. The Department of State agreed. Its primary objective was "to prevent the aircraft and ground equipment ... from reaching Chinese Communist hands inasmuch as the significant quantities of equipment would materially improve the Communist military potential." In March 1950 the U.S. Department of State "categorically warned" Sir Oliver Franks that failure to prevent the aircraft from falling into the hands of the communists might "seriously endanger the continuance of Marshall aid and of the Military Assistance Programme."[84]

Britain's delicate diplomatic situation with the United States had to be weighed against its political objectives regarding the Soviet Union and Communist China. Relations with both the United States and the PRC became strained as a result of the controversy. After heated discussion, the British cabinet agreed to use technical loopholes to prevent the planes from leaving Hong Kong, and on 24 April a divided cabinet cautiously decided in favour of the United States and agreed to issue an executive order that would enable the Hong Kong courts to consider an appeal. The cabinet decision was closely related to British attempts to maintain an Anglo-American partnership in Asia, but the ministers were angry about what they perceived to be interference in the domestic jurisdiction of British courts. Nevertheless, a telegram from the embassy in Washington had expressed the need to succumb to the American representations; Franks pointed out that if the communists retained the rights to the aircraft, recent British efforts to persuade the Americans to adopt a more realistic China policy would be destroyed. It would also be much more difficult for the United Kingdom to coordinate Western strategy for China and Southeast Asia at the upcoming London Conference in May if British and American differences over recognizing the Chinese regime were exacerbated by the aircraft issue.[85]

Despite British hopes that the United States could be persuaded at the London Conference to adopt a more moderate China policy, the United States did not alter its stance towards Mao's government in the months leading up to the Korean War; U.S. policymakers continued to be wary about the British Commonwealth's defensive containment strategy towards China. A memo of a tripartite meeting in London noted that Acheson did not believe anything useful would be gained by discussing Chinese representation at the United Nations. American containment strategy towards the Soviet Union was at stake. According to Acheson, "Russian tactics had been such that this question now involved a matter of principle"; it would be difficult "to give way on the question of Chinese representation without appearing to be giving into Russian intransigence and blackmail, and this impression would have a damaging effect on the morale in S.E. Asia." Although the situation in the United Nations was bad, argued Acheson, "it might be more dangerous from our position in Asia to give way on the China question."[86] Thus, British attempts to get American agreement on a policy for admitting the PRC into the United Nations were a failure.

Although Tucker and Warren Cohen have argued that Acheson was cautiously hoping to normalize American relations with the new republic, the United States' actions in regard to its allies in this period indicate that the literature has overestimated the extent to which American policy adhered to an acceptance of the Communist Chinese regime. Had the Americans wanted to work towards a genuine accommodation with the PRC, they could have promoted better Chinese-Western relations by encouraging the British. Instead, during the London negotiations Acheson campaigned against reaching a *modus vivendi* with the communists. The policy followed by the United States towards China until the Korean War was on the whole a defensive one, but strategists kept their options open for the possibility of following a more rigorous anticommunist line. The Korean War – or, more accurately, American policymakers' interpretation of Sino-Soviet objectives during the Korean War – brought the strategy of increased pressure on the Chinese periphery to the fore. But it was not a strategy conceived solely in light of the Korean conflict. It was also influenced very much by American objectives regarding the Soviet Union and by attempts to undermine what was described as pacifist and neutralist public opinion in NATO countries.

Acheson should not be made the focus of United States' China policy. Disillusionment with Chiang Kai-shek existed, but there was also a powerful tendency in official thinking which viewed the communists as illegitimate rulers of China. Jessup's comment to Pearson reflected this tendency to hope for a divided China or for replacement of the regime altogether. Many Americans believed that communism and nationalism were ultimately irreconcilable and contradictory forces. As Jessup wrote during the London Conference in May, the U.S. government was "convinced that national independence and democratic evolution is nonexistent in any area that falls within [the] network of Soviet imperialism." To some extent, Acheson himself believed in the China "myth" – the idea that American policy towards China in the twentieth century was built largely on altruism towards the Chinese people and Chinese "nationalism."[87] The perception that the Chinese communists, like their Vietnamese counterparts, were the antithesis of nationalism made it difficult for American policymakers to follow Britain's strategy of accommodation towards China. In this context, American "Titoist" policies should be seen in a different light from those of Britain. Insofar as U.S. officials refused to see communism as a legitimate form of nationalism, there was an element of counterrevolution implicit in America's China policy. This theme remained under the surface of America's "wedge" strategy, and in part it explains why American policymakers adopted a harsher stance towards the Chinese, especially after the Korean War.

There were other important reasons why the Truman administration did not adopt the cautious, piecemeal approach towards Communist China as wholeheartedly as Great Britain and other allies. As Gaddis has pointed out, there were pressures within the administration that worked against the policy alternative of letting the dust settle. Taiwan, for example, was seen by the military establishment as an important adjunct of America's defensive perimeter strategy, which was based on maintaining a line of defensive strength along the islands facing mainland Asia.[88] The major factor behind the United States' more intransigent China policy at this time, however, was the Truman administration's adherence to a harsher stance against the Soviet Union.

The London Conference temporarily delayed the implementation of Britain's strategy. The United States, France, and Britain had agreed that there was to be no attempt at seating the PRC until later that summer. Nevertheless, spurred on in part by telegrams from the Commonwealth Relations Office, Canada's Department of External Affairs continued to push its recommendations against cabinet cautiousness. In early May, Pearson convinced the cabinet to gets its representative in Peking, Chester Ronning, to make an informal oral communication to the Chinese authorities to find out, without any Canadian commitment, the PRC's response to the possibility of recognition by the Government of Canada. On 14 June, Pearson revealed that the response had been favourable and that Peking had "conceded that negotiations might be undertaken on procedural matters and agreement reached prior to the announcement of recognition. This would mean that Canada should not be subject to the difficulties in which the United Kingdom was involved after extending recognition."[89]

External Affairs continued to align its strategy with that of the United Kingdom. On 15 June, Noel Baker informed External that the United Kingdom would henceforth vote in favour of a changeover in Chinese representation in United Nations bodies whether or not there was likely to be a majority in favour of such a changeover. The United Kingdom's previous policy had caused friction in Anglo-Chinese relations, and British officials were now keen to get their defensive containment strategy on a stronger footing. Kenneth Younger, the minister of state, was an enthusiastic supporter of seating the Chinese. In advocating this position, he had in mind the preservation of Britain's interests in Asia. On 11 May he minuted to the foreign secretary that a failure to seat the PRC in the United Nations would undermine the prestige of that institution and weaken Britain's position in Hong Kong. Outside the United Nations the PRC might be driven into closer alliance with the Soviets, he argued; but if it was allowed to join the United Nations, there would be less likelihood that the Chinese would "allow themselves to be used by the Russians for a direct or indirect attack on Hong Kong."[90]

Britain hoped that the entrance of China into the United Nations would help normalize its relations with Peking and would result in a Soviet return to the Security Council. In London and New York important discussions were held with Soviet officials; British diplomats suggested that in return for support for seating Communist China in the United Nations, the Soviet Union should press the Chinese to work towards a *modus vivendi* with the British. On 15 June, Attlee gave his approval to this strategy and agreed that Britain would take the first step and vote for PRC membership to UNICEF on 19 June.[91]

On 16 June a telegram was sent to Washington telling Franks to inform the Americans of the British decision. It is significant that the United States had no prior knowledge of it. The Old Commonwealth, on the other hand, had been anticipating such a decision for months.

In June 1950, Canada was on the verge of recognizing the new Chinese government.

British and Canadian policies on this issue also must be examined in the light of their larger objectives in relation to the Sino-Soviet alliance. The seating of the PRC was a particular sore spot in Anglo-Chinese relations at this time. Since Britain believed that stable relations with Peking were required to help preserve its colonial power and world position, a way was needed to overcome American intransigence on Chinese recognition and representation in the United Nations; and when hopes for a closer Anglo-American agreement at the London Conference were dashed by the Americans, the British decided that they needed to force the issue by influencing and encouraging other governments to support their position in the United Nations. Besides putting pressure on the Commonwealth, the United Kingdom petitioned other members on the Security Council, including Iraq, Egypt, France, and Ecuador, to vote in favour of the changeover. Here, then, was an example where Britain was playing its own game of power politics on the margins of the Anglo-American special relationship.

British policy was geared to putting indirect pressure on the United States to accept the Government of the People's Republic of China. The British were well aware of the American position of agreeing to a majority decision of any United Nations body accepting PRC representation. With this in mind, they set out to force the hand of the United States. Britain had the support of Canada's Department of External Affairs, but External's hopes were weakened by the prime minister's fear of hurting the Canadian-American special relationship over a region in which Canada had few direct interests. However, there were indications that the French also were getting ready to accept the changeover. On 28 May, Georges Vanier reported that a French government official had the previous day told him that, barring unforeseen events, France would recognize China within two months. In this way, Vanier noted, "the deadlock would be broken."[92] If true, this French decision had more to do with France's overall objectives in the international system than with British representations for a change in French policy. Yet France's objectives were in line with many other members of the Western alliance. As Bevin had told the British cabinet in May, the French disagreed with American strategy at the London meetings. The United States had insisted that any statement of principles issued at the conference should "show no suggestion of weakness in the prosecution of the 'Cold War.' The French, on the other hand, wanted it to be moderate in tone and to contain some reference to the possibility of negotiating with the Soviet Union."[93] France's acceptance of China in the United Nations at this time would have been consistent with its more moderate approach to containing the Soviet Union. It was this more conciliatory policy that Acheson and the Americans objected to.

In the final analysis, the American response to the British initiative in the United Nations reflected the tougher American policy towards the Soviet Union as demonstrated in the early drafts of NSC 68. On 17 June the assistant secretary of state, Dean Rusk, informed Sir Oliver Franks that Acheson had been "greatly disturbed" by Britain's initiative. Acheson thought that the London meetings had confirmed that none of the three powers would take major action with respect to Chinese representation without consulting the others, and that none would enter into discussion with the Soviets without similar discussion. Unlike the British, American officials were unwilling to see the Soviet Union return to the United Nations as a consequence of the seating of Communist China. In their view, Soviet peace propaganda was an attempt to bully the West and blackmail it into making concessions. Any attempt to give into Soviet blackmail would thus constitute appeasement. Rusk told Franks that Acheson still believed, as he had in London, that it was "a great mistake to take action which implied surrendering to Russian blackmail."[94] In this way, American policy towards China was subordinated to its broader perceptions and objectives *vis-à-vis* the Soviet Union.

This is not to argue that the United States rejected all attempts to work out a common policy with its allies in the Far East. In particular, in the two weeks leading up to the Korean War, Acheson was working on securing bipartisan support for a China policy which could possibly have led to the United States accepting Chinese representation in the United Nations. This message was relayed to the British on 17 June. Because of the outbreak of the Korean War, it is unclear how such a policy would have worked itself out, but it is very unlikely that it would have represented any significant concession to either Soviet or Chinese communism. Perhaps Acheson's moves foreshadowed American attempts in early 1951 at the height of the war to offer a "deal" to the Chinese, involving Chinese rebuttal of its alliance with the Soviet Union in return for Western concessions on recognition. In April 1950, Andrew Cordier and Dr Ralph Bunche told Pearson that they disagreed with their administration's China policies, and "they made ironical references to the present State Department efforts to justify non-recognition because of the possibility that the new regime might prove ineffective in South China." In their estimation, the State Department "would be quite happy to find some formula by which the representatives of Peiping could be admitted to the United Nations and the deadlock ended without United States recognition of the Communists."[95]

The United Kingdom decided once again to alter its policy, and it abstained on the UNICEF vote on 19 June. It was about to formulate a strategy for another vote on 3 July when the Korean War put an end to attempts to resolve the issue.[96] To Bevin's and Pearson's disappointment, there was little agreement within the North Atlantic alliance on how to deal with China. The alliance was unable to formulate an Asian containment strategy for the continent as a whole. On issues such as the need to uphold Western power in Indochina, there was more apparent agreement, but even here solidarity could sometimes give way to underlying competition for spheres of influence amongst the Great Powers. It is possible that if the French or the British had helped to overturn the American position towards seating China, a crisis within the alliance would have ensued between the Europeans and the Americans. After the Korean War, Western rearmament might then have been much more difficult to legitimize. It was just such a crisis in NATO relations that St Laurent wanted to avoid. A crisis was averted, however, because Bevin realized that his strategy required American support. Without that, Britain's other international objectives would be endangered. In the event, the Korean War presented a framework in which the West's dilemma towards the Soviet Union and China would be resolved in favour of a much harsher stance.

3 Containing the Soviet Empire: The North Atlantic Triangle and the Korean War, 1950–1951

The theory behind informal empire on the East Asian periphery was not the immediate concern of American strategists and diplomats in the first months of the Korean War. Their minds were focused initially on containing the North Korean attack, and then with a means of rolling back the communists. In September and October 1950, some thought was given to the economic reconstruction needs of a new unified Korea, but such considerations were quickly shelved with the intervention of the Chinese communists. In short, military and strategic considerations predominated in this period – the attempt to develop Korea as part of a pro-Western anticommunist proxy partner of the Cold War was a secondary consideration of policymakers.

American officialdom believed that the Soviet Union was the major motivating force behind the North Korean attack on 25 June 1950. The possibility of Soviet aggression in peripheral areas had been foreseen in the policy paper NSC 68, and the North Korean attack was interpreted as a Soviet-inspired move towards the larger goal of world domination; by getting its satellites to drive back Western spheres of influence, Moscow could remain relatively detached from the responsibilities of conflict while its global objectives were being accomplished. In a significant way, the Korean War served to give further impetus to America's informal empire. As a result of its perception of Soviet policy in Korea, the United States expanded its military and economic aid programs on a global scale, and in Asia it intensified its efforts to establish pro-Western proxy containment partners in Vietnam and Korea.

China's actions in Korea also had tremendous implications for American policy towards Asia. In the initial stages of U.S. intervention, American containment policy towards Korea was based on "rollback" – the notion that Moscow's satellite had to be eliminated militarily and replaced by a unified Korea that was pro-Western and anticommunist. The Chinese decision to counter rollback with force resulted in a less threatening U.S. containment policy for Korea, but it also had the long-term effect of directing more U.S. animosity towards the People's Republic of China. The rehabilitation and military build-up of South Korea after 1951 was designed both to hold back possible North Korean incursion and to bolster America's more aggressive policies towards China.

An important consequence of the war was the integration of China into a more belligerent U.S. containment strategy for continental East Asia as a whole. In the short term, Korea was seen as the test case of a successful containment and rollback strategy – a Western military response in "the land of the morning calm" would deter further Soviet moves in other areas of the globe. In the long term, however, indigenous anticommunist forces positioned on the two eastern peripheries of China would help limit Korean, Vietnamese, and Chinese communist influence in all of Asia.

The strategy of preventing further Soviet-inspired aggression by using military force against the North Koreans was an American idea, but it was supported forcefully by America's allies throughout the conflict. Although important differences among the allies arose during the course of the war, these related to differences over China and not to the need to defeat Soviet proxy aggression and teach the Soviet Union a lesson in "collective security."

As with Britain's anticommunist strategies in Asia generally, its containment policies during the Korean War were dictated by two somewhat contradictory impulses: the need to defend colonial interests in the Far East, and a reliance on the Anglo-American "special relationship" to help defend Britain's position in Europe. Whereas British concern for Hong Kong and Malaya required peaceful coexistence with the People's Republic of China, the United States' perceptions of global communism and its strategic and economic interests permitted consideration of a more belligerent stance towards mainland China.

Although top American officials continued to view Western Europe as the key to their global power, after the outbreak of hostilities in Korea, they tended to associate containment policies in the Far East with containment strategies for Europe. It was felt that a failure in Korea would result in a failure in Europe in two ways: it would encourage both Soviet expansionism and American feelings of isolationism. To the United States, a forceful response to the North Korean invasion was important not only for defending the Western position in Europe but also for defending American economic and strategic interests in Japan, the Philippines, and Taiwan. The war had exposed vulnerabilities in the "defensive perimeter" island strategy.

Canada's role in the Korean conflict was not based on any colonial or substantial regional interest. Principally, Canada's participation in the war was the result of its attempts to work within the North Atlantic alliance to further its own political and economic objectives, which were inextricably linked with the containment of Soviet communism. Broadly speaking, Canada followed its two main allies in containing the perceived international communist threat in Korea in order to help consolidate its relationship with the United States and Western Europe. Its policy reflected attempts to strengthen the Western "system" in an Eastern setting, and Canadian policymakers continued to be influenced by the more limited containment goals which other commonwealth counties, particularly Britain, had set for Asia.

In the first five months of the conflict, United Nations objectives in Korea were enthusiastically pursued. Although the Old Commonwealth was initially reluctant to raise troops for the cause, Britain, Canada, Australia, and New Zealand generally supported the broad American goals of meeting Soviet aggression and enhancing Western prestige in Asia. They backed the decision to cross the 38th parallel, and there was agreement on the ultimate objective for an independent and unified Korea.

Communist China's intervention precipitated a crisis in Western and Atlantic diplomacy in the winter of 1950. The entrance of the Chinese volunteers brought out underlying differences within the United Nations on how best to deal with the Chinese communists. Significantly, compromises were made on all sides during this crucial stage of the war, and despite fears that the American initiative branding the Chinese as aggressors might result in escalation of the conflict, the war remained limited.

In most of the writing dealing with the theme of "the diplomacy of constraint" there is an implicit understanding that constraining U.S. actions was a necessary and important function of allied diplomacy. In certain cases, allied efforts to contain American enthusiasm for bringing the war to China did play an important role in influencing American decisions. To this extent, constraint was a wise strategy to follow. Rosemary Foot notes that "British intervention at a time when this loss of confidence and international criticism were at their height reinforced still further U.S. doubts about entering into a new and more dangerous phase of the conflict in which America would stand virtually alone."[1]

This approach has merits, but it tends to exaggerate both the degree to which the United States' allies influenced American actions and the extent of the differences, particularly in the first year of the war, within the alliance on the issue of containing communism. Like its allies, the United States was fearful of a prolonged war with the Chinese. Implicit in much of the historiography on this issue is the notion that if the allies had pursued these policies more forcefully, in certain circumstances a more successful outcome to the conflict might have emerged. William Stueck argues that British support of the crossing of the 38th parallel was in some ways a lost opportunity: "Had the British joined with the French in pressing a cautious policy on Washington, the effort might have had some effect, especially if the pressure had come prior to mid-September, when a sudden reversal of the military balance on the peninsula created strong momentum for a campaign in the north."[2] In Stueck's argument, the limits of influence lay not in the strategy itself but in its application.

However, there were broader considerations of strategy which prevented America's allies from vigorously applying their policies of constraint and which required them to make compromises to the American position. These considerations stemmed from the need to maintain a special relationship with the United States and to show a united front against the Soviet Union in the event of global war. Ultimately, there was recognition in Great Britain, Canada, and other allied countries that if either the conflict in Korea or American policy towards China precipitated a global war, there would be little choice for the allies but to follow the American lead. The diplomacy of constraint emerged naturally from these considerations. Underlying the policy of restraining the United States lay important limits to the strategy itself.

Britain tended to pursue its strategy of restraining the United States with more vigour than Canada did. The position of those in the United Kingdom who argued for greater independence from the United States on issues related to the Korean conflict was strengthened when Ernest Bevin, the major architect of the Anglo-American special relationship, fell ill early in 1951. But the need for unity against the Soviet Union, coupled with several changes in the wording of the resolution, were the compelling factors that propelled Britain and Canada towards compromise with the United States. Seen in this light, the allies' decision to back the aggressor resolution in January 1951 was a significant precedent for their decision to give public support to the American strategy for ending the war in the spring of 1953. There was greater allied concern about U.S. policies towards China in 1953, however, and the Eisenhower-Dulles containment program proved a much greater threat to Western unity.

On an important level, allied diplomacy in the winter of 1950–51 did sustain the possibilities for negotiating a settlement to the war. But there remained substantial agreement on objectives. Canada and Great Britain consistently backed American diplomatic initiatives, and the United States was prepared to make concessions to its allies, though these were not major compromises. The United States altered the tone of some of its U.N. proposals, not simply as a result of allied pressure but because it acknowledged that a united front was crucial for its own objectives as well as for those of its allies.

In short, despite differences in method between the three North Atlantic nations' diplomacy, similar goals and objectives underlay their strategies in this stage of the Korean War. Through compromises on all sides, a relatively consistent and united effort was forged. Although the compromises engendered animosity, ultimately a united program was followed, and the need to prevent general hostilities emerging from the conflict was agreed to by all participants.

THE DIPLOMACY OF CONSTRAINT AND THE SOVIET THREAT, JUNE–JULY 1950

The American response to the North Korean offensive was motivated primarily by political reasoning. The attack was viewed as an integral part of Soviet global strategy; consequently, a U.S. military response was necessary to maintain U.S. prestige in Asia and elsewhere and to teach the communists, particularly the Soviets, that the Western alliance would not tolerate aggressive imperialism. Militarily, Korea was of minor importance in global strategy, but on 25 June the Estimates Group of the Office of Intelligence Research, Department of State, argued that a refusal to meet communist aggression in Korea would have far-reaching negative consequences: it would weaken Japanese confidence in the American ability to protect Japan; it might cause more Chinese Nationalists to defect to the mainland and increase the possibilities of the People's Republic intervening in Southeast Asia; and in Europe, America's allies might question the might and will of the United States.[3] George Kennan was given a copy of this report, and he used its conclusions to brief the twelve ambassadors of the North Atlantic Pact on 27 June. Kennan was regarded by many of the ambassadors as level-headed, and they were relieved to hear that the United States would not take an openly hostile position towards the Soviet Union. The lesson the Soviets would learn would be an indirect one, calculated not to initiate global war. As Kennan put it, "American forces would be acting against Korean dissidents, not against the manipulators of the adventure."[4] This satisfied the Commonwealth representatives at the meeting, who understood the importance of "firmness and patience" in containing Soviet-backed aggression.

The United States' decision to commit air and naval forces (and, later, ground forces) to Korea, and the decision to obtain United Nations support cannot be considered separately: from the start of hostilities, the policymakers realized that in committing themselves to fight in Korea, they would also be engaging the prestige of the Soviets and Chinese communists. As Sir Pierson Dixon, the deputy under-secretary of state in the Foreign Office, minuted on the 28 June, "If the situation develops into a general war between the United States and the Soviet Union, we shall have entered it automatically."[5] A collective effort was required to deter the communists from escalating the conflict to encompass global war, and the United Nations offered the best forum for presenting the Soviet Union with a unified war effort. Allied backing for American actions in Korea would provide the necessary deterrent to further Soviet actions. A united response circumvented the pitfalls of appeasement, and it would teach the communists a valuable lesson. However, the American and allied governments realized that the converse was also true: failure to support the United States in Korea would be a sign of allied disagreement, of which the Soviets could take advantage. In this context, a Soviet invasion or even a threatened invasion of Western Europe might persuade the Europeans to sue for a "peace" on Soviet terms. In general, the Soviet Union would be more willing to risk a third world war.

Officials in the United States believed that the Soviet Union did not intend to provoke a major war. The united response was meant as a challenge and a threat to the USSR. Since any Soviet action against United Nations forces would result in escalation of the war, and since the Soviets did not want war, they would not intervene. At an executive level meeting with the president on 25 June, General Omar Bradley, the chairman of the Joint Chiefs of Staff, argued: "Russia is not ready for war. The Korean situation offered as good an occasion for action in drawing the line as anywhere else." The chief of naval operations, Admiral Forrest Sherman, agreed with Bradley and piped: "The Russians do not want war now but if they do they will have it."[6] In short, the Americans believed that the United States would be able to carry out its objectives through the United Nations and make officials in Moscow frustrated at their impotence. This logic was consistent with America's more coercive strategy to resist Soviet expansionism adopted in NSC 68. According to that document, "Our policy and actions must be such as to foster a fundamental change in the nature of the Soviet system, a change toward which the frustration of the design is the first and perhaps the most important step."[7]

Both the United Kingdom and Canada recognized the importance of supporting a U.N. effort in Korea. They supported the Security Council resolution of June 25, which called for a cessation of hostilities and withdrawal of North Korean troops to the 38th parallel. They also endorsed the resolution of 27 June, which recommended that members of the United Nations "furnish such assistance to the Republic of Korea as may be necessary to repel the armed attack and to restore international peace and security in the area."[8] There was general agreement to back U.S. military actions and prestige.

On 27 June the British cabinet "at once agreed that the United Kingdom Government should support the [27 June] resolution" of the Security Council. The next day, the Cabinet Defence Committee agreed to ask the Commonwealth Relations Office to make a request for military support from other Commonwealth countries. It was felt that although these countries had commitments elsewhere, they could "be asked to do their utmost in the interests of solidarity." The British themselves were reluctant to provide more than token military support for the operation. Dixon was concerned that "an offer of a naval contribution may only be the first step towards having to offer land forces."[9] In the House of Commons the next day, Prime Minister Attlee announced that ships of the Royal Navy, then at sea near Japan, would be placed under American command for use around Korea.

In Canada there was also general agreement with American objectives in Korea. Canadian diplomats understood the potential consequences of involvement in the Korean War. On 27 June, the day before Seoul fell to the communists for the first time, the Canadian secretary of state for external affairs described to the cabinet the reasoning behind American actions. Drawing on Kennan's discussion with Hume Wrong and the other ambassadors, Pearson concluded that "if the U.S. action was effective, the result would be helpful in the cold war." However, "the worst of all policies would be intervention that was not successful," he added; the limited American response thus far of authorizing naval and air support "could be expected to lead to all-out intervention if necessary." At this stage in the conflict, Canada was prepared to make only a limited military contribution to the allied effort. On 28 June, after Pearson had pointed out that messages from London had indicated that the British might place a naval force at the disposal of General MacArthur, the minister of national defence, Brooke Claxton, told his cabinet colleagues that "the only practical contribution" that Canada could make "appeared to be provision of a number of Canadian destroyers and possibly a small squadron of transport aircraft." A Canadian contribution to the fighting was a "desirable gesture"; but like the British, the Canadians were cautious about committing their limited military resources to the region. On 30 June, Prime Minister Louis St Laurent told a supportive House of Commons that Canada would make a naval contribution to aid United Nations operations.[10]

It is instructive for comparative reasons to describe briefly the Australian perspective on the crisis. Australia was, like Canada, a Commonwealth "middle power." But in terms of global strategy, Australian officials were unlike their Canadian counterparts in that they did not hold a Eurocentric view of the Cold War. This was reflected in the fact that they were not part of NATO but became members of the Australian–New Zealand–United States (ANZUS) treaty organization, which was signed in 1951. Australian priorities lay in Southeast Asia and, to a lesser degree, in the Middle East. Nevertheless, NATO and Commonwealth diplomacy had a significant impact on the way Australians perceived the Cold War in Asia. In Southeast Asia the Australians tended, more than Canada, to associate their security with the dominant European colonial powers. Consequently, the Conservative government of Prime Minister Robert G. Menzies was more willing than Liberal leader Louis St Laurent to provide military aid to help the French and British fight their anticommunist colonial wars in Malaya and Indochina. In a public statement on 27 June, Menzies argued that although the military attack in Korea was led by North Koreans, they represented communist expansionism; the attack was "a Communist inspired and directed move." The conflict in Korea was not "remote from our interests and safety," Menzies proclaimed. There was also a communist danger in Indochina and, much closer to home, in Malaya: "There are the operations of the Communist guerrillas in Malaya who are making it their business to render British control of Malaya difficult and who, if they succeed, will make it impossible. These operations may well be stimulated by events in Korea." One of the first Australian cabinet decisions after the war broke out was to send a squadron of Lincoln bombers and military advisers to Malaya. Then, on 29 June, Menzies dedicated several Australian naval vessels to Korean operations, and on 30 June an air squadron stationed in Japan was committed to Korea.[11] Thus, although the Old Commonwealth viewed the outbreak of the Korean War from different geostrategic points of view, its initial military contribution to the conflict was roughly similar.

Like the Canadians and Australians, the British wanted to limit the conflict to Korea. Britain had more to lose if the war escalated: any expansion of the war involving China or the Soviet Union would have grave implications for Britain's Great Power status. Officials in the Foreign Office were very uneasy with President Truman's proposed statement of 27 June condemning the "centrally-directed Communist imperialism" of the North Koreans. They felt it was too belligerent and too threatening to the Soviets. The cabinet pointed out that "there might have been advantage in seeking to isolate this incident and to deal with it as an act of aggression committed by the North Koreans on their own initiative. This would have enabled the Soviet Government to withdraw, without loss of prestige, any encouragement or support which they might have been giving to the North Koreans."[12]

The British were much more fearful of the American decision of 25 June to station the Seventh Fleet in the Formosa Straits. This was done in order to prevent the military seizure of Taiwan by the communists. U.S. military authorities argued that in a general Asian war the island would serve as a critical bombing base and therefore it should not be lost to the communists. The action was referred to as the "neutralization" of Formosa because it also prevented the Nationalists from continuing their amphibious assaults on the mainland. In Britain, there was much concern over this decision: the People's Republic of China was intent on capturing the island from the Nationalists; it had been preparing for an armed assault prior to the war in Korea and had expected an eventual victory. "Neutralization" might therefore exacerbate British relations with the People's Republic and contribute to hostilities between China and Britain's Southeast Asian colonies, especially Hong Kong. On 27 June the British cabinet noted that the American decision to employ the Seventh Fleet in the Formosa Straits "might embarrass the United Kingdom Government in their relations with the Communist Government of China and might even provoke that Government to attack Hong Kong or to foment disorder there."[13] While the British did not publicly do anything to endanger the U.S.–U.N. effort in Korea, they privately informed the Americans of their concern. Peaceful relations with Communist China were critical for promoting Britain's global and regional objectives. The diplomacy of constraint emerged from Britain's limited Cold War objectives in Asia, a decision to preserve its formal empire in Southeast Asia, and a determination to maintain its global status as a Great Power.

An important objective of U.S. diplomacy was to keep the war confined to the peninsula. But unlike the British cabinet, officials in the American executive branch were more willing to engage the Soviet Union and China in a battle for world prestige over Korea. Despite the fact that President Truman did not publicly use the phrase "centrally directed Communist imperialism" to describe the North Korean attack, privately his perceptions were more aggressive. On 26 June, the assistant secretary of state for Far Eastern affairs, Dean Rusk, suggested to Truman that if the Soviets decided to enter the Security Council and veto United Nations actions, the United States should argue that their actions were within the scope of the United Nations Charter. The president replied that "that was right. He rather wished they would veto ... We needed to lay a base for our action in Formosa."[14] This need to punish Soviet military adventurism was a lesson that Truman believed history had taught, and it conditioned the U.S. response to Soviet and communist moves towards resolving the conflict through diplomatic means.

The first attempt to discuss a possible settlement of the conflict came from the Soviet foreign minister, Andrei Gromyko. On 6 July, Gromyko invited the British ambassador to the Soviet Union, Sir David Kelly, to his office. Gromyko stated that his government wanted a peaceful settlement and he asked Kelly for proposals. Kelly responded that the British government wanted the Soviets to exert their influence over the North Koreans and get them to withdraw their forces from South Korea. The British wanted to end the war and restore the status quo. He added that he would see Gromyko again if the Soviets requested it.[15]

The Americans viewed Gromyko's *démarche* as a genuine attempt to achieve a settlement without any undue loss of prestige, but for a price not revealed by the foreign minister. The Americans' attitude to the *démarche* indicated that they were prepared to consider a negotiated settlement with the Soviet Union over Korea, but only one based on American interests and objectives. Anything less would amount to appeasement. On 7 July, in a telegram to London, Dean Acheson wrote that it was of the "greatest importance" that any further discussions with Gromyko be "wholly within [the] framework of UNSC Korea Resolutions of June 25 and 27." Negotiations would not involve any other issues on which the Soviets "might attempt to extort concessions (e.g. Chinese representation in U.N. or Formosa)." A settlement required the immediate end of hostilities, stated Acheson, and a withdrawal behind the 38th parallel observed by the United Nations Commission on Korea (UNCOK). The *status quo ante bellum* might be restored, but in the "ultimate settlement," UNCOK should be allowed to implement a policy recommended by the United Nations General Assembly.[16]

This last requirement was significant, revealing American intentions early on in the war to establish a unified and democratic Korea by bringing the issue to the Western-dominated General Assembly, thereby effectively overriding any possibility of a Soviet veto in the Security Council. If a settlement were made, it would be one that enhanced American and U.N. prestige at the expense of world communism.

The Canadian government was kept informed of the discussions in Moscow. Pearson was uncertain about the motivation of the recent Soviet *démarche* but emphasized the need to prevent an extension of the conflict. Canada, like the United Kingdom, had relatively little interest in Korea beyond supporting the United Nations containment effort. An overcommitment in Korea would result in weakening the West's position in Europe. "The Russians," Pearson warned, "would probably welcome any situation which would tie up Western forces." Pearson shared Bevin's concerns about American policy towards Taiwan. He told the Canadian cabinet that "it was important to make clear that our contribution was in support of the United Nations only and that U.N. operations against Korea should not be confused with U.S. operations in other parts of the Far East, particularly with regard to Formosa."[17]

Implicit in British, Canadian, and American strategies for preventing Western troops getting bogged down in a war in the Northeast Asian land perimeter was a recognition that if a long-term solution was to be found, then strong local indigenous forces would be required. The consensus that emerged from the conflict was that the allies would develop Korea's economic and military strength, and that ideally Korea should accept Western concepts for containing Soviet and global communism.

On the more immediate issue of Far Eastern strategy, the American government interpreted the allied positions on Taiwan and China as a form of appeasement of the enemy. A telegram for the foreign secretary dated 10 July indicated the United States' unwillingness to alter its Taiwan policy. Taiwan was too closely linked with Korea. Acheson wrote: "We have faced squarely a calculated act of aggression and in so doing we are profoundly convinced that we are acting for the entire free world." Emphasizing the importance of defeating the North Koreans and containing Soviet expansionist tendencies, Acheson argued that the "future peace of the world in our view hangs directly upon the success we expect to achieve in defeating the first overt act of aggression since the end of the war." His letter reflected the belief of U.S. policymakers that there was a high level of coordination between the communist parties in Asia and the Soviet Union. America's allies were providing their "overwhelming support," he said, precisely because they recognized that "the whole future of the free world is at stake." The overriding objective of the free world was "to defeat the present aggression in Korea and to forestall its possible outbreak elsewhere in the Far East."[18] The tragedy of the 1930s had demonstrated that the only hope of preserving the peace of the world was to stop aggression in its initial stages. On Taiwan, there were limits to which British, Canadian, and other allied representations influenced American strategy.

It is possible to get an exaggerated sense of Anglo-American differences from these representations. United Kingdom officials viewed their diplomacy not in terms of appeasement but as a matter of prudence. There was a consensus on the need to meet Soviet aggression in Korea. Although the British hoped that the Soviets could be convinced to return to the United Nations on peaceful terms, Bevin wrote to Acheson on 14 July, "We are just as determined not to submit to Soviet blackmail as you are ... We could not agree with you more whole-heartedly when you say that you have faced squarely a calculated act of aggression. We ourselves, and I think the whole right-thinking world, appreciate to the full the stand which the United States Government has taken in Korea on behalf of us all." A few days earlier Hume Wrong had written to Ottawa welcoming America's new role in international affairs "After all," he wrote, "what has taken place has occurred less than nine years since the Japanese attack on Pearl Harbor finally ended the widely prevalent belief that the United States could stand aloof from world affairs"; in the context of international relations since the Great War, America's new-found internationalism marked "a very welcome and almost incredible change in the international scene."[19]

Acheson's telegram of 10 July reflected the American administration's desire to get its allies to broaden their commitment to Korea. The United States was pressing the U.N. secretary general, Trygve Lie, to make an appeal to the fifty-two U.N. countries to provide more military support in Korea. When Lie did so on 14 July, Canadian and British officials were upset. At a meeting the next day in London, Sir Pierson Dixon complained that the Americans had unilaterally approached Lie "without consultation with other members of the Security Council." With moderate British temper, he described the secretary general as the "stooge of Wall Street." In New York, John Holmes, the Canadian representative to the United Nations, told Lie's executive assistant, Andrew Cordier, that Pearson "had been upset" by the secretary's message. Pearson thought "it was inappropriate to hear a message of this kind for the first time from press reports of the Secretary-General's press conference." A request like this "ought not to have been taken without consultation at least with the countries which might be expected to contribute."[20]

The responses of the United Kingdom and Canada to Lie's request underlined their continued reluctance to provide more than a token military force to Korea. The British assistant under-secretary of state, Esler Dening, reiterated that Britain had only one reserve brigade in Asia and that according to the vice-chief of the Imperial General Staff, "it would hardly be possible for us to supply in the immediate future even one battalion as a token force without seriously jeopardising our reserves for existing commitments in that area." Similarly, the strength of Canada's armed forces in mid-1950 gave Canadian diplomats rea-

Table 2
Force Levels: United States, Britain, and Canada, 1949–1954
(force levels, expressed in 000's)

	1949	1950	1951	1952	1953	1954
United States	1,610	1,481	3,279	3,661	3,590	3,331
Britain	737	666	804	848	841	816
Canada	47	68	95	104	112	114

Sources: Millet and Maslowski, Common Defense, 491; Rosecrance, Defense, table 2; Canada, Department of National Defence, Reports.

son for concern. Altogether, in 1949–50, there were only 47,185 active servicemen in Canada's navy, army, and air force. Although this was a slight increase from the postwar low of 34,759 in 1947–48, it represented a vast cutback from the Second World War, which in 1944–45 had produced over 672,000 active servicemen.[21] As in the United States, postwar demobilization in Canada was rapid. In 1950 Canada's limited forces were being integrated within the NATO structure, which meant that their major focus would be on Europe. American requests for troops in Asia might distract Canada from its major strategic objective of reinforcing the European continent. On 18 July, Under-Secretary A.D.P. Heeney wrote Pearson that there was no reason to believe that Europe had been supplanted as "the main theatre"; it would be unfortunate, he said, "if our attention should be diverted from Europe by reason of Korea." A Canadian military contribution to that conflict "should not be at the expense of our capacity to fulfil our responsibilities for the direct defence of Canada under the North Atlantic Treaty." The Korean "incident," Heeney noted, had in fact demonstrated the need to accelerate Canada's defence preparations.[22] (For force levels and A-B-C defence expenditure, 1949–54, see tables 2 and 3).

Britain and Canada each had its own strategic rationale for limiting its participation in Korea. Similar concerns were expressed in Paris (because of France's commitment to fighting colonial wars in Indochina) and in Canberra (because of Australia's responsibilities for the Middle East and Malaya). There was a general reluctance in the West in the early stages of the war to commit ground troops; Canadian and British considerations were representative of deliberations other allied governments were making.

Efforts to maintain and consolidate the Anglo-American and Canadian-American "special relationships" in the Cold War international situation following the Korean War were a critical factor in influencing the Canadians and British to contribute troops to the conflict. On 25 July, Prime Minister Attlee sent a Commonwealth Relations Office tele-

Table 3
Expenditure on Defence as a Percentage of Total Government Expenditure

	1949	1950	1951	1952	1953	1954
United States	32.2	30.4	49.1	64.7	65.6	65.7
Britain	20.3	21.3	25.6	30.2	30.6	29.5
Canada	9.7	14.9	25.1	35.6	43.2	41.1

Sources: U.S. Bureau of the Census, *Statistical Abstract 1955* (figures for major national security expenditures); Gaddis, *Strategies*, app.; Rosecrance, *Defense*, table 1; Canada, Department of National Defence, *Reports.*

gram to the prime ministers of the Old Dominions stating that, from a strategic point of view, it was still "extremely hard" for the United Kingdom to provide forces to Korea; however, the British cabinet had agreed that the question of contributing soldiers was "at least in part if not mainly political." The decision to send troops was directly linked to the wider issue of Anglo-American solidarity in the Cold War, noted Attlee. Thus, an early public announcement of a decision to send reinforcements "would be of immense political value, as showing unity of purpose in United Nations, as a help to securing next military aid appropriations, and as a morale-builder to all troops engaged." For these reasons, the United Kingdom would make an offer of ground troops.[23]

The next day, after the announcement to send troops had been made in the British House of Commons, the American ambassador in Ottawa, Stanley Woodward, approached Lester Pearson with an urgent request for troops. Woodward told Pearson that the U.S. government was "particularly anxious that Canada should participate"; Canada was the "nearest neighbour and closest friend of the United States," and the symbolic significance of a Canadian contribution "would be very great." Pearson made no commitments but stated that Canada had accepted the implications of making the effort in Korea a United Nations one.[24]

Pearson elaborated on these remarks to a receptive cabinet on 27 July. "Canada had every interest in strengthening the U.S. position as leader in the struggle against Communism," he argued. The importance of Korea lay in its beneficial effects for Canada's wider Cold War stance: "The lesson of effective United Nations co-operation would not be lost on the u.s.s.r." The minister of national defence agreed. For Claxton, the British precedent was important. Despite the concerns of Britain's Chiefs of Staff regarding forces available for the United Kingdom, the British had decided to send a brigade group to Korea. The "political considerations which led the United Kingdom to that decision applied with even greater force to Canada," argued Claxton. C.D.

Howe, the powerful minister of trade and commerce, thought that pressure on Canada would be "irresistible" once Britain, Australia, and New Zealand acted; and Robert Mayhew, the fisheries minister, who had accompanied Pearson to Colombo several months earlier, argued that he "did not see how Canada could honourably fail to come to the aid of the United States."[25]

The role of public opinion is a neglected aspect of allied diplomacy in this period of the war, yet it was a vital consideration, shaping the perceptions and policies of all three North Atlantic countries. In Canada, it was important partly because of concern with French-Canadian opinions towards war. The cabinet was well aware of Quebec's traditional fear of conscription and its opposition to Canadian participation in overseas wars. A poll conducted in early August by the Canadian Institute of Public Opinion showed that 59 per cent of Canadians felt Canada should send equipment and 34 per cent thought soldiers should be offered; 39 per cent of all Canadians were against a contribution of both equipment and troops, but in Quebec 62 per cent disapproved of sending ground troops. Quebec opinion reinforced Canadian caution. As early as 20 July, Pearson wrote to the Canadian ambassador in Washington that Quebec opinion was relatively calm but that a false step might destroy any tendency in Quebec to provide stronger support for the U.N. action. The Canadian government's real fear was that a crisis in domestic opinion about the Cold War might force a re-evaluation of Canada's place in NATO. In a significant sentence, Pearson wrote that it was "in the interests of the U.S. as well as ourselves" that Canada take a careful approach to the issue of raising ground troops.[26]

In the United States international public opinion was directly linked to issues of rearmament and the Korean War. Rearmament was needed to demonstrate that the United States was prepared to meet the communist threat with general war if necessary. At a cabinet meeting on 4 July, Acheson argued that the world situation was one of "extreme danger and tension," and that further Soviet probes or an escalation of the war in Korea could lead to "general hostilities." It was becoming apparent to the world that the United States did not have the resources to meet the threat, he observed, and "the feeling in Europe is changing from one of elation that the United States has come into the Korean crisis to petrified fright." International opinion of the United States was dropping, noted Acheson, and people "are questioning whether NAT really means anything, since it means only what we are able to do." In Asia there was evidence that the Japanese "believe association with the U.S. is dangerous to them." The solution was rearmament, he stated: the president must announce that the United States is expanding its force levels. "He must ask for money, and if it is a question of asking for too little or too much, he should ask for too much."[27]

For Acheson, the war also provided the perfect reason for getting the U.S. public to support the tougher stance against the Soviet Union which he had been campaining for and which had been articulated in the first drafts of NSC 68. At the end of July, Acheson met with Pearson to discuss Korea and the international situation. He stressed the need for America's allies to rearm and make a military contribution to Korea because of the impact it would have on U.S. public opinion. "If the United States had to do all the fighting in Korea," he warned, "there was a real danger that public opinion in the United States would favour preparing in isolation for the larger conflict ahead and writing its allies off." If properly promoted to the American public, Canadian, British, and other allied contributions to Korea would help support American as well as Western rearmament. Acheson told Pearson that he was "intensely concerned, as the President was, that the struggle ahead should not be one of the United States v. the U.S.S.R., but of the free world vs. the Communist world. The American people could be convinced of this if we all acted together on the Korean front as members of the United Nations, and if we worked together to strengthen our defences generally." Allied action in Korea would deter the Soviets from escalating the conflict and "would make a coordinated international effort for further rearmament far more acceptable to public opinion." In short, Western rearmament was tied directly to largely symbolic contributions to Korea from America's allies. For Acheson, the "main thing" was for the North Atlantic countries to "strengthen their defences and their war economies immediately." He told Pearson that the United States was planning defence expenditures in the order of $30 billion in the next eighteen months; Congress had just been asked by the president for another $10 billion, and there would be a request for an extra $4 billion for military assistance to other nations. This, he said, was "surely positive evidence" of American determination in the Cold War, but the United States was "most anxious to have it matched with equal determination in friendly countries." Contributions to the Korean cause would be of "tremendous importance," especially if it came from countries like Canada who "have prestige and influence and command respect." Reflecting on the substance of the meeting, Pearson noted: "Personally, I think the whole question [of providing an international force] should be explored energetically and sympathetically to see if it is practicable and, if so, how it should be carried out." Echoing the conclusions of Attlee's letter to

Table 4
U.N. Command, Ground Forces, 1951–1953

	30 June 1951	30 June 1952	31 July 1953
Republic of Korea	273,266	376,418	590,911
United States	253,250	265,864	302,483
United Kingdom	8,273	13,043	14,198
Canada	5,403	5,155	6,146
Turkey	4,602	4,878	5,455
Australia	912	1,844	2,282
Thailand	1,057	2,274	1,294
Philippines	1,143	1,494	1,496
Ethiopia	1,153	1,094	1,271
New Zealand	797	1,111	1,389
Greece	1,027	899	1,263
Columbia	1,050	1,007	1,068
France	738	1,185	1,119
Belgium[1]	602	623	944
Netherlands	725	565	819
India[2]	333	276	70
Sweden[2]	162	148	154
Norway[2]	79	109	105
Italy[2]	0	64	72

Source: Hermes, Truce Tent, app. A.
[1] Includes Luxembourg contingent of about 44 men.
[2] Noncombat medical units.

St Laurent a few days earlier, he pointed out: "Its practical importance might be considerable and its political international significance much greater."[28] (See table 4 for relative troop contributions to Korea.)

On the same day that Pearson reported to the cabinet his conversations with Acheson, St Laurent made a public announcement that the Canadian government would establish a special volunteer brigade for Korea. Existing front-line army personnel would not be sent, but the prime minister made an appeal for "young men, physically fit, mentally alert, single or married, particularly, just as many veterans of the Second World War as possible."[29] This did not completely satisfy American authorities, who wanted an immediate Canadian contribution, but for officials in Ottawa it represented an attempt to support the broader objectives of Western rearmament and containment of the Soviet Union.

Attlee described Britain's plans for rearmament to St Laurent on 3 August. The British were generally satisfied with their manpower levels because one million men had received compulsory military training since 1945. Since 1949 that training had been followed up with a four-year compulsory reserve service. The real requirement was the production of defence equipment. This would entail a vast increase in defence expenditure. Prior to Korea, the British defence budget was about £780 million per year. Now it was expected to total £3.4 billion over the next three years – an average of £1.1 billion per year. The Labour government understood the burden that the program would have on the already overstretched British economy. The added expenditure would delay the postwar recovery and would "entail very heavy costs in payment of necessary dollar imports, loss of exports and reduction of essential home investment." In simple terms, it would at a minimum postpone any improvement in the standard of living. For these reasons it was important to maintain the Anglo-American special relationship, explained Attlee: "It would be impossible to carry out the full programme without substantial United States assistance in addition to the completion of the European Recovery Programme."[30]

In Canada, decisions about accelerating defence expenditures were also made at this time. The impact of rearmament on the Canadian economy would be much less drastic than the cost of rearmament would be in Britain. Although the Canadian finance minister, Douglas Abbott, thought that Canada, like other Western countries, would have to go on a "semi-war" economy over the next few years, C.D. Howe pointed out that the increased expenditure on defence would not have "any strong impact on the economy for some six months or more. Only food and certain imported commodities would experience a serious rise in prices in the next few months." On 7 August the Canadian cabinet agreed that $90 million more would be allocated for Canadian defence.[31] Between 1950 and 1952, defence spending in Canada was to rise from $385 million to $1.415 billion.

Overall, this stage of the war had demonstrated a consensus of opinion among the major participants. The Americans had asked for allied contributions of forces because the provision of these would bolster their efforts to shape a favourable domestic attitude towards the Cold War. Allied troops in Korea would help Western rearmament efforts and demonstrate the importance of working with the North Atlantic Treaty powers in international affairs. The allies understood the importance of these considerations for their own containment policies and responded in kind. Their largely symbolic contributions to Korea were meant to help consolidate the United States' new-found role as leader of the West in the Cold War.

THE KOREAN WAR AND THE ANGLO-CANADIAN "SPECIAL RELATIONSHIP" WITH INDIA

Maintaining Indian support for United Nations actions was a concern of Canada and Britain throughout the Korean War. British and Canadian diplomats emphasized the advantages to Western diplomacy if India supported their containment strategy towards Asia. On 4 September 1950, Bevin told the British cabinet that he wanted the United States to accept a greater role for South Asia in America's Asian policies. Britain had taken the lead in guiding the forces of nationalism in South and Southeast Asia, but "the United States had been much slower to recognise the new independence in Asia and had even now to be reminded of the important role which India could play in Asian affairs." In Canada, Escott Reid, the deputy under-secretary of state and a moderate socialist, held great expectations for an Indian-Canadian partnership in the Asian Cold War. Reid believed that India, as a Commonwealth nation and the only major Asian state with a significant degree of experience with Western democracy, could play a vital role in communicating Western ideals to other Asian states. Reid even used the term "special relationship" to describe Canadian-Indian diplomatic relations.[32]

In practice, the Old Commonwealth remained sceptical about Indian initiatives in the bipolar Cold War. The Commonwealth Relations Office operated a two-tiered telegraphic system, one for the old white Commonwealth and another for the new "coloured" Commonwealth, and it was very cautious about bringing the New Commonwealth into the inner circle of British strategic and diplomatic thinking. Differences between old and new were reflected during the Korean War. The Old Commonwealth was not prepared to accept the Indian position on admitting the People's Republic of China to the Security Council. In July the Soviet Union indicated to both the British and the Indians that the first step in any settlement should be the seating of the Chinese representative in the Security Council. Prime Minister Nehru agreed and saw this proposal as encouraging. The British cabinet did not. On 18 July it noted that "the procedure proposed by the Soviet Government could not be accepted."[33] Such concessions were also unacceptable to the Canadians. But the need to contain aggression overrode any considerations the Indians had about seating the Chinese. As in other cases during the war when there was open disagreement between the Americans and Indians, the British and Canadians sided with the Americans. Ultimately, preserving the special relationship with the United States was much more important than catering to what was perceived by disappointed British and Canadian officials as the Indian diplomacy of appeasement.

The British and Canadian support for the United States against Indian arguments illustrates the limitations and dilemmas of the allied diplomatic strategy of constraint. On 30 September, Secretary Acheson presented a resolution to the General Assembly which gave General MacArthur implicit authority to cross the 38th parallel. MacArthur had launched a successful amphibious assault at Inchon two weeks before, and the North Korean army was in retreat. Acheson was now laying the groundwork for the eventual military reunification of Korea. Britain and six other nations co-sponsored this "eight-power" resolution, which recommended that "conditions of stability throughout Korea" be created, that elections for a unified and democratic Korea be held under U.N. auspices, and that the people and representative bodies of North and South Korea be invited to cooperate with the United Nations in setting up a new independent state. U.N. forces were to remain in any part of the peninsula only as long as was needed to preserve stability. A U.N. Commission for the Unification and Rehabilitation of Korea was also envisaged.[34] Canada, Britain, the United States, and forty-six other nations passed the resolution in the General Assembly on 7 October 1950. Although India had supported the U.N. decision to cross the 38th parallel, concern about Chinese intervention was growing and it voted against this resolution. On 27 September the secretary general of the Indian Ministry of External Affairs, Girja S. Bajpai, said that his government believed "there was real danger Peking might intervene" if the U.N. forces crossed into North Korea.[35]

Like the Americans, the British were sceptical of this information. On the twenty-ninth, the American ambassador in India, Loy Henderson, reported that Bevin had written to Nehru expressing doubts that "Peking would be so foolish as to intervene in Korea at this stage." The allies supported the U.S. position and, as Bevin's message illustrates, did little to constrain the United States on this issue. According to Henderson, Bevin pointed out to Nehru that "unless U.N. forces entered North Korea there seemed to be no way to effect unification of Korea." The foreign secretary hoped that Nehru would co-sponsor the U.N. proposal.[36] Arguments that a stronger British push for caution in crossing the parallel may have made a difference in the conduct of the war thus do not stand up to the realities of British strategy at the time. British and Canadian officials wanted greater Indian support for the U.N. strategy, not vice versa. There were definite limits to the strategy of restraint.

The British wanted to assure the Chinese that the U.N. forces did not represent a threat to Chinese security, and they suggested to the

Americans that representatives of the mainland government be invited to discussions in the Security Council. When Acheson explained to Kenneth Younger that this might delay the passing of the eight-power resolution, Younger said he would not have difficulty explaining this to Bevin.[37] In the event, the Americans agreed with the British that an invitation to attend the Security Council might allay Chinese fears, and they agreed that the Chinese be invited for discussions, though not on an American initiative.

The Canadian government hoped that Chinese attendance in the Security Council would modify India's reluctance to support the United Nations' decisions on Korea. A Canadian cabinet memo entitled "Asian Questions before the General Assembly" argued: "If the Chinese communists were given the chance to state their own case and did so in the intemperate language they have learned from the Soviets the Indians might be constrained to adopt a more objective attitude than they are now assuming." The Canadians hoped to forge a stronger U.N. position with regard to Korea and believed that Indian support of the U.N. policy would achieve this goal. In their view, it was the Indian as well as the American position that needed to be "constrained." Pearson wrote from New York on 9 October that "the inability to bring India along with the majority ... cannot be regarded as anything less than an important setback." The Indian position did suggest an alternative approach to the issue, he noted, but India "failed to make any real contribution which might have brought the majority position closer to her own, thereby giving rise to the suspicion that New Delhi is perhaps more concerned with the appearances of compromise than with finding an acceptable solution to the Korean problem."[38]

British and Canadian policy towards Asia took concepts borrowed from an older framework of empire and attempted to apply them to the bipolar post-1945 world. On many levels the argument for Indian support for Western Cold War initiatives in Korea was more symbolic than real. That both countries actively tried to get India to support U.N. policies in Korea can perhaps be seen as representing a certain idealism in their Korean policies. Rhetoric that stressed India's role as an Asian power faced many practical difficulties that did not seem to be fully understood. It is significant that India's Asian policy was not looked on favourably by the South Korean government. The acting officer in charge of Korean affairs in the Department of State, R.B. Emmons, wrote in a memo that the Korean ambassador and the Korean foreign minister had "expressed enthusiasm" for the admission of Pakistan on the new U.N. commission overseeing the rehabilitation of Korea: "Indian participation ... had tended to make their relations with the old [U.N.] Commission difficult in the past."[39]

THE REPUBLIC OF KOREA AND ROLLBACK

The South Korean government was not fighting a limited war; it demanded the eradication and complete elimination of North Korean communism. South Korean government representatives were the most vocal advocates of rollback policies. Little fear was shown of the possibility of extended war with the People's Republic of China or even the Soviet Union. South Korean rhetoric implicitly supported the need to fight any communist group that continued to threaten Korean unity. Dr John Chang, the Korean ambassador to the United States, who later became president of the ill-fated Second Republic, wrote to Dean Acheson on 21 September: "It is the view of my Government that the forces of the United Nations ... should not lose sight of the ultimate goal of crushing the communist invaders of Korea."[40]

South Korean anticommunist rhetoric had many similarities with American perceptions of communism. Like the Americans, the South Koreans placed responsibility for the invasion on the Soviets. Chang argued that Soviet imperialism, in its efforts to advance its aims, had "blocked all attempts to bring about unification of my country." The Russians had "consistently defied the will of the Korean people in this attempt to enslave them." The "most earnest hope" of the Republic of Korea (ROK) and the Korean people, said Chang, was "that the forces of the United Nations will march beyond the 38th parallel ... The traditional boundary of Korea must be the boundary of Korea after the present military action is concluded, since the 38th parallel has no legal basis as a division."[41] Although American officials believed that the views of the South Koreans gave added legitimacy to their cause, the ROK had very little influence on American decision making during the war. The asymmetry in South Korean–United States relations which had been characteristic of their association before the war was heightened by the outbreak of hostilities. During the war the South Korean government depended on the United States for its very existence.

President Rhee continued to pressure the United States to adopt unlimited rollback strategies, but tensions between the United Nations and the ROK during the war were settled in favour of American and allied objectives and policies. On one level, Rhee's policies and pronouncements can be seen as an attempt to assert his will as the recognized leader of the Republic of Korea over United Nations goals for Korea. But the obstacles he encountered and the limits of his influence on allied strategy demonstrate the extent to which South Korean objectives were secondary to the larger allied goals of rearmament and of undermining Soviet prestige and power in the bipolar world.

During October 1950, relations between ROK and the United Nations were strained as a result of conflicts between President Rhee – who called for the South Korean government to administer North Korea after the defeat of the communist forces – and the United Nations Command (UNC), which was developing a separate strategy for the reunification of Korea. On 12 October the U.N. Interim Committee on Korea adopted a resolution that advised the UNC "to assume provisionally all responsibilities for the government and civil administration of those parts of Korea which had not been recognized by the U.N. as being under the effective control of the government of the ROK at the outbreak of hostilities, and which may now come under occupation by U.N. forces, pending consideration by the U.N. Commission for the Unification and Rehabilitation of Korea of the administration of these territories."[42]

Three days later, President Truman met Douglas MacArthur at Wake Island. This meeting is usually treated in the context of the Truman-MacArthur power struggle. MacArthur believed that the Eighth Army would be able to withdraw to Japan by Christmas. When asked by Truman about the possibilities of Chinese intervention in Korea, he boasted: "We are no longer fearful of intervention … Only 50/60,000 could be gotten across the Yalu River. They have no Air Force. Now that we have bases for our air force in Korea, if the Chinese tried to get down to Pyongyang there would be the greatest slaughter."[43] The conference was also significant for its discussion about the future of a unified Korea. Virtually every aspect of the internal administration of the country was touched on by the conference participants. In addition to the president and MacArthur, the participants included Arthur Radford, the commander-in-chief of the U.S. Pacific Fleet; the secretary of the army, Frank Pace; the ambassador, John Muccio; the ambassador-at-large, Philip Jessup; the assistant secretary of state, Dean Rusk; and the Soviet expert, soon to be appointed head of the Mutual Security Program, Averell Harriman. No Korean officials were in attendance at the meeting, nor were any invited to attend.

Plans for northern rehabilitation reflected American objectives for the southern peninsula: the north, under U.S.-led occupation forces, would be integrated economically and politically into a unified anti-communist Korea. Essentially, the meeting was an executive-level discussion for the second U.S. occupation of Korea. When MacArthur argued that the American effort would take three years, Ambassador John Muccio pointed out that this was the first time the United States had moved into a country that had been dominated by communists; it represented a "challenging opportunity." Pace then asked about the Korean Military Advisory Group (KMAG) and MacArthur gave it high praise. "The group has been wonderful," and its five hundred officers and men "should be continued indefinitely," he said. It would provide the training for the Korean soldiers until their civilian administrators took over. Muccio agreed that the mission had done "a great job training the young Koreans." The Economic Cooperation Administration (ECA) would temporarily be responsible for rehabilitating the railways and utilities, but economic reconstruction was only part of the job. Harriman asked about "psychological rehabilitation," and Muccio stated that this was one area where more Koreans should be brought in: "We should provide them with radios and text books and also scientific guidance. We could set up a very effective system with a radio or loudspeaker in every school and village center." He also had sound trucks that had been very effective, he reported. Previously, without radio or newspapers, "we sent them out to rural districts and village centers." Truman was familiar with such techniques. "I believe in sound trucks," he joked. "I won two elections with them." Rusk was more serious. It was important not to undermine the Rhee government, he observed. Although Rhee would not like it, it should be possible to maintain a regional government in the north with Rhee holding the South. "And then it will be almost time for the 1952 elections throughout the country." In the interim, General MacArthur noted, "North Korea will be under military control." MacArthur stated that until the Southern Korean officials were allowed to take over, the military would freeze land tenure, banks and currency: "I will keep the North Korean currency in effect in North Korea without setting a rate to the dollar or ROK won until the civilian government can take over." It was only after this overview of occupation plans that Truman asked about Chinese and Soviet intervention.[44]

The comments at the meeting reflected the continuity in goals of American policy towards Korea since the initial U.S. occupation in 1945. The KMAG and ECA would be extended northwards; Rhee would be kept in the background until the framework had been established, and then elections would be held in which he would be the likely victor. Formal occupation would give way to a pro-Western proxy ally, who would require continued "guidance" in economic and military affairs. This state building in Korea provided the background experience for many U.S. officials who were later involved in Vietnam.

Before the conference broke up, Rusk and MacArthur expressed their concern about U.N. attitudes towards Rhee. Rusk warned Truman that there was an effective propaganda campaign in the United Nations against Rhee's government. The president understood the implications of this for U.S. policy. For Truman, Rhee had become analogous to a member of the "Pendergast machine." He thought of Rhee

as one of America's boys: "We must make it plain that we are supporting the Rhee Government and propaganda can 'go to hell.'"[45] Truman
would support the Korean president as long as it was expedient. In a
private meeting between Rusk and Muccio, the ambassador said that
he had made "repeated efforts to keep Rhee moving in the right direction," but despite his "repeated and strong representations" he had
"thought a great deal about an alternative to Rhee." The problem was
that he had "thus far not been able to think of anyone who could do
the job." The new Korean military leadership "was about the only possible source for a successor."[46]

Rhee was interested in expedience as well, but it was an expedience
built on the knowledge that Koreans had been prevented from determining their own national policies by thirty-five years of Japanese colonial rule and three years of American and Soviet occupation. While
Rhee understood that American "informal empire" was preferable to
Japanese rule, he was determined to assert Korean "independence"
from all foreign attempts to impose developmental frameworks on Korea. He wanted to unify the North immediately on the basis of the existing constitution of the ROK, and on 16 October he sent a message to
General MacArthur stating that the interim committee's resolution was
unacceptable to the Korean government. Rhee argued that Korea had
not participated in the resolution and would not adhere to it. This was
the sovereign right of the constituted Government of Korea: "This government is taking over the civilian administration whenever hostilities
cease by dispatching the Governors appointed two years ago for five
provinces of the North to restore peace and order." He further believed that the UNC would not be able to eliminate communist influence in northern Korea. The U.N. committee's proposals would only
result in the protection and revival of communism in the north, to the
detriment of the ROK. Rhee's adherence to Korean sovereignty was
coupled with a fierce anticommunism: "To allow any nation or nations
even U.N. to interfere with the internal administration [of Korea] in
cooperation with the existing communist organizations imposed upon
the people by alien [Soviet] power is impossible."[47]

The Korean president feared that left-wing northern voters might
elect people's representatives who would not be favourable to his continued rule. It is possible that strong left-wing opposition would have
emerged, but the ROK had its own methods of dealing with that. Rusk
was probably correct in predicting an eventual victory for the existing
president. But Rhee was not willing to have this strategy imposed on
his government. In the end he was faced with the ugly reality that he
himself was not an independent actor and that the UNC held the balance of power.

Had the Canadians or British read this message, they would have thought it fantastic to associate UNC operations in North Korea with appeasement of communism. As a general rule, the Commonwealth was much more openly critical of Rhee than the Americans were. As members of the UNC, they were unconcerned and indeed afraid of Rhee's anticommunism, usually because Rhee's statements seemed to threaten their more moderate prescriptions for dealing with the over-all communist threat in Asia. For them, Rhee's internal sovereignty was not important, and there was no apparent need to consult with the Koreans themselves over issues revolving around the Korean War. Canada at this time did not even have full diplomatic relations with the ROK: it depended on the British ambassador in Seoul for diplomatic niceties. British, Canadian, and other allied actions in Korea were legitimized entirely through the United Nations, a body with no Korean representation. On the whole, the allies supported American objectives *vis-a-vis* the Korean government.

MacArthur understood that many members of the United Nations would not agree with Rhee, and he told Truman that "he should carefully avoid any action which might encourage further public controversy." Rhee did not take UNC representations with a good grace. A CIA report dated 18 October pointed out that Rhee's attitude was one of "defiance" of the United Nations: "Late press reports from Seoul state that Rhee has dispatched governors to the liberated North Korean provinces and quote him as promising 'land reform' in North Korea as soon as possible."[48]

On 27 October, Bevin told Sir Oliver Franks to relay to the State Department the United Kingdom's hopes that the administration of North Korea lay with the Unified Command and the United Nations Commission, not with President Rhee. Bevin felt that the Rhee government was acting arbitrarily on this matter and that the Unified Command would be subjected to criticism.[49] American officials also were concerned, for Rhee's efforts might undermine their plan for a unified Korea and weaken the United States' relations with its allies. On 31 October the American chargé in Korea, Everett Drumright, wrote to Acheson that if Rhee could be assured that North Koreans would not be used in the interim administration and that South Koreans and northern refugees would be used instead, then "Rhee's principal points of opposition will have been surmounted."[50]

It is uncertain whether the UNC would actually have barred North Koreans from elections. However, the United Nations was not much longer to be concerned with the administration of North Korea, for in late November the Chinese mounted an offensive which within a few months once again brought communist forces south of Seoul. Consequently, the dilemmas of informal empire on the peninsula were once again shelved in favour of more immediate military and strategic considerations.

TWILIGHT WAR: 25 OCTOBER TO 26 NOVEMBER

The decision to expand the "police action" into North Korea was taken with the understanding that it might provoke the Soviet Union or China into intervening. Despite warnings from the People's Republic of China and from Indian officials and other sources, neither Canada nor Great Britain, nor the United States believed that Chinese intervention was likely. However, some steps were taken to assure the Chinese that U.N. forces would not invade mainland China. On 28 September, when the American delegation to the United Nations discussed the Korean situation, the secretary of state pointed out that hearing the Chinese communists in the Security Council "might reassure them with respect to our intentions in Korea." Although the United States had to be careful about appeasing the communists, he said, it would be helpful to explain to the Chinese that "we were not fortifying the border." The issue was not worth fighting over, "since many other government[s], whose cooperation we needed, regarded the Chinese Communists as the Government of China, and if this issue were debated at length, we would lose more than we would gain."[51]

On 25 October the first Chinese units were reported to have clashed with ROK soldiers in North Korea about 65 kilometres south of the Chinese border. In the West, efforts to reassure the Chinese were accelerated. In early November, as the Chinese were building up their military strength south of the Yalu, the British, French, and American delegations at the United Nations introduced a resolution which affirmed "the policy of the United Nations to hold the Chinese frontier inviolate and fully to protect Chinese legitimate interests in the frontier zone." The resolution also pointed to the "grave danger" which Chinese intervention entailed.[52]

There is little indication that the United States wanted war with the Chinese communists at this time. Leighton Stuart, the acting officer in charge of political affairs, Office of Chinese Affairs, reflected on 3 November: "Major hostilities with Communist China would be contrary to our interests and to the interests of the Chinese people." On 9 November the U.S. Joint Chiefs of Staff concluded: "Every effort should be expended as a matter of urgency to settle the problem of Chinese Communist intervention in Korea by political means, preferably through the United Nations, to include reassurances to the Chinese

Communists with respect to our intent, direct negotiations through our Allies and the Interim Committee with the Chinese Communist Government, and by any other available means."[53]

The position of the United States on this issue was not unequivocal; the logic of its need to force a lesson on the communists conflicted with its perceptions of limited war. The result was a certain ambiguity in U.S. policies and the presence of escalatory thinking. "Even though the United States makes every effort to localize the present conflict," wrote the Joint Chiefs of Staff, "a review of its probable eventualities leads to the conclusion that there now exists a greatly increased risk of global war."[54]

Dean Acheson, who viewed the crossing of the 38th parallel as somewhat of a gamble anyway, also recognized the difficulties of American containment strategy in Korea in the light of China's intervention. He was torn between the need to meet the communists head-on and the need to prevent the extension of the conflict. On 6 November he wrote to the embassy in the United Kingdom that "if Peiping discovers that nothing at all happens in the face of its intervention it will be emboldened to act even more aggressively by what it might consider proof of weakness or nervousness on our part." On the other hand, he said, "We do not wish to extend the fighting in Korea to China by pressing and proving a case of aggression ... certainly not at this stage." On balance, he hoped the U.S. gamble would pay off: "Our purpose should be to emphasize that we are trying to limit the fighting to Korea and to do everything we can not to spread the hostilities."[55]

American actions in the fighting did not always match private thoughts regarding limited war, and to some extent the momentum of the conflict itself resulted in obscuring the limited war precept. On the same day that Acheson wrote the above telegram, the Department of State received notice that the U.S. Air Force had orders to bomb a bridge that spanned the Yalu River from Sinuiju in North Korea to Antung in Manchuria. Alarmed, Dean Rusk, George Marshall, and Deputy Secretary of Defense Robert Lovett agreed that the action was provocative and that permission should be obtained from the president. In a phone call, Truman told Acheson that if it was necessary to protect U.S. forces, the bridge should be bombed, though the American position would be stronger if they could consult their allies first. MacArthur subsequently reiterated the need to bomb, and the Joint Chiefs of Staff gave authorization with the caveat that only the Korean side of the bridge be bombed and not dams or power plants on the river. "Extreme care" was to be taken to avoid violating Manchurian airspace and territory.[56] The belief that U.N. actions should demonstrate that Chinese territory was inviolable had only been partially fulfilled. Although the bombing of the bridge was consistent with short-term strategic objectives, it could have done little to alleviate Chinese fears that the United Nations was intending to extend hostilities to Manchuria, the launching point for Japan's aggression against China in the 1930s. In calling for this action, MacArthur may have been bending the rules a bit, though he was still working within the American game plan.

So, too, were America's allies. In late November, in the light of Mac-Arthur's upcoming offensive, which was supposed to be the last big U.N. push to the Yalu, Bevin agreed to delay proposals for a buffer zone across the neck of Korea. On 22 November he sent a message to Chou En-lai stating that the United Nations had "no hostile intent" against China and that the Chinese frontier would not be violated. Canadian officials maintained their allegiance as well. On 22 November, Lester Pearson told the cabinet that "the United Nations should make every effort to ensure that Korea were united under a democratically elected government and started back on the road to recovery through essential rehabilitation and reconstruction measures." On the whole, the allies continued to work within the American framework of containment. In general, the diplomacy of constraint worked best where it reinforced existing U.S. policy. The issue of "hot pursuit" – the possibility that U.N. planes would attack enemy planes for up to three minutes inside Manchurian air space – was one such case where Canada and Great Britain, in conjunction with other allies, reinforced American policy. Many Americans agreed with the basic tenets of allied representations urging caution. Rusk told the Canadian ambassador that "everyone in the State Department shared the apprehensions over the possible consequences expressed by the Canadian and other Governments." Hot pursuit would only be necessary, he said, "in the event of serious military necessity"; only "large-scale bombing operations from Manchuria" against U.N. supply depots would create the need for U.N. air action over China. Furthermore, there had been little air activity originating in Manchuria during the past week, and "he hoped that the need to apply the proposal would not arise."[57] On 26 November, however, two days after MacArthur's "end of the war" offensive, the Chinese attacked U.N. and ROK positions with the full force of an estimated seven armies. Initial intelligence surveys pegged their forces at about 200,000 men. The new war had begun.

LIMITED WAR AND THE TRUMAN-ATTLEE DISCUSSIONS

Chinese intervention in the Korean War exacerbated allied tensions and threatened the policy consensus that had been pursued in Korea.

It also exacerbated fears about possible war with the USSR. The United States, Great Britain, and other North Atlantic allies undertook a limited mobilization of forces and again accelerated their defence spending. On 16 December, President Truman proclaimed a national emergency. The period of crisis was most acute after China's New Year offensive and the second communist march past Seoul in early January.

As before the intervention, the United States was more willing than either Canada or the United Kingdom to challenge aggression. At a cabinet meeting on 28 November, Acheson argued that it was clear "we should charge the Chinese Communists with aggression. We should see what pressures we can put on the Chinese Communists to make life harder for them." But the United States should be careful to avoid escalating the war, he cautioned, for this would only bring in the Russians. What was important was "to find a line that we can hold, and hold it."[58]

The discussions between British and American officials between 4 and 8 December 1950 were important in illustrating the common objectives and disagreements of the two allies. During the meetings, both sides agreed that their short-term strategy should be to attempt a cease-fire arrangement. This would prevent escalation and would provide time for U.N. reinforcements to take position in Korea. During a session on 4 December, President Truman said that despite pessimistic reports from his military advisers, he hoped "the line could be held in Korea until the situation was better for negotiation." Attlee agreed. U.S. and U.N. prestige was at stake. On the seventh, the prime minister argued: "We should hold out until we were obliged to get out. A cease fire may be secured; then we could begin to talk … This was really a United Nations business, but our enemies are always trying to present the matter as if it were really a quarrel between the United States and China." Truman responded that Attlee was right: "We did not want that impression."[59]

In global strategic terms, there was a consensus on keeping the war limited to Korea. Attending a Canadian cabinet meeting after the Anglo-American discussions were completed, Attlee stated that it was crucial that the U.N. character of the Korean operations be maintained: "The organization could not afford to fail in the first real challenge of aggression." Yet it would be "equally fatal to pour the resources of the democratic nations into a war with China which would leave the Soviet Union free to act in Europe. In Washington it became clear that the U.S. administration was in complete agreement."[60]

On the more sensitive and longer-standing issue of the recognition of the People's Republic of China and its seating in the United Nations, there remained substantial differences between the two allies.

During the Truman-Attlee meetings, the prime minister pointed out that unlike the Americans, the British believed that the Chinese were not pawns of the Soviets. They might be communist and Marxist and still "not bow to Stalin"; Chinese nationalism instinctively disliked dictation by the Soviets.[61] Such arguments were meant to reinforce the importance of adopting a cautious policy towards the People's Republic of China. They were also a means of preserving Britain's formal colonial interests in Hong Kong and Malaya. But there were definite limits to which the Americans were prepared to come to a *modus vivendi* with the new China. They continued to reject any possibility of recognizing the People's Republic, seating it on the Security Council, or returning Taiwan in exchange for a settlement in Korea. American officials stated firmly that they would not do so. Truman concurred, noting that he would "have a great deal of difficulty with our people" if the Chinese were admitted to the United Nations.[62]

The basis for unity stemmed from concern about containing the Soviet Union. Sir Oliver Franks pointed out: "We were agreed on what we hoped to do in Korea. This attitude flowed naturally from the decisions which had already been made concerning aggression." Prime Minister Attlee agreed with Franks's remark that negotiations would not be made at any price. A joint communiqué issued at the end of the conference noted the British and American divergence on policies towards China but stated that they were "determined to prevent it from interfering with our united effort in support of our common objectives."[63] The communiqué thus recognized the overriding strategic priority of presenting a united front to the Sino-Soviet alliance.

Subtle differences with regard to the containment of communism in Asia were reflected in the proceedings of the conference. In particular, despite the fact that the British and Americans wanted to keep the war limited, they had different ideas of what "limited war" meant. In general, there was more of a consensus in Great Britain and Canada than in the United States as to the meaning of the term. To the British, it meant that military activities should be strictly confined to Korea and not involve China in any way. As Attlee said, "The United Kingdom does not approve of limited warfare against the Chinese if this were not directed to the immediate terrain of Korea but became a kind of war around the perimeter of China."[64] In Ottawa, Pearson reminded cabinet on 29 November that "on a number of occasions" Canada had "expressed concern over the possibilities of reckless action in Korea and had done whatever possible to discourage aggressive or provocative moves in an attempt to confine the extent of hostilities."[65]

The Americans, too, wanted a "limited war," but their tendency to exact retribution led Dean Rusk, General Omar Bradley, George Kennan, and General MacArthur to believe that an expansion of the war into China would not necessarily lead to global escalation or pro-longed regional conflict.[66] Even Dean Acheson and George Marshall considered the possibility of attacking China from the defensive island perimeter if the United Nations forces were forced to evacuate the peninsula. Although such ideas did not dominate American strategy or diplomacy and although, overall, care was taken not to take actions that would escalate the war, nevertheless these ideas were an important source of friction with America's Atlantic allies.

Another important cause of tension was the difference of opinion regarding the application of the containment strategy. Compared with its allies, there was more of a crusading tone to American anticommu-nism. More so than Britain, Canada, France, and others, the United States tended to perceive its actions in Korea in a moralistic and self-righteous manner. The American usage of the term "free world" with regard to collective security action is indicative of this trend: led by America, the United Nations had undertaken military actions that were in the best interests of all "free" people. The moral imperative of acting against Soviet totalitarian aggression was seen in somewhat sim-plistic, black-and-white terms. A heroic image of the United States was invoked: American democratic values were triumphing over the evil and illegitimate representatives of oppressed peoples. Like the Pro-gressives in the early twentieth century, there was a crusading element to American containment policy. In the context of the Korean War, a fundamental distinction was made between legality, legitimacy, and moral values defined in Western and American democratic terms and the basic corruptness of Soviet and communist societies. Democratic values were, a priori, legitimate and legal; communism was totalitarian and therefore both illegitimate and illegal. Thus, the West had a moral obligation to undermine this social system.

The term "police action" can be viewed in this light. In international law, a "war" could imply a recognition of the legitimacy of a belligerent state; a "police action," on the other hand, implied an act of legal retri-bution against an illegal force. It appealed to the American imagina-tion and invoked a kind of populist image of a cops-and-robbers drama. The phrase is a telling indicator of the ideology behind Ameri-can containment strategy during the Korean War.

A memorandum written by the director of the Department of State's Northeast Asian Affairs Division, John Allison, is representative of this trend of thought. Early in the conflict, Allison had complained about a draft National Security Council paper that recommended as a short-term American objective in Korea the status quo ante bellum. "The whole tone of the present [NSC] paper," he complained, "implies that the North Korean regime has a legal status and that the area north of the 38th parallel is, in fact, a separate nation. This has no foundation in fact or in morality. The North Korean regime is a creature of the Soviet Union set up in defiance of the will of the majority of the Korean people." America had nothing to gain if it compromised its "clear moral principles," argued Allison, or if it shirked its duty "to make clear once and for all that aggression does not pay – that he who violates the decent opinions of mankind must take the consequences and that he who takes the sword must die by the sword." Allison's views found a sympathetic hearing in the U.S. administration, and at the end of July he became the officer responsible for coordinating the department's future policy towards North Korea.[67] These sentiments did not dominate U.S. strategy, however, and they must be analysed alongside concern about expanding the war and maintaining allied support.

Nevertheless, it was the crusading tone of American containment strategy that British and Canadian officials feared and objected to. The Commonwealth tended to associate U.S. belligerence and possibly even unreliability with a strong emotional strain in American thinking. In a memo dated 30 March 1951, R.L. Rogers of the Canadian Far Eastern Division stated that one cause of differences between Canada and the United States was that the latter "follows a rapidly changing, almost mercurial policy."[68] At the height of the policy crisis over Korea, Sir William Strang, the permanent under-secretary of the Foreign Office, wrote that the United States "often behaves insufferably to its allies. Americans are apt to behave insufferably to each other." He added that the Americans were inexperienced in taking on the responsibilities of world power and had not yet learned "to tolerate the frustrations and bitterness of defeat." It was thus the job of the United Kingdom to "deflect the Americans from unwise or dangerous courses without making a breach in the united front."[69]

While there was a zealous aspect to American containment policy, there was much more to American policies towards Korea than wayward emotional sentiment. The United States' willingness to defend its interests during the Korean War was related to the extension of its power on a global scale. "Foreign policy in the East and in Western Europe cannot be separated," Dean Acheson said. "We must have a single foreign policy for both sides of the world." As Truman told Attlee, "The United States has responsibilities in the East and the West. We naturally consider European defense primary, but we equally have responsibilities in Korea, Japan and the Philippines."[70]

Truman's allusion to the "defensive perimeter" concept was significant. America's interests in Japan and the Philippines and in the defence of its western shores gave its containment strategy greater regional scope than those of its allies. The secretary of state believed that if the United States bowed to the communists, a huge row of dominoes might collapse: "If we surrendered Formosa, the Japanese would react to our surrender to the display of Chinese force. If we give up Korea by agreement the Filipinos and Japanese would run for cover. In this connection the Russian opposition to our proposal for holding the Ryukyus shows a general plan to oust us from our island defenses."[71]

The British fear that the Americans might provoke a global war or a regional conflict with the Chinese was also grounded in concrete global and regional interests. In regional terms, it was important that Great Britain should neither antagonize China nor pull U.N. forces out of Korea entirely in anticipation of air attacks on the mainland. The British feared Chinese retribution against Hong Kong, Indochina, and Malaya. An attack on these areas would seriously undermine Britain's colonial prestige and power in Asia. During the Truman-Attlee discussions, British Air Marshal Lord Tedder related British interests in Asia to its European interests: "If war started with the Chinese, the Russians might wait in Europe until it suited their book to come in. The Chinese would probably go on attacking Hong Kong and Indochina, hoping our troops would be drawn to Malaya, and at that point there might be a Russian strike in Europe. We must avoid that if we can."[72] Thus, Great Britain's colonial position in Asia influenced its Cold War policies in Korea and contributed to tension in Anglo-American relations. The underlying cause of these strains was a conflict of national interest between British colonial objectives and American objectives regarding its Pacific perimeter.

Although allied and American containment policy for Korea was troubled with internal contradictions, the common concerns outweighed the differences. The United States' more bellicose stance was tempered by the realization of the primacy of its position in Western Europe and also by the belief that the West was still militarily too weak to tie itself down in a regional conflict or risk global war. Britain's policies were responsive to its colonial interests in Asia and a perceived vulnerability in Western Europe, but the British agreed on the need to rearm and to contain Soviet global imperialism. Canada had no significant interests in Asia itself, but its strategic interests in containing the Soviet Union and its participation in the North Atlantic Treaty Organization reinforced its willingness to work with its two major allies in the Korean War.

ATOMIC DIPLOMACY AND THE AGGRESSOR RESOLUTION

Two factors that influenced British and Canadian caution over American attempts to get allied support for a U.N. resolution branding

China as an aggressor at this time were the weak state of the West's conventional military strength and scepticism about the political and military value of the atomic bomb. In discussing the outcome of the Washington meetings in the presence of the Canadian cabinet, Attlee, and Field Marshal Sir William Slim, Prime Minister St Laurent reported: "With regard to the use of the bomb ... [Truman] was as anxious as was the Canadian government that it should not be used and that it would be particularly unfortunate if it were used for a second time in Asia." Like Britain, Canada had requested the United States for consultation prior to its use. Pearson told the British and Canadian officials that Canada had received a "reassuring interim reply" on the use of the bomb: "It appeared that the consultation referred to in the communique issued by the President and the Prime Minister included Canada."[73]

The Attlee-Truman discussions had only temporarily soothed allied fears, and concern about the bomb's use re-emerged in the context of the Chinese offensive at the end of December. The limits of the bomb's military power were most evident against China, and the possibility that its use in Asia might provoke the Soviet Union made Canadian diplomats and military officials very worried. Pearson told cabinet at the end of December that "the present military weakness in western Europe supported the Canadian contention that all possible steps should be taken to avoid becoming embroiled in a war with Communist China. In such a war, a decision would be almost impossible to secure even with the aid of atomic weapons."[74]

British officials were also very worried. In early January, at what was perhaps the height of British uncertainty regarding American intentions in East Asia, the Chiefs of Staff wrote to Air Marshal Lord Tedder, the chairman of the British Joint Services in Washington, that an evacuation of Korea would be "lamentable" and "could hardly fail to encourage the Communist Powers to further adventures with little fear of effective resistance." In such a situation, he said, Britain's security for several years would "rest solely on the somewhat uncertain foundations of the Atom bomb."[75] This was less than reassuring. Despite President Truman's promise to Prime Minister Attlee during their discussions in early December the British and Canadians remained extremely agitated about the military situation in Korea. The possibility of unilateral American military action remained and officials in both countries continued to emphasize the difference between being fully consulted and simply being informed about a decision to drop the atomic bomb. In the latter case allied influence on the Americans regarding the use of the ultimate weapon would be minimal. Both governments seemed certain only of the United States' commitment to inform them of developments that might lead to the use of the bomb. Everything remained dependent on stemming the Chinese New Year offensive. Allied concerns and trepidations about Truman's apparent assurances were expressed in a memo by Sir Roger Makins on 19 January 1951.[76] He wrote that although the "Prime Minister has received a personal undertaking from the President which we can feel sure will be honoured while President Truman remains in office," the United Kingdom would make no effort to "pin the Americans down" on the issue.[77]

That the Soviets possessed the bomb was not the greatest fear of some Britons. The minister of war, John Strachey, wrote to Bevin on 2 January 1951: "Our responsible military advisers tell us that long range weapons of the v.i and v.ii type, which are at Russia's disposal, would render the whole Southern and South-Western parts of Britain, including London, uninhabitable or at least 'unworkable.' These, rather than atomic weapons, are surely the real and potentially fatal menace to the existence of this country."[78] Such sentiments pushed Western officials towards massive conventional rearmament in the early 1950s.

The lack of existing forces was an important factor in getting the allies to delay consideration of the American resolution condemning China as an aggressor. However, it also underlined the need to maintain the Anglo-American special relationship. Attlee told his cabinet of the necessity of increasing expenditure on defence. On 18 December he noted that the United States was programming its own expenditure on the possibility that war might come as early as 1951, and he concluded that some further acceleration was "unavoidable" if the Anglo-American special relationship was to be consolidated. In Washington, he said, he had "persuaded the Americans to accept Anglo-American partnership as the mainspring of Atlantic defence," but this advantage would be lost and Britain would be treated simply as another European nation if it did not take the lead and urge the others to do more: "One could not ignore the risk, however remote it might seem, that the United States might lose interest in the defence of Europe, if her allies in the North Atlantic Treaty Organisation failed to play their larger part."[79]

Canada's reasoning was similar to Britain's. It too was worried about a further escalation of hostilities, and it believed that the West was not yet militarily prepared to enter into a global conflict – certainly not one that began in Asia, stretching even more the military power of the allies. Nevertheless, the Canadians supported action in Korea as part of a policy of maintaining collective security against the Soviet Union. Military mobilization after mid-1950 reflected uncertainty about Soviet intentions, the course of the war in Asia, and the importance of maintaining Canada's alliance with the United States. Pearson told cabinet in late December that "the events of the last few weeks had clearly indicated that, even if a third world war could be avoided for some time being, the forces of Soviet imperialism throughout the world might be able to seize so many additional areas in Asia and Europe that the position of North America would eventually become very serious." Like their British counterparts, the Canadian officials saw their salvation in an alignment with the United States and through the North Atlantic Treaty Organization. Reflecting the conclusions of the British memorandum, PUSC 22, on the need to consolidate the Western alliance on the basis of a special relationship with the United States, Pearson stated that a "successful defence of the west depended largely on continued and increased participation and assistance by the United States." It was therefore essential that Canada re-examine its defence program with a view to greater expenditures and commitments: "All N.A.T.O. countries would be required to press forward at a much accelerated speed if the free world was to attain the goal of security set by the North Atlantic Treaty."[80]

These considerations had important implications for British and Canadian policy towards the Far East, for failure to support American initiatives in Asia might harm the broader aspects of the "special relationship." Even more dangerous, a loss of Western unity might present the Soviets with an opportunity to exacerbate rifts in the alliance over East Asian issues. If war broke out, the allies would be forced by circumstance to side with the Americans against the Soviet Empire; British and Canadian diplomats believed it was better to try to influence American diplomacy and present the Soviets with a united position than to risk a split in the alliance. There was no room for neutrality. This was the logical conclusion of those who accepted PUSC 22.

Through December 1950 and January 1951 the Canadians and British, along with other Commonwealth countries, hoped that the United Nations would be able to negotiate a cease-fire with the Chinese, and between 4 and 12 January the Commonwealth prime ministers met in London to try to work out a compromise plan that both sides would accept. A guidance letter sent to all British representatives overseas pointed out that the conference wanted to "bring representatives of the United States government and the Central People's Government of China to a conference table." The essence of the plan was that a cease-fire in Korea would be followed by the creation of a committee composed of representatives of Britain, the United States, the Soviet Union, and the People's Republic of China. The committee's objective would be to achieve a settlement "of Far Eastern problems including, among other[s], those of Formosa and of representation of China in the United Nations."[81] The proposals were not accepted, however, and on 18 January the Chinese submitted counter-proposals rejecting an initial cease-fire and requiring withdrawal of the United States from Taiwan, the seating of the Chinese on the Security Council, and the convening of a seven-nation conference in China to discuss Far Eastern problems. The Americans were outraged, and in an attempt to force their allies' hand, they unilaterally introduced a resolution in the General Assembly calling the Chinese "aggressors."

In the short term the American initiative was a failure. On 22 January a vote on the resolution was delayed by forty-eight hours after the Indian representative, Benegal Rau, announced that he had received a message from the Chinese that might lead to further discussions. The outlook for negotiation seemed more optimistic, and Canada and Great Britain helped delay the vote.

They succeeded in gaining time, but a decision was still needed with regard to the resolution. Bevin argued that "some means should, if possible, be found of handling that situation without any rift between the Commonwealth and the United States." The chief of the air staff, Sir John Slessor, went further. In discussions with the JCS chairman, General Omar Bradley, Slessor had been convinced that the American position was not as belligerent as the cabinet believed. He held that the resolution was precautionary in intent. Bradley had told Slessor that "no action under the resolution would be taken until the United Nations forces had been withdrawn from Korea," and that the United States would consult Britain thereafter. Slessor revealed that it was not the intention of the United States to unleash Chiang Kai-shek's forces or to authorize an aerial attack on China unless, in the latter case, the U.N. forces were attacked in force by enemy aircraft. He stressed "the need for avoiding at this stage any action which might give the isolationists in the United States an opportunity to jeopardise the all-important contribution which the United States were making towards strengthening the defence of Western Europe."[82] In short, the linkage between American policies in Asia and Europe were seen as too interconnected to try to separate. If the United Kingdom wanted to preserve its power within the North Atlantic alliance, it should support American policy in Korea.

This sentiment had wide support among officials in the Foreign Office. On 6 January 1951, Pierson Dixon had minuted that there was little doubt that "the danger of a Russian attack would be great if the U.S., Great Britain and the Commonwealth were seriously divided." The permanent under-secretary, Sir William Strang, also commented on 6 January that the problem was not insoluble: "In the last resort the Americans want the same kind of thing as we do. We have in fact no alternative but to work with them." In the context of the bipolar world, the alternative of joining the Soviet bloc was "unthinkable," and the "establishment of a neutral or independent European bloc, manoeuvring between the Soviet Union and the United States," had been "repeatedly examined and as often rejected."[83]

The foreign secretary had based much of his strategy on the Anglo-American relationship, and he agreed with Strang's conclusions. On 12 January he wrote to Attlee warning of an American armed isolationism: "We have to imagine what it would be like to live in a world with a hostile Communist bloc, an unco-operative America, a Commonwealth pulled in two directions, and a disillusioned Europe which would be deprived of support in the form of American troops and American involvement in active European defence."[84]

On 22 January, however, Bevin took ill once again. He was replaced by Kenneth Younger, who did not share his enthusiasm for the Anglo-American special relationship and was more determined to put pressure on the United States to alter its aggressor resolution. Younger's influence was felt on 25 January when the British cabinet decided not to vote for the American resolution. But this decision was only temporary and the need to support the United States at some level had been recognized by Attlee. On 23 January he had stated, "We should be prepared to support some condemnation of Chinese action in Korea."[85]

On the twenty-fourth, Canada decided to support the resolution, though with reservations. Pearson's recommendation, which was accepted by the Canadian cabinet, was that Canada should vote with the United States but should state that the resolution did not "grant automatic authorization to the Unified Command to carry out active operational engagements against Chinese territory." In making this decision, the Canadians underlined the importance of American support against the Soviet Union in the bipolar world. The decision was implicit in the late December cabinet discussions. The minister of national health and welfare, Paul Martin, summed up the Canadian approach: the resolution had created a "regrettable divergence of views between the United States and Canada. Every care should be taken to avoid any widening of this rift and indeed everything should be done to facilitate complete unity of views between western democracies."[86]

The next day, the British received a further indication of China's apparent willingness to negotiate, but it also heard that the non-Asian Commonwealth and most European countries were prepared to vote for the American resolution. At its second meeting that day, the British cabinet rejected American concessions regarding the final paragraph of the draft resolution, which requested members of the Collective

Measures Committee to consider further sanctions to meet the aggression. A majority of the cabinet agreed that the United Kingdom representative at the United Nations should vote against the resolution as it stood. However, further concessions were forthcoming. An American suggestion that "the Collective Measures Committee would be authorized to defer their report against China if the Committee of Three to be appointed ... reported satisfactory progress in its efforts" was accepted by the British government. The decision on the twenty-fifth had not been sustained, and the broader forces demanding compromise and a maintenance of the special relationship had won out over the more independent line advocated by Younger.[87] On 1 February 1951, the resolution passed the General Assembly. A united front was preserved.

Both the British and the Canadians were pleased with the outcome. Pearson told his colleagues that he was encouraged at "the extent to which U.S. representatives had gone in modifying ... their resolution ... at the suggestion of other western countries. As the west's greatest power, they could probably have forced their views on others to satisfy Congressional and public opinion in the United States which was generally clamouring for the adoption of much more radical measures." Attlee also agreed that the compromise would meet British objectives of keeping negotiations open – sanctions would be imposed only after further negotiation.[88] In the eyes of the British and Canadian governments, then, their diplomacy had been successful. They had upheld their special relationship with the United States and had demonstrated their ability to influence and moderate American actions.

There had been compromises on both sides, however, and the allies tended to underestimate the extent to which they had moved closer to the American position. The passing of the aggressor resolution was also a success for American foreign policy. The Canadians were more ready to yield to the Americans than the British were, but ultimately both sides supported the American initiative. Their support underlined the dominant role and leadership of the United States within the Atlantic alliance, as well as the asymmetrical nature of interdependence between the United States and its allies in the bipolar world.

British and Canadian support for the resolution also illustrated the weakness of their "special relationship" with India. Both allies paid lipservice to the Indians when it was advantageous to do so, but their final decision reflected where they believed their interests lay. As Attlee pointed out, the Indian government had opposed the reference to sanctions in the resolution "and had reiterated their view that such a mention would bar the way to any further negotiations with the Chinese." Nevertheless, the compromise that had been reached with the

Americans "would re-establish a common policy between the United States and the older members of the Commonwealth, and would also emphasize our acceptance of our obligations as a member of the United Nations." Pearson's opinion of the Indians was more critical. "Throughout this episode the Indian position had been rather uncompromising," he told cabinet in February 1951.[89]

After the end of January, U.N. prospects began to improve. A Chinese offensive in late January failed and U.N. forces pushed northwards once again. By the end of March, they had re-established themselves along the 38th parallel. Military success was thus crucial in preventing the further escalation of the war. By the end of February, there was a new consensus in the U.S. government to maintain the containment line along the line of battle around the 38th parallel. This was reflected in the removal of MacArthur and the acceptance of the conclusions of a new National Security Council document for Asia, NSC 48/5. By spring, U.S. policymakers realized that their goal of a unified Korea was an illusion and that they would have to return to political and economic means of unifying the country. South Korea would need to be rebuilt with economic and military aid. In July 1951 negotiations for a settlement in Korea had begun; the initial period of danger had passed. Although the Americans continued to demand retribution, as Rosemary Foot has pointed out, "both Britain and Canada had indicated their reluctance to provide additional reinforcements for Korea, as well as general concern regarding a blockade of China; overall, however, U.S. and allied views on how to respond to a failure of the armistice negotiations were seen to be 'closely parallel.'"[90]

THE EARLY WAR IN RETROSPECT

The war in Korea had important implications for U.S. containment strategies. The conflict resulted in an augmented American effort to consolidate the power of pro-Western governments in peripheral regions around the globe. The supply of armaments and military advice to the underdeveloped world took on new significance in the post-Korean War globalization of American containment policy. Additional emphasis was placed on rearming and preserving Western spheres of influence in peripheral areas threatened by Soviet proxies. The development of indigenous military power in both Korea and Vietnam was now critical. Local forces were cheaper to maintain and would allow the West to concentrate its resources in more important areas of the globe where rearmament was required – namely, Western Europe.

As a complement to the build-up of Western proxies through military aid, the United States stressed the importance of accelerating its global economic aid programs. Averell Harriman told the British in early December 1950 that the only way the West could preserve its strength and morale was to "follow a vigorous policy to strengthen others." This would be done by preserving "a defense in depth in Southeast Asia by economic aid to Indonesia and similar countries, by strengthening the Middle East through our economic programs and mainly getting ahead with the NATO plans."[91] The Korean War thus accelerated America's involvement in the political and economic development of the Third World.

The events of November 1950 to February 1951 also set the tone for the debate surrounding the end of the war in the spring of 1953. Many of the considerations undertaken in that winter were repeated in 1953 when the United States implicitly threatened China with attack involving nuclear weapons if the communists did not comply with the U.N. Command's final negotiating stance. As had been the case during the negotiations over the aggressor resolution, America's allies were very worried about the American stance but felt compelled to support the United States publicly on this risky diplomatic strategy. The reasons for supporting the U.S. position in both 1951 and 1953 were based on similar considerations: the need to preserve Western unity in order to deter Soviet involvement and maintain strength against the Sino-Soviet alliance. By 1953, however, that consensus had weakened and there was greater division within the alliance on matters pertaining to Korea and China. The high point in Anglo-American relations had been reached in 1950–51. The Korean War made the relative power differentials between Britain and America more obvious. Bevin's death, the costs of European rearmament, and the emergence of a more active U.S. containment strategy for Asia all contributed to a decline in the special relationship after 1951.

4 Defending Southeast Asia: Informal Empire and Containment in Vietnam, 1950–1953

The North Korean attack confirmed American fears that communism was a world movement, relatively integrated and cohesive, striving to undermine Western capitalist society. This belief laid the basis for the United States' vastly accelerated rearmament program after 1950. The Korean War "globalized" U.S. foreign policy: henceforth, distinctions between peripheral and vital interests were skewed. Containment became associated even more with the development of the West's military strength. According to John Lewis Gaddis, U.S. foreign policy in the 1950s and 1960s tended to "view world order as an undifferentiated whole, and to regard Communist threats to that order anywhere as endangering the structure of peace everywhere ... Since U.S. interests were equated with the maintenance of peace, they, like peace, were considered indivisible."[1] Fear of further incursions in developing areas made U.S. policymakers more determined to support pro-Western allies on the periphery of the communist empire. The Korean War consolidated the Cold War in the Third World. The Joint Chiefs of Staff noted in January 1951 that the "long-range objective of the communists in Indochina, as in all other parts of the world, is clear and immutable – the conquest of the world by communism."[2]

By the early 1950s, the loss of Western influence in regions once peripheral to U.S. diplomacy was seen in apocalyptic terms – as potentially resulting in the fall of Western civilization to Soviet communism. This was one of the conclusions of NSC 135/3, "Reappraisal of United States Objectives and Strategy for National Security." Accepted by the Truman administration in the autumn of 1952, this policy paper said that the "most immediate danger" was that "a progressive and cumulative loss of positions of importance to the United States (either as a result of deterioration within the free nations or of communist cold war actions or a process involving both) could eventually reduce the United States, short of general war, to an isolated and critically vulnerable position."[3]

Competition between the two rival world blocs was viewed not only in terms of power politics but also from a moral perspective. NSC 135/3 did not reject the moral convictions of previous National Security pronouncements; on the contrary, it reaffirmed the correctness of the American stance. It argued that the "fundamental purpose" of the United States was "to assure the integrity and vitality of our free society founded upon the dignity and worth of the individual, while promoting peace and order among nations in a system based on freedom and justice as contemplated in the charter of the United Nations." The document bluntly stated that the general policy of the United States was to "develop throughout the world positive appeals superior to those of communism."[4] This statement was an apt description of some of the ideological bases of American containment policy in this period. There was an element of idealism in America's informal empire. The idealism was posited as the ability to achieve "freedom" by throwing off the shackles of communism. However, there was a contradiction between the moral stance enunciated in these NSC pronouncements and the realities underlying the evolution of the United States' informal empire in Vietnam after 1945.

The underlying contradiction between, on the one hand, the United States' attempts to foster an indigenous Western-oriented power grouping in Vietnam and, on the other, its need to control and shape the political, economic, and military development of that state is an important theme of this chapter. The irony of the American containment strategy for Vietnam was that it required an increased formal presence to achieve it. In short, policies designed to create an "independent" anticommunist elite were accompanied by actions associated more with formal colonial rule than informal empire. The ideal was decentralized control in the hands of pro-Western "moderate" nationalists; the emerging reality was closer to traditional imperial control. Yet this is a long-term view. In the period before the end of direct French rule, before 1954, the contradictions of informal empire in Vietnam were played out in the context of America's reluctant support of France's colonial policies in Indochina. American policymakers legitimized their support for France by claiming that it was necessary for the short term only. Acheson and Dulles knew that the nationalists in Vietnam were very weak; they understood that even if France formally declared Bao Dai's independence, the Vietnamese anticommunists would be incapable of attracting popular support. Nevertheless, the possibility that the nationalists could develop as proxy Western partners underlay much of U.S. thinking in the period. The belief that the Viet Minh could be destroyed proved illusory, however, and the United States gradually replaced France as a semi-formal imperial power in Vietnam.

THE DOMINO THEORY

The Korean War had an immediate impact on the United States' informal empire strategies for Indochina. The war galvanized support for the anticommunist crusade in Vietnam and accelerated American aid to support the French and indigenous anticommunists. On 27 June 1950, President Truman announced that more military assistance would be provided to France and the associated states. A military mission would be dispatched "to provide close working relations with those forces" that were against the Viet Minh. On 8 July the president approved a request by Acheson for an additional $16 million from funds under Section 303 of the Mutual Defense Assistance Act.[5] Of the three means available to the administration to effect its informal empire (political support, military supplies, and economic aid), emphasis was maintained on increasing the military power of the French and the indigenous noncommunist alternative in Vietnam.

Feelings of insecurity, exacerbated by the Korean War, had abated somewhat by 1952. NSC 135/3 noted that the United States and its allies had successfully responded to "the perilous situation of 1950, had improved the security of Western Europe and the Pacific and had mobilized in greater readiness for war." But work still remained to be done; the Soviet empire had developed industry and technology that threatened the West, and further containment of Soviet expansionism was needed: "The free world with its superior resources should be able to build and maintain, for whatever length of time proves to be necessary, such strength that the Soviet orbit will be unable to make significant advances in expanding its power, either geographically or politically."[6]

One region which the United States wanted to integrate into the Western nexus was Southeast Asia. It was felt that the resources of the region, especially tin, rubber, and petroleum, in the hands of the Soviet empire, would enhance communist industrial and strategic power and would undermine the favourable balance of Western power. Western rearmament resulted in an increased appreciation of the West's need for the region's resources. In 1949 Southeast Asia had been viewed as important but not vital to American interests. NSC 48/1 had pointed out that Asian tin and rubber were of "strategic importance" but that "the United States could, as in World War II, rely on other sources if necessary."[7] After Korea, this assessment was altered. NSC 48/5, dated 17 May 1951, noted the increased importance of the region in light of the redoubled effort to contain Soviet power. Producing virtually all of the world's natural rubber, 60 per cent of the tin, and significant amounts of oil, manganese, jute, and atomic materials, the area contributed "greatly" to American security needs. Access to these resources "would be of great assistance in time of war if they remained available," and they would continue to be required as long as stockpiling continued. American economic and military programs were to be geared towards maximizing the "availabilities of the material resources of the Asian area to the United States and the free world."[8] To accomplish this, a further integration of the region into the West's sphere of influence would be necessary. Here was one source of the economic relationship between core and periphery in the bipolar Cold War.

Economic considerations foreshadowed political ones. The greatest danger to Southeast Asia lay in a victory of the Vietnamese communists over the French Union forces in Indochina. Indochina was seen as the key strategic corridor to all of Southeast Asia – it had to be held if the West's interests in the rest of the area were to be salvaged. The threat did not arise primarily out of the possibility of Viet Minh military expansion. Rather, it arose from Western interpretations of how indigenous states in Southeast Asia would react to the presence of a communist Vietnam on their borders. The domino theory rested on simplistic political and psychological assumptions. Thai politicians in particular were viewed in an historical context of bending with the wind and accommodating to the strongest regional actor. Thailand "could not be expected to resist Communist pressure if Indochina or Burma fell."[9] After token resistance the Thais would "install a government acceptable to the Communists in the hope of retaining at least a semblance of autonomy."[10]

Exponents of the theory disagreed on the timing and the extent to which other nations in Southeast Asia would be forced to accommodate to communist pressures, but there was a consensus that the loss of Indochina would threaten directly or indirectly all of the region, with repercussions in South Asia, the Middle East, and, ultimately, Western Europe. According to NSC 124, entitled "United States Objectives and Courses of Action with Respect to Communist Aggression in Southeast Asia" and dated 13 February 1952, a communist success in Indochina would result in "an alignment with communism of the rest of Southeast Asia and India, and in the longer term, of the Middle East (with the probable exceptions of at least Pakistan and Turkey) would progressively follow." This would "endanger the stability and security of Europe and nullify the psychological advantages accruing to the free world by reason of its response to the aggression in Korea."[11] Communist victory in Indochina would have far-reaching global repercussions.

JAPAN, SOUTHEAST ASIA, AND THE PRC: ECONOMIC LINKAGES AND REGIONAL CONTAINMENT

Strategic considerations underlay American concerns about communism in Indochina, but the defence of Southeast Asia was also related to America's regional containment policy involving Japan. Indochina had to be maintained within the Western orbit so that the raw materials of other Southeast Asian nations could be retained for Western and Japanese consumption. NSC 124/2 had concluded that Japan needed access to these materials if it was to remain oriented towards the West in the Cold War. The United States was anxious to stabilize the Japanese economy and help solve Japan's dependence on U.S. procurement dollars by reorienting Japan's economic relations with other countries in the Pacific.

Although much of the literature on Japan–U.S. economic relations has emphasized the role of Southeast Asia in U.S. plans for the Japanese economy, the relationship between the resources of Southeast Asia, Japan, and the Vietnam War should not be overemphasized. One aspect of American policy that has been neglected is the importance officials placed on opening China's market for Japanese goods. Even in the early 1950s, U.S. policymakers recognized the difficulties of promoting bilateral trade between Japan and the nations of Southeast Asia. Nor was Southeast Asian trade with Japan always seen as a long-term solution to Japan's economic ills. Both President Eisenhower and Secretary Dulles believed that, eventually, greater trade with mainland China would be required. In early April 1953, Dulles told the National Security Council that Japanese economic history since the 1930s had shown that "a revival of Japanese trade with the various free nations of Asia" was only "a temporary substitute for Japanese control of portions of the Chinese mainland"; in the long term, "the Japanese would have to have access again to mainland areas like Manchuria."[12]

President Eisenhower took up this theme at an NSC meeting in late 1953. One means of achieving the dual policy goals of containment and of sustaining Japan's economy was through increased Western trade with Communist China. Referring to remarks made by the CIA director, Allen Dulles, on the need to weaken the Sino-Soviet alliance, the president said that "trade might be a very useful tool in accomplishing this purpose." He would even sell jet aircraft to the Chinese communists if it held advantages for the United States. But for Eisenhower, the Japanese economy was a priority: the United States "could not afford to forget about Japan and its need for economic viability in any discussion of Communist China." If America "could get the Japanese to send harmless manufactured goods, such as crockery, knives and forks, and wholly non-strategic materials, and sell them to China, this would serve the dual purpose of relieving Communist China's dependence on the USSR and Japan's dependence upon our own Treasury."[13] The desire to sustain Japan's economy and maintain Japan's pro-Western orientation thus provided an impetus for containing communism not only in Southeast Asia but also at the core of communist power in East Asia – the People's Republic of China.

VIETNAM'S "NATIONALIST" ALTERNATIVE: INFORMAL EMPIRE DELAYED

The United States continued to support an indigenous political alternative to the Vietnamese communist movement. This meant legitimating the Bao Dai government in the eyes of the Vietnamese and working with the French to create, as had been done in Korea, a stable pro-Western and anticommunist regime that was capable of dealing with its internal security problems and competing with communists for nationalist sentiment.

The situation in Vietnam was more complicated than that in the Republic of Korea because of the necessity to work through French colonialism to implement policies for Indochina. American officials continued to experience frustration with French colonialism. In January 1951 the American minister in Saigon, Donald Heath, congratulated the participants of the 1950 Pau Conference for their decisions to transfer economic power from France to Vietnam and to activate the Vietnamese national army. However, he complained that these decisions had come too late; if the French had made concessions two years ago and had given Bao Dai two years of administrative experience, there would have been a "radically different" situation existing in the associated states. French tardiness threatened the American strategy for establishing a proxy Western ally in Vietnam. The basic political issue, Heath argued, was "whether there is time enough to utilize [a] new political framework to mobilize mass allegiance behind Bao Dai."[14]

Heath also wanted the new state in Vietnam to have the support of Vietnamese citizens. The United States needed to press the French and the Vietnamese for a government that would implement a "liberal program [of] social educational, and economic betterment (with present and if necessary increased ECA funds) and would set in motion machinery for ... representative organs." In American parlance, and as Heath put it, "As long as Bao Dai is our candidate he must be ingeniously 'sold.'" In the short term, however, military containment took precedence: "In the next six months military effort must be given priority, although in long run economic assistance through capital development and improved technology" would be necessary to put the three states on a "truly sound economic base."[15] The measures designed to consolidate the internal legitimacy of Bao Dai took second place to the need to defeat the Viet Minh. As a report on U.S. policy in Vietnam noted in mid-March 1951, "American military aid furnished the [Associated] States' forces and the Army of the French Union may have been the decisive factor in the preservation of the area against Communist aggression."[16]

Vietnam was different from Korea in another way too, for the army and the indigenous political forces were unable to assume central control over the political and military situation. This situation stemmed from the nature of French colonial policy, which was more interested in preserving its position in Indochina than in fostering democratic government and compromising with nationalist politicians. The noncommunist Vietnamese politicians who were involved in negotiations with the French were often found to be defending their own personal or local interests. They lacked a cohesive national program for their country. Heath pointed out that the "Viet Government has thus far failed to display any real dynamism and has not yet won confidence of public in its ability to provide security or welfare. The Chief of State has yet to exhibit sustained energy or the know-how of leadership, its cabinet lacks stature, colour, and broad representativeness; its administrators are generally inexperienced and frequently venal."[17] In Heath's mind, the objective of the United States was to establish the basis for a popular anticommunist state. A CIA national intelligence report of August 1951 agreed. According to this estimate, the French had failed to take advantage of a change in government in Vietnam in early 1951. Instead of forming a broad-based Vietnamese cabinet representing many noncommunist groups, the French authorities had directed the formation of a cabinet composed of Premier Tran Van Huu's own pro-French faction. The intelligence report noted that the composition of the cabinet and its perceived status as a "French puppet" limited its popular appeal and alienated important nationalist groups in Tonkin. Viet Minh penetration into formerly held French areas had also "discouraged many people from allying themselves with the government."[18] The impetus for American-sponsored state building in Vietnam was thus created during the French colonial period, and it came about partly as a consequence of U.S. perceptions of the wrongs of traditional French colonial policies.

If the military situation was precarious, the political situation created dilemmas for American policymakers. These problems stemmed from some of the very same considerations that had motivated the need to develop proxy partners in Vietnam – namely, military weakness in Western Europe and a decision to base American strategic defensive principles on the island perimeter. America's global commitments and perceived strategic vulnerability required the maintenance of French military power in the associated states. The principle of primary French responsibility in Vietnam could not be violated because the consequences of a French withdrawal or negotiated settlement with the Viet Minh were too dangerous for the Western position in the Cold War. Strategic and political considerations underlay the United States' decision to underwrite France's direct military involvement and presence in Vietnam. American policies were shaped to cohabit with older patterns of empire in the international system, for in the early 1950s there were limits to which the United States could implement its informal empire strategy of developing the power base of the Vietnamese pro-Western nationalists. American policy towards Vietnam was guided by contradictory considerations: the need to support the French military effort and the need to convey to Asians and to the world that the United States was not simply another imperialist world power backing colonialism. Informal empire was meant in part to be a response to the latter, while the need to contain communism in Southeast Asia led to the adoption of the methods of the former.

A persistent theme in American policy for defeating the Viet Minh was the perceived need to establish a strong Vietnamese national army. Such an army would undertake the defence of Vietnam and would help France with its European defence needs by substituting indigenous French Union troops with local cadres. A local army would bolster the goal of creating a stronger Vietnamese state, and it would temper criticism that the United States backed French colonialism in Indochina. The American ambassador in France, David Bruce, wrote in the fall of 1950 that the political and military advantages of creating a national army in Indochina would be substantial. The project was accepted by both the French and the Vietnamese, and there seemed "no other course which would on the one hand provide a basis for French withdrawal of their own forces, which are so badly needed for the defense of the European continent, and on the other serve to give outward and visible expression to Vietnamese nationalist aspirations."[19]

Short-term policy was meant to enhance the military effectiveness of the French against the Viet Minh. This was to be achieved primarily through the granting of Mutual Defense Assistance Program aid. By 1952, the United States was subsidizing about one-third of French costs in Vietnam. By the end of 1953, it was footing two-thirds of the French bill. To this degree, the Americans supported the French colonial regime in Indochina. However, American policymakers disliked direct rule and formal colonial empire. Many of them would have preferred not to underwrite French colonial policies in Indochina, but they also failed to see the negative implications of their own policies in Vietnam. This was not a consequence of naive beliefs about the indigenous moderates; from the beginning of American involvement, U.S. officials recognized that the Vietnamese nationalists were not sufficiently powerful to fight the Viet Minh threat unilaterally. "The new states have thus far failed to develop a solid anti-communist front," Dean Rusk lamented in September 1950. "Their efforts and fears remain largely anti-colonial, a form of government which they know and dislike, rather than anti-communist, which is to them still a relatively unknown and unrecognized threat."[20]

The weakness of the anticommunist nationalists in Vietnam made Americans wary about any French attempts to negotiate a settlement in Indochina. In early 1952, Assistant Secretary of State John Allison wrote to Acheson that the feebleness of the native government and the uncertain attitudes of the population meant it was "highly probable that any settlement based on a withdrawal of French forces would be tantamount to handing over Indochina to communism." The United States should therefore "continue to oppose any negotiated settlement with the Vietminh."[21] These fears persisted throughout both the Truman and the Eisenhower administrations and were one indication of the continuity of U.S. policy towards Vietnam.

The United States may have been wary about supporting French colonialism in Southeast Asia but was not prepared to abandon it. The French military presence served the dual purpose of containing the Viet Minh and preserving hopes for a resurgence of the noncommunist nationalists. It was in this context that Ambassador Donald Heath wrote from Saigon in late 1952: "Our sympathy with [the] aspirations [of] these peoples for independence implies no opposition to their remaining within [the] French Union." In Heath's opinion, the associated states had "no other choice"; if it were not for the forces of the French Union, "the three states would be in effect vassal members of

[the] Soviet Union."[22] The United States helped France sustain the Bao Dai solution in the context of a longer-term strategy of fostering a Western-oriented state against Soviet totalitarian control. To argue that the United States supported French colonialism simply because it was itself an imperial power avoids the very important issue of the nature of the American empire after 1945.

The United States hoped to resolve the tensions in its dual policy of supporting the French and developing a nationalist alternative to the Viet Minh. The objective was to establish a regime that was less dependent on a colonial framework for its survival. Attempts were made to convince the French of the necessity of decentralizing their empire and of creating a relationship with the indigenous leaders that would allow the moderates comparative freedom in decision making. The long-term relationship which American officials envisaged for Vietnam and the West was not one of colonial control; what sustained American policy in Vietnam was a determination to make the nationalists led by Bao Dai a viable political solution. Ironically, these beliefs, which formed the ideological basis of their informal empire, brought the Americans into increased direct responsibilities for preserving the region against communism.

As part of the process of devolving more power onto the Vietnamese anticommunists, there was a tendency within U.S. official thinking to criticize the need to obtain French consent for aid going to Vietnam. State Department officials recognized the extent to which the Vietnamese distrusted the French, and they understood that in the long run the Vietnamese could only be successful if they were given their "independence." American aid was not aimed at supporting French colonialism, the acting secretary of state wrote in mid-1952; it was designed to assist the Vietnamese people in preserving their freedom against communist aggression.[23] However, these concepts of freedom and independence were shallow and illusory: they were circumscribed by the Great Power objectives of the United States in Southeast Asia.

Many Americans believed that French influence in the region would weaken and eventually dissipate. France was viewed as a declining colonial power in Southeast Asia. In March 1952 the CIA warned that a general economic crisis in France had undermined the country's ability to maintain its position in Indochina and pay for the rearmament program; in the long term, the economic costs of the war and rearmament would adversely affect France's will to continue the conflict, and this would have an adverse impact on Vietnamese morale.[24] Philip Bonsal, a counsellor in the American embassy in Paris, put it bluntly when he wrote that the French "are finished in Indochina." The key was to keep the French committed to their colony until the indigenous nationalists were able to strengthen their position against the communists. Although the associated states were constitutionally linked to the French Union, in formal terms this link might be something of a constitutional nicety. Later in the year, Bonsal argued that "no reasonable man can have any illusions as to the ability of the French to continue to maintain a colonial relationship with Indochina; they are through and they know it."[25]

French rule in Indochina was viewed as a transitory phase leading ultimately to the "independence" of the Indochinese states. In this transitional phase, the crucial goal was to get the Vietnamese to forge the political will to kill the Viet Minh. In October 1951, Edmond A. Gullion, the United States chargé d'affaires in Saigon, pointed out to the State Department that the Viet Minh were helping to create this morale but that the men in the new national armies "must also believe they are fighting for their own good and for independence. [A way] must be found in the present transitional phase of IC independence to make the future real."[26]

Military officials in the American administration were even less enthusiastic about supporting French colonialism in Indochina. Calling for a more "dynamic" strategy, the secretaries of the American forces complained to Secretary of Defense Robert Lovett in April 1952 that State Department policies preserved the status quo: "A continuation of the current program is an expression of a sit tight philosophy without definitive goals." On the need for a transitional stage in Vietnamese political independence, the military agreed with the State Department. The secretaries argued for an acceleration of the transition period: "Seen in the perspective of time, the problem for U.S. policy is not to keep the French indefinitely committed to Indochina, but to facilitate the inevitable transition from colonialism to independence in such a way that there is no opportunity for communism to flow into an intervening power vacuum."[27]

The objectives of defeating the communists and ensuring the success of an anticommunist regime in Vietnam were complementary. There was no timetable for U.S. informal empire-consolidating policies, but the implications of American diplomatic strategies for Vietnam were clear: an end to communist expansion on the periphery and the creation of a political system oriented to the West.

Until 1952 at least, the State Department viewed its policies towards French Indochina as a success. Assistant Secretary of State John Allison wrote to the Joint Chiefs of Staff that American policy, "initiated by the Dept of State but validated on several occasions by the National Security Council, has contributed to the preservation of Indochina from Communist domination for nearly two and a half years."[28] After 1952, there were growing pressures on policymakers which undermined their sense of relative security about the region. Among the factors that made officials nervous were the apparent French and British willingness to negotiate a Far Eastern settlement with the Soviets and Chinese, the deteriorating military situation in Indochina itself (especially Vietnamese successes in Laos in early 1953), the lack of French military spirit, and the continued political ineffectiveness of the noncommunist nationalists. These factors, accompanied by Secretary of State John Foster Dulles's dislike of colonialism, served to galvanize increased support for military solutions to the war in Vietnam.

IMPLEMENTING INFORMAL EMPIRE IN VIETNAM

To sustain the French and the anticommuist Vietnamese, the Americans sent economic and technical aid to Vietnam. Economic aid was administered initially through the Economic Cooperation Administration (ECA), and after 1951 through its successor organizations, the Mutual Security Agency (MSA), headed by Averell Harriman, and the Foreign Operations Administration (FOA), led by Governor Harold Stassen.

The philosophy behind economic aid to the developing world varied from country to country, but in general it was believed that money for social projects would enhance the ability of local governments to reject communism and orient themselves closer to the United States. According to a document written by ECA officials in 1951: "In Asia, provision of material economic assistance is the most effective method of promoting the security of the free world."[29] In most Far Eastern countries, the main danger was an internal security one and problems were socially rooted: "The promptest and surest way yet developed by the U.S. Government to meet this threat is to attack these problems with all available tools at once – technical assistance, material aid, and the support inherent in the presence of a U.S. economic mission." Economic assistance was viewed in terms of the global competition for spheres of influence with the Soviet Union: it would "reduce the risk of losing this whole area to the Soviet Bloc through internal subversion of new, inexperienced governments."[30]

In Vietnam, STEMs (Special Technical and Economic Missions) were established to strengthen and modernize the infrastructure of the rural-based economy. Health officers worked to end disease, and engineers built dams and roads. Some progress was made in a Western sense in mod-

Table 5
United States Military and Economic Aid to Indochina, FY 1951–1954 (in millions of dollars)

FY 1951–53	Procurement and delivery program (military aid)	940.4
	General defence support and technical cooperation (economic aid)	101.8
	Total	1,042.2
FY 1954	Direct-forces support (new program created for FY 1954 to reimburse France for its expenditures on behalf of the associated states)	745.0
	Procurement and delivery program (military aid)	348.0
	General defence support and technical cooperation (economic aid)	25.0
	Total	1,118.0

Sources: National Archives, RG 59, lot 55, D388, box 5, "U.S. Programs of Military and Economic Assistance in the Far East," 1 April 1953; Mutual Security Administration, *Mutual Security: A Six Month Report*, 30 June 1954.

ernizing the country. For the communists, however, the root of Vietnam's ills lay not in its inadequate infrastructure or health system, but in the political system of domination which flourished in French colonial rule.

American economic aid was subordinated to the larger military and strategic goals of defeating and eliminating the Viet Minh. "In the Associated States of Indochina the major aim of the programs of technical and economic assistance is to complement the program of military assistance," a 1952 Mutual Security Program pamphlet declared. This was done by providing aid to areas recently "pacified" by troops of the French Union or Vietnamese government. "By helping the people of Indochina to achieve better health, more food, and economic ability, the economic and technical assistance programs ... helped to strengthen the will and ability of the Indochinese to fight the Communist insurgents, and in this way the program aided the military effort."[31]

The emphasis on a military solution to the communist threat is indicated in the relative amounts of military and economic aid provided to Indochina (through the French) in fiscal years 1951–53. Of a total of just over $1 billion of aid, $940.4 million went for military supplies, while $101.8 million was spent on economic aid[32] (see table 5).

There were important local obstacles to the successful achievement of America's goals in Vietnam during this period. One was a consequence of the tension in the U.S. policy of supporting the French and yet working for greater "nationalist" independence. The French were very wary of American policies designed to strengthen Bao Dai's power and popularity, and there was competition for influence and power over the Bao Dai government between the Americans and the French. Although official American policy tried to downplay the conflict, the French were fearful that the United States was working to supplant them.

Local French officials were in some respects the most suspicious. On 14 June 1951, Donald Heath reported to Dean Acheson that French administrators in Vietnam believed that American policy would inevitably conflict not only with French plans to retain Vietnam in the French Union but also with France's conception of the way the rest of its colonial empire should evolve. The French were especially worried about American technical and economic aid to Vietnam. Robert Blum, chief of the United States' Special Technical and Economic Mission (STEM), wrote in mid-1951 that the French "are not very sympathetic with our program"; they would have preferred to see American funds used as military "expenditures and to cover budgetary deficits of the three states or the debts inherited by them" from France.[33]

American policymakers tried their best to placate French fears. "We must do everything we can [to] avoid undermining the Fr[ench] position," cabled Blum. But it was also important, he stated, to guide the anticolonialism of the Vietnamese moderates. French weakness was a result of their own long-term failure to work with the nationalists. The best the United States could hope for, Blum wrote, was "to conduct here a kind of holding operation until something else happens in another place." If this happened and the French withdrew entirely, "unless we are willing to abandon this area indefinitely we sh[ould] try [to] maintain [a] position of influence in this part of [the] world where only [a] break with [the] past offers a firm foundation for the future."[34]

The Americans faced other obstacles to their policies of developing the strength of the Vietnamese under Bao Dai. Local corruption and regionalism are notable examples of this. The government headed by Tran Van Huu (1951–52) was dominated by ministers from Cochin China and had little national appeal. Furthermore, despite some important local projects such as the initiation of health care to rural areas, the United States relied on the French and Vietnamese to implement reforms. American policy was thus dependent on a top-down approach to social change which failed to achieve substantial grass-roots support. Moreover, U.S. propaganda did not always address crucial issues, and it reflected cultural bias: the first book translated by the Americans into Vietnamese was a history of the United States.[35]

Although it remained an American priority to get other Asian states to support the fledgling "government" in Vietnam, the United States and other Western nations were only partially successful in getting

Asian diplomats and politicians to believe that the West was fighting an anticommunist and not a colonial war. The Indian government remained critical of French colonialism in Indochina and was sympathetic to the nationalism of the communists. In a speech before the Indian parliament on 12 June 1952, Prime Minister Pandit Nehru criticized what he called the colonialism of NATO powers. At a press conference a few days later he elaborated on his criticisms, observing that there was a tendency within "the Atlantic Treaty to include within its scope the protection of the colonial territories owned by NATO powers." He believed that "this was something essentially in opposition to the basic principles of the United Nations Charter." When asked if he was thinking of French territory in Indochina, he replied: "Certainly yes; if you start on the basis of protecting a colonial power or territory it is the wrong approach."[36]

On a superficial level at least, more success was made in getting Thailand to align itself with the West in the Asian Cold War. In this alignment the Korean War was crucial: Thailand was the first Asian nation to offer troops to the U.N. effort. In 1951 the Thais exchanged diplomatic representatives with Vietnam and Cambodia. Thailand in fact had much to gain by aligning itself with the West: its rice was exported to British colonies and Japan, and the United States was providing it with military and economic aid.

There is evidence to suggest that Thai officials disliked the French colonial presence and retained some sympathy for the communists' goals. Some were critical of the domino theory and disclaimed the possibility that communism could undermine the Thai government's authority. On 10 March 1953, the United Kingdom's ambassador to Thailand, G.A. Wallinger, spoke with the head of Thailand's police, General Phao. Phao believed that Britain's fears of communism were exaggerated, and he dismissed the ambassador's analogy that since the communists in Vietnam had convinced the peasants to accept their ideology, the same thing could happen to Thailand. "It was French mismanagement and exploitation which had caused the rot in Indo-China," said Phao. The British had been smarter in Malaya, but in Thailand "there would be no trouble."[37]

Some of the principal Western Cold War axioms therefore looked very different to local actors. The theoretical differences between formal and informal empire may have appeared debatable to Asian leaders such as Nehru and other "neutralists," but it was precisely this difference between East and West that worried the American and British officials.

GREAT BRITAIN AND THE DOMINO THEORY

Like the Americans, British officials adhered to the principal tenets of the domino theory. However, the British were concerned with the regional aspects of the theory as it pertained to British colonial interests in Southeast Asia, and they focused their attention on the economic consequences which the pull of Thailand into the communist orbit would have on Malaya and Hong Kong. Of particular concern was the British colonies' dependence on rice supplies from Thailand. In 1950, for example, 94 per cent of Malaya's rice and 88 per cent of Hong Kong's came from Thailand. A Foreign Office memo recorded: "The establishment of Communist control on the frontier of Siam ... would probably gravely weaken the pro-Western alignment of the present Siamese Government and might eventually lead to its replacement by a government of elements favourable to the Vietminh." This would severely disrupt supplies of rice for Malaya and Hong Kong, and perhaps Burma. Psychologically, a belief in the success of communism might lead to renewed Chinese communist successes in Malaya and a deterioration in the security situation in the British colony.[38]

A loss of French control in Indochina thus threatened British colonial power in Southeast Asia. The British dependence on Thai food supplies meant that the Thai government could use rice as a diplomatic weapon. A memo to Ernest Bevin dated 15 September 1950 noted that rice was a staple food of the region and that a serious shortage would have potentially disastrous effects on the "present rather delicate balance ... between the appeals of Communism and those of the democratic system."[39]

The British greatly feared the effects of a communist success in Vietnam on their position as a colonial power in Southeast Asia. The United States, on the other hand, viewed the problem in the context of denying the Soviet-led communist empire a resource-rich and strategically important region of the world. For somewhat different though compatible reasons, both the United States and the United Kingdom agreed that it was in their national interests to contain the Vietnamese threat from spreading into Southeast Asia and beyond.

ANGLO-AMERICAN RELATIONS AND VIETNAM, 1950–1953

The change in the British government in late 1951 in favour of the Conservatives headed by Winston Churchill did not alter the premises underlying British strategy towards Asia. Following on from Britain's acceptance of the domino theory, the United Kingdom continued to support America's broad policy goals towards Vietnam. A brief for the British secretary of state's visit to Paris in early 1952 summarized British objectives towards France and Indochina: the defence of Tonkin was vital for the protection of Malaya and Southeast Asia, since a continuing drain on French resources would weaken France's military commitment to Western Europe. "We have therefore been supporting French policy in Indo-China which is broadly to restore law and order, to build up the Viet Nam forces with the utmost speed and to create stable Governments in the three Associate States."[40] This statement reflected Britain's broad degree of support for the U.S. strategy of state building in Vietnam.

The British realized that the development of the armies of the associated states represented a long-term solution to the Viet Minh revolution, for the indigenous noncommunist nationals were too feeble to act independently of the French. The difficulty was that local politicians had insufficient experience and ability to govern. Nationalists were often associated with communism, and the associate states were "still widely regarded ... as French puppet governments." This dilemma was "an extremely serious one for the French Government" and was "a problem which closely affects British interests in South East Asia."[41]

In conjunction with American policy, the British wanted to encourage stronger anticommunist and pro-Western sentiment among the Indochinese states, and one of the best means of indicating the autonomy of the three associated states was through the build-up of their armies. Robert Scott of the Far Eastern Department recommended that Foreign Secretary Anthony Eden assure French Foreign Minister Maurice Schuman "of our full support for French policy in Indo-China." The United Kingdom would "encourage the French government to press on with their plans for building up the Viet Nam army and for promoting political stability through policies which will attract popular support for the established Governments of the Associate States."[42]

This policy complemented the United Kingdom's regional strategy involving India and Southeast Asia. Indian recognition and support of the Indochinese states would lend prestige and credibility to Western policies in Asia, and one way of gaining the diplomatic support of India was to demonstrate to Indian officials that the Indochinese governments were not simply pawns of the French.

In the meantime, however, France had to be prodded to maintain its will to defeat the Viet Minh. Foreign Office officials realized that only in the short term could the French Union army prevent a communist military success. A memo produced for Prime Minister Churchill's use in the summer of 1953 reflected this belief. It argued that the French were drifting towards an eventual collapse: "This year may be the last chance for France to act to save the situation."[43] The memo reflected British anger and frustration with French colonial policy on Indochina. Churchill himself believed that the French were incompetent as colonial administrators – they needed to operate more closely on British colonial principles. Like the Americans, the British were critical of France's more centralized approach to empire in Indochina.

The British conception of empire in Vietnam was ultimately closer to the American than the French, but the British were not as optimistic as the Americans about moving forward with the local anticommunist candidates. Also, they tended to be less willing to do things that might jeopardize French colonial power. It was not that colonialism itself was wrong in British eyes; rather, that French colonial policies were poorly conceived and carried out. An evolution of French colonial policies on the basis of the Commonwealth would prove more fruitful. Although Britain should not offer detailed advice, the French required a more imaginative approach. In addition to political, economic, and military concessions, what was needed was "at least the promise of an eventual status equivalent to that of Commonwealth countries, with freedom to secede from the French Union."[44] In this way, British officials could justify their actions as progressive and could continue to pursue policies in line with British colonial interests.

The Conservative colonial secretary, Oliver Lyttleton, agreed with the memo's military recommendations – the United Kingdom needed to pressure the French government to enact a two-year military conscription program and to send more troops to Indochina. Writing to the acting secretary of state for foreign affairs on 7 July 1953, Lyttleton argued: "Any further deterioration in Indo-China would hit Malaya hard; and if the trouble spread to Siam the effect on Malaya would be little short of disastrous … It is thus vital to the security of Malaya that the French should achieve victory in Indo-China."[45]

The major weakness of the United Kingdom's policy towards French Indochina was its lack of military and financial resources. The British depended heavily on American interest in preventing Indochina from falling to the communists. They recognized the importance of American power in the region and consciously sided with it to help preserve British colonial interests. An unsigned draft memo entitled "Future Policy for Indochina" pointed out:

Vital United Kingdom interests in South East Asia are at stake, but as the United Kingdom is not playing a major part in supplying or fighting the Indo-China war, she has little real *locus standi* to advise. Any suggestions for an increased French effort will be met with requests for increased aid of one kind or another. The resources of the United Kingdom are fully strained and further commitments as regards EDC would present great difficulties. The United States have a much stronger bargaining position (though they must use great tact in availing themselves of it) and the United Kingdom can act most effectively in concert with the United States.[46]

Here was one area where Britain's special relationship with the United States could have positive consequences for British interests in Asia. The memo concluded that "the United Kingdom should act in concert with the United States, using United Kingdom experience and influence with both the United States and French Governments."[47]

ANGLO-AMERICAN RELATIONS AND THE COLOMBO PLAN

As in the period before the Korean War, the United Kingdom continued to seek ways and means of increasing America's commitment to Southeast Asia. The Colombo Plan was one such strategy. A memo dated March 1952 argued that the United Kingdom should "continue to persuade the countries in the area of the need to concentrate their development plans, as far as possible, on objectives which will really strengthen their economies and to take every possible step to attract United States capital for investment of this kind."[48] The economic situation had changed since early 1950, largely because of the impact of the Korean War on the global economy. The war had a negative impact on America's relations with some of the countries in the region, especially India. But the increase in price in primary products which resulted from the conflict meant that capital for development projects was no longer the major problem. The "general availability of finance" was not the major "limiting factor on the rate of carrying out their programmes," the memo stated.[49]

New economic difficulties for Britain emerged in the wake of the war. The economic burden of rearmament was tremendous and resulted in a severe curtailment of British foreign aid. In general, the gap between British rhetoric and global capabilities widened after 1950. On the one hand, a telegram from the Commonwealth Relations Office could argue that the Colombo Plan represented "a co-operative attack on the problems of poverty and undernourishment in a region of vast populations ... vital strategic importance, and great actual and potential resources." The raising of standards of living in this area was "a challenge to the whole of the free world."[50] On the other hand, a Treasury official suggested to J.D. Murray of the Foreign Office that the United Kingdom's economic problems might result in a recommendation to India, Pakistan, and Ceylon that they "order their affairs [so] as not to have to draw down their sterling balances to the full extent provided by the existing agreements." British officials going to the Colombo Plan meeting in Karachi in 1952 were told that "the pressure of rearmament on steel supplies and on the engineering industry in the United Kingdom must inevitably limit any great increase in expenditure on capital goods in the next few years."[51]

It is in this context that British economic policy towards Vietnam must be viewed. On 3 October 1952, J.G. Tahourdin wrote to H.A. Graves in Saigon that the prospect of additional British aid for economic development in Southeast Asia was "less hopeful now than ever. It would be hard to counter the argument that money put up to support Indo-China could be more usefully employed elsewhere." Recently, said Tahourdin, the government had acknowledged "the necessity of encouraging long-term measures to increase rice production in the colonies by making available up to three million pounds to finance the necessary preliminary investigations," and this would leave "still less in the kitty for other projects." Consequently, he said, "We must drop the question of the United Kingdom aid for the present."[52]

Canada was able to offer aid to the Vietnamese. On 3 August 1951, Herbert Graves told Vietnamese authorities that three Vietnamese citizens had been accepted for a study program in Canada; but they had been prevented from taking up their scholarships because of a mobilization order in Vietnam which prevented them from leaving the country.[53] Although the Canadian minister of trade and commerce, Clarence Decatur Howe, was somewhat sceptical of Canadian aid to South and Southeast Asia, other politicians remained enthusiastic about the principle. J. Thomson of the British High Commission in Ottawa wrote on 2 September 1952 that "it was Mr. St. Laurent's view that it would be most disastrous for technical assistance from the West to South-East Asia to cease with the end of the Colombo Plan, and that such technical assistance should be carried on by United Nations."[54]

There was an inconsistency in Canadian policy towards Vietnam in this period, one that reflected tensions in Canadian objectives. Prime Minister St Laurent was concerned about publicly supporting French colonialism in Indochina, yet both he and Pearson were moving towards increasing their support of Western objectives in the region. Significantly, Canada's offer of technical aid to Vietnam came before Canada had even officially recognized any of the associated states. This initiative through the Colombo Plan was symbolic and representative of Canada's willingness to underwrite the Bao Dai solution.[55]

CANADA, NATO, AND THE DEFENCE OF
SOUTHEAST ASIA

Pressure on Canada to recognize the associated states came in the context of Western efforts to internationalize the war. As we have seen, Canadian involvement in Vietnam was an outgrowth of its participation and membership in the North Atlantic Treaty Organization. At the NATO meetings in Lisbon in February 1952, the French prime minister had asked whether "our Allies consider Indochina a specific French problem or an international problem." Increased pressure from Canada's NATO partners and concern about the role that Canada's Western allies were playing in Vietnam led the Canadian government to recognize the associated states in late 1952. Dana Wilgress, who was then the under-secretary of state for external affairs, wrote to Pearson: "There is evidence that recognition on our part would be greatly appreciated by the French, and that it might have a beneficial effect within NATO. Moreover we would be in good company in extending recognition to the three associate states." In December 1952, the North Atlantic Council adopted a resolution that supported French action against communism in Indochina and agreed that "the campaign waged by the French Union forces in Indo-China deserves the continuing support from NATO governments."[56]

Although Canadian officials were hopeful that sustained economic aid and political support would bolster the Vietnamese anticommunist nationalists, they were even more wary than the Americans and British about getting militarily involved in Vietnam. The global and colonial commitments of Canada's allies had made Canada recognize the Western interest in defending Southeast Asia against communism, but the Canadian policy community was worried about the military implications of the Indochina war. While the military planners understood the importance of coordinating global strategy, they feared that an escalation of the war would compel Canada to contribute forces to the region. The chairman of the Chiefs of Staff, Charles Foulkes, pointed out that Canada should not press for Canadian observers at the five-power talks on the defence of Southeast Asia, because Canadian pressure "may be misinterpreted as our future intention to take action or make a contribution to that particular area." The chairman was apprehensive that the use of American or British ground troops in Indochina might "provoke more widespread Chinese or even Soviet action in South-East Asia."[57] Also, an allocation of allied resources and troops in Vietnam might make it necessary for Canada to make a greater contribution to the defence of Western Europe. It would be preferable, stated Foulkes, for the French to withdraw divisions from Europe and send them to Indochina, but the problem was that these troops might have to be replaced "by other NATO nations who are reluctant to assume responsibilities outside the NATO area for fighting communism." This would have "very serious implications" for Canada.

Political concerns reinforced these military conclusions. Speaking about his government's role in Southeast Asia in early 1951, Lester Pearson said that Canada must be careful not to overextend itself. External Affairs official R.E. Collins noted afterwards: "The Minister obviously wished to play down any statement on Canadian policy in Southeast Asia on the grounds that there is very little that we can contribute in this area beyond limited economic assistance through the Colombo Plan and good advice if we feel justified in offering it."[58]

Canadian diplomatic initiatives towards Southeast Asia were circumscribed by a determination not to get too deeply involved in a region of relatively peripheral interest. Nevertheless, Canada's enthusiasm for economic aid for Vietnam and its recognition of Bao Dai demonstrated its willingness to consolidate its junior membership within the alliance. Like the Americans, Canadian government officials supported the devolution of more power onto Bao Dai and were critical of the French effort in Vietnam; Pearson criticized France's "quasi-colonial" position there. In the long term, as Douglas Ross has noted, "Canadian interests lay in helping the French retreat from Indochina."[59] Despite the gap between Canada's recognition of Vietnam's sovereignty and the political and military weakness of the moderate nationalists, Canada provided both material and moral support for the U.S. goal of creating a noncommunist alternative in Vietnam. Canadians were generally less enthusiastic than their allies about using military force to contain communism in Indochina, but they accepted the necessity of the fighting and believed in the importance of establishing a pro-Western state on China's southern periphery.

Compared with Canada, the Australians were more directly implicated in the events in Southeast Asia. Although they shared the Old Commonwealth scepticism of French efforts in Vietnam, they sustained the largest Commonwealth commitment to Vietnam. Like Canada, Australia supported the French effort as part of "an essential contribution to the common security of the free world." But unlike Canada, Australia was prepared to supply direct military aid to the French. The acting minister for Australian external affairs, James Plimsoll, told the Canadian high commissioner in March 1953 that Australia was planning on sending Mustang aircraft to Indochina to help the French stock up on spare parts. Australia would also provide $250,000 in Columbo aid, most of it in the form of machinery, livestock, and railway rolling stock. Early in the month, the French minister for the associated states, Jean Letourneau, visited Australia, and his comments during the trip foreshadowed French policy for the coming year. One of his main preoccupations was to prevent Chinese intervention in Vietnam. He said that Chinese involvement was not extensive and that the Chinese were mainly involved in providing the Viet Minh with advisers and training camps; but that might change if the war was internationalized. As he told Richard Casey, "If non-Vietnam and non-French troops were to become engaged (i.e. American or British or Australian, etc.) the war would assume an international aspect." This would provide the Chinese with an excuse to "inject themselves into it." For this reason, the French government did not seek the help of troops from other countries. Only if the Chinese intervened unilaterally would France consider internationalizing the conflict. The implication was that France would seek a negotiated settlement to the conflict. Letourneau pointed out that France "could no more *solve* the problem in Indo-China than the British could solve it in Malaya or the United Nations in Korea," and that the French would not be able to resolve the Indochinese question through military means.[60] In fact, the British were successful in defeating the Malayan insurgency, but Letourneau's comments are important for establishing France's defensive Cold War posture on China and its predisposition towards partitioning Vietnam. Within a year, this French position would lead to increased tensions with the United States and a greater American determination to supplant France's dwindling commitment.

BRITAIN, THE UNITED STATES, AND THE DEFENCE OF SOUTHEAST ASIA

British officials were happy to see America's increased commitment to Southeast Asia after 1950. Like the French, they remained anxious to secure a greater American determination to defend the region on the basis of a defensive containment strategy *vis-à-vis* the People's Republic of China (PRC). A defensive alignment with the United States on the mainland would serve to protect European and Western interests and would demonstrate the value of the Anglo-American special relationship. An American military commitment to Southeast Asia, in conjunction with an acceptance of the Chinese communist regime, would act as a deterrent to Chinese revolutionary expansionism and would provide a framework for the preservation of Britain's colonial power and the successful destruction of indigenous communist movements in the region.

The United States' refusal to recognize the legitimacy of the regime in Peking and its more provocative stance towards the PRC posed a threat to British and French interests in the area. In early 1951 Roger Makins wrote, "The American outlook in this part of the world seems to us ... to be most out of focus in relation to the strategy of containment which we are pursuing."[61] British diplomats wanted the United States to extend its defensive perimeter to encompass mainland Southeast Asia in a defensive posture against China. In the context of the Korean War, an American guarantee to Southeast Asia was important because the signing of an armistice in Korea might result in the release of Chinese troops for an invasion. Robert Scott, the under-secretary of state in charge of Far Eastern and Southeast Asian affairs, expressed these concerns in late 1951, arguing that it was "futile to build a boulder Dam in Korea if the Communist flood is thereby diverted and spills over the weak levees in the south." The Americans, he said, had so far demonstrated "great reluctance to commit themselves in the south or to engage in military staff talks on South East Asian defence even in limited war"; the British objective was to "secure American agreement to such talks, in which Australia should also take part, and which should lead to American support for the defence of South East Asia at least in limited war." This might result in some regional defence arrangement, he hoped. Such statements reflected British frustration with the Anglo-American relationship in Asia, and the difficulties they faced in creating a "special relationship" in that part of the world. As Scott told the Canadian high commissioner in London (who at this time was Dana Wilgress), more effort was needed to interest the United States in the general question of the defence of Southeast Asia.[62]

The United States was of course very concerned with Southeast Asia and did make plans for its defence, but not on the basis of the British Commonwealth's or France's defensive containment strategy. Despite British hopes, the Americans were wary about committing American ground troops to the region, and until 1952 they rejected any possibility of extending their defensive perimeter strategy to encompass all of mainland Southeast Asia.

The policy paper NSC 48/5, "United States Objectives, Policies and Courses of Action in Asia," stated: "In the event of overt Chinese aggression, it is not now in the overall interests of the United States to commit any United States armed forces to the defense of the mainland states of Southeast Asia. Therefore, the United States cannot guarantee the denial of Southeast Asia to communism." The Americans would continue to promote programs designed to undermine communist power on the continent and to develop South Vietnam as a proxy ally, but their primary strategic interest was the building up of the off-shore defensive perimeter: "The United States should continue ... to strengthen the will and ability to resist the Chinese Communists, to render Communist military operations as costly as possible, and to gain time for the United States and its allies to build up the defenses of the off-shore chain and weaken communist power at its source." The Korean War initially made further commitments on the mainland unlikely. Admiral Radford, the American commander-in-chief in the Pacific, who was later chairman of the Joint Chiefs of Staff, pointed out in his memoirs that "Chinese intervention in Korea had placed such heavy demands on American fighting strength that the JCS could visualize no practical means of assisting Indochina other than increasing the flow of supplies in the event of emergency."[63]

The United States was doubtful that its European allies had the strength to defend Southeast Asia and also meet their commitments to NATO. The United Kingdom was a declining power in the region and the JCS were not prepared to underwrite the security of Britain's colonies in Southeast Asia. A related concern was the perception that Asians would have if the United States and other Western powers became members of a non-Asian defensive pact with Britain. Secretary Dulles remarked at the second meeting of the ANZUS council in 1953 that "British inclusion would be deeply resented by our Asian friends."[64]

The strategic impasse between Britain and the United States was aptly summarized by Charles Ritchie of the Canadian Department of External Affairs. In a memo to Pearson, Ritchie reflected on the broader issues underlying Anglo-American differences: "Until there is a common policy toward Communist China and Japan there appears to be little possibility of developing an overall strategy in the Pacific area acceptable to all the non-communist powers concerned." The United States had not shown enthusiasm for sharing responsibility with European powers in the development of its Pacific strategy, noted Ritchie. It preferred "to enter into separate arrangements with individual countries (Japan, the Philippines, Australia and New Zealand) on limited aspects of the overall problem and has reserved to itself the vital matter of the post-war development of Japan." The United Kingdom on the other hand, was "most anxious to obtain an effective voice in Pacific strategy and planning and has apparently sought to achieve this objective, first through membership in ANZUS and more recently through proposals for a five-power staff agency in South East Asia."[65]

Until 1952 there was no explicit American policy regarding its allies in the event of Chinese aggression in Southeast Asia. Only in the light of experience during the Korean conflict did American policymakers develop a strategy for defending Southeast Asia from possible Chinese intervention. Ironically, British representations for an increased American commitment to Southeast Asia may have contributed to the emergence of a harsher policy towards the PRC.

NSC 124/2, "United States Objectives and Courses of Action with Respect to Southeast Asia," was approved by President Truman on 25 June 1952. This was an important turning point in American policy towards both the region and its allies. The document emerged as part of the United States' military commitment to defeat the Viet Minh in Indochina. A vital part of this strategy was to prevent the Chinese communists from intervening in Indochina. The Americans were determined to avoid another "defeat" in a land war in continental East Asia. The policy paper committed the United States to the defence of Southeast Asia in the event that overt or covert Chinese communist actions threatened the ability of the French to hold Tonkin in North Vietnam. In such a situation, the United States would try to brand China as an aggressor in the United Nations and would seek maximum international support for U.N. action. In the absence of such action, the United States would provide air and naval support to the Indochinese and would disrupt Chinese communication lines in China. Token British and French forces were expected to back the American initiatives. In addition to these "minimum courses of action," the policy statement argued that the United States should seek to institute a naval blockade of China in conjunction with Great Britain and France, to assist Britain in evacuating Hong Kong if required, and to utilize, if necessary, Chinese Nationalist forces in Southeast Asia, Korea, or China. The document forecast possible expanded allied action against China: if the Americans decided, with French and British support, that the situation required military action against the PRC, "the United States should take air and naval action in conjunction with at least France and the U.K. against all suitable military targets in China, avoiding insofar as practicable those targets in areas near the boundaries of the USSR in order not to increase the risk of direct Soviet involvement." If, however, the United Kingdom and France refused to undertake expanded military action against the Chinese, the United States "should consider taking unilateral action."[66] Thus, by mid-1952 the United States had approved contingency plans for Southeast Asia which called for a limited war with China, probably using nuclear weapons, if the Chinese communists attacked the region.

NSC 124/2 was somewhat of a compromise statement, leaving the United States with flexibility according to a given situation. Nevertheless, it is very significant that American officials saw the need to take collective action against China. It was believed by some that failure to get allied agreement on this crucial issue might lead to a rift within the Atlantic alliance. America's experience in Korea was important in shaping its policies in Vietnam. The strategic considerations that had required a united effort in Korea were present in American thinking about defending Southeast Asia against Chinese attack. As Charles Bohlen, the counsellor at the Department of State, pointed out, "We have to get French and British support if we are going to war with Communist China, for without their support we might lose the whole NATO structure."[67]

Since NSC 124/2 was a function of American attempts to achieve a military solution in Vietnam, it did not describe what the background to a Chinese attack in the region might be – whether the Chinese would have initiated an unprovoked attack or whether they would have been responding to actions undertaken by allied forces in Vietnam. In this sense, it conflicted with the more defensive Southeast Asian strategy advocated by the Europeans and other allies. It was important for articulating some of the assumptions underlying Dulles's strategy in the spring of 1954 to defeat the Viet Minh.

The United Kingdom was not prepared to accept the American terms for the collective defence of Southeast Asia. As early as 16 February 1952, Rob Scott noted, "The real difference of opinion is over the risk, which we rate higher than the Americans do, that direct retaliation may lead to general war."[68] The British and French were no more prepared to support American policy statements after NSC 124/2 was approved. The U.S. ambassador in London, Walter Gifford, complained that the United Kingdom and France had an "obsession" with the "avoidance [of] action which might lead to Soviet involvement."[69] Just as they had feared an expanded war against China during the Korean conflict, America's allies were fearful that such a war might originate in Southeast Asia. The basic lines of allied debate over Indochina were in place by 1952.

Despite disagreements, further military discussions involving the United States, the United Kingdom, France, Australia, and New Zealand were held after 1952. The latter two countries were included because of their geographical proximity and their interest in preserving the Western sphere of influence in the region, and because of their participation in ANZUS and in tripartite defence planning with the United Kingdom. NSC 124/2 suggested that the United States should seek agreement with these four nations with respect to issuing a joint warning to Communist China of the "grave consequences of Chinese aggression against Southeast Asia." Such a warning would only be issued after the allies had agreed on action to be taken against China – that is, action as defined in NSC 124/2. The United States was not prepared to issue a five-power warning statement that would not be backed by the other powers on American terms. The United Kingdom also saw the advantage of participating in the five-power military discussions: it would help fill the gap in United Kingdom strategy that had been created by Britain's exclusion from ANZUS, and it might result in an expanded American commitment to the defence of Southeast Asia on British terms.

The first five-power military conference to discuss the defence of Southeast Asia in the event of Chinese aggression was held 6–17 October 1952. The conference report concluded that the best means of causing Communist China to cease its aggression was "a combination of all coercive measures," including a naval blockade and "air attacks on all suitable targets of military significance in China."[70] This prompted the U.S. Joint Chiefs of Staff to write that the conference had "special significance in relation to the objectives of NSC 124/2 as regards expanded action against Communist China," and that the conclusions "should serve as a basis for negotiating further political agreements on the issuance of a joint warning to Communist China."[71] Progress was made towards goals set out in NSC 124/2, but subsequent conferences from 6 to 10 April and from 15 June to 1 July 1953 did not resolve the political disagreements between the United States on the one hand, and the United Kingdom, France, and the antipodean countries on the other, regarding expanded action against the People's Republic. The underlying competition for spheres of influence within the alliance and the difficulties of forging a unified Western response to the Chinese threat in peripheral regions of the globe were not overcome.

The United States' more belligerent strategy towards China dominated its policies of undermining the sources of communist power in the Far East. American containment policy on the Chinese perimeter was not static: it was meant to revise the status quo not only in Asia but globally. The United States continued to encourage ways of undermining Chinese power without provoking global war; its policies towards Korea and Vietnam reflected the vague hope that these policies might someday result in the overthrow or reorientation of Communist China's government. NSC 48/5 had declared that U.S. policy should "detach China as an effective ally of the USSR and support the development of an independent China which has renounced aggression." Independence was associated with a noncommunist China. U.S. goals would be achieved if the communist regime was replaced, if it developed policies of " 'leaning toward' the free world," or if China became politically fragmented, with "local regimes pursuing policies at variance with those of the central government."[72]

Although America's allies agreed with the need to weaken the Sino-Soviet alliance, they disagreed with U.S. methods. Allied policy papers were much more cautious than American ones and did not openly discuss the possibility of replacing the Chinese regime or encouraging southern China to develop independently of northern China. America's Western allies were much more willing to accept the People's Republic and to work with it in the international system than the United States was. A telegram from the Canadian high commissioner in London, Norman Robertson, on 1 December 1953, outlined the Foreign Office's perspective: "On China the position is that while the United Kingdom agrees with the policy of containing Communism by defence support to neighbouring countries, it would seek to put across the point to the United States that it is unwise and undesirable to maintain a belligerent or provocative attitude from behind the defence wall."[73] Too much emphasis on America's "defensive" containment strategy *vis-à-vis* the Chinese distorts this important distinction between U.S. and allied policies towards China.

The American attempts to create pro-Western regimes in Korea and Vietnam were part of a larger strategy of undermining communist power in continental East Asia. Unlike its position in Korea and Vietnam, however, the United States lacked the direct means of influencing the internal orientation of the Chinese government. The methods used for establishing informal empire in Vietnam and Korea were therefore inapplicable to the Chinese situation. Since they were unable to use military and economic aid to help direct the development of the PRC, American policymakers resorted to the threat of force and covert activities to undermine the Chinese communist regime. NSC 124/2 was thus consistent with America's more belligerent strategy of containing the PRC.

Allied differences over which policy to adopt towards a Chinese invasion of Southeast Asia pertained to a hypothetical situation. It is difficult to say to what extent America's allies would have cooperated with the United States if China had indeed invaded. A relatively united effort was forged during the Korean conflict, and it is probable that all sides would have developed a common position once again. But in the absence of unprovoked Chinese aggression, the British and French were very wary about supporting what they regarded as American rollback strategies in Southeast Asia. For them, the colonial and global stakes were simply too great.

THE INVASION OF LAOS

The internationalization of the war in Vietnam is usually associated with Dulles's "United Action" strategy during the Geneva Conference in the spring of 1954, but its roots lie in this comparatively neglected early period of the war and in the inter-allied debate about the most efficacious means of defending the region from communism.

In April 1953, Viet Minh forces invaded Laos. The invasion, and Western responses to it, underlined the differences within the West regarding the means of containing communism in Indochina. In particular, it demonstrated how European colonial considerations and a cautious stance towards Communist China conflicted with some of the premises underpinning American policy. Britain's disagreement with U.S. attempts to internationalize the war in Vietnam after the Viet Minh invaded Laos in 1953 demonstrated its concern with preserving its colonial power and not antagonizing the Chinese.

On 14 April 1953 the Royal Government of Laos issued a statement that requested the United Nations formally to condemn "Viet Minh aggression." At this juncture, American officials were disturbed about the lack of French military aggressiveness in Indochina. What was needed was a military victory. If no military progress was made, the situation would deteriorate even further. Philip Bonsal, who at this time was director of the Philippine and Southeast Asian Affairs Division of the State Department, wrote on April 20, "French ineptitude and the deteriorating military situation are counteracting progress earlier made in the political field." Military officials agreed with this sentiment. "The whole French position seems to be a defensive one and one of not really wanting to fight the war to a conclusion," the U.S. Air Force chief of staff, Hoyt Vandenburg, told a combined Joint Chiefs of Staff and State Department meeting on 24 April. "I feel that if the French keep on in this manner, we will be pouring money down a rathole."[74]

Officials believed that in the absence of military success, the United States should try to draw more international support behind the Indochinese governments by bringing the issue to the United Nations. There were many arguments in favour of such action: it would encourage the pro-Western nationalists in Vietnam who had faith in the United Nations; it might lay the base for further military actions at a later date; by the internationalization of the war, American public opinion would be more prepared to support United States aid to France; it would place America in a stronger position in relation to the communists if the United States deemed it desirable to negotiate a settlement; and inaction might be interpreted by the communists as a sign of weakness. Internationalization would also help remove the " 'colonial war' stigma."[75] In general, it would lend support to the U.S. goal of accelerating the transition from centralized French colonial control to increased indigenous responsibility under more indirect American influence and supervision; it would facilitate the evolution of an informal empire.

Secretary of State Dulles was particularly enthusiastic about bringing the issue to the United Nations, anticipating his attempts to internationalize the war in 1954. Dulles told British and French representatives during a tripartite meeting in Paris on 25 April 1953 that the conflict had "not yet fully received the status of an international war or an international act of aggression." It would therefore be wise "if at some appropriate time the French government were to give consideration to the possibility of a complaint being made by Laos or by France, or jointly or both, in the Security Council, about the invasion of Laos." This would make the conflict "more readily a subject for international negotiation and settlement, which it is not today," argued Dulles.[76]

Both the French and the British refused to take such a step, however. They feared that bringing the issue to the United Nations would hurt their international status as colonial powers and would threaten their position in relation to China. The French ambassador in Washington, Henri Bonnet, told Philip Bonsal that an appeal to the United Nations might encourage Chinese intervention in support of the Viet Minh; and that it would also "probably encourage a lot of futile discussion of the issue of 'colonialism' and would not therefore be particularly helpful in the struggle against Communist aggression in Indochina."[77]

The British also disagreed with the Americans on this issue, though not as vehemently as the French. At the tripartite discussions in April 1953, the minister of state, Selwyn Lloyd, told Dulles that "with respect to a complaint to the Security Council by Laos or by France or by both, the British government would follow the wishes of the French government."[78] A few days later, M.S. Williams of the Foreign Office's United Nations Political Department minuted: "From the point of view of British interests, it would seem extraordinarily dangerous to bring the U.N. into the Indo-Chinese dispute by indicting one of the parties to the civil war." He warned that this "would create an immediate precedent for raising Mau-Mau in Kenya and the Communist terrorist activities in Malaya."[79]

The Foreign Office did, however, see some advantage in bringing the issue to the United Nations. For example, this would weaken the public perception that France was fighting a purely colonial war. But, on balance, it was believed that no United Nations action should be undertaken unless a charge of complicity was also made against the Chinese. This way, the issue would be debated in the context of international aggression and not a colonial war. Nevertheless, such a linkage would raise the troublesome issue of Chinese representation in the United Nations and would risk a widening of the conflict. It was therefore of "doubtful value."[80]

In May, even as the Viet Minh forces began to withdraw from Laos, Dulles continued to advocate an internationalization of the war. He pressed Thailand to raise the issue at the Security Council in the hope that a vocal Thai appeal to preserve its border security would provide added impetus in the U.S. Congress and the international arena for an intensified effort against the Viet Minh. For the British, Australians, and Canadians, this appeal was less threatening than Dulles's earlier proposals. First, it was limited to asking the Security Council to dispatch a Peace Observation Commission to the endangered border region. This was perceived as a positive move by the British, who, like the Americans, wanted a greater Thai commitment to fighting the Cold War. A British telegram to the Commonwealth high commissioners stated: "Siamese decision has certain advantages. Continued Siamese adherence to anti-Communist cause is vital to stability of South East Asia"; the telegram added that provided the appeal did not make reference to Indochina or China, "it might be possible to avoid embarrassment to France."[81] Significantly, Canadian diplomats also wanted to avoid any discussion of colonial issues that would hurt the prestige of their European allies. The Canadian permanent representative to the United Nations, David Johnson, told Ottawa that he wanted to avoid "the embarrassment which a full-dress discussion in the Security Council" might create for the French and, to a lesser degree, the British. It would also be wise not to antagonize the Soviets, given the delicate stage of the Korean armistice negotiations. The acting secretary of state for external affairs, Charles Ritchie, pointed out that as long as the Thai resolution did not condemn anyone, "the question may not prove to be particularly explosive."

Dulles's concerns about political instability in France delayed the Thai appeal, and on 14 August Kenneth Landon, the person responsible for Thailand affairs in the American Department of State, told the Canadian ambassador in Washington, Arnold Heeney, that the appeal was dormant and was not expected to be raised again unless Thailand's security was again threatened by the Viet Minh.[82]

This initial attempt at internationalizing the war had failed, and the issue demonstrated that there were limits to which the United States, the British Commonwealth, and France were able to agree on the methods of containing communism in Vietnam. The trend was towards a devolution of French power in Indochina and a corresponding increase in American responsibilities, but disagreement existed on a multiplicity of levels. Unlike the Korean situation, the process of consolidating an American informal empire in Vietnam was complicated by the strength of the communists, the weakness of the nationalists, and an implicit competition for spheres of influence and prestige among the Western powers. Different strategies for containing China also worked against America's attempts to create an informal empire on the communist periphery at this time.

The American efforts to bring the issue to the United Nations had demonstrated a certain disregard for French colonial power. But there were limits also to Anglo-French feelings of colonial solidarity. British officials tended to view the French as bumblers. Britain's quandary was that, isolated from the sources of power in Vietnam, it needed to maintain its "special relationship" with the United States; in the end, the British could only hope for continued U.S. aid to Vietnam and for greater French effort in Indochina. Prime Minister Winston Churchill demonstrated his own attitude towards colonial questions when he wrote that "the French are naturally afraid of being 'Dutched out' of Indo China by the same sloppy United Nations' methods as lost Indonesia." Churchill was frustrated with France's inability to prosecute the war: "On the other hand, they will not take the only step which could restore their position, namely 2 years military service and sending conscripts to the front. France cannot be a great Nation."[83]

VIETNAM AND FRANCO-AMERICAN RELATIONS, JUNE–DECEMBER 1953

The Eisenhower administration tended to downplay potential rifts among the Western allies over China in favour of an active policy of doing more to fight the Viet Minh. In discussions with French officials in 1953, Dulles stated that it would be wise to make plans on the premise that the Chinese would not provide airplanes or volunteers to the Viet Minh. In July 1953 he told the French foreign minister, Georges Bidault, that it was reasonable "to make plans in Indochina on the basis that there would be no such development because ... the Communist[s] know that it is probable that such an operation would lead to a rather general war in the Pacific area and that sea and air forces from the United States might be brought to bear in areas other than Indochina."[84]

For their part, the French were keen on getting the United States to underwrite more of the costs of their anticommunist colonial war. In June 1953 the newly appointed French commander in Indochina, General Navarre, presented a memo to Lieutenant-General John ("Iron Mike") O'Daniel, the commander-in-chief of the U.S. Army in the Pacific. This document, which met American demands for increased military effort on the part of the French, recommended "a new military offensive with emphasis on guerrilla warfare, the development of local armies with greater leadership responsibility, and the organization of army units with larger components."[85]

In conversations with American officials, French diplomats argued that the plan would only be approved by the their government if the United States agreed to subsidize the effort with $400 million in aid. On 29 August 1953, the American ambassador in Paris, Douglas Dillon, wrote to the Department of State conveying Prime Minister Joseph Laniel's position: "As to the Navarre Plan he said the decision to send out the 9 additional battalions was definite provided of course the funds were available from the United States to carry out the rest of the plan, i.e., the creation of the necessary additional Associated States forces." In an earlier discussion with Dillon, Laniel had said: "The additional troops will not be sent unless France is assured of adequate assistance from the United States to create the necessary local forces."

After receiving further assurances from the French that they would carry out their part of the agreement, the U.S. National Security Council (NSC) agreed to supply the French government with $385 million more for the 1954 calendar year.[86]

For a short period in the fall of 1953 there was a feeling of hopeful optimism among American officials about France's prospects for success in Indochina. At the NSC meeting which recommended that the president approve the French request for financial aid, Dulles "expressed his firm conviction that Premier Laniel was really disposed to make this additional effort in Indochina." Dulles believed that "for the first time" there was a French government that saw "the necessity of building strength in Indochina." He predicted that "it would probably take two or even three years to achieve a real decision in the Indochina war. A marked improvement in the situation, however, would be visible much sooner."[87]

The day after the State Department received France's assurance that it would carry out the plan if the Americans provided the funds, Dulles issued a warning to China. On 2 September 1953, at a speech before the St Louis chapter of the American Legion, he warned that the United States did not view the Korean War as an isolated event, but saw it as "one part of the worldwide effort of communism to conquer freedom." Communist China, he said, was sending supplies and training the Indochinese communists, and there was a risk that "as in Korea, Red China might send its own army into Indochina." The Chinese needed to understand that "a second aggression could not occur without grave consequences which might not be confined to Indochina."[88]

Dulles's speech was calculated to support the French will to continue the fight in Southeast Asia and to contain the People's Republic of China. The Secretary of State realized that the French government was fearful of Chinese intervention, and his speech was designed to make the intervention less likely. It was clear to the American administration at least that Dulles was using an implicit atomic threat to the Chinese; the minutes of the National Security Council meeting record that it "was with the objective of making Chinese Communist intervention less likely that he had made his statement, and Secretary Dulles enumerated possible actions by the United States to execute this threat which the Chinese Communists would not find pleasant to contemplate."[89] Despite recent evaluations of the pragmatic nature of Dulles's diplomacy,[90] he was neither timid about wielding the atomic threat nor willing to accommodate the Chinese in international diplomacy. The notion of the dynamic, so important to understanding Dulles's thinking, was translated into specific threats and action. Although

Eisenhower was generally more concerned than Dulles about preserving Western unity over Asia, he gave his general support to Dulles's foreign policy style.

CORE AND PERIPHERY: VIETNAM AND THE SINO-SOVIET RELATIONSHIP IN WESTERN STRATEGY

The key issue and centre of allied disagreement in this period remained the relationship between the peripheral outposts of Western influence in Asia – Vietnam and Korea – and the People's Republic of China. The problem of how Western hopes for creating pro-Western governments in Vietnam and Korea related to their China policies was not resolved in the period 1949–54. The Americans wanted indigenous Asian governments to serve as a bulwark to continued communist expansion and in the longer term as a means of undermining Soviet and communist bloc power. To the United States, the containment of communism in Asia was part of a larger strategy linked to the rolling back of the Soviet system. The British and French, however, were more interested in coming to a *modus vivendi* with both the Soviets and the Chinese. They were willing to work towards an implicit spheres-of-influence agreement in Asia. Their primary aim was to prevent the outbreak of a regional war that would threaten their colonial interests and divert resources into a secondary theatre of combat. In general, more difficulties were encountered in Southeast Asia than in Northeast Asia, and it was in Southeast Asia that allied disagreements were made manifest.

There was broad agreement among the North Atlantic countries on the need to contain Vietnamese communism and to create a Western sphere of influence in Vietnam. The sources of this commitment differed, however, and each country pursued policies which it believed was consistent with its regional and global interests. Much of the debate within the alliance focused on opposing views on how to contain Communist China's continuing aid to the Viet Minh. All parties were afraid of involving the Soviet Union in a regional war with China, but the United States was more willing than its allies to test the strength of the Sino-Soviet partnership. The differences among the allies were largely over a hypothetical situation of a Chinese invasion, but even hypothetical discussions had important implications for policy. All the governments recognized the delicate nature of their disagreements, however, and a united front was an important objective of all the Western nations in this period.

In view of the fact that American policymakers perceived European power in Southeast Asia as a declining commodity, they were prepared to respond to Chinese aggression unilaterally if they felt the situation dictated it. But the need to preserve a united front to the Soviet Union tempered American plans for unilateral action against China. Ultimately, the weakness of European power in Southeast Asia drove the United States towards other partners in the region, such as Thailand, Australia, the Philippines, and South Korea. But in the early 1950s, the Americans still needed to work within an older framework for Western action in the region. This meant accommodating their policy to French and, to a lesser extent, British colonialism.

5 The North Atlantic Triangle, China, and the Korean Armistice Negotiations, 1951–1953

In the period 1951–53 the United States and its allies were able to maintain their relative unity over Korean issues. There was still basic agreement in the Western alliance that the decision to contain communist advances in Korea was a wise and correct one. Nevertheless, the negotiations leading to the armistice agreement generated severe tensions within the North Atlantic alliance. The British and Canadian special relationship with the United States remained the determining factor in their Korean strategies, but the Americans' policies towards the People's Republic tended to undermine their allies' regional defensive containment strategy regarding China.

For Britain especially, there was acute tension between the need to maintain a good Anglo-American relationship and the hope of moving towards a *modus vivendi* with China. The Churchill government worried that America's China policy would prevent peaceful settlement of the Korean conflict, distract the Western alliance from Western Europe, create a context for further Chinese aggression in Asia, and solidify the Sino-Soviet alliance. The British were supported by other Western governments which had similar interests in keeping the conflict confined to Korea. Like British officials, Canadian diplomats emphasized the need to meet the communists at the bargaining table, not on the battlefield.

The United States showed no interest in accommodating the new China in this period. For American strategists, the Korean War represented an opportunity to weaken Communist China's industrial and military power. Increased military pressure on the Chinese would stem industrialization efforts, exacerbate divergences within the communist alliance, and divert Chinese resources to military ends. On the day that armistice negotiations began at Kaesong, a U.S. National Intelligence Estimate reported: "The Korean War has placed strains upon the internal political, military and economic position of the Chinese Communist regime. While these strains have not yet become critical, they may well become so if the war is prolonged."[1]

U.S. policymakers coordinated their strategy of greater pressure on the Chinese communists with their limited war aims. Early in this period, the concept of limited war was altered to include the possibility of a restricted extension of operations into China. American and allied differences over the definition of "limited war," apparent in the early stages of the conflict, became more pronounced after 1951.

There was, however, still substantial agreement on the overall prosecution of the war. In conjunction with the United States, Canada and Great Britain extended their list of embargoed goods going to China, supported the United States on the issue of non-forcible repatriation of prisoners of war, and agreed that hostilities in Asia should not initiate a general war with the Soviet Union. The bipolar international system continued to exert an influence on allied diplomacy, and the need to contain Soviet military might remained the cardinal aim of Western strategy in this period.

In the fall of 1952, an outward appearance of unity was maintained when the United States and its principal allies voted for a United Nations resolution which reiterated their position on the prisoner-of-war issue. The resolution had initially been introduced by the Indian delegation, and America's adherence to the final draft represented the commitment its allies had hoped for: a settlement of the conflict through continued negotiations, not through increased military pressure. But the apparent allied victory proved illusory, for the new Republican administration of Dwight D. Eisenhower privately revoked its support of a negotiated settlement through established diplomatic means. On 11 February the National Security Council (NSC) noted President Eisenhower's desire that Secretary Dulles "undertake promptly to secure the agreement of our allies to termination of the existing arrangements in Korea connected with the armistice negotiations."[2] By May, the administration had decided that the best way to put an end to the fighting and engender conflict in the Sino-Soviet relationship was to obliquely and indirectly threaten an expansion of the war, possibly to include the use of atomic weapons against China.

There is a fairly extensive literature on this issue.[3] In an important article, Roger Dingman has pointed out that atomic diplomacy was an element of American strategy throughout the war, and not just in its final stages. Turning earlier historiography on its head, Dingman emphasizes that the Eisenhower administration acted more cautiously than its predecessor in considering the use of atomic threats.[4] However, both Dulles and Eisenhower often argued that atomic bombs should be viewed like other weapons of destruction and not treated as a special category of weapon. Atomic weapons could therefore be included in the negotiating process when it was militarily feasible to do so. This is the context in which atomic weapons were discussed in the months leading up to the armistice. Dean Acheson, on the other hand, was critical of using the bomb as a political weapon. In late January 1951, he told an NSC meeting that "the threat represented by our stockpile of atomic bombs was not a political advantage or asset, but, rather, a political liability." The threat of atomic retaliation would "frighten our allies to death," but it would not cause much concern in enemy quarters. "In any case," Acheson concluded, "such a step needed much talking about before it was taken."[5]

The Truman administration did use the weapons to support its diplomacy in Asia. But the circumstances surrounding the two administrations' resort to atomic diplomacy were very different. In 1950–51 the U.S. government considered a nuclear response in a much more desperate military situation *vis-à-vis* the communist armies. As Dingman writes, when Truman ordered B-29s to ferry atomic weapons across the Pacific in April 1951, he did so "in the gravest circumstances."[6] In the spring of 1951, the decision to resort to atomic diplomacy was taken initially in the face of a feared Soviet attack and, later, in the light of the Chinese communists' spring offensive. The context of these American decisions was therefore defensive. Truman was hoping to deter further Soviet and Chinese offensive action.

The military situation in the spring of 1953 was the converse of this. The Chinese had shown signs of war weariness, and American officials believed that the Soviet Union was willing to end the war in Korea. In this light, the use of atomic diplomacy by the Eisenhower administration was provocative. Dingman argues, however, that Washington was involved not in nuclear diplomacy in April–May 1953 but in "nonnuclear persuasive diplomacy"; although Eisenhower did approve the transfer of nuclear weapons on the eve of the negotiated agreement, his decision "was not part of an atomic diplomacy scheme. It appears to have been shaped more by long-term strategic, rather than immediate Korean War-related, concerns."[7] However, long-term strategic considerations were crucial to Eisenhower's thinking on the Korean issue, and they were an integral part of the decision to employ the weapons. The policy paper NSC 147 made this clear. The decision to use atomic weapons if necessary was one that would have been implemented through a series of escalatory steps, but the threat to the Soviets and Chinese underlay American diplomacy in the period leading up to the armistice. Moreover, the communists and America's allies understood long before the spring of 1953 the deadly ramifications of a breakdown in the armistice negotiations.[8] This underlying threat of atomic retaliation was the critical factor behind allied efforts to get the Truman and Eisenhower administrations to negotiate with the communists at the bargaining table. Eisenhower merely confirmed the legitimacy of these fears when he told an NSC meeting on 20 May 1953 that if the armistice negotiations were not successful and a decision was made to escalate the war, "it would be necessary to use the atomic bomb." He wanted to ensure that atomic operations against China were mounted quickly to lessen the danger of Soviet air attacks on Japan. "Everything ... should be in readiness before the [atomic] blow actually fell." The president noted that he did not want to get involved in a global war over Manchuria, but he was less concerned over Chinese military capabilities, "since the blow would fall so swiftly and with such force as to eliminate Chinese Communist intervention."[9] An atomic attack on China was therefore also meant to scare the Soviets and prevent them from intervening. That a negotiated settlement occurred without an escalation of the war was probably due more to the war weariness of the Chinese than to any specific successful application of atomic diplomacy. Secretary Dulles's arguments that the threatened use of atomic weapons was a crucial factor in getting the communists to agree to American terms were an exaggeration.[10]

One gap in the literature of the conflict is an evaluation of U.S. aims regarding the Sino-Soviet alliance at the end of the war. Containing Soviet power remained America's priority in this period, and American policymakers saw the negotiations surrounding the end of the war as an opportunity to create rifts in the Soviet–Chinese relationship. Their diplomacy in April and May 1953 should thus be seen in the context of an application of the "wedge strategy," forcing apart Soviet and Chinese strategic interests in East Asia. This was a risky strategy, and it was implicit in their threats to use atomic weapons in the Korean and Chinese theatres if a settlement was not forthcoming. The attempt to create rifts in the alliance would also further America's position in the Republic of Korea and Vietnam, for cracks in the alliance would weaken the Soviet Union's ability to use China as a means of spreading communist influence throughout East Asia. If China became alienated from Soviet control, the U.S. objective of orienting China towards the West would be one step closer to fruition. In the zero-sum game of Cold War politics, any loss of prestige or power by the Soviet Union was seen as a gain for the United States and the West.

American policymakers recognized the importance of getting their allies' support if the war was to be expanded. Dingman implies that one of Eisenhower's reasons for not advocating the nuclear threat was his fear that the allies might not support it. The allies were reluctant to back America's final negotiating position; but, for Eisenhower, allied support was all the more important because he understood the implications of a breakdown in the negotiating process.

It is at this point that the United States' relations with its allies in the earlier part of the war become relevant. The allies' considerations in the early winter of 1950–51 regarding the aggressor resolution, and their ultimate decision to compromise their preferred policies to present a unified stance towards the Soviet Union, serve as a useful backdrop to their decisions in May 1953. Once again, the need to deter conflict with the communists, the willingness of the United States and its allies to come to a compromise position, and the fear of the implications of a public break in the allied front brought the United States and the other Western nations together.

Both Britain and Canada were very exercised about American diplomacy in this period. The United States' decision to present a tough negotiating stance and its implicit threat to end discussions resulted in extreme tensions within the alliance. Britain and Canada initially objected strenuously to the possibility of breaking off negotiations, especially since it appeared that the communists were on the verge of accepting a negotiated agreement. But as in 1951, a compromise position was put together, one that accepted the basic tenets of American strategy. Though the allies argued that the U.S. position should not become the basis for a breakdown in the negotiations, their public adherence to the American final position implied to the Chinese at least tacit support of America's nuclear threat against the Sino-Soviet alliance. The need to preserve unity with the United States was utmost in Canadian and British minds. Churchill especially wanted to preserve the remnants of the wartime special relationship, and he believed, as did some Canadian officials, that the communists would accept the final position of the U.N. Command.

The costs of maintaining unity were high: the American tendency to take unfavourable decisions with regard to the Far East had been underlined once again. From this point onwards, allied policy towards continental East Asia was on a precarious footing. The United States' stance on ending the war had further demonstrated to its allies the necessity for a settlement of Far Eastern issues. The decision to threaten an expansion of hostilities contributed to a growing divergence between the United States and its principal NATO allies on the best methods for containing communism in Asia. These differences revealed themselves again in the context of the Geneva Conference on Indochina in the spring and summer of 1954.

CHINA AND KOREA POLICY, 1951

The fundamental principles behind the formulation of U.S. policy towards Korea and the People's Republic of China after 1951 were laid out in NSC 48/5, "United States Objectives, Policies and Courses of Action in Asia." This NSC document is best viewed in the light of U.S. objectives concerning the Sino-Soviet alliance. Echoing the conclusions of earlier NSC papers, it regarded Communist China as an extension of Soviet power in Asia: "Current Soviet tactics appear to concentrate on bringing the principal mainland of Eastern Asia and eventually Japan and the other principal off-shore islands in the Western Pacific under Soviet control, primarily through Soviet exploitation of the resources of communist China." A successful strategy to contain China should work also to undermine Soviet strength.

In view of hostilities in Korea, NSC 48/5 recommended that the United States continue "economic restrictions against China, continue to oppose seating Communist China in the U.N., intensify efforts to persuade other nations to adopt similar positions, and foster the imposition of United Nations political and economic sanctions." To American policymakers, the war represented an opportunity to weaken Chinese power and disrupt Soviet strategy in the Far East. It was up to the United States to maintain the lead in bringing about a reduction in Sino-Soviet power in Asia. The ultimate objective was to "detach China as an effective ally of the USSR and support the development of an independent China which has renounced aggression." This could be achieved by fostering anticommunist Chinese forces and "expanding resistance in China to the Peiping regime's control, particularly in South China."[11]

British and American differences over China stemmed in large part from divergent assessments of how best to contain Chinese communism. Britain's containment strategy for Asia, formulated in 1949, called for a defensive containment of the People's Republic. This was made evident in 1949 and early 1950 with Britain's recognition of the new regime and its diplomatic efforts to seat the Peking government in the United Nations. The essential element of this strategy was negative: to prevent the communists from viewing Western diplomacy as provocative. The policy was substantially compromised as a result of the perceived necessity to respond to Soviet aggression in Korea and by the Chinese government's decision to intervene in late 1950. However U.N. success in stemming the communist offensive in the spring of 1951 and the opening of armistice negotiations in July provided a setting for the United Kingdom, Canada, and other allies to press for a better working relationship with the communists and a return to the original defensive containment concept. These revived hopes conflicted with America's evolving strategy and served to contribute to tensions in Anglo-American relations.

The British position on China was described in a memo by the head of the Foreign Office's Far Eastern Department, Robert Scott. Writing in September 1951, Scott argued that the American approach precluded any possibility of an accommodation with the government of the People's Republic. Whereas the United States hoped ultimately to initiate a chain of events that would result in the overthrow of the communist regime, the United Kingdom recognized that the communists were securely in power and could only be removed with resort to war, which should be avoided at all costs. In view of China's military power relative to British resources and the vulnerability of British colonial possessions in Asia, British officials deemed it wise to accept the communist state and react against it only when it had committed an act of overt aggression, as it had in Korea. The continuance of the war and America's greater enthusiasm to take action against the communists undercut British strategy. Scott lamented: "Perhaps because they believe a major war is in the offing, [the Americans] want to weaken the new Chinese Government by every means in their power." He held that Great Britain should continue to exert its influence on the United States to modify its stance. A *modus vivendi* with the Chinese was necessary to "restore stability in the Far East and avoid cementing a permanent Chinese-Soviet alliance." British policy, said Scott, was "not to rely on the stick alone, but to apply a mixture of carrot and stick – keep in touch, maintain some trading and diplomatic contacts, but stop the Chinese if they interfere in other peoples' affairs outside China."[12]

This was essentially the strategy that successive foreign secretaries followed, with minor differences in emphasis. In a discussion with American officials in September 1951, Herbert Morrison pointed out that the Soviet Union and China should not be driven closer together and that such contacts as the West had with the Chinese government should be retained. On issues relating solely to Korea, however, the foreign secretary stated that the United States and Britain were in "general agreement." If the armistice negotiations were successful, the

British government would promote the principle of an independent and united Korea.[13]

Like British policymakers, Canadian officials supported the broad American and Western objectives regarding Korea. They also impressed on American diplomats the advantages of pursuing a less forceful policy towards the People's Republic. Lester Pearson attempted to restrain America's China policies and publicly warned of the consequences of war with China. In a speech on 5 June 1951, he argued, "We are not in an all-out war with the People's Republic of China; we are engaged in a limited United Nations action to defeat aggression in Korea." An open war with China would, "in all likelihood," lead to global conflict, he said. "This is the disastrous outcome we are striving to prevent."[14]

The U.S. government agreed that global war should be avoided. However, the policymakers believed that their tougher position on China was consistent with policies designed to avoid escalation, because the Soviet Union could be discouraged from entering into any potential conflict with the People's Republic of China. The more belligerent nature of U.S. strategy towards China compared with its major allies was reflected in the United States' policies on trade with China, its concept of limited war, and its negotiating strategy to end the Korean conflict.

ANGLO-AMERICAN RELATIONS AND TRADE
WITH CHINA: CONTAINING REVOLUTION
FROM WITHIN AND WITHOUT

One method by which American officials hoped to create pressure on China was through the imposition of collective economic sanctions. After 1951 the United States continued to pressure its allies to adopt tougher restrictions on their trade with the People's Republic. These efforts were only partially successful: the United States was unable to get allied backing for a blockade of the China coast in the event of further hostilities in Korea, and though the British agreed to restrict the export of strategic materials going to the Chinese state, they consistently refused to bow to American pressure to impose a blockade or complete embargo on China. These decisions stemmed largely from their evaluation of the best means of preserving British colonial power in Asia.

There was fundamental agreement between the Labour and Conservative governments of the period that the U.S. containment policy for China should not be permitted to threaten the existence of Hong Kong. British officials feared the effect that an embargo or blockade would have on the population of Hong Kong. They argued that an end to the trade between the colony and the mainland would create social tensions that would threaten revolution. On 12 February 1951, Mr Paskin, the Colonial Office representative on the cabinet's Far Eastern Official Committee (FEOC) argued that "a complete embargo would have little effect from the short term point of view and for that matter on the war in Korea, whilst at the same time it would affect Hong Kong's trade most adversely causing unemployment and all that goes with it."[15] The containment of revolution in Hong Kong required a defensive containment of China; it was important to stem the tide of the Chinese revolution within China's own borders and prevent its export into the colonies.

A report of the Working Party on Economic Sanctions against China made the connection between trade and revolution explicit. An end to Hong Kong's trade with China "would be of the utmost gravity and might indeed lead to the loss of the island as a British possession." Hong Kong's vulnerability to Chinese actions contributed to the United Kingdom's reservations about supporting the U.S. policy on China. It was precisely the value that China placed on Hong Kong as a means of supply that prevented it from taking action to undermine British power: "The value of Hong Kong to China is at present one of the principal guarantees against a Chinese attack," the working party noted.[16] Britain wanted to maintain the informal agreement with China which made Hong Kong mutually advantageous to the mainland and to its colonial mother. For these reasons, officials regarded British trade with China, indirectly through Hong Kong, as an important factor in supporting British power and helping to maintain Britain's status as a major actor in world affairs.

The British Chiefs of Staff supported the diplomats' position on economic sanctions against China. A report by the military commanders entitled "The Strategic Consequences of the Application of Economic Sanctions against China" stated that sanctions would increase the intensity of Chinese military operations. While the commanders noted China's threat to European colonial powers, they argued that global strategy ruled out any unnecessary or provocative action against China. "We have no delusions," they warned, "as to China's ultimate policy to eliminate European influence from the Far East and South East Asia"; but although China would try to embarrass the West in Asia, there was no evidence that it would provoke war. It was thus of the "greatest importance, not only to our position and that of France in the Far East but in relation to the defence of the West, that we should gain time and not get embroiled in a major war in Asia."[17] The United Kingdom's resources were at the time too weak to risk increased fighting in Asia, a risk brought closer to reality by the U.S. policy on economic sanctions on China.

The British government did take some additional economic measures against China, in part to placate U.S. demands but also out of a realization that Britain should not increase the military power of China, especially in the context of the fighting in Korea, by exporting to China goods of strategic value. On 10 May 1951, the cabinet agreed that the United Kingdom would not allow any more rubber to be exported to China for the remainder of the year. On 18 May it supported a U.S.-sponsored resolution calling for more stringent measures against Communist China. And in November transshipment controls were introduced for goods with China as their ultimate destination.[18] But when the U.S. government suggested in the fall of 1952 that the British block all Chinese assets, deny port facilities to ships going to the mainland, and institute an embargo if the Chinese refused to accept the principle of voluntary repatriation of prisoners of war, the Foreign Office objected. The Americans were notified that such actions would endanger Hong Kong and risk the loss of the British embassy in Peking.[19]

The British did, however, agree to some minor concessions to the American position, and in March 1953 a voyage-licensing system was instituted to prevent U.K.-registered ships from going to Chinese ports without notifying the British government. A cabinet memo produced that month by the president of the Board of Trade, Peter Thorneycroft, demonstrated that his government's objectives and fears had not substantially changed since 1951. An embargo of the mainland involving Hong Kong would "cripple" the colony, and the Peking government might try to foster unrest in Hong Kong, possibly as a prelude to an all-out attack: "Any proposal to extend the range of trade to be covered by our controls would therefore call for very careful scrutiny."[20]

The Canadian position was in basic agreement with the British. Like its former colonial mother, Canada prohibited the export of strategic materials to North Korea and China. It was also reluctant to participate in a Western embargo or blockade of the mainland. In June 1951, Lester Pearson stated publicly that a complete embargo or naval blockade of China would only bring China closer to the Soviet camp: it would not substantially alter China's ability to wage war against the United Nations forces in Korea. Like the British, Canadian officials saw the wisdom of supporting a defensive containment strategy in a region of peripheral interest. "We should not seek to put a complete embargo on all trade with her," Pearson said in 1951, "unless the policy of the Peking Government gives us no alternative in the matter."[21]

Canada's diplomatic support of Britain's containment strategy was based mainly on its own global strategic objectives, goals that it shared with the United Kingdom. Nevertheless, the Canadian position provided added credibility to British policy. It cannot be argued that Canada inadvertently supported British colonialism in Asia; a fairer position might be that despite St Laurent's careful avoidance of overt material support for Britain's colonies, Canadian policy towards Asia indirectly supported British colonial objectives in the region in the context of its own anticommunist policies. Although Canada was critical of old-style European colonialism, its stance on issues relating to decolonization was one of caution and non-interference. The promotion of self-government in colonial areas was a goal of Canadian policy, but it was important as well to moderate nationalist criticisms of the colonial powers. It was hoped that the Arab-Asian bloc could be persuaded that the administering powers could play a "positive and necessary role" in the assertion of Third World sovereignty. Lester Pearson summed up the Canadian position in February 1952 when he wrote that the European colonial nations had a "heavy responsibility to make sure that their colonies are ready for independence before it is granted to them." Although sympathetic to the moderate nationalists, Canada also worked closely with the Europeans. In 1952 Pearson pointed out that in the United Nations, Canada, "generally speaking, side[d] with the colonial powers."[22] Canadian officials accepted the fundamental premises of the memorandum PUSC 22. It was not in the interests of the Canadian government to destabilize British or Western European powers. On the contrary, in the bipolar international system, a close alignment with the Anglo-American Western Alliance was a crucial element of containment policy. Attempts to restrain America's China policy reflected Canada's implicit support of Britain's Great Power objectives in Asia. This "flip side" of Canada's "diplomacy of constraint" has been inadequately understood and has been passed over in traditional Canadian historiography, which has centred on exploring the nature of Canada's special relationship with the United States.

"LIMITED WAR" AND THE CHURCHILL ADMINISTRATION, 1951–1952

Late in 1951 the American administration undertook a re-evaluation of its Korean policy. On 27 September the executive secretary of the Natonal Security Council, James Lay, told his senior staff that since negotiations at Kaesong might drag on indefinitely, "any realistic report on U.S. courses of action in Korea would have to be based on the contingency of a continued stalemate as well as on the contingency of a formal breakdown of the armistice negotiations." The staff agreed and expressed their "very great doubt" that actions outlined in NSC 48/5 "would prove sufficient to achieve the desired settlement in Korea." The result of this reformulation of the problem was NSC 118/2, "United States Objectives and Courses of Action in Korea." This document, approved by President Truman on 20 December 1951, has been described as "a major restatement of the limited-war objectives outlined in NSC 48/5 of May 1951."[23]

It was through its limited war objectives that the United States felt it could undermine Chinese power. Attempts to reorient the Chinese regime towards the West by provocative threats went hand in hand with attempts to weaken the bases of Chinese strength. An NSC staff study accompanying the executive document anticipated that "a *de facto* war with Communist China in Korea continues to provide a significant strategic opportunity, perhaps the last opportunity, for the United States to weaken and undermine the Soviet Union's principal ally, possibly without the costs of a general war either with the USSR or with Communist China itself."[24] What was to be avoided was a prolonged war with China. Korea presented opportunities, but the United States had to be careful in deciding which methods it chose to exploit them. The cardinal principle of American strategy in the Pacific, the defensive perimeter concept, could not be jeopardized. The United States had committed itself to rolling back communism in Korea in 1950, but this decision was a temporary extension of the defensive perimeter onto the mainland. The communists held the capabilities of keeping American and allied forces tied down indefinitely, and the West would be vulnerable to Soviet aggression elsewhere. In short, "even a decisive military victory in Korea and its unification by force might be a hollow victory in the short term, and a major strategic error in the long term."[25]

NSC 118/2 modified the U.S. limited war objectives as defined in NSC 48/5. The latter document foresaw the possibility of increased economic and military pressure against China, but only in the event that "U.N. forces are forced to evacuate Korea." By the end of 1951, U.N. forces were fairly secure in their positions, and the chances of a forced evacuation from Korea were slim. In these circumstances, the staff study argued that it might be wise for the United States not to seek its maximum objectives in Korea and to continue to pursue the goals outlined in NSC 48/5. "At the same time," the study continued, "it may become necessary to increase military and other pressures on the enemy to achieve our limited objectives."[26] Whereas NSC 48/5 had foreseen defensive manoeuvres against the communists, the revised

NSC stance envisaged the possibility of increased pressure against China. As early as 1951, under the Truman administration, the U.S. strategy for ending the war was taking root: a restricted expansion of military and other actions was seen as consistent with the pursuit of "limited war." This hardening of America's China policy in relation to the Korean conflict contributed to tensions within the Western alliance.

The Conservative government in Britain did not substantially alter the previous Labour government's dual policy of containment and *modus vivendi* towards Communist China. Although Churchill himself tended to be less emphatic about pressing Britain's China policy on American officials, in practice his administration continued the policies adopted by Labour to contain communism in Asia.

Foreign Secretary Anthony Eden was even more wary than previous foreign ministers had been about committing Britain to American containment policies in Korea and Southeast Asia. In part this stemmed from the United States' greater willingness to take a harsh stance towards the People's Republic. However, it also represented Eden's anti-Americanism and his personal attempts to act independently of the United States when he felt those actions were in Britain's interest. Although Eden recognized the pragmatic value of the Anglo-American relationship, he placed greater value on developing and asserting Britain's independence in world affairs than either Morrison or Bevin had done. It is significant that after returning from Anglo-American discussions in Washington in early 1952, Eden told the cabinet of his "renewed conviction of our need to do everything possible to re-establish our economic and financial independence," and he pointed out that the United States' attitude "was fundamentally affected by our dependent situation and would be substantially changed once we were standing on our own feet."[27] These attitudes extended to foreign relations, and Eden resented Britain's declining influence in world affairs relative to the United States.

British officialdom reacted with some concern in early 1952 when it became apparent that the United States was pursuing a tougher policy towards China. American intransigence threatened hopes for a settlement of Far Eastern issues not only in Korea but in Southeast Asia as well. The costs of rearmament gave additional impetus to British hopes for a settlement. But it was not simply that Great Britain sought a friendly accommodation with the Chinese. What was in British minds was a form of implicit spheres-of-influence agreement, whereby European and Asian powers would agree not to interfere in each others' territory. It was an attempt to draw frontiers where, in some cases, none existed. British diplomats believed that the Korean War presented the greatest immediate threat to their containment strategy for

China. As a result, they directed their energy to negotiating a settlement of the war and getting the United States to accept the reality of the Chinese regime in Asia.

In March 1952 a series of Foreign Office minutes illustrated the exasperation which British policymakers associated with America's tougher Chinese policy. On 7 March, George Toplas of the China and Korea Department worried that the Americans were considering the possibility that the Chinese would commit a further aggression in Asia. This was "at complete variance" with a PUSC paper which argued that "the case for or against Chinese aggression is not proved." One danger with U.S. strategy, Toplas noted, was that "policies will inevitably be adopted, the whole basic thinking of which leaves out any possibility of a return to moderation *even if* the Chinese by their future attitude clearly show that they are anxious to reach a *modus vivendi*."[28]

J.M. Addis, who later became the head of the Far Eastern Department, agreed. Britain and China should learn to coexist with each other: "That is still our objective if we can secure a Korean armistice and can avoid a worsening of relations in other areas of the Chinese perimeter."[29] A peaceful solution to the conflict in East Asia would allow for a redistribution of United Kingdom resources for internal economic consolidation and would contain Soviet attempts to set up other communist states in the Far East.

Despite their wishes, British diplomats were not optimistic about the possibilities of reaching a broader settlement with the Peking government. Only part of the reason for this was the U.S. dislike of the regime; another was that the tactics of the Chinese had not up to that point demonstrated that an accommodation might be possible. The PUSC paper had warned that the actions of the Chinese government were "open to influences and temptations favouring expansion." As C.H. Johnston remarked, the risk was "that these influences and temptations may, in China's case, have the same result in practice as the inherent dynamism of their situations did, say, for Napoleon or Hitler." However, British diplomats preferred not to create situations that would tempt the Chinese to use force. What was important was that China was not an inherently expansionist power – it did not need to rely on expansion for its existence. Even though Chinese policy in Korea and Tibet, and towards Taiwan, offered further possibilities for aggression, the Foreign Office did not believe that the case had yet been decided. Most of all, it felt that American policies should not exacerbate tension between China and the West. The British favoured a reactive policy of containment towards Mao's government.[30]

Canadian officialdom also was sceptical about the advantages of supporting the U.S. concept of limited warfare on the Northeast Asian perimeter. Like the British, Canadian diplomats saw contradictions between U.S. attempts to negotiate a settlement of the Korean War and U.S. policy on China. When the assistant secretary of state, Dean Rusk, told the public in May 1951 that the Peking regime was not the government of China or even Chinese, America's allies were outraged. John Holmes, Canada's delegate at the United Nations, wrote to Pearson that what was alarming about Rusk's speech was that it put forth "a fundamental policy in dealing with China which the rest of us have not accepted and I presume still do not accept." There was very little apparent logic or consistency in American policy towards China, noted Holmes. In the United Nations, American officials emphasized the need for peace; but on the other hand, Rusk made this "public statement indicating that the Peking Government are usurpers, the valid government of China is Chiang's, and implies that the policy of the United States is to aid Chiang in overthrowing the Peking regime. Are the State Department so stupid that they believe Mao would dare to negotiate with a government pledged to his overthrow?" Holmes went on to criticize the U.S. crusade against the evil enemy, observing that to support diplomatic sanctions against China would be "an absurd example of cutting off our noses to spite our faces in order to appease a neurotic American public which has inherited from its ancestors in Salem superstitions about those who consort with the devil." Holmes reflected departmental attitudes and placed his hopes on British policy: "If the British remain unprovocative, the excitement in this country might subside."[31] British strategy, however, was not attractive to many American policymakers, because it did not satisfy the regional or emotional needs underlying their China policy. There is nonetheless much irony in Holmes's criticism of American self-righteousness.

The U.S. containment strategy on China's periphery had significant provocative aspects. The policymakers were not innocent in wielding power, and towards the People's Republic they took advantage of opportunities to undermine Chinese prestige and power. There was thus a tension between America's defensive perimeter strategy and its need to weaken the People's Republic, a tension that contributed to feelings of frustration over U.S. policy on China.

There are other factors that need to be taken into account in examining the U.S. policy on China in this period. It is plausible to argue that in taking the lead against North Korean aggression, the United States acted in an essentially moral manner, and that its China policy was simply a logical consequence of that original decision. This argument is partly true. American officials initially viewed their decision to intervene in moral as well as strategic terms. Furthermore, Kim Il Sung sought to extend complete control over Korea when North Korea's forces attacked in June 1950. But allied policy was more determined to lay the basis for rearmament and to counter the perceived global Soviet threat than it was to defend a weak nation on the East Asian periphery. The lesson is perhaps that one must be cautious about accepting American rhetoric about the essentially moral nature of its decision to roll back communism. The South Koreans were only part players in a global strategy. Great Power politics explains much better the motivations of Western policymakers towards Korea.

BRITISH AND AMERICAN POLICY TOWARDS THE SINO-SOVIET ALLIANCE

The American government deliberately chose to use the Korean War to further its goal of weakening the combined power of the Soviet Union and China. The hope of creating divergences in the alliance followed logically from the containment of Soviet power. The objective was to exacerbate tensions that already had surfaced in the Sino-Soviet alliance. One of these differences was noted in National Intelligence Estimate 58, "Relations Between the Chinese Communist Regime and the USSR: Their Present Character and Probable Future Courses." Dated 10 September 1952, this document argued that Soviet Far Eastern objectives were pursued in the context of a global strategy but that Soviet officials were not prepared to engage the West in a general war beginning in Asia. The Chinese, on the other hand, were more sensitive to Western containment strategies in East Asia. Chinese diplomats might "view the accomplishment of Far Eastern objectives with more urgency and impatience than do the Soviets." It was believed that the Chinese might make demands that were inconsistent with Soviet global strategy, and that America's limited war strategy could create tensions within the communist alliance. As National Intelligence Estimate 58 pointed out, the Korean War was "a potential source of friction to the two regimes."[32]

The potential friction engendered as a result of U.S. policy was not seen to be great enough to disrupt the alliance seriously. The Sino-Soviet partnership was too strong to be broken by Western diplomatic initiatives alone. Military pressures, however, might contribute to tensions that might prepare the way for a split within the communist system. The negotiations surrounding the end of the Korean War in the spring of 1953 presented one opportunity to test these assumptions. It was an opportunity, moreover, that American policymakers took advantage of.

British and Canadian officials feared the risks involved in supporting America's Sino-Soviet strategy: military pressure might simply bring the two communist allies closer together and result in a further drain of Western resources to the area. To Canadians in the Department of External Affairs, Sino-Soviet discussions in the fall of 1952 illustrated the complementary nature of the alliance. The decision taken during these meetings to operate Port Arthur jointly was seen as consistent with the overall aims of the 1950 Sino-Soviet treaty. Further pressure on China would only solidify the partnership to the detriment of Western interests. "The Treaty was designed for safeguarding China and Russia against Japan and any ally," the department wrote to Canadian embassies in Washington and London. "External pressure on China has only increased the determination to remain in the embrace of Russia."[33] Diplomatic policies which brought the Soviets and Chinese closer together were seen in a negative light. On this level, Britain and Canada did not disagree with the American goal of reorienting China in the direction of the West. For both countries, a defensive containment strategy towards China would bolster their objectives *vis-à-vis* the Soviet Union. Canadian and British policy cannot be dissociated from their anticommunist programs involving the Soviet Union, which were centred in Europe. Like the Americans, these two allies recognized that differences existed between China and the Soviet Union, but they chose different means of exploiting these tensions. In general, they sought a diplomatic solution to the potential threat of Chinese power in Asia. PUSC (52)6, "Future Policy Towards China," pointed out the basic differences in Anglo-American strategy. Although the United Kingdom hoped for a rapprochement with the People's Republic of China, the United States discounted the possibility "of ever reaching a *modus vivendi* with the c.p.g." Instead, it put faith in the possibility "of an alternative Government succeeding in the foreseeable future, or at least of the partition of China into Communist and non-Communist regions."[34]

Hume Wrong, Canada's ambassador in the United States, also supported a *modus vivendi* with the communists. He told State Department officials in February 1952 that "the effect of extending hostilities to the mainland of China would be to cement relations between Communist China and Russia, whereas without further pressure the Chinese might become increasingly aware of the substantial differences between Chinese and Soviet interests." American diplomats agreed that all-out war with China would be a mistake, but they believed that their policy could force China into realizing the disadvantages of its alliance with the Soviet Union. Paul Nitze of the Policy Planning Staff told Wrong that "the State Department was inclined to exclude consideration of possible effects on Sino-Soviet relations in making up its mind about the course of action to be adopted in the Far East in any given set of circumstances." This statement was not entirely consistent with American hopes to exacerbate tensions within that alliance. What Nitze had in mind was that American pressure on China would not necessarily mean immediate Soviet intervention to save its ally. The Americans implied to their Canadian audience that the Korean War presented an opportunity for creating tensions between the two communist powers: "The Russians would be prepared to see the Chinese absorb a lot of punishment before going to their assistance." Doc Matthews and Nitze concluded that the Soviet Union would not intervene "if attacks were delivered against Communist China strictly in connection with the Korean operations."[35] This is a significant statement, indicating the U.S. view that limited war with China on the Northeast Asian periphery might present opportunities to weaken the communist alliance. The roots of the Eisenhower administration's provocative strategy for ending the war lay in the Truman period.

The Sino-Soviet alliance did not represent as great a threat to the United States as it did to that country's North Atlantic partners. From the allied point of view, American thinking was risky and might initiate a series of chain reactions leading to global war. If those emotions could be tempered, U.S. strategy would be more prudent. Motivated in part by feelings of retribution and frustration, U.S. policy nevertheless was based on a logical and plausible assessment of Sino-Soviet relations. But it was a potentially high-risk one that could lead to trouble if the assessments turned out to be wrong. It would be wise, however, to avoid associating British and Canadian policy with superior moral justification. In terms of power politics, the allies simply preferred to pursue a more cautious policy. Differences arose over tactics but not over the basic requirements of containment.

THE UNITED NATIONS RESOLUTION, DECEMBER 1952

In the fall of 1952 the United States introduced a resolution into the United Nations which reaffirmed the right of prisoners of war (POWs) to decide individually about repatriation. Allied support for this resolution deteriorated, however, when India's foreign minister, Krishna Menon, proposed that a neutral commission be established to discuss the ultimate fate of the POWs. The British and Canadians welcomed this initiative, but the U.S. government refused to be committed to it because of ambiguities in the proposal regarding the period of time POWs would be held by the commission. To American policymakers, the Indian position represented appeasement of the communists. During the ensuing allied debate over the Indian resolution, Dean

Acheson put "enormous pressure" on both Britain and Canada to reject it. Echoing the conclusions of NSC 118/2, the U.S. secretary of defense, Robert Lovett, warned that if an honourable settlement was not achieved, there would be "a strong possibility" that the United States would resort to military force.[36]

The eventual U.S. decision to vote for the resolution in December 1952 represented a partial victory for allied diplomacy. It demonstrated that the Commonwealth could influence the United States in favour of India's position on important issues at the United Nations. In other ways, however, the victory was a pyrrhic one. At the United Nations, Andrei Vyshinsky criticized the Indian initiative on November 10 and 24, and his actions may have been instrumental in bringing the United States and India closer together. His attacks made it clear that the resolution would not be accepted by the communists, who still insisted on unconditional repatriation.

British and Canadian officials were sceptical about the ultimate success of the Indian resolution anyway, but the Indian government hoped that its resolution might open up opportunities for a breakthrough in the negotiations. Pearson and Eden, along with Selwyn Lloyd, Britain's representative at the United Nations, worked closely with Menon to alter the resolution to make it more acceptable to the American delegation. The original idea underlying the proposal – that of putting as little stress as possible on the principle of non-forcible repatriation – was thereby distorted. Under strong Commonwealth pressure, the Indians made considerable compromises on their original proposal.

The final resolution specified that prisoners who refused repatriation sixty days after a political conference on Korea would be handed over to a U.N. commission; as well, it affirmed the principle of non-forcible repatriation in its preamble and in annexed proposals. In the end it was the Indians, not the Americans, who had substantially altered their position. As a British memo pointed out on 24 November, Acheson had "recognised the great value of an Indian resolution embodying our principle of no forced repatriation."[37] In essence, the West viewed India's support on the POW issue as a propaganda victory; none of the Western powers seriously expected the communists to accept the resolution, which was adopted by the General Assembly on 3 December by a vote of 54–5.

Attempts by Britain and Canada to get Indian agreement on the United Nations resolution demonstrated their continued hopes for an Indian diplomatic presence in the settlement of Far Eastern issues. For Foreign Secretary Anthony Eden, India's vote was good publicity for Western policy in Asia and "represented the beginning of an alignment of Asian opinion in a more positive sense on the side of the free world."[38] The Canadian prime minister, Louis St Laurent, agreed with this assessment. Meeting with the United Kingdom cabinet at the beginning of December 1952, he stated that India's initiative at the United Nations "had given great encouragement to all Commonwealth Governments," and that the large number of states that had supported the resolution "was an encouraging demonstration of the strength and solidarity of democratic feeling throughout the world." Nevertheless, the Indian partnership in Asia remained of secondary importance – as British and Canadian attempts to change the character of the initial proposals and get American approval demonstrated. At one point in the discussions, Eden assured Acheson that if it came down to a choice, the United Kingdom would vote with the United States over India.[39]

The propaganda victory which India's support for the resolution represented proved ultimately to be hollow. In 1953 a decision was taken by the Eisenhower administration that threatened to extend the hostilities if no settlement was reached. The disagreements that arose in the alliance in the process of negotiating the compromise position presented to the communists at the end of May were indicative of a widening of opinion between the United States and its allies over the best methods of achieving a settlement in Korea. Although the outward appearance of unity was reached, the allied debates in May exacerbated tensions within the Atlantic alliance.

THE EISENHOWER ADMINISTRATION AND THE KOREAN ARMISTICE, JANUARY– JULY 1953

The Truman administration considered ways of undermining the Sino-Soviet alliance through increased pressure on the Chinese periphery. In the context of its emerging "New Look" strategy, the Eisenhower administration implemented a policy designed to achieve a successful negotiation of the Korean War and put strains on the Sino-Soviet alliance. A rift in the alliance would separate China from the source of communist power. It would also reinforce America's attempts to establish its proxy allies on China's periphery: if Chinese support to communist movements in North Korea and Vietnam was reduced, America's informal empire would have a greater chance of success. The chosen method of splitting the Sino-Soviet alliance was integral to the New Look: a combination of allied support to deter Sino-Soviet machinations, and the use of informal atomic diplomacy.

The new administration's strategy was also part of larger trends in its diplomacy towards the Chinese and Soviet regimes. On 9 April 1953,

Secretary of State John Foster Dulles mentioned that it might be more economical to "combine operations in Korea and from Formosa rather than to attempt to do the job in Korea alone." The Chinese, uncertain of U.S.–U.N. intentions, would stretch their military capabilities, making it harder for them to prosecute the war in Korea. For Dulles, this "was an ideal opportunity for exploiting sea and air power." He was sure that if the United States was willing to exploit the situation, "this would place a strain on China and Russia. This would give us the best chance of securing our objectives either with fighting or without fighting."[40] U.S. policy towards Formosa and Korea in the first half of 1953 was part of a larger regional objective of weakening Chinese power and Soviet influence in East Asia.

The British cabinet received an early indication of the new Republican government's policy towards China at the end of December 1952. The foreign secretary warned his colleagues that the Americans "might seek to free their hands in dealing with the Korean situation by repudiating President Truman's declaration that the Formosa Straits would be neutralised." America's policy towards Taiwan was a thorn in the side of Britain's containment of China. Like an economic embargo, or an extension of hostilities in Korea, U.S. actions respecting Taiwan threatened the possibilities for a regional settlement of Far Eastern issues. "From the political angle there would be great disadvantage in taking this limited and unproductive step," Eden warned, and it was up to the United Kingdom "to dissuade the new United States Government from taking it, at any rate until there had been an opportunity for full Anglo-American discussion on the whole Far Eastern situation."[41]

President Eisenhower and Dulles met with Prime Minister Churchill and Eden in early January 1953, but British representations regarding Taiwan were unsuccessful. On 30 January, Assistant Secretary of State John Allison told the British counsellor in Washington that the United States could no longer "continue a situation which in effect has meant that the U.S. Navy has served as a defensive arm of the Chinese Communist aggressors, so that they can with greater impunity kill United States and U.N. troops in Korea."[42] A message from Eden to the U.S. government on 2 February noted Britain's "serious misgivings" regarding the American decision; it observed that the political consequences would outweigh any military advantages and that it would not help "in any way towards a solution of the Korean conflict."[43] The next day, in his State of the Union address, Eisenhower told the American public that the fleet would no longer shield the Chinese mainland. The U.S. government had thus demonstrated that it was prepared to negotiate with China only on terms of its own choosing.

The threat to the government of the People's Republic also became more explicit. A study prepared by the National Security Council (NSC) in the spring of 1953 pointed out that the detachment of China from the Soviet Union might not be possible. In an apocalyptic allusion, the authors of the study wrote: "In such a case nothing less than [the] complete obliteration of the regime would satisfy U.S. objectives."[44]

The rollback of Chinese communism remained more of a theoretical than real goal of the administration. In late 1953 the Joint Chiefs of Staff recommended that the United States should state "as an ultimate though not an immediate objective the removal of the present Chinese Communist regime and its replacement by a regime not hostile to the U.S.". At the NSC meeting held to discuss the proposal, General Bedell Smith summed up the consensus by noting that he had no objection to the chiefs' recommendations but the current situation "offered very little prospect of upsetting the present regime."[45]

The destruction of the mainland communist regime through the deployment of Nationalist troops was not defined as a policy objective in this period. The only way the Nationalists would be able to overthrow the communists would be with overt U.S. aid, a condition that would probably ignite global war – something the Americans wanted to avoid. The Sino-Soviet alliance did act as a deterrent to American strategy, but there was no long-term commitment not to replace the central People's government with Chiang Kai-shek's forces. At a meeting of the Joint Chiefs of Staff and the Department of State in April 1952, Paul Nitze argued: "We want to have as much strength as we can have. Contingencies may arise in which we will want to use Chinese Nationalists. Apart from that there is the problem of developing capabilities to bring down the Communist Chinese regime at some time." Dulles agreed with this evaluation, though after the decision to release Chiang was made, he remained concerned that Chiang's military adventures against the mainland might lead the United States into a war with China.[46]

The NSC staff study prepared in the spring of 1953 mentioned that there was no contradiction between America's limited Taiwanese strategy and its eventual hopes to displace the communist regime. It concluded that increased pressure on China that fell short of direct military intervention promoted the detachment of China from the Soviet Union while not excluding the possibility of overthrowing the communist government.[47] Despite the fact that the United States demanded and received a formal commitment from the Nationalists to consult with it in any major offensive directed against the mainland, the U.S. government did not rule out the possibility that Chiang might

replace Mao Tse-tung as head of China. The United States was prepared to export counterrevolution in the Third World if its global interests would thus be served. This was consistent with the U.S. policy of
not recognizing the Peking government, and its tendency to view communism as an illegitimate social and political force.

These perceptions help account for the U.S. involvement in counterrevolutionary movements in Asia generally. At this level, American
attempts at creating an informal empire in continental East Asia can
be seen in counterrevolutionary terms. Local centres of power were
needed on the communist Chinese periphery to support U.S. goals for
Japan and the defensive perimeter and to help stem the tide of global
communist bloc power. A noncommunist China or a China more
closely oriented towards the West would further these objectives.

U.S. policies towards China remained constrained to creating pressure on the communist periphery. This was a situation that America's
allies reluctantly accepted. The Canadian government was concerned
about the decision to unleash Chiang's forces, but it was powerless to
prevent the American decision. Like Great Britain, Canada recognized
the United States' dominant power position in the Pacific. Broader
concerns relating to the Canadian-American partnership prevented
any public criticism of American policy towards Taiwan. For Canada,
"quiet diplomacy" was often a synonym for reluctant agreement to
American policy initiatives. In this case, Lester Pearson was also as-
suaged by American officials, who told him that the U.S. action was not
a serious threat to broader Western objectives. Pearson told the Canadian House of Commons that Canada would "follow developments
with the closest possible attention and take appropriate action to make
our views known if and when the occasion so warrants." In the meantime, Pearson stated, "I think it would be unwise and premature to
jump to dogmatic or critical conclusions concerning the step taken by
the United States Government, and announced in a statement by President Eisenhower which contained so much that was wise and heartening to us all."[48] The Taiwan issue was simply not important enough to
risk a public break with the United States.

The decision to remove the Seventh Fleet was somewhat of a diver-
sionary tactic of the administration and was not meant as an immediate threat to Mao's rule. American strategy for ending the war in Korea
was potentially much more threatening for Chinese communist power.

An indication of the new administration's containment policy came
at a meeting between Lester Pearson and Secretary Dulles in mid-Feb-
ruary 1953. The secretary told a horrified Pearson that "it was Eisenhower's policy to create situations which would worry the Kremlin by
creating threats to Soviet influence at various points in the world."

When Pearson expressed concern that such a strategy would also create "uneasiness among the allies of the United States," Dulles replied that "such a war of nerves" would be difficult but that "it would be of great help if political leaders in other countries could try to increase this fund of confidence even on occasions when it might not be possible for them to explain fully United States plans and actions."[49] This did not soothe Pearson's fears. Dulles had approached Pearson in an effort to lay the basis for the administration's Cold War "New Look" tactics. The allies had been forewarned, and the Americans expected their support.

To some extent it is unfair to describe American policies towards the armistice negotiations as "strategies" because, as Edward Keefer has pointed out, the administration lacked a coherent strategy for ending the war until May 1953.[50] Nevertheless, the decision of the National Security Council on 20 May to extend air and ground operations "if conditions arise requiring more positive action in Korea" can only be seen in the backdrop of the earlier considerations of the Truman and Eisenhower administrations. This decision confirmed that the administration was willing to use tactical atomic weapons against Manchuria in order to achieve an "honourable" settlement.

After the event, both Eisenhower and Dulles argued that U.S. threats played a critical role in getting the communists to agree to the armistice proposals tabled by the United Nations Command (UNC). The decision to resort to atomic diplomacy, however, was not an invention of the Republican administration; it was implicit in the Truman administration's policies for ending the war. As the study accompanying NSC 118/2 had warned, an American decision to break off negotiations "would imply willingness to increase substantially the scale of military action and to extend the conflict."[51] The Republican government's strategy was the logical product of American officials' conception of "limited war." The allies understood this and were very wary about giving support to a position which they felt was both unnecessary and too provocative. Despite these reservations, they recognized the need to give public support to the American initiative against the Sino-Soviet alliance and to uphold a united front. As in the winter of 1950–51, the broader goals of the North Atlantic alliance on the Northeast Asian periphery were upheld.

The major factors forming the background to the American decision were the need to enhance the United States' global security position by disengaging troops from Korea, a feeling of disillusionment about the possibilities of negotiating a truce through the United Nations, and a belief that the armistice negotiations, combined with the death of Stalin, presented an opportunity to create tensions within the

Sino-Soviet alliance. This last aspect was particularly important, and it has been ignored in the historiography on the war.

On 30 March, Chou En-lai, China's foreign minister, broadcast a speech in which he announced that his government would agree to an exchange of sick and wounded prisoners. Chou also proposed that POWs unwilling to be repatriated should be transferred to a neutral state. America's allies viewed the speech as a significant compromise, but American officials did not interpret it as an opportunity to achieve an early armistice. Instead, a series of decisions were taken which culminated in the threat to use further force if UNC terms were not accepted. In part, American policymakers were hoping to capitalize on possible Sino-Soviet differences over the Korean prisoners-of-war issue.

Various State Department and NSC papers provided the context for the American strategy, but the death of Stalin appears to have been the critical catalyst. On 7 March, two days after Stalin's death was announced, Charles Bohlen, soon to be America's new ambassador to the Soviet Union, wrote: "Our plans should be directed for exploiting 'an emerging situation' which, of course, we must watch from day to day, e.g., helping to stir up some of the developments in China and the satellite states if and as we see them taking form."[52]

Several days later, a memo by Paul Nitze, entitled "Exploitation of Stalin's Death," noted that "a real possibility" to exploit his death might arise in the next few months. Nitze recommended that the United States "make a settlement of the Korean armistice the principle immediate target" of this strategy. A successful settlement in Korea would improve America's strategic and political flexibility and create "a situation in which the possibilities of developing rifts between Mao and Malenkov, would be enhanced"; the United States should be prepared to take "substantial risks and pay substantial costs to achieve success." Anticipating elements of the American negotiating strategy in May, Nitze recommended that the UNC should release the 35,000 North Korean detainees and have Bohlen in Moscow approach Molotov "to initiate negotiations." Finally, Nitze recognized that the United States should be militarily prepared to extend the conflict: "Our position should contain an overtone of really significant military action in the event the negotiations were unsuccessful. This overtone should be no mere bluff."[53] This is a significant statement, demonstrating the overall trend towards a harsher line on China in an attempt to undermine the core of communist power and orient the Chinese government away from the Soviet Union.

C.D. Jackson and the Psychological Strategy Board (PSB) were intimately associated with these moves. A telegram delivered to the PSB from the Department of the Army in Yokahama, Japan, pointed out that all UNC "radio exploitation" of Stalin's death was based on the objective of lowering the morale of Chinese and North Korean soldiers and civilians. The best means of achieving this goal was by arguing that the "war would continue, at great sacrifice by China and Korea, none by Russia, while Russian underlings compete for succession to Stalin[']s power." In this context, the satellites "would suffer even more brutally as pawns of every Russian leader anxious to gain preferment."[54]

The key was the prisoners-of-war issue. On 31 March, Lewis Clark of the Far Eastern Division noted: "We should search diligently for some crack in Sino-Soviet relations into which we could slip a wedge. We may be on the verge of momentous developments in Asia." He defined the nature of this wedge in terms of opening a possible disagreement between the Soviet Union and China on ending the war in Korea. After Stalin's death, Mao might attempt a more independent course, he said. In this case, "Mao would be restless under the restraints placed upon him because of his complete dependence on Moscow for his ability to prosecute the war in Korea. What more likely, therefore, than a move on Mao's part at this time to gain greater freedom of action by bringing about an armistice in Korea."[55] The critical intelligence assumption here was that the Soviet Union would not support the Chinese in a military confrontation with the West. The death of Stalin was important, not only because it ushered in a change in the nature of Soviet leadership but also because it changed the context in which Sino-Soviet relations operated.

A CIA memo of 8 April, prepared for Allen Dulles's use at an NSC meeting of the same day, pointed out that the Soviet Union had been engaged in a peace offensive since Stalin's death. Specific steps included the acceptance of the U.N. proposal for the exchange of sick and wounded POWs, new proposals for disarmament, the initiation of four-power discussions regarding air safety over the Berlin air corridor, the toning down of propaganda, and increased social fraternization with Western officials. The offensive constituted "a clear departure from the recent tactics of the Stalin regime." Russia's objectives, stated the memo, were to lessen the danger of war, end Western and Japanese rearmament, and defeat the European Defence Community project in Europe. The one region where the Soviet Union feared war was now Korea: "They have seen a stiffening of our own Far Eastern policy and recognize the possibility that the Korean War, if continued, might be enlarged to the Chinese theatre ... An armistice would postpone this danger." The death of Stalin made world war over Korea less likely, the memo argued: "All our estimates have been unanimous in the view that the Soviet Union has no desire to provoke or become involved in a general war *at this time*. It is not ready with sufficient atomic weapons or adequate means for delivering such weapons. Also it recognizes its present industrial inferiority to the West."[56] In the context of this Soviet desire for peace, the United States decided to risk an expansion of the Korean War into China. It was a decision inspired by calculations of power politics and Kissingerian *realpolitik.*

The American strategy appears ingenious – the idea that if the UNC threatened an expansion of the war in Korea on the POW issue, the Chinese might realize that their position in Asia was isolated and weak; and they might come to understand the extent to which the Soviet Union was prepared to let them suffer in a "limited" war with the West. It was hoped that the Chinese would eventually see that the Soviet Union was simply using China for its own purposes in East Asia, that the Soviets had little interest in China, and that Soviet objectives were dictated not by a treaty of friendship with the Chinese but by cynical political considerations. This might orient the People's Republic closer towards the West, or it might spark anti-Soviet nationalism in the People's Republic. Chinese nationalism could thus be used as a force to counter Soviet imperialism in Asia. This was part of the logic behind American thinking regarding an end to the conflict on the basis of an agreement acceptable to the United States.

The decision to increase American pressure to achieve a satisfactory settlement on Korea was taken in late April, when President Eisenhower approved NSC 149/2, "Basic National Security Policies and Programs in Relation to Their Costs." This was a major document, which related national security to the economic well-being of the United States. Paragraphs 5 and 6 defined American objectives towards China and the Soviet Union. The former underlined the need to deter the Chinese and Soviets from aggressive war and to "continue to exploit the vulnerabilities of the Soviets and their satellites." The fundamental objective remained directed at the Soviet core: the United States was to pursue these policies "with a view to the ultimate retraction and reduction of the Soviet system to a point which no longer constitutes a threat to the security of the United States." In carrying out the goals defined in paragraph 5, paragraph 6 stated that the United States should *increase* its emphasis on "bringing the Korean war to a final settlement acceptable to us."[57] Here, then, lay the linkage between the Korean War, American objectives towards the Sino-Soviet alliance, and the decision not to bargain with the communists on the basis of Chou En-lai's proposals of the previous month.

It is significant that the decision to increase pressure on the Sino-Soviet alliance relative to Korea was taken in the context of a document concerned about strengthening the economic bases of American national security. "A vital factor in the long-term survival of the free world is the maintenance by the United States of a sound, strong economy," the report noted. Current levels of government spending and the high rate of taxation were seen as threats to the long-term health of the United States economy: "For the United States to continue a high rate of Federal spending in excess of Federal income, at a time of heavy taxation, will weaken and might eventually destroy that economy." The costs of the Korean War exacerbated the problem: "So long as there is war in Korea, the United States should not substantially reduce the level, though it may change the form, of its Federal taxation."[58] The key was to find fiscal and national security programs that were consistent with the strengthening of American power.

Economic considerations thus acted as a brake on the extension of America's international undertakings, but in the short term the Republican government gave priority to its containment policies. At a meeting with congressional leaders on 30 April, the day after NSC 149/2 was approved, the president "dealt at length with the dual threat facing the United States: the external threat of Communism and the internal threat of a weakened economy. He asserted that the administration would follow a new policy which would continue to give primary consideration to the external threat but would no longer ignore the internal threat."[59] An expansion of the Korean War and its resulting added costs might not contradict the administration's economic objectives if the war resulted in a retraction of communist power.

Eisenhower himself did not see a contradiction between the use of atomic weapons and achieving a victory in Korea. On 31 March he told NSC members that "it would be worth the cost if, through [the] use of atomic weapons, we could (1) achieve a substantial victory over the Communist forces and (2) get to a line at the waist of Korea."[60] The decision to accept NSC 149/2 on 29 April was consistent with Eisenhower's thoughts on this matter.

Finally, NSC 147 defined the military context for the possible use of atomic weapons in the war in Korea. This document spelled out six alternative strategies that the administration could pursue in expanding the war to achieve its political objectives. These ranged from a build-up of ROK forces to the coordination of a large-scale offensive and air attacks in Korea and Manchuria. A report by the Joint Strategic Plans Committee, entitled "Future Courses of Action in Connection with the Situation in Korea" and dated 11 May, argued: "None of the courses which extend military action outside Korea can be effectively pursued without employing atomic weapons." Even increased military pressure in Korea might require air attack in Manchuria: "Extension of activity inside Korea would probably require action, at least against enemy bases in nearby Manchuria. This too could be effectively accomplished only by using the atomic bomb."[61] Thus, additional military action could lead logically to extended limited nuclear war with China. The courses of action defined in NSC 147 should be seen not in terms of any one strategy but as a series of incremental steps that could be taken if the war was escalated. Increased pressure could be continued until the political and/or military objectives of the United States were achieved. Intelligence estimates had concluded that the Soviet Union was not willing to risk or initiate global war in the Far East. Thus, the Americans viewed their strategy as a calculated risk. They reasoned that after the death of Stalin, the Soviet Union was willing to make compromises with the West and that added pressure on the communists would result in more concessions. Their concept of limited war was seen to have strategic advantages in relation to the Sino-Soviet alliance, for they did not believe that an extension of the war into Manchuria would initiate global war. The strategy for ending the war was consistent with America's limited war aims. It was logical as far as it went, but risky. Dependent on intelligence sources, it failed to take into account the broader bases of the Sino-Soviet partnership, especially in the areas of ideology and economic cooperation.

The risks of the new policy were well understood by high-level American officials. Their concern was reflected in numerous memos and letters written in May. On the seventh, the deputy executive secretary of the NSC, S. Everett Gleason, wrote to Robert Cutler, the special assistant to Eisenhower for national security affairs, stating that, with respect to America's alternatives in Korea if the armistice negotiations failed, "the Vice-President observed to me and Jimmy [Lay] that he thought the Council was fast approaching the point of being willing to take decisions which have been confronting it since the new administration took over." Vice-President Nixon had said that any discussion about what to do if the armistice negotiations failed had to deal with a much larger issue: the possession by the Soviet Union in the near future of "a stockpile of atomic weapons sufficient to deal this country a very heavy blow." The vice-president, noted Gleason, firmly believed that "the immediate problem of our future courses of action in Korea should be discussed by the Council with an eye to the prospect of a large Soviet stockpile."[62]

There were other indications of American concern. C.D. Jackson, the head of the Psychological Strategy Board, shared Eisenhower's fears cited earlier about Soviet intervention if the war escalated. In a letter to Assistant Secretary ("Beedle") Smith on the eleventh, Jackson attempted to convince himself that the administration's policy would not lead to global war. "In March," he wrote, "we pretty well agreed that the new Russian foreign policy would turn its attention away from the East and back to Europe. They would seek an end to fighting in Korea, and they would be willing to make certain concessions to bring this about." Events had so far proved American thinking correct, he observed. The Russians "apparently" wanted a settlement. The communists had shown a willingness for compromise, and "they will either make more or at least they will not call everything off because we refuse to fall for phoney neutral nations or an exaggeratedly long re-education." And then Jackson's final comment to Smith: "Please tell me I shouldn't worry."[63] Smith himself was not in an optimistic mood. On the sixth he persuaded Eisenhower to reschedule an NSC discussion on the political and military alternatives in Korea. Originally, the NSC had been scheduled to meet in two weeks' time. The discussion was moved up because of Smith's estimation that "it was quite possible that the armistice negotiations would break down during that [two-week] interval."[64]

The final decision to escalate the war if there was no adequate armistice was taken at an NSC meeting on 20 May. On that day, President Eisenhower approved a report by the Joint Chiefs of Staff which outlined the three most provocative scenarios of NSC 147, all of which included the use of the atomic bomb. Eisenhower said: "If circumstances arose which would force the United States to an expanded effort in Korea, the plan selected by the Joint Chiefs of Staff was most likely to achieve the objectives we sought."[65] The decision to expand the war if necessary represented one method of rolling back Soviet and Chinese influence in the Far East. Even if expanded action did not result in the overthrow of the Chinese regime, it would substantially reduce the ability of that government to undertake revolutionary actions in Asia. Limited war would destroy the bases of Chinese communist power in the short and medium term and would aid in the consolidation of pro-Western elites on the East Asian perimeter. Atomic diplomacy was consistent with the evolution of America's informal empire in Asia.

The United States was very anxious to obtain allied agreement for its decision to achieve a settlement in Korea by increasing pressure on the communists. Allied support was a fundamental objective of the administration's emerging international security strategy; it was a crucial aspect of American Cold War strategy which carried over from the Truman administration. Consideration of Soviet power was the major factor in the United States' need to get its allies' approval. A unified stance would serve as a warning to the Soviet Union and China and would fulfil the deterrent objectives set forth in NSC 149/2. In short, Western unity would diminish the risks of global war. Conversely, if a united stance was not achieved, the Soviet Union and possibly China might wish to take advantage of perceived divisions in the West by initiating war in the Far East or undertaking aggressive action elsewhere. In late May 1953, President Eisenhower told the press that "our whole policy" was based on the theory that "no single free nation can live alone in the world. We have to have friends ... We have to have that unity in basic purposes that comes from a recognition of common interests. That is what we are up against."[66]

The United States faced great pressure from its allies after presenting its counter-proposals of 13 May to the communists. The proposals included the release of all North Korean POWs on the signing of an armistice, the requirement of a unanimous vote in the proposed commission to oversee the POW issue, and a fixed date for POW release after an armistice was signed.

The Commonwealth allies of the United States were very agitated by the proposal. Prime Minister Churchill protested to the assistant secretary of state, Walter Bedell Smith, that the U.S. terms introduced a new aspect to the negotiations which "the Communists could not be expected to accept easily."[67] The Canadian high commissioner in London, Norman Robertson, reported on 14 May that Robert Scott of the Foreign Office believed that "the Communists regarded the continued demand of the United Nations negotiators to spell out the arrangements concerning prisoners as totally unnecessary bargaining."[68] Other European nations, including Holland and France, were similarly concerned; and in India, Foreign Minister R.K. Nehru and Prime Minister Pandit Nehru were upset with the American position. Pandit Nehru said he was sympathetic to the concerns expressed by Pearson. From New Dehli, Escott Reid pointed out that "suspicions here have deepened during the past few months"; increasingly, there was a feeling that the West was refusing to take advantage of the Soviet desire to reduce international tensions because of American intransigence: "If armistice negotiations fail, it will be difficult to persuade people here that the fault did not lie with the United States."[69]

In Canada, the prime minister and the secretary of state for external affairs were perplexed by the latest American bargaining position. The Canadian government soon made it clear to the United States that the proposals of the thirteenth should not be made a breaking point. On 14 May, Pearson told Hume Wrong that if the negotiations broke down over this issue, there would be widespread criticism in Canada that the reason for the breakdown was the abandonment by the United States "of principles which they had accepted at the U.N. last December." Pearson was angry at the absence of American consultation: "There would be no disposition on the part of the government to defend the recent U.S. Armistice initiative which introduced without consultation, such important changes."[70]

The United States did not have allied support for this initiative at Panmunjom. In presenting their views to the Americans, the allies recognized the implications of a breakdown in the talks. They were not prepared to support the provocative and risky American negotiating position when, in their view, the Chinese were willing to negotiate a fair armistice. Risking limited nuclear war with China on this issue was seen as the height of folly.

American and allied attempts to bring each other closer to their own position created serious strains. More than any other issue during the Korean War, the debate over the best means of achieving an armistice, in the context of apparent Chinese concessions, threatened the allied effort in Korea. At the NSC meeting on 13 May, Eisenhower stated that Anglo-American relations "had become worse in the last few weeks than at any time since the end of the war." Bedell Smith agreed that relations were "not good," and on 18 May he informed the president that the "Korean negotiations are at a crisis. Our position vis-à-vis our Allies is deteriorating daily."[71] The importance of holding the coalition together was emphasized by U. Alexis Johnson: "If we can get our Allies committed in advance to support us, we would be in a much better position to handle any U.N. action and therefore the Indian Resolution would be easier to live with." Significantly, Johnson rejected a suggestion by the chairman of the Joint Chiefs of Staff, Omar Bradley, to "tell our Allies now that we were going to void all previous agreements."[72]

The U.S. administration was prepared to make concessions on its final negotiating position to be presented to the communists. To some extent the proposals of 13 May had been designed as part of a larger strategy requiring further compromise. On 19 May, Bedell Smith outlined those concessions to the Commonwealth and stressed the need for unity. The United States had agreed to drop the requirement for releasing Korean POWs on the signing of the armistice. This did not entirely satisfy the allies, who were still reluctant to support any threat to break with the communists. Thus, when Eisenhower approved the Joint Chiefs of Staff study on 20 May, he did so without full support of the allies; perhaps this was an indication of his determination to carry out the strategy. But it was another five days before the final negotiating position of the United Nations Command (UNC) would be presented to the communists.

On 22 May the Foreign Office sent a telegram to Washington which argued that procedural matters regarding the proposed Neutral Nations Repatriation Commission should not be made the basis for a break. On the twenty-third the administration made another compromise, stating that it was prepared to accept a majority position on the commission. On the same day, Eisenhower wrote to Churchill to get

Britain's support, stating that the United States would present its final negotiating stance on the twenty-fifth: "I believe that a prompt public and unequivocal statement that the United Kingdom was fully consulted and fully supports the position which the United Nations Command is taking in the forthcoming Executive Sessions would assure an armistice promptly, if in fact the Communists want one on the basis acceptable to us."[73]

The American concessions reassured the British and Canadians somewhat, but they remained extremely reluctant to go ahead with an expansion of the war if the communists refused this "final" position. Other governments agreed. In a telegram to its embassy in Washington, the Australian External Affairs Department noted that it was "disturbed" at the NSC conclusion that if the "Communists do not accept United Nations proposals on Korea within a week or if they make no counter proposals within principles laid down General Clark will be instructed to break off negotiations, to cease to recognize demilitarized zone, to bomb Kaesong, to step up military and air operations, and to release Chinese and Korean prisoners who do not wish to be repatriated."[74]

Despite such reservations, the allies gave their public support to the proposals submitted by the UNC on 25 May. After receiving Eisenhower's message, Prime Minister Churchill supported the American negotiating position in the House of Commons on the twenty-sixth. Lester Pearson followed suit on the twenty-seventh, stating in a speech to the Canadian Club in Vancouver that the proposals "should – if the Communists are acting in good faith – provide the basis for an honourable and acceptable armistice in Korea." Canada, he said, along with the United Kingdom, the United States, and others, stood "firmly behind these proposals as fair and reasonable and in accord with the resolution of the United Nations General Assembly which was supported by 54 of its members. The Communists should not think, or try to make others think, that we are divided on this issue. We are not."[75]

Nevertheless, the allies maintained their reservations about the American proposals, and they were still unprepared to give the Americans a *carte blanche* for further military operations if the armistice terms were rejected. Canada's Department of External Affairs wrote to its embassy in Washington on the twenty-eighth: "The Australian and New Zealand Governments have expressed concern to their Embassies in Washington regarding the action contemplated by the U.S. National Security Council. We are also aware that Churchill has urged that the decision to adopt these measures be withheld until 'the break is inevitable.'"[76] The Canadian, British, and other allied representations might not have had any effect, however, for on 23 May the American Joint Chiefs of Staff had written to the U.N. commander, Mark Clark:

"If on resumption negotiations following one week recess ... Commies reject UNC proposals, make no proposal of their own incorporating basic principles of UNC proposals or otherwise provide no basis for further useful negotiations we consider that negotiations should be *terminated* rather than recessed, and agreements affecting the Kaesong-Panmunjom-Munsan area should be voided."[77] This would be the first stage of a broader escalation, which would include, if required, atomic weapons.

In making their decision to support the American position publicly, Britain, Canada, and Australia reaffirmed their special relationship with the United States. Their decision also reflected a perceived need to maintain a credible Western deterrent to the Soviet Union. A break between the allies on this issue would have represented a major danger: it might have threatened America's commitment in Europe, enflamed the fires of isolationism, and perhaps led to an even more dangerous American unilateral decision in the Far Eastern theatre. On 30 May, Hume Wrong wrote that the "present critical stage in Korean developments is dominated by the intransigence and unreasoning tendency to 'go it alone' by the extremists." Wrong lamely recommended Canadian support of Eisenhower's Cold War policies: "In this situation the moderating and steadying influence of President Eisenhower is more important than ever and merits our support."[78]

The allied consensus was summed up aptly by the prime minister of Australia, Arthur Menzies. Writing to Sir Percy Spender in Washington, Menzies reported that although there was still a "substantial risk" that the war would escalate if started up again, "we must exercise considerable caution in pressing the United States for further delays or concessions." He felt that "we should be careful in criticising Americans for an 'interventionist' policy even at times when such intervention may appear to be over-zealous ... It is not so very long since we were criticising [the] United States for pursuing an isolationist policy." Although it was important, he said, to "do our utmost to modify American policy in accordance with our wishes, so as to prevent adoption of extreme courses which seem to us unwise, we must at the same time remember that the world could suffer no greater catastrophe than reversion by United States to a policy of isolationism. Recent trends in this direction are too significant to be under-estimated."[79]

During the crisis over Korea in the winter of 1950–51, there had been limits to the allies' "diplomacy of constraint." In 1953 both sides again compromised their preferred positions to come to an agreed strategy to present to the communists. America's allies supported a modified American position: their special relationships with the United States over the Korean issue were again upheld.

Any discussion of what the allies would have done if the communists had not accepted the UNC position is hypothetical. However, the importance of the special relationship and the need to maintain a united stance in the light of possible Soviet intervention points to the conclusion that they would have reluctantly supported a further expansion of the war, including the use of atomic weapons.

In the event, the communists accepted the U.S. proposal of the twenty-fifth, and the long-drawn-out negotiating process came to an end on 27 July when an armistice was finally signed. It is difficult to say if the American strategy had any impact on Sino-Soviet relations. In the long term, it may have contributed to tensions regarding China's interest in developing nuclear capabilities. In the short term, however, the Soviet Union denied that it had any influence over the negotiations at Panmunjom. It also appears that the Soviets were satisfied with the armistice. In early June the Soviet foreign minister, Vyacheslav Molotov, wrote to Churchill that he could "state with satisfaction that the path to a successful conclusion of the negotiations has already been marked out."[80] Now that formal hostilities in Northeast Asia had ceased, America's allies could heave a sigh of relief and look forward to possibilities for a broader settlement of Far Eastern and global issues with the Soviet Union.

THE ARMISTICE NEGOTIATIONS AND INFORMAL EMPIRE

In accord with its containment objectives, the United States strengthened the military power of the Republic of Korea (ROK) after 1951. NSC 118/2 announced that allied forces would be replaced with indigenous units; national security interests required the United States to "develop and equip dependable ROK military units, as rapidly as possible and in sufficient strength, with a view to their assuming eventually responsibility for the defense of Korea."[81] This decentralization of the U.S. presence in Korea was given further impetus by the need to redeploy troops to areas of greater strategic concern. The costs of utilizing indigenous forces were far less than the expense of keeping trained Western armies in the republic. By 1953 the United States was prepared to equip and train twenty ROK divisions representing several hundred thousand men, but it also told Korean diplomats that the ROK had to provide assurances that it would support the armistice and agree to achieve unification through peaceful means.

Politically, the Rhee government keenly asserted foreign and domestic policy goals that often conflicted with America's regional containment policy; in military issues, the South Korean position on the armistice negotiations differed substantially from American containment policies. The Korean position was summed up in early 1952 by the acting prime minister, who pointed out that the ROK would not accept an armistice unless all Chinese forces were evacuated, the North Korean military disarmed, and full representation given to the ROK at an international conference. The ROK also wanted to retain its sovereignty in issues related to North Korea, and argued that no aid be provided to the communist regime. In essence, these demands represented South Korea's attempts to retain full control over the process by which the North would be integrated into the South. Although Secretary of State Dulles was sympathetic to the South Korean bargaining position on some issues and although he toyed with the idea of neutralizing a unified Korea, on the whole the Americans purposely limited the ROK's role in the armistice negotiations. American officials generally recognized the position of the Koreans and tried their best not to exacerbate the differences between the two countries. On 10 July 1952 the U.S. ambassador, John Muccio, wrote to the State Department warning that the ROK hoped for a breakdown in the ceasefire talks: "ROK leaders, recognizing their powerlessness to influence turn of events, are understandably sensitive to minor role they permitted to play in negotiations ... I have suggested to Ridgway importance of playing up, particularly from publicity point of view, participation of ROK representatives."[82]

In the months leading to the armistice, Rhee continued to demand the immediate reunification of the entire peninsula through the use of military force; large public rallies were held throughout the country protesting the armistice terms and demanding the surrender of the North Korean army and the withdrawal of all Chinese soldiers from the peninsula.[83]

There is little evidence to suggest that until early May 1953 the United States took seriously the ROK's position on the armistice negotiations. On 12 May, General Mark Clark wrote to the Joint Chiefs of Staff: "To the best of my knowledge since the armistice negotiations commenced the UNC has never been required to obtain, nor have we solicited, the approval of the ROK Government in advance of taking any of our negotiatory positions or in our negotiating tactics."[84] The UNC's proposals of 13 May were in part designed to placate Korean protests against the armistice terms, but this strategy was unsuccessful. Again without prior consultation, on the twenty-fifth the United States requested the Korean government to support the armistice proposals. Korean compliance was not forthcoming. On 29 May, President Rhee insisted that unless the conflict was continued, he would remove eighteen ROK army divisions from UNC control. These units would then be ordered either to make a suicidal attack on the North or to withdraw from their positions, thus inviting a northern push southward. The following day, Acting Secretary Bedell Smith told Ambassador Hume Wrong that the United States was having "extremely acute difficulties" with Rhee, who was being "completely uncompromising." The threat appeared to be real, since the South Korean chief of staff had told Smith a few days earlier that "he would, as a soldier, execute any orders given by his government even though he knew they were suicidal."[85]

President Rhee's rhetoric threatened to engulf the United States and its allies in an extended war with China. In an ironic twist, he became a force undermining the bases of America's informal empire in Korea. Further exertion was required to ensure that the ROK pursued policies that were in accord with U.S. strategy for the peninsula. To prevent the ROK army from acting unilaterally, the United States provided it with a limited three-day supply of ammunition.

Despite Rhee's threats, the Korean troops held their ground, in part because the United States agreed to negotiate a mutual defence treaty with the Republic of Korea. However, Rhee understood his government's great dependence on U.S. favour for its survival, so although he was willing to press the Americans to the full extent of his abilities, he believed that there was little choice for Korea but to follow America's lead. U.S. officials recognized this as well. Ambassador Briggs wrote to Dulles on 5 June: "Rhee clearly understands that the issue is drawn and also that, unless he collaborates, he cannot expect to receive U.S. support – military, economic or otherwise – which if he collaborated, American people would be glad to extend." Through a combination of dissuasion and some concession, Rhee was effectively prevented from carrying out his threats. General Mark Clark put it succinctly when he said that Rhee understood "the facts of life." South Korean officials would have disputed Dulles's claim on 15 July when he told British and Canadian officials that the UNC "had been obliged to point out to the Communists that it could not give an absolute guarantee regarding the action of the government of the Republic of Korea, which was a sovereign government." In the grey area between "absolute guarantee" and formal "sovereignty" lay America's informal empire in Korea.[86]

The United States and its allies received another scare from Rhee on the eve of the armistice when he unilaterally issued orders for the release of the North Korean prisoners. This action was potentially dangerous, but relative to Rhee's threats to withdraw from the line or attack unilaterally, his action proved ineffective. However, it may have been important psychologically in restraining him from taking actions which threatened the further extension of hostilities. The Korean civil war, a product of international tensions between two rival cores of power, had been effectively contained on the basis of an implicit spheres-of-influence agreement. There was little Rhee could do to change this situation. The fighting was over.

THE EXTENSION OF WAR BY OTHER MEANS: ECONOMIC CONTAINMENT IN KOREA

The war was stalemated, but U.S. policymakers did not lose hope of recovering a unified Korea in the Western camp; plans were laid that were meant eventually to orient North Korea towards the West. Thus, the armistice did not put an end to American containment goals towards Korea; it only altered the methods employed to retract the power of communism on the peninsula.

U.S. economic aid to the South Korean government was designed to work as a magnet and to make North Koreans realize the material benefits of Western capitalism. The reconstruction of the Republic's economy was perceived as a peaceful means of weakening communist influence in the North. After 1951, the Americans became increasingly concerned about the state of the ROK economy. The major U.S. objective in this respect was to stabilize the Korean economic situation by maintaining a low inflation rate. This was proving difficult because of the ROK's determination to spend huge sums of money on its military machine. The 1948 Economic Cooperation Administration (ECA) agreement had required the ROK to establish a "counterpart fund" that was subject to joint control by the two states and was equal to the value, in local currency, of U.S. dollar aid. However, the Americans argued that their role in the Korean economy was insufficient for them to control the economic situation. More interference in the Korean economy was therefore necessary. In early 1952 the United States attempted to negotiate an agreement for the further coordination of economic aid, but in March Ambassador Muccio told Washington officials that relations between the ROK and representatives of the commander-in-chief, UNC, had "become so acerbated that any further attempts at negotiations by same officers from Tokyo would be most inadvisable." What was needed, reported Muccio, was a high-level joint economic coordination committee "empowered to take such steps as are necessary to stabilize local economic and financial situation."[87] In effect, he called for further direct American intervention in the Korean economy. Subsequent events demonstrated the dynamics of the economic aspects of the American informal empire in Korea.

In April 1952 a special presidential mission was dispatched to Korea headed by Clarence Meyer, a man with significant experience with the ECA in Europe. The concerns of the ROK government with respect

to this new American initiative to direct the Korean economy were expressed during the mission's second meeting with ROK representatives. Both Pyun Yong-T'ae, the ROK foreign minister, and Paik Tu-
Chin, the minister of finance, raised questions about the scope of the
proposed Combined Economic Board (CEB). According to the minutes of the meeting, Mr Pyun pointed out that the mission chart of
the CEB "presupposed a rather complicated organization practically
paralleling that of the ROK government." Paek agreed, noting that the
American proposals "would get the Board involved in internal administrative matters which should be the sole concern of the ROK Government," and he said that the joint board should restrict itself to
working with the U.N. relief programs and support for the ROK economy. This suggestion clearly undercut the objective of the U.S. mission, and Meyer "stressed the need for a joint organization with
authority to coordinate all economic aspects of the combined UC-ROK
effort in Korea"; the committee had to be able to deal with all the
"fundamental problems in the economic sphere ... Continuous joint
action was required to combat inflation and other problems." Meyer
continued to press and "expressed amazement at the hesitance of the
ROK delegation to enter into the formation of a joint organization."[88]
After he threatened to depart without an aid agreement, the Koreans
agreed to the establishment of the joint board. Thus, the United
States successfully tied its economic aid agreement to further control
over the ROK economy.

The Combined Economic Board effectively replaced the Joint Economic Stabilization Committee to coordinate American and Korean
policy on Korean economic issues. The 1952 agreement had given the
United States an equal share in economic decisions dealing with the
use of Korean dollars that had been received from the United States in
repayment of hwan that had been spent on U.S. military operations.
By the terms of the agreement, the Americans had an effective veto
over the use of ROK foreign exchange credit coming from the United
States. Although foreign exchange derived from ROK exports was theo-
retically to be controlled by the Korean government, another clause of
the 1952 agreement said that both types of foreign exchange were to
be "coordinated by the Board, in order to integrate the use made of
such foreign exchange with the imports included in the Unified Command assistance programs."[89] The Combined Economic Board was
thus a significant mechanism through which the United States hoped
to control ROK inflation and build up the Korean military establishment consistent with American containment objectives. The board initially consisted of a representative of the ROK, Prime Minister Paik
Tu-Chin, and an American representative from the UNC.

In an effort to define the needs of the Korean economy further, President Eisenhower sent an economic mission to Korea in the spring of 1953. The special representative for Korean economic affairs, Henry Tasca, forwarded the mission's recommendations to the president in mid-June. In his letter of transmittal, Tasca recommended a "three-year integrated economic program of military support, relief and reconstruction" totalling approximately $1 billion. He emphasized the need to provide logistical and moral support to the South Korean armed forces, to replace American troops with Koreans, to develop Korea as a market for Japan, and to provide "an example to the rest of free Asia and the free world generally that resistance to aggression will bring forth effective moral and material assistance from other nations of the free world."[90]

The enthusiasm accompanying U.S. efforts to rehabilitate Korea were truly amazing and fuelled the administration's world struggle against communism. The post-armistice era in Korea was seen as a showcase of America's power and wealth. In a meeting with fourteen other nations that had participated in the conflict, Dulles revealed that the United States was "extremely anxious to start the economic rehabilitation of South Korea in a way that would be impressive not only in Asia but throughout the world as an example of what the free nations can do." He believed that the free world, led by the United States, could peacefully undermine the bases of communist power. Economic aid had "the best chance of bringing about the peaceful unification of Korea as it would make Korea an almost irresistible force attracting the North Koreans."[91] Eisenhower, too, was very optimistic about the role the U.S. armed forces could play in providing peacetime assistance to Korea. In a draft letter to Dulles and the mutual security administrator, Harold Stassen, he wrote: "It strikes me that never before have the armed forces of the United States had a better opportunity to contribute more effectively than they now have in Korea toward helping win the cold war, just as they have done their share in the hot war in Korea."[92] Economic aid was a very important means of consolidating America's objectives towards Korea in the post-armistice era.

American aid to Korea was also intended to help achieve broader containment policies and to reinforce the regional power dominance of Japan as the bulwark of anticommunism. There was concern in the United States about how the end of the Korean War would affect the Japanese economy, especially given America's hope that Japan would act as a stabilizing factor against Asian communism. The economic future of Japan depended on its ability to trade with the free world, for Japan's traditional market source of supply in China had been cut off as a consequence of the Chinese revolution. But tariff barriers in the United States also worked to the detriment of Japanese economic security.[93] A partial solution to these problems lay in expanded trade with South Korea. Tasca argued that economic assistance to Korea would provide "strong collateral support to the Japanese economy and Japanese economic orientation toward the free world by developing increased trade between Japan and Korea at a time when potential reduction in U.S. military procurement in Japan and continued loss of a large export market in China may tempt Japan to seek additional markets in Communist areas."[94] Korean rehabilitation would help alleviate the strains caused by the imbalance in world trade and the rise of communism in Asia, and would promote the ROK as a regional containment actor. Rhee appeared satisfied with these American goals. On the day the armistice was signed, he wrote to Eisenhower: "I have much for which to be grateful to you, and cause to rejoice that in these desperate days our beleaguered nation has found so good a friend. Your great generosity in rushing through this last week of the Congressional session an immediate appropriation of two hundred million dollars to speed our reconstruction is appreciated from the depths of our hearts."[95]

Despite this welcoming attitude towards U.S. aid, Rhee disliked America's ability to direct specific aspects of South Korea's internal economic development. The Tasca mission helped set in motion a debate between the United States and ROK economic officials over the Korean-American Combined Economic Board. In the fall of 1953, in line with Tasca's recommendations to the president, a new civilian coordinator was appointed to serve on the board. Tyler C. Wood, the economic adviser to the commander-in-chief of the U.N. Command, was appointed to the board as "economic coordinator."

One of Wood's most important duties in the first few months of his appointment was to negotiate an economic agreement with the ROK that would strengthen the position of the dollar in relation to the hwan. In late October, on the eve of an apparent agreement, Paik told Wood that Rhee wanted omitted from the agreement any reference to the coordination of ROK free dollars through the Combined Economic Board. Wood was instructed by the U.S. government to stand firm, and the difficult negotiations continued. Another conversation between Woods and Paik, however, confirmed that the "ROK govt wishes to amend or ignore provision of May 1952 Economic Coordination Agreement which explicitly gives CEB control over ROK dollars ... and instead merely to supply information as ROK is supposed to do in the case of dollars derived from exports." The prime minister had told Wood that if this and other demands were not met, "I am afraid President will say let us have no aid program."[96] Despite these warnings, the South Korean government lacked the resources to carry out such threats. Its eventual reluctant acquiescence to U.S. demands reflected how dependent the ROK was on U.S. aid in order to survive. On 14 December an agreement was reached that met most of the American requirements. A report from the U.S. Embassy in Seoul on 18 December 1953 noted that the economic coordinator's "success in obtaining ROK signature without further concession ... may prove helpful in future relation[s] with [the] ROK Govt." The critical factor forcing the Koreans into agreement had been Wood's "resolute firmness in refusing [to] send Washington further firm requests for procurement until agreement had been reached." Although Wood had demonstrated "tact, patience, and consideration for ROK sensibilities,"[97] the United States had won another important battle in achieving its goals for Korea. The negotiations had helped to sustain its informal empire in South Korea.

6 The Political Economy of Containment and Detente, 1953–1954

Recent accounts of East-West relations after the death of Stalin centre on Churchill's search for a *modus vivendi* with the Soviets.[1] Although these analyses rightly emphasize the European dimension of Churchill's diplomacy, there are two important components to his government's strategy that have been largely ignored. First, historians have tended to downplay the economic factors that impelled the Conservative government towards a détente in East–West relations. Second, the role that the Far East played in the overall British strategy of working for détente has been inadequately explored. The diplomatic strategy of the Conservative government will be analysed in the light of these two factors.

The relationship between economic considerations and foreign policy goals will be made with specific reference to the administrations of President Eisenhower and Prime Minister Churchill in the early 1950s. Economic difficulties in Great Britain created pressure for détente with the Soviet Union; American foreign economic goals, on the other hand, underlined the need for a continuing and uncompromising stance against the global communist threat. These somewhat contradictory assessments of what British and American national security interests required were evident in the two nations' Far Eastern diplomacy, especially after the Korean armistice was signed. The United States and Great Britain sought different objectives in their diplomacy in East Asia, objectives that were in part determined by their overall strategies for containing communism.

The United Kingdom hoped that the removal of pressure on China's periphery would serve to lessen tensions not only in Asia but with the Soviet Union as well. With its economic difficulties at home in mind, the British government sought a means of retracting its overextended global security commitments, preserving its colonial power in Asia, and reducing superpower tensions. Churchill himself recognized the economic strains imposed on the British economy partly as a consequence of Britain's rearmament program after 1950, and he sought to de-emphasize international conflict in order to alleviate these strains. Yet there remained a dichotomy between the United Kingdom's economic objectives and its global security needs, a dichotomy which on the whole was resolved in favour of maintaining a strong defence effort against the Soviet Union. As the prime minister told the House of Commons on 5 March 1953, Britain was devoting a "disproportionately large slice" of economic resources to defence, but it was better to err on the side of strength than to lay the country open to criticism that it was not doing its part in the defence of the free world. He remarked that Britain's defence effort was "the absolute maximum of which we are capable."[2]

Unlike Great Britain, the United States did not view the achievement of the Korean armistice as a starting point for a general lessening of international tensions with the communist bloc. In Korea, overt military conflict with the communists was replaced by a more subtle means of retracting communist power in Asia. After the war, the United States concentrated on consolidating its informal empire in Korea as a means of redistributing its men and resources to more vital areas of the globe. This process, it was hoped, would in the long term require less direct American commitment in the region. What emerged was a containment strategy that placed more emphasis on building up the economic strength of South Korea. Although the new armistice line legitimized a diminished American presence in the peninsula, U.S. policymakers believed that a revitalized South Korean economy would act as a magnet, pulling North Korea into the Western capitalist orbit. U.S. policy at the Geneva Conference on Korea in the spring of 1954 was meant only superficially to confirm the borders of the two Koreas within the international system.

American containment policy in Korea reflected the overall U.S. goal of undermining communist power on a global scale. By 1953, the United States had come to see itself as the leader of the Western camp against the totalitarian methods of communism. American officials recognized that both the United Kingdom and France were on the decline as Great Powers; pressures in these countries favouring negotiated settlements with the communists in peripheral areas only weakened Western security. Rearmament had not disrupted the American economy, and the need for increased access to markets and raw materials in the Third World strengthened arguments for continued vigilance against international communism. East Asia – and Vietnam in particular – came to be seen as an area where increased vigilance was necessary.

By 1953 America's global containment policies encompassed areas of traditional concern to the Great Powers. The limits of West European power in the nuclear age only accelerated this trend. Secretary Dulles told the National Security Council at the end of March 1953 that one factor in preventing global war "was a firm policy to hold the vital outpost positions around the periphery of the Soviet bloc"; these areas included Japan, Indochina, India, Pakistan, Iran, and the NATO region – and the loss "of any one of such positions would produce a chain reaction which would cost us the remainder."[3] The Cold War front encompassed the underdeveloped Third World.

American competition with communist movements for spheres of influence in the Third World further distanced the United States' worldwide strategy from that of its European allies. Increasingly, as European power retracted, France and Britain found themselves peripheral actors in America's struggle for power with the Soviet Union. Both 1953 and 1954 were transitional years in this process, when the French presence in Indochina was still important enough to the United States to require the Americans to make certain concessions to French public and governmental opinion regarding negotiations with the communists.

Like the British, the French hoped that the Korean armistice would open up possibilities for further settlements in Asia. However, the French government was under pressure from the United States to maintain its military effort against the Viet Minh. As we have seen, American officials hoped to forestall the premature military and political collapse of French power in Indochina. The Joseph Laniel government, which came to power in May 1953, was under strong domestic pressure to negotiate a political settlement with the communists. This led the United States reluctantly to agree to hold an international conference to discuss Indochina. From the American point of view, this concession was needed to prevent the European Defence Community from being destroyed and was a necessary step for the short-term preservation of French commitment to Vietnam.

IMPERIAL OVERSTRETCH: THE CONSERVATIVE GOVERNMENT'S SEARCH FOR DÉTENTE WITH THE SOVIET UNION

The Churchill government came to power in the midst of an economic crisis, and economic concerns defined the context of much of its domestic policy for the next several years. In the foreign policy sphere, the government cut back on successive defence budgets and sought a relaxation in international tensions. The objective was to divert resources going to military goods into civilian production for the export market. In the very first cabinet memo of the new government, the chancellor of the exchequer, Richard A. Butler, pointed out that the British economy was overloaded. The United Kingdom was in the middle of a balance-of-payments crisis which threatened Britain's reserves and economic solvency: "This very serious deterioration in our position, coming as it does at the inception and not during the full impact of the rearmament programme, threatens the whole position of sterling and of the United Kingdom in the sterling area." In addition to "serious underlying weaknesses" in the United Kingdom's position, external confidence in its ability to deal with these weaknesses was "greatly impaired." Part of the solution to the country's economic ills lay in a further expansion of engineering exports. The problem was that there was a lack of manpower for both an expansion in engineering exports and defence production. Pressure was put on the government to reduce the defence preparedness of the United Kingdom: "The fundamental question here is the priority to be given to exports as against defence orders ... the Government would need to re-emphasise the existing policy of putting full weight behind the export drive." The chancellor of the exchequer recognized that his recommendations involved a "defence risk," but in his view "the danger to our defence effort of a balance of payments crisis involving inability to buy essential food and raw materials far exceeds the defence risk of postponing stockpiling."[4]

In subsequent cabinet memos leading into mid-1952, Butler outlined a series of "remedies" designed to meet the crisis. These included cuts in social spending and defence, and a transfer of production for the home market to the external market. Recommendations were made to delay rural electrification, reduce the number of cars destined for the home market, and make a 10 per cent reduction in shipbuilding. The basic problem was outlined in a memo to the cabinet in mid-December 1951. It indicated that Cold War obligations had played a critical role in weakening Britain's economic strength. The problem was that the government was undertaking too many tasks. These included rearmament, attempting to maintain the standard of living, the sterling system, health and social services, global commitments, and overseas aid. Other problems, such as the increase in the cost of imports, the loss of Abadan, and the fall in prices of the major raw material exports of the sterling area, were beyond the ability of the United Kingdom to control. The economy had become "seriously overloaded"; there was no flexibility to deal with new difficulties, and the United Kingdom could no longer even meet previous commitments. "In consequence," the memo declared, "we are faced with a continual crisis, both internally and externally."5

Foreign Secretary Anthony Eden also was concerned about Britain's financial difficulties. But he was somewhat reluctant to face up to the limitations imposed on Britain's external policy by the economic crisis. This was particularly true of Britain's commitments in Western Europe. A cabinet memo, "German Financial Contribution to Defence," illustrated the Foreign Office's concern with the political and strategic obligations of Britain as a Great Power. One problem facing the United Kingdom was that the German financial contribution to the allied forces would fall as Germany built up its own military forces. It was estimated that by mid-1953, Britain would lose £130 million. Yet Eden and the Foreign Office were unprepared to limit Britain's obligations: "There are very strong strategic and political objections to making a large reduction in the level of our forces in Germany, so long as there is no real reduction of tension with the Soviet Union and no major change in the present situation in Europe. Any such reduction would add most seriously to the difficulties of our European policy." Eden did not believe that the solution lay in relying on the United States. This was compatible with his belief in Britain's Great Power status. The Americans would not give any guarantees regarding aid, Eden argued, and "it would be folly for us to lay our plans on the assumption that additional aid would be forthcoming."6

On the whole, Churchill was more optimistic about the Anglo-American special relationship than Eden was, but he sided with his foreign secretary on the issue of maintaining military force as a deterrent to Soviet power. In March 1954, Churchill criticized those opposition members in the House of Commons who supported German rearmament and a diminution of Britain's military power. To Churchill, a weakened defence effort meant defeat by the forces of Stalin; weakness would be an "inordinate danger to the cause of peace." Furthermore, the consequences in Germany and France "of our making a definite gesture of diminution and disarmament would be wholly bad."7 Despite these observations, Churchill was more concerned than his foreign secretary about the economic difficulties facing Britain. His attempts to advance a détente in superpower relations through personal diplomacy represented his own solution to the underlying problems of the British economy.

Although the balance-of-payments crisis lessened in 1953, there still existed structural bottlenecks associated with rearmament which posed difficulties for the government's policy of expanding engineering exports to meet the costs of imports. A paper prepared for the prime minister's discussions at Bermuda in December 1953 pointed out that the United Kingdom's defence effort had increased by more than two-thirds since 1950. Per capita expenditure on defence was the highest in Europe. The defence effort continued to affect the country's balance of payments, especially in relation to lost export opportunities. Defence production put heavy demands on Britain's engineering industries, and these companies provided 40 per cent of the country's exports. Coupled with a shortage of steel, defence requirements were "a major cause of the sharp check to the expansion of these exports during the past three years and of the marked fall in the United Kingdom's share of world trade in engineering products. Quite apart from this, high defence expenditure, by adding to the weight of taxation, has a generally discouraging effect on export enterprise."[8]

Such considerations led Churchill to recognize the need to cut British defence expenditures, but only in the context of diminished international tensions with the Soviet Union. Above all, an increase in superpower conflict should be avoided. Churchill pursued his goal in a series of speeches and advances to the Soviet Union after 1953. In a meeting with the Soviet ambassador to the United Kingdom, Mr Jacob Malik, Churchill proposed a figurative toast to "more cows and less cannons." This was a Churchillian ploy, ironical and clever, deceptively innocent. He told Malik that "the world needed opportunities for peaceful scientific development which could only be brought about by the lessening of tension and decrease of armaments." Churchill's goal was to get the Soviets to agree to mutual security guarantees against aggression, similar to the principles underlying the Locarno Treaty. He hoped to define more clearly the spheres of interest of East and West, and he wanted the Soviets to accept German rearmament without any corresponding rise in international tensions. As he told Malik, "Everybody agreed that Russia should be freed from the fear of another aggression such as that which took place in 1941. Russia had the right to be safeguarded against another Hitler."[9]

It is within this context of economic overload and European security that British policy towards the Far East should be viewed. The Korean armistice was welcomed as a factor in decreasing Western tensions with the Soviet Union, and British policymakers hoped that peace in Asia might lead to broader spheres of interest agreements between the two power blocs. The idea of a Locarno-type agreement for Southeast Asia was conceived by Eden in early 1954. Furthermore, it was convenient to fall back on a proposed détente in the Far East when it became apparent that there was little prospect for agreement on a unified Germany. This became British strategy during the Berlin Conference in January and February 1954.

THE ECONOMICS OF AMERICAN NATIONAL SECURITY POLICY

American containment policies towards East Asia after 1953 were representative of larger trends within American national security policy. These differed greatly from the British efforts to contain the Soviets through a *modus vivendi* and an informal spheres-of-influence agreement. British economic weakness called for diminishing superpower tensions, but American foreign policy in the 1950s attempted to extend Western spheres of influence on a global scale, particularly in the Third World. There were important economic considerations underpinning this expansionism. The most important were the global balance-of-payments problems and long-term access to raw materials. The economic considerations that affected Britain's search for a *modus vivendi* with the Soviet Bloc were absent in the United States.

There was a great disparity between American and British economic strength in the early 1950s: Western rearmament did not affect the American economy nearly as harshly as it did the British. The president's mid-year economic report to Congress in 1952 pointed out that the "facts reveal beyond question that the security programs now being undertaken are not even threatening – much less depleting or impairing – the strength of our domestic economy." Although defence expenditure represented a "real burden," "our business system has been doing better and our people have been living better than ever before." Western Europe's economic problems, however, worried U.S. officials.[10]

To alleviate strains caused by rearmament, the American executive branch undertook a multipronged strategy towards Europe, which involved mutual aid, increased imports, and improved Western access to the raw materials and markets of the Third World. The Mutual Security Program was designed with economic and rearmament issues in mind. The program supplied European nations with dollars so that they would be able to maintain both their rearmament efforts and their standard of living.[11] As a 1952 Bureau of the Budget memo on the Mutual Security Program pointed out to President Truman, the dollar gap must "continue to be a matter of profound concern to our national policy: European economic and political health will be jeopardized unless Europe can earn more dollars to buy from us military goods and goods vital to the functioning of its economy."[12] The aid was meant more as a stop-gap measure than as a permanent feature of U.S.–European relations. More important in the longer term was the need to provide European goods with greater access to the American market.

In 1953 the assistant secretary of state for economic affairs, Robert Asher, wrote that Europe "has had difficulty in obtaining dependable markets in the United States for its exports, and in competing with American exporters in Latin America and Asia." Both the Truman and Eisenhower administrations rejected any cutback in American exports abroad as a solution. Any such restriction would hurt America's economy and threaten European standards of living and political stability. The solution to Europe's trade imbalance with the United States, wrote Asher, was to be found in "increased production and productivity within Europe, the further development of Asia and Africa as sources of supply and markets for European products, as well as increased European exports to the United States and the dollar area."[13]

An important economic factor underlying U.S. attempts to maintain global security against the communist threat was the growing demand for the world's raw materials. The global material resources upon which the United States was dependent included tin, rubber, manganese, and tungsten. A report submitted by President Truman's Materials Policy Commission in mid-1952 stated that in twenty to twenty-five years, the United States would need three to four times its present volume of net materials imports to sustain an expanding economy. To the director of Mutual Security, Averell Harriman, the implications of the report were clear: "If we are to have access to the raw materials we shall need so desperately in the next two decades the producing nations must remain free from Soviet domination and friendly to the rest of the free world."[14] In the context of the Soviet-American competition for the periphery, the Third World took on a new importance. Continued economic strength was vital to sustaining the containment policies of the Western powers. As another assistant secretary for economic affairs, Samuel C. Waugh, put it, "Our common military forces in the free world and indispensable political stability rest upon an economic foundation."[15]

The key resources of Southeast Asia needed protection, and the domino theory posited that if Indochina was lost, they might fall into communist hands: a military defeat would force other pro-Western regimes to fall under the spell of communism, nullifying Southeast Asia as a rich and vital source of supply for the West. The power of the communist bloc would then be greatly enhanced. To counter the threat, the United States employed a combination of political, economic, and military techniques. The objective was defined not in terms of a partial victory through a political settlement with the Soviet Union and China, but through a complete defeat of communist forces in Southeast Asia. Unlike the Europeans, U.S. officials believed that they had both the political will and the necessary resources to roll back communism to China's borders in this region of the East Asian periphery.

British policy towards Asia after the Korean armistice continued to be premised on defensive lines of containment, ones designed to accept spheres of influence for the Soviets and Chinese. U.K. Far Eastern strategy was related to the combined policy objectives of containment and of establishing a working agreement with the communist world.

In Southeast Asia, British policymakers recognized the possible pitfalls of a Soviet-French agreement involving the European Defence Community and Indochina – they were thus more cautious about moving towards an accommodation with the communists in that region, lest their own interests in Malaya be threatened. As a safeguard against French enthusiasm for a negotiated settlement in Vietnam, British Foreign Office officials emphasized the importance of making progress in the Korean Political Conference before agreeing to discussions on Indochina. The British diplomats worked for an acceptance of the status quo in Korea. Denis Allen, the head of the Foreign Office's Far Eastern Division, put it succinctly: "We regard the Korean problem primarily in terms of the balance of power, between the two opposed groups of world powers, whose spheres of interest touch in the territory of Korea." The prospects for maintaining the status quo appeared bright: U.N. forces in Korea had proved a strategic disadvantage to the communists, and the Chinese had been taught their lesson.[16]

Canadian officials also looked towards reduced international tensions emerging from an acceptance of communist and Western spheres of interest in Korea. In May 1953 the Far Eastern Division of the Department of External Affairs produced a memo for Pearson entitled "Far Eastern Problems Other than Korea for Consideration by One or More Political Conferences after a Korean Armistice." Korean policy was part of a larger defensive containment strategy designed to accommodate the communists and preserve Western spheres of power in the Far East. Canada's defensive containment policy for East Asia, based on a consideration of its primary interests in Western Europe, reinforced the British position. Like policymakers in the United Kingdom, the Canadian officials saw the prospect of a détente in Asia in the context of reduced tensions between the two superpowers. Korea was only one of a number of problems in Asia that required "agreement between the West on the one hand

and Communist China and the Soviet Union on the other." A political settlement in Korea "would create a favourable climate for negotiations on other problems," including the conflict in Vietnam, Formosa, and recognition of the People's Republic of China. Canada favoured "individual consideration [of each issue] in the belief that each problem which is resolved will result in an easing of tension which in turn will make it easier for subsequent agreement to be reached on another point at issue."[17]

After the armistice, both Pearson and Eden hoped to convene a political conference on Korea as a means of achieving their broader political goals. Both men wanted Indian participation in a round table conference with the communists, a kind of meeting of minds to deal with Korea and, if successful, broader issues. India was needed as a mediator between the two power blocs and might prove a useful diplomatic tool when it came to discussing issues relating to the People's Republic. As president of the General Assembly, Pearson reconvened the seventh session in early August 1953 for the purpose of drawing up a resolution laying the groundwork for the Korean Political Conference.

THE ROAD TO BERLIN: JULY–DECEMBER 1953

The United States was not as interested as its allies in seeing a general lessening of tension in relations with the Soviet Union. Dulles's diplomacy after mid–1953 was based on his determination not to make concessions to the Chinese communists and to get the European Defence Community established. On 5 June 1953 he told the National Security Council that if the armistice was signed, all hell would break loose. There would be increased pressure from the allies for a less severe policy towards Asia and communism generally. The United States, he said, should maintain its embargo of goods against the People's Republic, because "it appeared to be causing the Communist Chinese economic suffering and might be one reason why they wanted an armistice." It would be difficult, however, to get the allies to maintain trade sanctions against China and Eastern Europe, because they were getting paid in dollars and food. In Eastern Europe, the United States had kept up the pressure by threatening to reduce aid. But as U.S. aid to Europe would soon be reduced, it would be necessary to allow the Europeans to increase some aspects of their trade with the satellites, as long as strategic goods were not exported.[18]

Dulles's strategy was formulated on two contradictory fears. He worried that a diminution of global tension might provide more ammunition to the opponents of the European Defence Community in France; on the other hand, unless some U.S. concessions were made regarding discussions for Indochina, anti-American sentiment in France might destroy the prospects for the passage of the Treaty. Above all, it was essential to avoid an East-West discussion linking Korea with Vietnam. It was vital to isolate the issues of possible disagreement, because France's commitment to fighting the communists in Indochina was diminishing.

NSC 162/2, "Basic National Security Policy," dated 3 October 1953, outlined some of the weaknesses in the allied coalition. One source of concern was European colonialism. In Asia and Africa, stated this document, the colonial problem "has not only weakened our European allies but has left those areas in a state of ferment which weakens the whole free world." European opinion was now less inclined to follow American initiatives and leadership: "Many Europeans fear that American policies, particularly in the Far East, may involve Europe in general war, or will indefinitely prolong cold-war tensions." The tone of the paper contrasted sharply with the allied goals of meeting the communists at the bargaining table. It argued that the alliance's cohesion was undermined by the fact that America's partners tended to view Soviet aggression as "less imminent" than the United States did; and that these factors led to "allied pressure in favour of new major efforts to negotiate with the USSR, as the only hope of ending the present tension, fear and frustration."[19]

Concern about Europe's security continued to dominate U.S. global strategy. American national security depended above all on the industrial power of Western Europe. In a restatement of George Kennan's basic thesis, NSC 162/2 insisted that without these allies, the United States could not afford to meet its defence requirements. It needed "to have aligned on its side in the world struggle, in peace and in war, the armed forces and economic resources and materials of the major highly-industrialized non-communist states." If these states fell into the Soviet sphere of influence, the world balance of power would be altered to the extent of endangering "the capacity of the United States to win in the event of general war or to maintain an adequate defense without undermining its fundamental institutions."[20] American officials recognized the importance of not alienating their allies in the Cold War. The dilemma was that their Asian and global strategies for undermining communism conflicted with this basic premise.

The ratification of the European Defence Community (EDC) by the French parliament was the cornerstone of the Eisenhower administration's European strategy at this time; the EDC would permit the rearmament of West Germany and would bolster the military deterrent against the Soviet Union. The integration of West Germany into the anticommunist core went beyond pure military reasoning; it underpinned America's global containment strategy of denying further industrial and economic potential to the Soviet Union. During discussions with British and French officials in London in October 1953, Dulles noted that the future of Europe and all Western civilization depended on this "opportunity to integrate Germany with the West." He warned that "unless Europe moves forward" with the EDC, the United States "will be forced against our will to explore new alternatives." Dulles advised his colleagues against any Locarno-type agreements with the Soviet Union before the treaty was passed.[21] Locarno had been the precursor of appeasement, and he refused to alter his dynamic containment strategy against the Soviet Union.

For the United States, the greatest challenge to the ratification of the EDC came not from France or Britain but from Soviet moves designed to reduce tensions and weaken the alliance's unity in Europe. The method the Soviets chose for weakening Western solidarity was the proposal of a five-power conference that would include Communist China. By linking Far Eastern and Western security concerns, the Soviets hoped to lower the general level of world tension, destroy the impetus for German rearmament within the EDC framework, create tensions in the alliance, and allow a breathing space for Soviet domestic goals to be achieved.

On 4 August 1953, before the General Assembly reconvened to discuss the Korean Political Conference, the USSR responded to a Western tripartite request for a four-power conference on Germany by proposing a five-power meeting. The Soviet note argued that "responsibility for the maintenance of peace and international security rests primarily ... on five powers." It adroitly suggested a possible détente in Great Power relations: "It is precisely at this time when efforts of peace-loving governments have made it possible to put an end to war in Korea and conclude an armistice that favorable conditions have been created for achieving a lessening of tension in the international situation." Moreover, the need for an examination of international issues was dictated not only by the state of affairs in Europe: "the situation of the countries of Asia" also contributed to the impetus to decrease tensions. From this it followed that "the participation of the Chinese People's Republic is necessary in a discussion of questions concerning measures for lessening tension in international relations."[22]

This theme was repeated by Chinese and Korean authorities with reference to the ongoing negotiations over the Korean Political Conference. In a letter to the secretary general of the United Nations, the vice-minister for foreign affairs of the Democratic People's Republic of Korea, Li Dong Ken, argued that the political conference would "not only discuss the question of establishing a genuine peace in Korea, but will, at the same time, discuss important questions of vital bearing on peace in Asia and the whole world."[23] The Chinese and North Koreans emphasized the importance of "neutral participants" in the conference, especially India and the Soviet Union. The communists coordinated their strategies on this issue; as Western intelligence emphasized in this period, there was a high level of coordination within the Sino-Soviet alliance. China, like the Soviet Union, was determined to work on its economic development. A detente in superpower relations would help accomplish this goal.[24]

The United States refused to concede to these communist power plays. By indicating that it would participate in the Korean conference only as a neutral, the Soviet Union was in effect averting any responsibility for involvement in Korea; this was advantageous for Soviet diplomacy in that it would prevent attempts by the West to blame the Soviet Union for a breakdown of the conference itself. Soviet demands may also have reflected a belief that there would be no agreement on Korean unification. Given British and American demands that progress be made on Korea before discussions on Indochina could begin, it is not surprising that the Soviets continued to try to get Far Eastern issues discussed as a group, and with Chinese participation, and not independently beginning with Korea, as some Western states demanded. In this context, discussions became stalemated. The new Canadian ambassador in the United States, Arnold Heeney, pointed out that Dulles realized that the Soviets did not want to meet to discuss problems of international tension on America's terms. As Dulles had told him, "United States authorities were being compelled to the conclusion that the Communists did not now want a conference to take place. Every indication seemed to confirm this."[25]

With the negative communist response to the U.N. resolutions of 28 August inviting China and the Soviet Union to a political conference on Korea, and the failure to come to any agreement regarding five-power talks, America's allies were becoming frustrated. Returning to his post in early October after an illness, Eden quipped that he was unhappy about "the present state of affairs." To the British ambassador in Washington, he complained that the Americans had taken "a contrary view to us in their conception of the Political Conference as a two-sided affair, i.e., a sort of political Panmunjom"; they had criticized British support for the presence of India at the discussions – since 28 August the British "had tried to support the decisions taken." Eden was anxious about these developments: "My fear is that failure to have the Conference may be blamed more upon the United States and its allies than upon the Communists."[26]

The French were even more anxious than the British to convene a Korean conference. They hoped that discussions would lead to talks on Indochina. On 8 October the French ambassador in Canada told Canadian officials that France was considering its own unilateral approach to China and that it hoped for British support. This information was dispatched to Heeney in Washington and was almost certainly conveyed to the American authorities. On the ninth, Pearson himself suggested to the British a modified five-power conference regarding the Far East, to begin with Korean issues. The Foreign Office did not reject the Canadian minister's proposal, but it preferred to await further developments before putting the idea to the United States.[27]

Discussions between communist and American authorities were held in Panmunjom in the autumn of 1953, but the stalemate in East-West negotiations was not broken until the end of November, when the Soviet Union decided to drop its demand for a five-power meeting and request instead a four-power meeting for Germany and Austria. The United States appeared to have won a substantial diplomatic victory. From Moscow, Charles Bohlen wrote that the "chief substantive difference" in the latest Soviet reply was the abandonment of including China in the conference. The proposed conference now posed fewer threats. Bohlen contended that since there was little reason to believe that Soviet support of East Germany had changed, "we have everything to gain and nothing to lose by agreeing to [the] Soviet proposal as soon as possible."[28] The Western response to the note was drafted during the tripartite meetings in Bermuda in early December, and at the end of the conference the two camps agreed to convene a four-power meeting in Berlin on 24 January 1954.

Although the State Department realized that the Soviets would raise the issue of a five-power conference when they met in Berlin, American officials felt that the consequences of not agreeing to the Berlin Conference might have a serious and negative impact on its European allies. The U.S. chargé in Paris, Ted Achilles, warned the department that it was best to meet with the Soviets and demonstrate to the French the essential correctness of the U.S. position. Everything should be done "which will contribute to ensuring that our role will be presented in [the] most accurate and most favorable light."[29] Ten days before the conference began, Achilles soothed some fears regarding French policy towards Germany, saying that the Laniel government would not "go any appreciable distance in possible bilateral dealings with Soviets regarding Germany." Indochina presented more difficulties. Achilles pointed out that no contemporary French government could refuse to listen to Soviet proposals on Indochina. Nevertheless, the Laniel government represented the best among other alternatives, and it was considered unwise "to discourage, or hinder, its representatives in Berlin if bilateral soundings take place." The embassy was satisfied that the French would not take the initiative with the Soviets.[30]

The difficult balancing act that the Americans pursued *vis-à-vis* the French demonstrated America's continued dependence on Great Power strength in the context of its global containment strategies. In the case of Indochina, however, it was becoming clear that there were some unwanted consequences. This transitional period in international affairs, characterized by the imperial overstretch of the traditional Great Powers, witnessed a greater willingness by the Americans to defend the endangered outposts of Western power and to assume greater responsibility for consolidating these spheres into the American-led capitalist camp. The fight against communism on the periphery was increasingly being fought by the extension of American power. This expansion manifested itself in accelerated programs of economic and military aid to proxy partners in East Asia. In Korea, the United States was in the process of consolidating its informal empire. In Vietnam, the process of substituting French influence for American was moving ahead slowly, in part because policies designed to establish semi-independent proxy collaborators were stalled by continued reliance on French colonial structures.

At Berlin, the American objective was not to let Soviet proposals undermine Western strength in Asia or Europe. But British and French hopes for a reprieve in the Cold War threatened the Eisenhower administration's more dynamic containment policies. The European countries could maintain their strength only in the context of a *modus vivendi* with the Soviet Union, however cynical such a position might be; meanwhile, American officials argued for expanded efforts of vigilance. An American position paper prepared for the Berlin conference argued, "We will endeavour to hold the French in line with respect to any overtures on Indochina."[31]

THE BERLIN CONFERENCE

The American objectives for the Berlin Conference were partially fulfilled. The three Western powers were able to maintain a united front on European issues, though the alliance was less successful with regard to the Far East. On the whole, however, a united effort was maintained and the alliance remained intact, despite important differences in objectives.

At the outset of the meetings, Eden wrote to Churchill suggesting that the United Kingdom search for a way of obtaining a five-power meeting on Far Eastern issues, and on 25 January the cabinet noted its "full sympathy" with Eden's proposals. The minutes recorded that "it would be inexpedient to resist a proposal for a Five Power meeting confined to East Asian questions and beginning with Korea." The cabinet hoped that Eden "might be able to persuade Dulles to fall in with this view."[32]

The Churchill administration's search for a détente with the communist powers did not involve any radical changes in Britain's perceptions regarding the ultimate goals of communism. Military strength was seen as the critical factor underlying deterrence strategies, and the Conservative government was not prepared to bargain away the integration of West Germany into the West. As Churchill remarked, "I do not consider that seeking friendly relationships with Russia is contradictory to forming the strongest combination possible against Soviet aggression. On the contrary it may well be true that the Russians can only be friends and live decently with those who are as strong or stronger than they are themselves."[33]

By early 1954, the Churchill administration's search for a *modus vivendi* with communism centred on the Far East. Since it was highly unlikely that any agreement would be reached over Germany, it was important to maintain at least the spirit of conciliation with the Soviets. Foreign Office officials believed that a five-power conference dealing with Asian issues would help avoid "the disappointment and danger that would follow" from failure to come to agreement over Germany. Such a conference "could do no harm and might do much good." It would involve no weakening of British military power, and it "would prevent the sense of a renewed breakdown between East and West." Even if the conference did not convene for several months, the benefits would be positive: "It would keep alive the atmosphere of easement and friendly, or at least civil, relationships between the two sides while in no way injuring our fundamental theme, namely, 'peace through strength.'"[34] The cabinet's proposals regarding the Far East emerged as a logical consequence of Britain's perceived need to work for less tensions with the Soviets and Chinese, and to maintain Western strength in Europe.

It was thus in areas of peripheral interest to the United Kingdom that it sought its objectives of détente. In these areas the crisis of British power was most obvious. Britain's policies in the Far East were subordinated to its global containment strategy. With little hope for a European settlement, East Asia was turned to in consolation. There was not much idealism involved in Churchill's "search for peace." A five-power meeting over the Far East would "cost us nothing substantial," he pointed out, and it would "make the world safer" if a conference including China "could be brought on to the scene as soon as possible, if only as a shock-absorber."[35]

The French pressed hard for a five-power meeting on Asia that would include discussions on Indochina. Foreign Minister Georges Bidault knew of American objections to such a conference, but he pointed out that the length of the war and French public opinion had made it impossible for France to elude an "honorable" negotiated settlement. On 26 January 1954 the French director for Asian affairs, Jacques Roux, told American officials that "the French expected a political conference on Korea ... and that a conference on Indochina might come immediately thereafter."[36]

Dulles was well aware of allied pressures regarding a five-power conference on the Far East. He was critical of Eden, writing to the Department of State that the British foreign minister was "very wobbly" on the issue.[37] To counter these pressures, Dulles emphasized that the success of a five-power conference would be largely dependent on the actions of Communist China: so far the People's Republic had not given any concrete examples that it had modified its aggressive behaviour. This argument reflected America's more aggressive containment strategy towards the Chinese East Asian periphery.

On 27 January, Dulles decided to make a minor concession to his European colleagues; he proposed that the four powers invite China, North and South Korea, and others for a meeting to settle the Korean problem. Out of this conference, "if Red China wants it," would arise another conference, which would deal with the "restoration of peace in Indochina." By placing the responsibility for a conference on Indochina on China, Dulles hoped that discussion on Indochina would occur only under the most favourable conditions for the West. Slyly, he realized that this was also the best method of placating European demands: "While I am far from sure that Molotov would accept ... I believe that it would result in holding [the] British and French in line, even if Molotov rejected it."[38]

The Soviets, for their part, were also anxious to reduce tensions, and they recognized that a settlement in Indochina would be a strong card for them to play. Charles Bohlen wrote from Moscow on 20 January that the new Soviet government "needs and genuinely desires some relaxation in international tension."[39] In early February, Molotov intimated that the Soviet Union was prepared to consider narrowing its conception of a five-power conference to encompass issues relating primarily to Asia. This encouraged European officials. On 10 February, Roux and Allen jointly proposed to the United States that references to China proving its good faith on Asian issues be eliminated from the conference communiqué. At the second restricted meeting, the French unilaterally proposed a text which incorporated this principle. After Eden replied that the French suggestion "represented a good compromise," Dulles was forced into a corner. Noting that the French text did not require China to demonstrate its peaceful intentions, Dulles said that "the U.S. preferred its text in this matter." There was not much use "in thinking of a conference for peace in Indochina unless, in fact, the Chinese Communists gave proof of their spirit of peace both in the Korean Political Conference and ... in Indochina." But he added that if the French proposal was agreeable to the other ministers, he would accept it.[40]

Further concessions were forthcoming. At the fourth restricted meeting, Bidault responded to a Soviet inquiry about the relationship between the Korean and Indochina conferences by stating that "there was no subordination of Indochina to Korea but both questions were subordinate to the will for peace."[41] This went beyond what the Americans wanted to concede and served to underline the tensions in the West's approach to Far Eastern issues. Capitalizing on these differences, the Soviets presented a proposal for two conferences, one for Korea and another for Indochina, both including Chinese participation, that would meet on 15 April 1954.

In accepting these proposals, the Americans had compromised their initial position regarding Far Eastern discussions. This, it was felt, had been necessary in order to maintain allied unity vis-à-vis the Soviet Union – a break with France on the issue would only increase anti-American sentiment in the country and would threaten both the EDC and France's commitment to prosecuting the war in Indochina. Ultimately, the American agreement to hold the Geneva conference represented an acknowledgement that French power was needed, in the short term in Indochina, and in the long term in Europe.

It is easy to exaggerate the degree to which the United States compromised its position at Berlin. As Dulles reported to the Department of State after the conference, the principle that there would be no five-power conference had been upheld; Communist China had not gained any prestige; and India had been excluded from the discussions. The French were still fighting in Indochina and the Navarre Plan predicted victory by 1956. Nor had the conference damaged the prospects for the EDC. Dulles did warn Bidault, however, that the upcoming conference would encourage the communists and that this would have to be met with a corresponding unity by the West if it was to have a solid negotiating position at Geneva.[42] For Dulles, then, the prospects for Indochina still appeared hopeful.

In the immediate aftermath of the Berlin Conference, the British also appeared content. Eden reported to the cabinet that the conference had not caused any break in the Western camp and that Dulles had even proved conciliatory. The basic objectives of maintaining support for the EDC and keeping a door open for further negotiations with the communists had been upheld. Churchill remarked that he was "not surprised or disappointed by the results of the Four Power Meeting. The agreement to hold a Five Power Meeting at Geneva meant that negotiations on Far Eastern problems would be continued. In Europe, the Russian attitude should help the French Parliament to proceed to ratification of the E.D.C."[43]

The twin objectives of maintaining British strength in Europe and opening avenues of negotiations with the Soviet Union did not amount to very large concessions to the Soviets. The détente which Churchill envisaged was illusory. At best – and this is what Churchill hoped for – was a period of lower risk of war and further consolidation of Western power, particularly in Europe. At base, the Conservative government's attempts to come to a *modus vivendi* with the communists rested on a recognition of the dangers of the overextension of the United Kingdom's resources. But the methods used to meet this problem did not do much to alleviate the stresses of the British economy. Overall, Great Britain continued to search for a means of retaining its Great Power status.

APPROACHING GENEVA: THE KOREAN POLITICAL CONFERENCE

American policies for Korea had broader regional containment objectives than British strategy did. In theory, the British also wanted to undermine communist power globally. But facing economic difficulties at home, and needing to placate the Chinese communists, Britain was wary of putting further pressure on this edge of Chinese territory. The British defensive strategy was aimed to a lesser extent than the American at containing global communism, and the British were more reluctant than the United States to roll back communist power in Korea. Only at the outset of the Korean War were they willing to engage their resources against the perceived threat from the communist core, the Soviet Union. They were much more cautious about maintaining that pressure once the sensitiveness of the Chinese to such action became apparent. After the armistice, the United Kingdom lacked the resources to make any important impact on the Korean economy. The job of rehabilitation fell largely on the United States, whose economic objectives for Korea reflected its greater enthusiasm for undermining Soviet influence in Asia.

The political goals concerning Korean unification were to be met through the Korean Political Conference. American officials were initially more optimistic than their British counterparts with respect to the possibilities of unification. After the armistice, the United States defined its Korean strategy in NSC 157/1. On 3 July 1953 the president approved the document's conclusion, which stated that the U.S. objective was "to secure a unified and neutralised Korea under a substantially unchanged ROK." It was hoped that the Chinese communists, in their zeal to get rid of American troops in Korea, might be willing to trade off North Korean positions. American goals "would entail Communist agreement to a unified Korea with U.S. political orientation, in exchange for U.S. agreement to remove U.S. forces and bases from Korea and not to conclude a mutual security pact with Korea."[44]

The Mutual Defense Treaty between the United States and the ROK was not seen as a threat to such an agreement, because it did not require the stationing of American troops on Korean soil. Dulles was favourable to the idea of a "neutralized Korea" at this time, and he felt that the United States was tied down too much to the demands and whims of President Rhee; a nominally neutral Korea would further American anticommunist goals and permit the United States greater flexibility in its foreign policy. However, Dulles was not willing to abandon informal empire for a united and truly neutral Korea. American influence would be sustained after unification. The United States' insistence on the constitution of the ROK as a basis for negotiation reflected its attempts to sustain the principles underlying its containment strategies for Korea. Not only would the country be politically oriented to the West, but economic aid would consolidate American influence in a united Korea.

In the fall of 1953, Dulles appeared hopeful that unification on American terms was possible. Discussing the issue with the British minister of state, Selwyn Lloyd, he said that he wanted a political conference on Korea to succeed: "The alternative was too unpleasant: i.e. a permanent United States base in Korea with the chance of Rhee starting up a war again. There was just a chance that the Chinese and Russians would also intensely dislike that alternative."[45]

While both the United States and its allies wanted the political conference to succeed, it was for different reasons. American security objectives necessitated at the very least a strengthened South Korean state, both militarily and economically. A unified Korea would be a bonus; the United States' Korean strategy held out the possibility for a further retraction of communist power in the North. Unlike its allies, though, the United States was not prepared to compromise its objective to achieve decreased tensions in Asia or Europe. Only on the basis of a unified Korea would it provide guarantees against an ROK attack on the Chinese periphery. Its attempts to achieve a unified Korea reflected a dynamic containment strategy, opposed to the more defensive ones advocated by its principal allies.

Dulles was willing to work within a strategy that was only superficially analogous to a "Locarno" framework. British officials were suspicious of it. The British minister in Seoul, Walter Graham, wrote to Lord Salisbury (who was filling in for an ailing Eden) that American goals for Korea at the conference differed in emphasis from those of Britain. Reflecting his fellow countrymen's suspicion and disregard for President Rhee, he thought American policy would augur poorly for the future of Korea and the West. The "American criterion of the success of the conference appears to be whether or not it results in the peaceful unification of Korea," he observed. For Graham, the peaceful unification of Korea was a "hallucination." Failure to unify the country "would probably lead to a resumption of the war on a far greater scale." Therefore, "some alternative must urgently be sought." The only feasible alternative was partition. If this was not accepted, the consequences might be a "war to death." Like other British officials, Graham believed that threats to the territorial integrity of the People's Republic would only lead to further trouble. Agreement based on existing spheres of power was infinitely preferable: "An anti-Communist power in control of North Korea would be as great a threat to China ... as Communist control of South Korea would be to Japan and the American defensive line in the Pacific ... There are other solutions besides unification. It may well be possible to reach a *modus vivendi*, under which the two sides, mutually antipathetic but no longer belligerent, will 'co-exist' indefinitely."[46] These goals were in line with Britain's weakened power and its need to maintain and protect its colonial interests in Southeast Asia.

On the unification issue, the British were in better touch with Chinese perceptions and objectives than the Americans were. Chinese propaganda after the armistice showed few signs of agreeing to unification on the basis of U.S. proposals. In addition, American concessions to Rhee only heightened suspicions. The United States' refusal to support the inclusion of India in the political conference, its opposition to a round table conference, and the Mutual Defense Treaty with the ROK all served to exacerbate the communists' suspicions regarding American and South Korean diplomacy.

A BBC monitoring report in September underlined the communist frustration with American policy. In a speech to the sixth plenary session of the Central Committee of the Korean Labour Party, Marshal Kim Il Sung warned that the South Koreans and Americans had made prearrangements to disrupt the conference. In addition, the "war merchant Dulles" had concluded a defence pact with Rhee to "provoke afresh a criminal aggressive war in Korea whenever necessary," he said; and despite the fact that the armistice agreement contained a clause regarding the withdrawal of foreign troops, this pact was an example of the sort of tactics that could be expected once the conference began.[47] Concrete evidence that both China and the Soviet Union preferred partition to unification lay in their respective aid agreements with North Korea in the fall of 1953. Margaret Meagher, a Canadian official in London, reported back to her colleagues in Ottawa that the Foreign Office believed the communist aid packages represented "not only a move to balance Western aid to South Korea but also a further indication that the Communists are not seriously expecting a unified Korea."[48]

THE GENEVA CONFERENCE ON KOREA, 26 APRIL TO 15 JUNE 1954

Western delegates to the Conference on Korea looked on the meetings as a good opportunity to demonstrate the intransigence of the communists on the issue of unification. In practice, however, the allies were not in complete agreement over the best means of presenting this propaganda to world opinion. In general, the European and Commonwealth representatives wanted to present a more detached and balanced perspective to the unification issue. Their major objective was to strengthen the armistice agreement. A flexible approach to the conference would ensure the continuance of the armistice, would ease tensions, and would allow for further negotiations on unification. The British plan, which the Canadian government basically adhered to, called for national elections based on proportional representation, the creation of a new constitution for Korea, and the establishment of a new all-Korean government. Elections would be internationally supervised, and only after the elections would Chinese and Western military forces withdraw from the peninsula.[49] The plan contained no explicit guarantee for the continuance of Rhee's government. The elections themselves would determine the new government, and the South Korean constitution would not be used as the foundation for the absorption of the North. These positions were "flexible," but only at a superficial level. Pearson and Eden both recognized that their proposals would result in the re-election of Rhee. So long as the principle of representation by population was adhered to, Chester Ronning wrote to Pearson, "Mr. Rhee need have no fears concerning the outcome of an election for the whole area." On 11 April, Eden wrote to the British ambassador in Washington, Sir Roger Makins, saying that the idea of simply integrating the North into the South "would be so obviously unacceptable to the Communists that it would cast doubts on our own desire to reach a settlement." But the United Kingdom had no intention of "doing away with the Republic of Korea." The Foreign Office wanted Rhee to accept its proposals for unification because "it is our belief that free elections would in fact return him to power."[50]

Within the Commonwealth, the New Zealanders tended to associate themselves with the Anglo-Canadian position. The Australians were more willing to support the Americans. On 29 April the external affairs minister, Richard Casey, told the conference that there was a strong case for arguing that elections should be held in the North only. However, it would be helpful if the South consented to supervised elections in all of Korea.[51] In general, allied proposals, apparently more balanced and fair minded in their presentation, sought the maintenance of the status quo in Korea. Unification terms implicitly backed the Rhee government and America's predominant position in the peninsula.

To an important degree, Indochinese considerations also affected the diplomacy of the Korean phase of the Geneva Conference. France and Britain in particular hoped that a "reasonable" approach to the Korean issue might contribute to a negotiated settlement in Indochina.

Violently opposed to even surface concessions to the communists, the ROK fought for the withdrawal of Chinese troops and the surrender of North Korean forces as a prerequisite to elections. President Rhee was very reluctant to agree to elections for the South and cited constitutional impediments to such elections. On 11 March he wrote to Eisenhower noting that the armistice had been signed six months ago "and now we have nothing to look forward to except a new round of fruitless talks at Geneva." The other allies insisted on "these endless conferences," he complained, but his government did not want to await unification any longer. If the UNC provided the Koreans with sufficient ammunition and air support, he said, "we shall secretly arrange with General Hull a full program of implementation." Chiang Kai-shek had agreed "to move his army on the mainland at the same time."[52]

The Americans were caught between the allied and Korean positions. They favoured national elections, but these were to be held in accordance with the constitutional processes of the South Korean government.[53] Unification based on the withdrawal of foreign forces would take place within the framework of the constitution of the ROK.

This essentially meant that a unified Korea would remain aligned to the West. The U.S. proposal, called Plan B, represented America's stake in maintaining the structure of its informal empire in a united Korea. It demonstrated that the heart of America's informal empire lay not in military or economic aid but in the political structure and Western orientation of the indigenous governments which U.S. diplomacy had helped bring to the foreground of national politics. Local collaboration was the base of informal empire, and economic and military aid its superstructure.

The major difficulties the United States faced in getting its allies to agree to its proposals were President Rhee's objections and the Commonwealth nations' tendency to work outside the formal context of the ROK political structure in formulating goals for unification. From the Commonwealth, the United States faced pressure to agree to a common negotiating position; proposals that recommended the formation of a new constitution for a unified Korea, thus rejecting the political legitimacy of the two existing governments, stemmed in part from hopes to reduce tensions in the international arena. Proposals that smacked of Western intransigence would undermine the larger objective of alleviating tension in Korea and the Far East.

The tendency to want to present a "fair" propaganda victory to the world was present in all the Commonwealth delegations. Lester Pearson described his impatience with the U.S. position in a telegram to the department on 17 May: "The American argument now being given to their impatient allies is that the Communists have so completely repudiated ... any United Nations role in a Korean settlement that it is unnecessary for us to worry about setting our own proposals. This argument, however, is not really acceptable."[54]

The United States hoped to put forward a proposal which both the allied and ROK delegations could accept. But President Rhee adamantly stuck to his position and only reluctantly agreed to make concessions to the U.S. proposals. Throughout the proceedings, Rhee tried to get American backing for a northern offensive against the communists. On 10 May he told Ambassador Briggs that if agreement was reached at Geneva to hold elections in North Korea, his army would move north to take the surrender of the DPRK troops. On 21 May, Briggs told the department that Rhee was afraid the United States was losing the war against communism and that it had already lost China and was in the process of negotiating away Korea and all of Southeast Asia. Rhee had insisted that Korea could not remain divided and that the "time to fight in North Korea was now."[55] At a time when the United States had decided to consolidate its position by providing economic aid and undertaking the training of local forces to replace

American manpower, Rhee threatened to tip the scales. President Eisenhower had called Rhee an "unsatisfactory ally" in mid-1953, and his administration was once again faced with Rhee's divergent diplomatic and military objectives.

Despite this, U.S. diplomats were able to keep the Korean president within acceptable bounds. Ambassador Briggs aptly summarized the Korean dependence on American-financed aid and the whole nature of the U.S. presence in South Korea in mid-May. Unification through force, he said, was "not consonant with our present global and strategic responsibilities"; nevertheless, the United States should continue to support the South Koreans "as long as that government really works with us, maintains mutual security pact as insurance against renewed Communist aggression, and seeks to rebuild Republic of Korea economy."[56]

Some covert methods were also employed to obtain greater allied unity on the Korean unification issue. When the ROK foreign minister, Pyun Yong-T'ae, put forth a fourteen-point proposal as the basis of the unification of the ROK, he did so with the consent of the Americans but without the consent of President Rhee. Point two represented a compromise to the American and allied positions on the part of the South Korean government. Initially it had called for elections in South Korea if the majority of people in the ROK wanted them. Under U.S. pressure, the final ROK proposals toned down these demands and provided for elections "in accordance with the constitutional processes of the Republic of Korea." Rhee was very upset when he learned of this diplomatic initiative, but he reluctantly accepted it and did not withdraw the ROK delegation from Geneva. The Commonwealth was satisfied with this compromise, though some nations wanted the ROK to go further on other points. Nevertheless, the United States emphasized that the new ROK position represented an important compromise. Officials argued that the conference should be adjourned and the issue brought back to the United Nations.

The political and strategic uncertainties of unification were now regarded as too high by both sides to take any risks. On 20 May, Dulles wrote that there was little likelihood of "achieving any political settlement." Attempts to unify the two Koreas might result in communist domination. American policymakers recognized the value of supporting some of the tenets of the ROK's proposals for unification. Rhee's remonstrations and threats to unify the peninsula by force both helped and hampered the U.S. attempts to undermine the status quo on the East Asian perimeter. But in the absence of a satisfactory settlement of the Korean issue, the Americans' strategic objectives required Rhee to accept the temporary division of the peninsula. The European allies accepted America's predominance in Korea. On 1 June, Foreign Secretary Anthony Eden noted that the British "would go along" with the Americans in Korea. On 2 June, the French foreign minister, Georges Bidault, concluded a discussion with Beddle Smith by noting that the United States was bearing the main burden in Korea as France was in Indochina. Bidault noted that he "would readily yield to [the U.S.] position."[57] Pearson, as a "middle power" representative at Geneva, was somewhat frustrated by these developments. He told Ottawa that the "British are unhappy but, like the French, [they are] inclined to avoid at almost any cost difference with the Americans on Korea." In effect, the traditional Great Powers implicitly agreed to a spheres-of-influence agreement on the Korean peninsula as a means of stabilizing the area. On 23 May, Molotov told Bedell Smith that Korea "would require a great deal of time to produce a solution ... Political settlement in Korea would come about possibly as a result of some years of living together."[58]

The conference contributed to some relaxation of tensions between East and West. But it also made the United States more sceptical of the benefits of aligning itself with the European powers in East Asia. Secretary Dulles viewed the debate over the Korean election proposals as "a minor technical point." For him, the real issue was the spread of communist power in Asia, not the merits of South Korea's unification proposals. The fall of Dien Bien Phu in the first week of May had made it even more imperative to support America's Asian and antipodean allies. On 10 May, Dulles wrote to the American delegation in Geneva: "In view of our desire to develop a strong anti-Communist position, with particular relation to Indochina, and the prospect that we might still intervene there and that this might involve a clash with Communist China, I think it important that we basically follow a line which will keep the confidence of our anti-Communist allies in Asia rather than seem to be working against them with a view to winning favor of Western European countries which are not disposed to be very helpful to us in Asia."[59]

The United States, for its part, tried to avoid a linkage between the Korean and Indochina conferences and worked towards ending the Korean phase without endangering its prospects for united action in Indochina. Differences amongst the allies over the proper strategy to pursue *vis-à-vis* Vietnam were mirrored in their diplomacy during the Korean discussions. Yet the Korean phase of the conference helped eliminate Korea as an area of Great Power struggle; the outcome of the Indochina phase accelerated America's involvement in a war that was to have an impact on international society well beyond the imagination of the policymakers of the day.

7   A Clash of Empires: The Indochina Conference, 1954

Much of the literature on the Indochina phase of the Geneva Conference emphasizes the cautious nature of the Eisenhower administration's "United Action" strategy. Writing in 1969, Robert Randle stated: "President Eisenhower and Secretary of State Dulles concluded, no later than the first or second of April 1954, that the United States should not become militarily involved in the Indochinese War unless the Chinese intervened." Melanie Billings-Yun also emphasizes the prudent attitude of the United States towards intervention. Most recently, Frederick Marks III has argued that Dulles "kept the nation from war" during the course of the conference.[1]

This chapter challenges these assumptions of American prudence and seeks to establish a broader context for understanding the evolution, continuity, and development of American policies towards Vietnam. This will be done through an examination of the relationship between the New Look, informal empire, and John Foster Dulles's United Action strategy. United Action, as proposed by the secretary of state, was a fluid and dynamic concept, involving complex negotiations and multiple participants. It was designed to maintain French involvement in the Indochina war, ward off Chinese aid to the Viet Minh, provide time to develop the indigenous Vietnamese forces, and lay the foundations for the military defeat of the Vietnamese communists. The strategy was compatible with the Navarre Plan, and it reflected Dulles's hopes of defeating the Viet Minh within two years. Taken as a whole, it held as its highest objective the consolidation of a pro-Western regime in Vietnam that was untinged by the criticism of being a colonial puppet yet was able to act as a Western proxy against the forces of communism.

Two critical factors prevented Dulles's proposal from being implemented. The United States had hoped to convince the French to maintain their military presence in Vietnam, but at Geneva both the French and the British insisted on giving the negotiations with the communists an opportunity to succeed. The allies refused to internationalize the war under the conditions set by the Americans. The political chaos and instability surrounding the Vietnamese noncommunist political factions also undermined the long-term objectives of United Action. During the course of the conference, it became evident to the United States that the Vietnamese regime could not sustain itself without the continued support of a Great Power. This, coupled with the persistent negative European response to Dulles's plan, resulted in an increased American determination to rebuild the noncommunist Vietnamese alternative themselves, replacing the French as the major power in Indochina. After 1954 the continued existence of South Vietnam was due primarily to American aid and support.

The conference marked a critical transition point in America's "state building" experiment in Vietnam. The failure of United Action demonstrated the precariousness of containing the Viet Minh through French military power. The result was a greater American commitment to get involved directly in the internal policy processes of the South Vietnamese government. The United States' diplomatic setback at Geneva accelerated its momentum towards acquiring an informal empire in Vietnam. Only through U.S. aid and guidance could the original objectives of United Action come to fruition.

American diplomacy at Geneva also reflected the principles of the New Look. Western unity and an implicit threat against Chinese intervention were two major premises of United Action. The Korean armistice had encouraged American diplomats and military planners to believe in the utility of using atomic diplomacy against the Sino-Soviet alliance. At various stages of the Geneva Conference, U.S. officials argued that the nuclear threat to China near the end of the Korean armistice negotiations had been a significant factor in the communist decision to sign the armistice. If Western nations could maintain their unity and continue the war against the Viet Minh, they would prevent Chinese intervention and establish the framework for the eventual defeat of communism in Southeast Asia. The perceived success of America's Korean strategy was thus followed by further pressure on the Chinese periphery in Southeast Asia. Building on the experience in Korea, America's New Look containment policy remained more risk-oriented than the policies of its European allies.

British and French actions during this phase of the Geneva Conference demonstrated the limits of American influence in a region in which the Europeans held substantial interests. Southeast Asia was an area of primary importance for America's European allies, and they were reluctant to follow the United States' diplomatic initiatives in this region. The determination of the British and French to negotiate a settlement to the war prevented the United States from organizing a coalition to intervene militarily in Vietnam. For the British, United Action was a volatile and dangerous concept which threatened to involve the Western alliance in global war with the Soviet Union and the People's Republic of China. As it had done during the Korean conflict, Britain attempted to restrain America's containment strategies involving China. United Action was discarded in favour of a more defensive containment policy, one based on an assessment of Britain's regional interests in Southeast Asia, its relative lack of resources to fight a war – especially in a peripheral setting – and a determination to work out a *modus vivendi* with China.

Other Commonwealth nations also were worried about America's more dynamic strategy for defeating communism in Vietnam. Nehru was critical of United Action, and Australia refused to consider joining the proposed alliance until after its national elections at the end of May. Canada was not directly involved in the Indochinese conference, but Canadians welcomed the opportunity to meet with Chinese diplomats. Lester Pearson's contacts with Chinese officials during the conference contrasted sharply with Dulles's abrupt reception of Chou En-lai. Pearson was also very concerned about the implications of United Action. He supported Eden at Geneva and sought to moderate the American position.

THE UNITED STATES AND UNITED ACTION

John Foster Dulles announced his proposals for United Action on 29 March 1954 amidst reports that the French fortress at Dien Bien Phu was losing the battle against the Viet Minh. The American ambassador in Paris had reported that French Premier Joseph Laniel was seeking a negotiated settlement to the conflict. The loss of the fortress would hurt French morale and could lead to concessions at the bargaining table at the upcoming Geneva talks. In this context, Dulles was resolved to maintain French military power in Indochina until more Vietnamese could be trained to fight. A French military commitment was needed in the short term as a means to contain the Viet Minh. In the longer term, greater indigenous military and political participation in the conflict would be required. At a meeting of the National Security

Council, Dulles said that the United States was witnessing "the collapse or evaporation of France as a great power in most areas of the world." The secretary told his audience that the "great rhetorical question was, who should fill the void left by the collapse of French power, particularly in the colonial areas. Would it be the Communists, or must it be the U.S.?" Dulles knew that his musings did not solve the immediate crisis. What was needed was further American support to bolster the French. On 26 March he told the cabinet that the United States had to help France "win" in Indochina.[2]

The U.S. government wanted a renewed commitment on the part of France to the principles of the Navarre Plan. But United Action was also premised on greater American and allied involvement in the region. Dulles envisaged a defence pact for Southeast Asia which would include the five Western regional powers and "interested" Asian states such as the Philippines and Thailand. The key members were the three associated states. A defensive coalition with Asian and allied participation would imply to the communists that the West was prepared to go to war to achieve its objectives. United Action was closely related to the formation of this alliance. Dulles envisaged short-term joint military action involving French Union troops, American sea and naval forces, British troops, an Australian and New Zealand naval presence, and the diplomatic support of the Philippines and Thailand.[3] The latter were required to placate Asian public opinion.

Dulles wanted to stand up to the communists with a unified and determined alliance. The deterrent value of the association was seen largely in terms of its impact on the People's Republic of China. If that country could be deterred from supporting the Viet Minh, the defeat of the Viet Minh would be a step closer to realization. The administration's strategy followed logically from the premises of NSC 124/2. As Dulles told British officials in Washington on 2 April, "If the Chinese Communists could be made to see that stepped-up activities on their part in Southeast Asia could lead to disastrous retaliation on our part by sea and air, perhaps they could be persuaded to refrain from adventures in that area. If so, Southeast Asia could be saved from communism and probably a world wide conflict avoided."[4] United Action was perceived as a means of deterring Chinese intervention while the West fought the communists in Vietnam. The lessons of the Korean War were incorporated into United Action: China would think twice about intervening if it was warned in advance of the West's response. In American eyes, a variant of United Action had proved successful in Korea. It could work equally well in Indochina. On 3 April 1954, Dulles told the French ambassador, Henri Bonnet: "We obtained an armistice in Korea primarily because the Chinese feared that we would knock out their industrial area north of the

Yalu. A coalition along the lines ... described would offer us an alternative at Geneva without which we would be lost."[5]

The United States wanted European support for its United Action plans, but in line with its evolving strategy of having the Vietnamese take a more prominent role in government, American officials continued to press France to decentralize its empire. U.S. officials demanded a larger role in the training of indigenous troops and in overall strategic planning. They wanted the French to grant political sovereignty to the associated states.[6] These U.S. efforts were meant to substitute formal French control in Vietnam with greater Vietnamese independence and American informal influence. Formal hegemony was to be replaced with less direct means of directing the anticommunist movement in the country. A form of containment by proxy was envisaged: local Vietnamese forces would be supported by a defensive organization backed by Western and Asian nations. Emphasizing the military aspects of informal empire, Eisenhower noted in late April that there were "plenty of people in Asia we can train to fight well." There was no reason for American ground troops to be committed to the region, nor was such a commitment required: "We can train their forces and it may be necessary for us eventually to use some of our planes or aircraft carriers off the coast and some of our fighting craft we have in that area for support."[7]

The idea of replacing formal empire with a decentralized system of influence and control, with increasing responsibility being given to indigenous elites, was consistent with traditional American criticisms of "empire." Both Eisenhower and Dulles were concerned about America's world image, and they believed that if American demands *vis-à-vis* France and the associated states were not met before intervention, the United States would be criticized for harbouring colonial aspirations. For Eisenhower, it was a principle of utmost importance that France grant full sovereignty to Vietnam so that American intervention could be legitimized by a Vietnamese request for assistance. On 8 May he said, "We could not go into Indochina unless the Associated States invited us."[8] Eisenhower and Dulles were critical of formal imperialism as conducted by the European colonial powers and they did not want similar criticisms to be levelled against the United States. In a personal letter to General Gruenther, the supreme allied commander in Europe, Eisenhower wrote that to intervene without the support of Asian and Western countries would "lay ourselves open to the charge of imperialism and colonialism – or at the very least – of objectionable paternalism."[9] Similarly, Dulles told C. Douglas Dillon in Paris that Vietnamese independence was necessary to gain the support of other Asian states and for the broader success of United Action. The removal of any taint of colonialism was critical to the success of Western intervention in Indochina. [10]

American diplomacy in the Cold War was different from that traditionally pursued by the European Great Powers. Formal empire in the postwar world was weakened by American attempts to change the structure of European colonial rule. To contain global communism, American officials believed that formal empire had to be replaced with informal control and greater indigenous responsibility. But the process was delicate because of the need to maintain unity in NATO. United Action thus attempted to sustain Western unity while altering the structure of formal European colonialism in Asia. At its centre lay the American dislike and qualified mistrust of direct colonial rule.

United Action emerged logically from American perceptions of the decline in European power on the world stage and was designed to foster a modern and "progressive" concept of empire for Indochina. For Dulles, a man who relished power, the events in Indochina presented an opportunity. As he told a National Security meeting in early April, the regional grouping "was a means of compelling some of our allies, and notably the British, to agree to join with us in creating a really effective Far Eastern policy." The American strategy would force the Europeans to re-examine their colonial policies, which had been "ruinous" to U.S. objectives in East Asia and the Middle East. Dulles warned that the "effort to compel these changes could, of course, have the effect of tearing the free world coalition to pieces." The special relationship on colonial issues that had existed between Bevin and Acheson had been replaced by a more critical stance. According to Dulles, the United States "could not go on forever avoiding these great issues. The peoples of the colonial states would never agree to fight Communism unless they were assured of their freedom."[11]

An association between the United States and other Western states would be necessary also for American public opinion and congressional action. A memo of a conference with congressional leaders on 3 April noted that Dulles "would attempt to get definite commitments from the English and other free nations." If such agreements were satisfactory, "the consensus was that a Congressional resolution could be passed, giving the President power to commit armed forces in the area."[12]

Dulles wanted to maintain the French military presence in Indochina. But the implications of America's strategy for containing the Viet Minh was clear. In the context of France's withdrawal, the United States would take France's place as the major Western power in Southeast Asia. Although Dulles qualified American involvement in Vietnam in 1954 in the context of his United Action strategy, the premises of his policy, once the French were removed from the scene, led logically to a greater formal American political and military presence in the region.

THE BRITISH COMMONWEALTH, FRANCE, AND UNITED ACTION

The objectives of United Action went beyond the containment of communism in Indochina. It was a regional strategy involving China as well. U.S. policymakers recognized the risks that the strategy entailed for British interests in Asia. "The British position was of crucial importance," Dulles told the National Security Council on 6 April. "If we can get the United Kingdom to line up with us throughout Asia in resistance to communism, and if the United Kingdom is prepared to risk the loss of Hong Kong in order to save Malaya, all of this might prove to be the beginning of the creation of a real United States policy in Asia." He had high expectations for British participation; he believed that at last there was a possibility that Britain might be steered over to the American position on containing communism in Asia: "The peril in Southeast Asia might forge the needed unity because the British stake in Malaya is so great and because Britain's two children, Australia and New Zealand, are likewise imperilled. If the British come in now they will gain assets for their position in Australia and New Zealand. If they do not, Britain will lose its remaining influence in the ANZUS countries."[13]

The British and French, however, were sceptical of the objectives and assumptions underlying United Action. For nations well versed in traditional methods of diplomacy, the concept was threatening. Far more used to settling disputes by drawing irrelevant borders on world maps, the French and British were more willing than the United States to accept a partition settlement for Vietnam. They were much less willing to provoke the People's Republic, and both wanted to give the conference an opportunity to come to a negotiated settlement.

The British wanted to extend the region of détente with the communists to include Southeast Asia. On 22 May, Foreign Secretary Eden wrote to Roger Makins in Washington that the United Kingdom's aim at Geneva "should be to draw a line and to create a *modus vivendi* in Asia of the kind already created in Europe." He added: "I have always recognized that these negotiations would involve concessions to the Communists, probably entailing creation of a buffer state on China's southern border." Eden contrasted British policy with the more aggressive American strategy, which appeared to have as its goal the reconquering of Indochina. He advocated a more defensive containment strategy, one with limited objectives regarding both the Chinese and the Viet Minh. However, he did want to support a policy of partition with a collective defence treaty for Southeast Asia that included the participation of Asian states. As he told Ambassador Makins, "My purpose is to reach an agreed settlement at Geneva of the Indochina problem and then to institute measures for the collective defence of South-East Asia in the light of that settlement."[14]

Churchill supported his foreign secretary on this issue. In a discussion in late April with Admiral Radford, the chairman of the Joint Chiefs of Staff, the prime minister made one of his off-the-cuff remarks: "No one in England gave a care for Indo-China." The debate about European colonialism in Southeast Asia was unimportant, he said, and he was not in a position "to convince the people of England that they should make any investment of their limited resources to hold Indo-China when a few years before they themselves had given up India." Churchill's attention was devoted to Western Europe, and throughout the conversation he referred to "the threat to the United Kingdom posed by the possession of atomic weapons by the U.S.S.R." Britain was "the bull's eye of the Russian's target." What was needed was political discussions with the Soviets; it would be folly, he said, "to squander our limited resources around the fringes."[15]

The military appreciation was critical, and the United Kingdom's Chiefs of Staff Committee affirmed Foreign Office scepticism about the viability of United Action. The military were concerned that the dispatch of air and naval forces to the region would require a contingency plan for a possible war in the Far East. The Chiefs of Staff rejected the American plan because it risked global war and threatened Britain's retention of Malaya and Hong Kong. A brief prepared by the Foreign Office for Eden stated that the United Kingdom could agree to a statement expressing concern about Indochina as long as it did not convey any warning to China.[16] The British wanted to restrict their containment program to a specifically defined area around the Chinese periphery. They hoped to consolidate a Western sphere of interest in southern Indochina, and to this degree they supported American attempts at creating informal empire in Vietnam; but they criticized U.S. efforts to force back the borders of communism and establish a new status quo in Asia.

The Chiefs of Staff also disagreed with the importance the Americans attached to cutting off Chinese support to the Viet Minh. In a prescient analysis, they argued that even if Chinese aid was stopped, the internal problem in Vietnam would remain. The military situation had "deteriorated to a point at which, even at best, a long term guerrilla problem of much more serious proportions than Malaya in the worst years is bound to remain for a considerable period."[17]

It is possible that the American strategy would have deterred the Chinese from open intervention, but even if that were true, in its haste to contain communism in Asia, the United States failed to heed warnings gained from experience by its European allies. The Eisenhower administration underestimated the momentum of America's growing involvement in the region. U.S. perceptions were based on a one-sided conception of justice and freedom; the Americans did not understand that the Viet Minh, too, were responding to injustice, albeit of a different sort. The West contributed to the radicalization of the regime that it was trying to destroy. On 10 April, Dulles said that Britain, France, and the United States needed "to join our strength and add it to the strength of others in order to create the conditions needed to assure that [the] conference will not lead to a loss of freedom in Southeast Asia but will preserve that freedom in peace and justice."[18]

Although they were critical of United Action, British officials were distressed about the military situation in Indochina. The Chiefs of Staff were concerned that a partition settlement in Indochina would "gravely increase our difficulties in Malaya."[19] However, like the Foreign Office, they regarded partition as the best of several unappealing possibilities. Furthermore, it coincided with Britain's strategy of maintaining French power in Europe; a lessening of France's commitment in Indochina would bolster its position within the Western alliance and against the Soviet threat. The chief of the Imperial General Staff, Sir John Harding, pointed out that the campaign in Southeast Asia was a drain on France's resources. French losses in Indochina were "probably greater," he observed, "than our combined commitments overseas. Militarily therefore it was essential to set a course leading to a reduction of the French commitment."[20]

The British policymakers were aware of the important role that Australia and New Zealand could play in the United Action scheme, and the Foreign Office and the Commonwealth Relations Office were busy coordinating their efforts to inform the Old Dominions of British policy towards Southeast Asia. It is difficult to judge the extent to which Britain influenced the Old Commonwealth or the extent to which its assessment coincided with that of the British. At a minimum, the Commonwealth Relations Office telegrams reinforced the perceived dangers of America's containment strategy. Broadly speaking, Australia, New Zealand, and Canada agreed with the British about the possibility of the war expanding to include China. From Ottawa the United Kingdom high commissioner reported that Lester Pearson was sympathetic to the British position and that the Canadian Chiefs of Staff agreed with the assessments of their British counterparts. Briefs prepared for the Canadian delegation at Geneva confirmed this observation. It seemed likely, one memo commented, "that intervention by the armed forces of western nations may lead to Communist Chinese intervention and a possible extension of the war."[21] In late April, Pearson wrote from Geneva that he would do what he could "to impress on the Americans the difficulty of the British position and the strength of the British arguments against the Dulles proposals." The American proposals contained a combination of "rashness and desperation," he said. They would not help the French or the situation in Indochina "and might even extend and intensify the present conflict."[22]

Although the Canadian delegation to Geneva played a small role in the negotiations on Indochina, the Canadians were kept informed of conference discussions and they provided a valuable sounding board for Chinese diplomacy at the conference. One of the Canadian delegation members, Chester Ronning, had grown up in China, spoke Chinese, and had met Chou En-lai in Chungking in 1945. Ronning was something of an admirer of Chou's intellect, if not his political ideology. At the conference, Chou asked Ronning to introduce him to Pearson. The two shook hands and talked briefly with each other. In discussions with Canadians and other Commonwealth diplomats, the Chinese emphasized the importance of working out a settlement to the conflict.

In May, Wang Ping-Nan, the director of the Staff Office of the Ministry of Foreign Affairs, told Ronning that the Chinese government was "very anxious to have the fighting in Vietnam stopped as soon as possible." He noted the "dangerous possibilities of continuing this war" and pointed out that "the United Kingdom was the great power in the best position to negotiate on behalf of the western nations." He also said that the conference participants should not focus their attention too much on the Soviet role in the talks: "Since the Soviet Union was so far removed from the scene, China might be the great power on the other side which was in the best position to negotiate." The Viet Minh, he stated, were willing to endorse an immediate cease-fire.[23] This was a significant discussion and reflected China's attempts to work with Britain's less aggressive containment strategy to achieve an agreement at the conference. It was an attempt also to isolate American power from its allies by appealing to the British Commonwealth's more moderate stance. In short, the Chinese played a significant role in limiting the appeal of Dulles's United Action proposals.

To complement this strategy, the Chinese also attempted to place their relations with Britain and Canada on better footing. Wang had told Ronning that his government would "be generous" to Canadian missionaries held in China. He stated that "all foreigners, business men or missionaries, were welcome in China on the condition that they did not oppose the government"; after all, the Canadian government would not tolerate opposition by Chinese residents in Canada. To this, Ronning politely pointed out that "criticism of the Canadian Government did not constitute basis for imprisonment in Canada."[24]

The Chinese also approached the British delegation in Geneva about formalizing the relationship between the People's Republic and the United Kingdom. Until then, China had not officially recognized the United Kingdom, despite the fact that the British had had a chargé d'affaires in Peking since early 1950. In mid-June, as a result of Chinese suggestions in Peking and Geneva, Eden and the British cabinet agreed to accept a Chinese chargé d'affaires in London. The British diplomatic mission in Peking was officially recognized, and in September 1954, Huan Xiang became the first People's Republic representative to London.[25]

Despite these improvements in China's relations with Britain and, to a lesser degree, with Canada, both countries remained concerned about the Viet Minh. Pearson's speeches covered general principles acceptable to Canada's Western allies. He argued that the "internationalist communist conspiracy" threatened the Western position in Asia, that a defensive arrangement for the region would be beneficial, and that covert military action by the Viet Minh represented the real threat to Indochina. In Washington, Arnold Heeney agreed that collective solidarity was a "sound principle" but felt that American tactics had been "hasty and ill-advised." He had sympathy for Dulles's position that communist aggression should be countered with "unity and resolution," but on the other hand he observed that "the suggestion that air intervention be extended over the border into China must have been alarming to everyone." Canadian and American public opinion was also a consideration. Earlier, when Heeney had pointed out to Dulles that the vestiges of French colonialism would have to be eliminated if United Action was to be accepted by the Canadian public, Dulles said that "the same was precisely true in the United States." St Laurent also was concerned about Canadian public opinion and augmenting Canada's involvement in the war. He wrote to Pearson during the conference: "We are not now committed to anything in respect of Indo-China so [we] can take no responsibility about decisions."[26]

Australia was the second most important Commonwealth participant in United Action, and it too was keen on promoting a negotiated settlement. The Australian prime minister, Arthur Menzies, wrote to Churchill on 6 April saying that Australia would wait until early May before reviewing the situation. If the French could hold on, this would "give us some months breathing space,"[27] he remarked. On 18 April, the Australian foreign minister, Richard Casey, told British officials in

Singapore that he could see no other solution than partition along the 16th parallel. Casey shared British reservations about the military costs of continued fighting against the Viet Minh, and possibly even China, saying that "he did not see how it would be possible to hold Indo-China and much less the whole of South East Asia by armed strength for an indefinite period and that the only hope seemed to lie in political arrangements though American policy seemed to make the area of manoeuvre a very limited one."[28] The Old Commonwealth thus acted as a deterrent to United Action, limiting the ability of the United States to implement its containment strategy in Vietnam.

The New Commonwealth, particularly India, was critical of both British and American policy. Nehru became much more anxious about events in Indochina after Dulles's United Action speech. A telegram from the United Kingdom high commissioner in India on 14 April noted that Nehru had been appalled by the idea of a Southeast Asian NATO and was worried that the United States might be trying to hem in India. Yet it remained an important part of Britain's regional containment strategy to retain India's support for an agreement that might be reached at Geneva. The Commonwealth Relations Office relayed a message to the high commissioner the next day saying that it wanted to keep open the possibility of India's associating itself with the defence organization.[29] In British eyes, Indian adherence to a defensive coalition would give the deterrent against further communist aggression in Southeast Asia additional credibility. Britain differed from the United States on this issue; the United States downplayed India's role and placed more emphasis on retaining the support of the Philippines and Thailand.

Indian criticism of the proposed coalition was one factor in Eden's decision to opt out of talks with the Americans scheduled for 20 April. The discussions were to centre on the formation of a regional defensive alliance, which would include the five Western powers, the associated states, Thailand, and the Philippines. Nehru sent Eden a personal letter saying he was pleased that the United Kingdom had not retained any obligation to the United States which might have endangered the upcoming Geneva Conference.[30] Eden did in fact want discussions leading eventually to a defensive coalition in the region, but he was afraid that the Americans would attempt to involve such an organization in immediate collective action against the Viet Minh.

The concentration on military solutions to what was essentially a political problem inside Vietnam was a common error of the three major Western powers in this period. A defensive organization might be able to secure the region from overt action by the communists, but it could do little against covert activities or continued civil war within the partitioned country. The strategists tended not to discriminate between areas where the concepts of informal empire could be enforced and areas where they would be difficult to implement.

On 25 April, Britain informed the United States of its position on intervention. This prevented any military action or joint announcement on the eve of the conference. At a cabinet meeting that day, it was agreed that the United Kingdom would not commit itself to the joint Anglo-American communiqué of 13 April, which had pledged British support for negotiations on a Southeast Asian defence grouping. The British would make no assurances regarding military action in Indochina before the Geneva Conference. They would support French efforts to obtain an honourable settlement and would try to guarantee this settlement through the formation of a Southeast Asian collective defence system. Britain's only concession to the United States was its stated willingness to study measures to ensure the security of Thailand and Southeast Asia in the event that part or all of Indochina was lost to the communists.[31]

LIMITED WAR AND ATOMIC DIPLOMACY ON THE SOUTHEAST ASIAN PERIPHERY

America's deterrent threat was much more escalatory. As had been the case during the negotiations to end the Korean conflict, American strategy relied on an implicit use of atomic diplomacy *vis-à-vis* the Sino-Soviet alliance. America's Korean experience was instrumental in determining its response to the Indochinese crisis. In January 1954 a report by the Joint Strategic Plans Committee, "Review of U.S. Policy toward Southeast Asia," noted: "Should there be overt Communist Chinese participation the U.S. will be faced with a radically altered military situation in the Far East. Such a possibility would precipitate a situation not unlike that of renewed Communist aggression in Korea."[32]

That the United States was considering the use of atomic weapons is seen from the Joint Chiefs of Staff records of the period. American military planners actively discussed the possibility that their strategy to keep Indochina out of the communist orbit might result in communist intervention and World War III. Atomic weapons were considered in the context of Chinese intervention and in the event of Western intervention in Vietnam leading to regional or global war. A Joint Chiefs of Staff memo to Secretary of Defense Charles Wilson dated 13 April stated that "U.S. Naval and Air Forces with the use of atomic capacities as may be appropriate, plus U.S. ground force training missions and special detachments for security of U.S. bases, would constitute the most suitable contribution to collective action in Indo-China" and that in the event of a Chinese offensive, the United States should be prepared "to neutralize the sources of Communist power in the Far East by U.S. air and naval action, employing atomic weapons as appropriate, against Communist China."[33]

The military job was to consider and formulate contingency plans to destroy communist power in Indochina. The Department of State wanted to prevent the global dangers associated with these plans from becoming a reality, so it searched for a deterrent that could make the destruction of the Viet Minh a safe military option. Dulles's pronouncements that Chinese intervention would be met with a response not necessarily confined to the area of attack were a direct warning to the communists. His call for United Action attempted to create a context in which limited war could be waged successfully against the Viet Minh on the southern perimeter of China.

The risks involved in the strategy became more apparent to U.S. officials during the first two weeks of discussions at Geneva. The communists attempted to undermine the possibilities for United Action. On 12 May the *People's Daily* issued counter-threats and alluded to China's actions during the Korean War. The focus of China's threat was the United States. If the U.S. "imperialists" dared to start another war, they should "recall the defeat of the United Nations forces in Korea and the fate of French forces at Dien Bien Phu." A world war, the paper said, would result in "the destruction of the capitalist system."[34]

These warnings were backed up by direct contacts between communist and Western representatives. On 1 May, a British official in Washington, M.L. Joy, transmitted a memo of a conversation held in that city between Mr Wade of New Zealand and Mr Smirovsky, the Soviet first secretary dealing with Far Eastern affairs. Smirovsky said that if the West decided in advance of the conference to reject any "reasonable" settlement and rely on intervention in Indochina, "there would not only be no settlement but there would be war." He emphasized the solidarity between the Soviet Union and China on this issue:

The Chinese Government was not prepared to have American troops on its borders. China had shown this quite clearly in the case of Korea and she would react in the same way if the West attempted to intervene in Indo-China. Several times during the conversation, he emphasized the inevitability of direct and immediate Chinese intervention if American troops were sent to Indo-China, and added that, in this event, he would not feel optimistic about the prospect of avoiding world war.[35]

The U.S. implicit atomic threats had been understood by both the Chinese and the Soviets. The Sino-Soviet alliance, too, was prepared to wield atomic diplomacy at the Geneva Conference.

The timing of these threats to coincide with the opening of the conference is curious. It could be that there was an element of bluff involved, particularly on the Soviet side. In late April, Heeney had reported from Washington that Soviet Embassy officials were "going out of their way to give the impression that the fighting can be stopped in Indo-China."[36] Nevertheless, these threats demonstrated that the United States had underestimated the degree of outward solidarity of the Chinese and Soviets on the issue of Indochina. The British had good reason to be sceptical of Dulles's containment strategy.

The Americans quickly recognized their error. At a National Security Council meeting on 6 May, Dulles pointed out that he had "a distinct impression" that the Soviets and Chinese "felt much greater confidence in the strength of their position than we had earlier estimated." But Dulles refused to be swayed by the communist threats; he maintained that his position was still a viable one. The British refusal to participate in United Action did not put an end to the scheme, he insisted, though this did make the proposition much less feasible: "If the United States intervened in Indochina and the U.K. stayed out ... there was a much greater chance of Chinese overt intervention than would be the case if the British were in it with us."[37] However, Dulles reasoned that the Chinese did not believe that the British would agree to intervene in the first place; thus, if Britain did agree to collective military action, the Chinese would be that much more fearful of intervening themselves. In short, the Chinese would take British participation in United Action more seriously than he had previously thought; the deterrence would be greater if Britain participated.

The principles underlying United Action were consistent with the U.S. containment strategy for Europe and Asia – they reflected the assumptions of the New Look. The common ground between the New Look and United Action was a recognition of the limits of American power in a peripheral setting. Allied support and assistance in the Cold War was fundamental to the New Look, and United Action was premised on the belief that the United States could not intervene unilaterally in Indochina. President Eisenhower and Secretary Dulles realized that unilateral intervention by the United States in a region of Great Power conflict would threaten the wrath of China and provoke the Soviet Union. Failure to present a united stance with America's European allies would increase the likelihood of a united communist military response with the hope of defeating both the coalition and the United States. In early June, President Eisenhower outlined his thinking to his special assistant for national security affairs, General Robert Cutler, and "expressed himself very strongly" that the United States "would not intervene in China on any basis except united action." This was the only strategically sound course of action: "The need for united action as a condition of U.S. intervention was not related merely to the regional grouping for the defense of Southeast Asia, but was also a necessity for U.S. intervention in response to Chinese communist overt aggression." Eisenhower's comments also implied that unilateral U.S. action against China in support of French colonialism would alienate American and world public opinion against the United States.[38] The one eventuality feared by both Eisenhower and Dulles was the isolation of the United States in a war with the major communist powers. United Action related America's local containment objectives for the Viet Minh with its broader global strategy of containing the Sino-Soviet alliance.

Dulles described in more detail his ideas about limited war with the Chinese at a meeting with the president and other National Security Council officials in late May. He pointed out that a NATO-type defensive arrangement for Southeast Asia would be valuable for its deterrent value against China. However, "to hold [our] allies" if the Chinese did attack, the United States would "have to limit its counter-measures to *targets having* a demonstrable connection with Chinese aggression." If American plans "were initially designed to destroy the total power of China," he said, "our allies would think we were heading toward general war." These "limited objectives" would also "risk a more general war"; but if the United States "leapt to general war all at once, our allies wouldn't leap with us."[39] It was precisely this type of thinking by Dulles that scared British Commonwealth and French diplomats. It contributed to their determination to promote a partition of the region between East and West.

Recent historiography evaluating Dulles has emphasized the pragmatic nature of his secretaryship. But although the internal logic of his thinking on United Action held elements of caution, these must be situated within his broader strategy of threatening the Chinese with war. Dulles's ideas held in them the possibility of full-scale escalation of the conflict, and he was willing to carry his strategy out. Despite overt communist warnings, the United States did not give up its risk-oriented containment strategy based on applying pressure on China's periphery.

The Americans continued to campaign actively for United Action. A joint warning to China by the Western powers and by the Asian powers concerned would bolster the American threat against Chinese action and pave the way for military action against the Viet Minh. In Geneva on 12 May, the under-secretary of state, Walter Bedell Smith, told Lester Pearson that the Chinese had stopped fighting and had negotiated a settlement in Korea as a consequence of the American threats. Furthermore, he said, a "threat of attack upon Chinese cities and lines of communication would be sufficient ... to prevent the Chinese from interfering in Indo-China, or elsewhere in Asia, if joint military action became necessary." Smith emphasized that it was still not too late to take preventive political action: "The calculated risk which can be taken now may not be possible three years from now."[40]

Like the British, the French recognized the deterrent value of maintaining negotiations with the United States on the conditions for internationalizing the conflict. The French had previously agreed to internationalize the war to save Dien Bien Phu, though not on all the terms requested by the United States. The French continued to try to get the United States to waive some of its preconditions for intervention. On 10 May, Douglas Dillon reported from Paris that many leading French officials had gone out of their way to criticize the British, especially Churchill, whom they pictured as the 1954 "version of Chamberlain at Munich." According to Dillon, the French knew that the United States was endeavouring to get the British in on United Action, and they hoped that the United States would be successful in these attempts or that the Americans would decide to internationalize the war without British participation. Dillon warned that if United Action died out, the French would feel abandoned, and this would strengthen the communist hand both in Geneva and in relation to the European Defence Community.[41]

It is difficult to determine the extent to which the French themselves were bluffing; certainly, Dulles was very sceptical about France's commitment to the concept. Nevertheless, the next day the National Security Council agreed that it would try to work out an agreement with France, the associated states, Thailand, the Philippines, Australia, and New Zealand. Britain was dropped from the list, though the possibility of it joining the coalition at a later date was foreseen. An important prerequisite for this altered version of United Action was that France grant the associated states full independence, including the right to secede from the French Union.[42]

THE UNITED STATES AND VIETNAM

The American policy towards Vietnam and Vietnam's relationship with United Action portray the evolution of America's informal empire in this period. The period witnessed increased American pressure on France to devolve further power on the Vietnamese anticommunist nationalists under Bao Dai. As early as 30 April, however, Robert Cutler noted that the French were unwilling to give Vietnam its independence until after the Geneva Conference. This would make it "impossible to meet the President's requirement that the indigenous peoples invite and actively desire U.S. intervention."[43] Dulles was less enamoured than his superior with the need to get the French to give independence to the associated states, and on 8 May he suggested that this requirement be omitted from a telegram describing American requirements for United Action, saying that it might result in French resentment. For Dulles, the weakness of the Vietnamese government meant that its "independence" was a moot issue. During a meeting on 11 May, he argued that the associated states would not in fact be able to take advantage of their independence. They had neither the personnel nor the leadership required to make a go of it: "If the Associated States were turned loose, it would be like putting a baby in a cage of hungry lions. The baby would rapidly be devoured."[44] Dulles understood the weakness of the Western position in Indochina, yet he underestimated the obstacles in creating a viable indigenous political grouping.

Eisenhower was more aware of the longer-term problems of the containment strategy that his administration was pursuing. In this respect, he was wise, but his insight into the long-term viability of fostering a pro-Western state in Vietnam was overshadowed by his own fears of communist domination of the area. With some anguish, Eisenhower supported the dynamic strategy of containment, with its imperial overtones, which his administration pursued towards Vietnam.

The crisis in the spring brought out some of the contradictions of creating informal empire in Vietnam. The inability of the anticommunist nationalists to consolidate and legitimize their power base was the major weakness of America's strategies of devolving power onto indigenous elites. It undermined the principle of a decentralized informal empire: the situation might now require a greater and more direct Western presence in the region to uphold indigenous political power. In the context of France's refusal to accept the premises of United Action, only the United States would be able to fulfil Vietnam's needs. Thus, in the process of replacing French colonialism, the Americans began to put in place the foundations of their own empire in Vietnam.

Internally, the central government of Vietnam, headed by Prime Minister Buu Loc, was in a political crisis at the time of the Geneva Conference. An appreciation made by American intelligence sources on 20 May pointed out that with the absence of Bao Dai and Buu Loc from Vietnam, "factionalism has become extreme and the Vietnamese central government is virtually paralysed. It is possible that the Vietnam central government will disintegrate during the next 30 days."[45]

There was no viable political structure upon which to build informal empire. U.S. officials realized this – it accounted in part for their determination to defeat the Viet Minh on the battlefield. However, the difficulties of defeating the Viet Minh and the tremendous obstacle of developing nationalist sentiment for a noncommunist government did not deter American policymakers. A new, mixed breed of imperialism was being born, one requiring more direct and long-term intervention. Its objective was to establish the context in which informal empire would eventually emerge. Its method would be the military destruction of a powerful communist movement through the use of U.S. military forces.

Although there were significant parallels between U.S. policy towards Korea and Vietnam, the internal situation in Vietnam was unique. Unlike Korea, the indigenous government in Vietnam was unable to consolidate its power or develop a sense of legitimacy amongst the population. For Dulles, United Action was required not only to help the French defeat the Viet Minh but also to create a new counter-revolutionary political culture that would foster the emergence of a strong pro-Western government. United Action was meant as a short-term strategy *vis-à-vis* France, and Dulles and Eisenhower still hoped that the Vietnamese army could take over the responsibilities of the United Action forces. The strategy failed, but the objectives underpinning United Action remained to be implemented – by the United States. United Action was thus an important and highly significant precursor to American military intervention under Presidents Kennedy and Johnson. The theoretical foundations of informal empire provided the ideological base for further military action.

That the government had effectively disintegrated was confirmed by the U.S. chargé in the Philippines on 25 May. Lacy wrote that the time when political deterioration became disintegration had been reached and passed in Vietnam, and there was now a "vacuum of political authority"; without a strong central government, he said, American advisers would have a very difficult time raising manpower for the "Nationalist Army."[46] The irony in his statement was unintended.

From Saigon, Robert McClintock underlined the desperateness of the situation. The French were simply sitting on boxes of champagne, he once wrote. He took Dulles's rhetorical question a step further by noting that the main issue for the United States now was "how to fill [the] power vacuum once French Expeditionary Corps leaves this peninsula and how therefore to establish a truly Vietnamese National Army."[47] The Vietnamese problem was not achieving independence but, more basically, maintaining existence.

Both McClintock and the French minister for the associated states, Maurice Dejean, had earlier agreed that "something radical" had to be done to improve morale in the army, especially since Vietnamese mobilization had thus far been a "total failure."[48] McClintock understood the implications of America's expanded role in Vietnam. He wrote that a Vietnamese national army would not fight better than the South Korean army after Korean-style MAAG training. Furthermore, it would not become a "ROK-type army" unless there was "some stiffening of foreign divisions alongside, whether American or French." He recommended that the United States work with some of the existing French military officials in this new phase of the war. In the future, however, French commanders should be subordinated to America's strategy for defeating the Viet Minh.

McClintock cautioned American military planners, who were currently discussing expanding America's role in the conflict. "Iron Mike" had spoken to General Paul Ely, the commissioner-general and commander of the French forces in Indochina. Ely "had agreed that a greatly enlarged MAAG training section should be established and that two large training camps would at once be turned over for American training of Vietnamese national troops." Americans would be permitted to serve in active Vietnamese units, and for the first time "this entailed possibility of U.S. military participation in combat." The Eisenhower administration laid the context for an expansion of its formal responsibilities in Indochina even as the conference was under way. McClintock did not object to America's expanded role in training, but he warned that the French might "expect us to train troops which they will use according to their own doctrine, while we will be training troops in expectation they will be used according to our doctrine."[49] The difference in doctrine represented the difference between formal colonial rule and the American approach to empire in Vietnam. On 10 June 1954, a joint meeting of representatives of the Departments of State and Defense heeded McClintock's warning and agreed to suspend discussions with the French regarding the training of Vietnamese forces "until the basic question of conditions versus commitments was clarified." By that point, however, there were already some 3,000 U.S. military training advisers in the country.[50]

The training discussions were suspended temporarily in the hope that the French might still accept United Action and an internationalization of the war. If this did not occur, the United States had plans for its future relationship with Indochina. As early as 26 May 1954, Dulles sent a cable to Dillon saying that contingency planning required that the associated states should play a role in the programming of American aid and should receive military aid directly. The secretary's cable pointed out that this might eventually require the renegotiation of the pentapartite agreement between France, the associated states, and the United States, whereby the United States had agreed to send its aid through French authorities. Nevertheless, he said, this fact should not delay the implementation of the recommended measure.[51] This was an important move towards taking over direct responsibility from the French.

The political crisis in Vietnam in the spring of 1954 further weakened the legitimacy of the Vietnamese government in the eyes of outside observers. The viability of the regime had been severely questioned even before the conference: the associated states had been recognized by very few Asian states, and Bao Dai's government was widely perceived as a puppet regime. The corollary to this was that the Viet Minh were seen as having some legitimacy. As Nehru said in mid-April, "The problem in Indo-China in its origin is derived from French colonialism and the popular national opposition to it. The methods 'contemplated or emerging' to resolve the conflict are foreign interventions." On 15 May, the Cambodian minister in Britain told British officials that the Vietnamese government had little real legitimacy.[52]

The imperialistic goals of the West became all the more apparent in the context of this political collapse of power in Vietnam. The anticommunist Vietnamese were wary of United Action, not because of its promise to defeat the Viet Minh but because it implied a continuation of French power in Vietnam, at least for the short term. Vietnamese officials were strongly anti-French, and they disliked the idea that United Action meant a continued French presence for some time to come. Bao Dai believed the Franco–Viet Minh negotiations were a plot, and he wanted American intervention to defeat the Viet Minh. The Eisenhower administration's attempts to get France formally to recognize Vietnam's independence reflected a need to placate the Vietnamese regarding United Action. The Vietnamese would have resented United Action if it was not to be accompanied by a declaration of their full independence from France. As the British minister in Saigon, Sir H. Graves, wrote on 4 May, "We know at present that the Viet Nam are opposed to armed intervention on their behalf."[53]

DETERRENT DIPLOMACY

Despite the difficulties with the allies, throughout the month of May, Dulles continued his efforts to get his United Action program accepted. Meanwhile, America's allies remained determined to stifle the provocative aspects of his proposals. Eden's diplomatic manoeuvring at this stage of the conference continued to underline the limits of the Anglo-American special relationship in this region of traditional Great Power concern. On 11 May, Eden told Bedell Smith that it would not be suitable at this time to make a commitment to the composition of the wider security organization for Southeast Asia; it would be "fatal" for the Geneva Conference to initiate discussions involving the ten-power group suggested by the United States. In a veiled reference to India, Eden said that to do this "before the results are known would destroy any prospect of bringing along the Asian Powers who really matter." Instead, Eden proposed discussions between the five-power staffs. These would act as a deterrent to Chinese intervention and might result in the formation of a regional defensive coalition. The five powers would keep the Colombo powers, Siam, and the Philippines informed of the progress of their deliberations.[54]

The British were worried that the United States was attempting to convert the five-power discussions into a forum for United Action. They were also concerned about the outcome of Franco-American discussions on intervention in Indochina. On 13 May, Dillon spoke to French Premier Joseph Laniel and reportedly told him that "the President was prepared to ask Congress for authority to intervene in Indo-China in the event of there being no agreement in Geneva, or of a French request in the meantime."[55] If the French agreed to American terms, increased pressure would be brought to bear on the United Kingdom to join. If the British delayed the formation of a military grouping and gave the conference participants an opportunity to settle their differences, their own limited containment strategy would have a better chance of success.

British fears were somewhat allayed when French Foreign Minister Georges Bidault assured Eden on 17 May that the French government would not seek to internationalize the war before the end of the conference. De Margerie confirmed this, stating that it would be impossible for the French National Assembly to agree to a commitment on U.S. terms. When news of this reached Churchill, he was relieved, and he agreed that the five-power talks should no longer be delayed: "The time had come when Anglo-American relations require strengthening."[56]

Like the French and British diplomats, Dulles believed that negotiations working towards a "defensive" arrangement for Southeast Asia would act as a deterrent to communist demands at Geneva. He was not optimistic about the Franco-American negotiations, and he wanted to strengthen the Western position at Geneva in the hope that the communists would moderate their demands on France. "The only ray of hope would be Communist fear of United States intervention in Indochina or of general war," Dulles mused on the twentieth. In the absence of United Action, this strategy was second best. The previous day, Eisenhower had suggested at a news conference that the United States could work out a collective defence system in Southeast Asia without the British, and Dulles said that "this knowledge was certainly not lost on the Communists." It was hoped that American initiatives outside the scope of the conference – such as the threat of Western support for an appeal by Thailand to the United Nations against aggression on its borders – would result in a stalemate and no negotiated settlement. If this occurred, the longer-term prospects for American strategy would be improved. As Dulles told Douglas MacArthur Jr that day, the United States did not want to wreck the discussions at Geneva; it wanted them stalemated.[57]

After the five powers had met and discussed various contingencies for action in Indochina in early June, the possibilities for United Action diminished. This was largely a consequence of the continuing military difficulties which the French Union forces experienced in Vietnam. The French had contracted their defensive perimeter around Hanoi and Haiphong, and there was some expectation of a Viet Minh attack on French forces stationed there. The weakened military power of the French in Vietnam was picked up by Beddell Smith and Dulles on 7 June. In a letter to the secretary, Smith recommended that the United States work for and accept the best of the worst scenarios – partition. This did not appeal to Dulles, but in his reply he agreed that the French were not taking American proposals for internationalization of the war seriously. The military situation was becoming so bad that internationalization might not be a viable alternative for much longer.[58] The prospects for United Action were waning.

The only bright spot from the American point of view was that it appeared that the conference was on its last legs and that a settlement might not be reached. On 9 June, Smith reported a discussion he had with Eden at Geneva in which Eden had said that on the issues of Cambodia and Laos, the status and power of the control system, and its composition, there appeared to be no way out of the deadlock. Eden expected the conference to split up soon.[59]

The prospect of the conference breaking up did not appeal to the British, who still maintained that their interests in the region required a spheres-of-influence agreement with the communists. In order to limit the possibility that China might see the end of the conference in a provocative light, Eden proposed that Laos and Cambodia make an appeal to the United Nations on the grounds that they had been invaded. Vietnam was purposely excluded from this appeal. To make this clear to the American authorities, he said that the appeal should be kept separate from the appeal which Thailand had presented to the Security Council on 29 May. Whether this was a viable strategy or not to limit the conflict is open to question. As a memo on the issue pointed out, "It appears preferable to work initially for the more limited objective of non-military action, but any decision must take account of the risks inherent in military intervention. The basic question is whether, in the last resort, we are prepared to participate in a conflict on the lines of Korea."[60] Dulles himself was sceptical of the plan. "A program for Laos and Cambodia, excluding Vietnam, will almost surely be interpreted in Vietnam and elsewhere as its total abandonment," he declared on 10 June. Until he saw no alternative to United Action, he would not promote action in the United Nations to save Cambodia and Laos alone.

At this point, the United States was still prepared to abandon the French at Geneva if the British sided with the Americans and the French refused to break off negotiations with the communists. According to Dulles, "If this happened and then we began the united-front talks which we had planned for early April, that in my opinion would prevent French continuance from thwarting our plans." Dulles's methods for United Action had altered since March and April, but the objective of defeating the Viet Minh and deterring China remained. The basic deterrent now rested with the United Kingdom. It is possible that the Anglo-American relationship had never appeared so important to the frustrated Dulles. He did not agree with the idea that "nothing can be salvaged from Vietnam." But the result depended on Britain. "I feel confident," he wrote, "that the Communists are prepared to stop wherever we are prepared to stand. However, that stand must be a united one to be effective, and the one element so far conspicuously lacking in that unity is the U.K."[61] President Eisenhower believed that the conference should be ended immediately. Discussions on Vietnam had been set up between the United States and Great Britain for the end of June, and the United States had made it clear that at those meetings they would discuss the possibility of intervening in Vietnam.

THE FALL OF THE LANIEL GOVERNMENT AND THE PARTITION OF VIETNAM

On the whole, Dulles realized by this time that it was unlikely that his United Action plan would be taken up by the allies. On 14 June he wrote to Dillon in Paris that "there is less disposition now than two months or one month ago to intervene in Indochina militarily." This was the consequence of military and political deterioration in Indochina, he said, which made "the problem of intervention and pacification more and more difficult." When his plan had initially been launched, French and Vietnamese forces had seemed strong enough to win the war with limited American military support. But since then, Vietnamese morale had "deteriorated gravely" and the entire Tonkin Delta might be lost to the Viet Minh. The situation would now require four or five U.S. divisions, which would "in effect commit our strategic reserve to a remote quarter of the world to go into action against a third-rate power." But the United States had never contemplated a substantial unilateral military action, and Dulles was considering other means of salvaging an anticommunist alternative in Vietnam. As he noted on 7 June, "We reserve the right to review the situation if by the time the French acted the situation had deteriorated beyond salvage. The latter seems to be happening." The *coup de grâce* to United Action was provided by the fall of the Laniel government on 15 June. On the sixteenth, Dulles told Bonnet in Washington that it was unlikely that the French National Assembly would agree to internationalize the war on U.S. terms. Speaking to Eisenhower the next day, he "commented that from time to time he thought it best to let the French get out of Indochina entirely and then to try to rebuild from the foundations."[62] Dulles realized this was impractical and that French cooperation would be necessary even if the country was partitioned; but the balance of power between the Americans and French in Vietnam was changing rapidly.

The events of May and June had shown the impossibility of successfully implementing the Navarre Plan. On 4 June, McClintock recommended that the U.S. government approach the French and point out that the "Navarre Plan no longer exists." This was not done, but on 25 June, during a joint State-Defense staff meeting discussing Mutual Defense Assistance Program aid to Indochina, the special assistant to the secretary of state for mutual security affairs, Frederick E. Nolting Jr, argued that the Americans had "solid grounds" for stopping payments of the $385 million promised to the French for operations related to the Navarre Plan.[63] The Americans were making plans to transfer their aid from the French to the Vietnamese. This was confirmed in a memo to Under-Secretary Smith on 12 August which recommended that the Navarre Plan funds be revoked, "since such aid in the future will be channelled directly to the Vietnamese Government."[64]

In the context of the virtual abandonment of the Navarre Plan in June, increased emphasis was placed on the United States developing the Vietnamese army. "Development of a Vietnamese national army constitutes ... the number one military objective toward which U.S. policy must be oriented," McClintock wrote from Saigon. Measures which the United States could and should initiate as soon as possible included direct assistance in training, authority for the chief of the Military Assistance and Advisory Group (MAAG) to organize such training, and an increase in the size of the MAAG to accommodate its new role. It was also imperative that the United States abrogate the existing pentalateral agreement and replace it with direct U.S. military aid to all three associated states. On June 16 and 20, General O'Daniel sent similar telegrams requesting an increased training role for the United States, and on the twenty-sixth Dulles informed Saigon and Paris that an additional ninety personnel would augment the existing MAAG group in Saigon.[65] The United States qualified its decision by noting that this was only an incremental American commitment and did not represent an approval for a training mission for all Vietnamese forces. Such an agreement was still awaiting French compliance with the American internationalization proposals. The decision was taken with the knowledge that United Action was unlikely and that a greater American presence in the associated states was desirable.

In the context of French failures on the battlefield, the Americans placed more emphasis on their relationship with the Vietnamese. This represented a logical evolution of the ideas underlying America's informal empire. American diplomats had to be careful not to alienate France, because it was important to get the French National Assembly to ratify the European Defence Community proposals. Yet the Americans realized that the Vietnamese had no respect for French colonialism and that to have any hope of fostering a pro-Western Vietnamese nationalism, the United States would ultimately have to align itself with the Vietnamese. Thus, the need to support Vietnamese anticommunists as part of its informal empire-building strategy weakened America's remaining support for sustaining the French military and colonial effort in Southeast Asia.

In a discussion with legislative leaders on 28 June, Dulles and Eisenhower defined in their own terms the new American empire. Responding to an inquiry by Congressman John M. Vorys, Dulles pointed out that if the American proposals of March and April had been accepted, "a greater part of the area would have been held that has since been lost." The fall of the Laniel government was unfortunate, he said, but Laniel and Bidault had been "living on borrowed time." The United States had never wanted to associate itself with the unpopular colonial policies of the French, and there was now "the possibility of salvaging something free of the taint of French colonialism that will have the backing of the states of Asia." The United States had the opportunity of establishing a new military line. "We must hold that line and also hold the area behind that line against the same kind of subversion which has gone on to date," the secretary informed the audience. He stressed a new role for the United States in Southeast Asia; to achieve American goals would require a considerable expansion of economic and military aid. The Navarre Plan was "finished," but "alternative efforts" would require "an equal output by the United States." Eisenhower then noted, "We are establishing international outposts where people can develop their strength to defend themselves. Here we are sitting in the center, and with high mobility and destructive forces we can swiftly respond when our vital interests are affected ... We cannot publicly call our allies outposts ... but we are trying to get that result."[66]

GENEVA

Accompanying the fall of the Laniel government was a moderation in the communist position on Indochina. This gave the European powers greater hope for a settlement. On 16 June, Eden wrote to the Foreign Office that he had the impression from a discussion with Chou En-lai that the Chinese wanted a settlement in Indochina and that Chou "was anxious that this part of the conference should not break down." Chou's major concern was that the United States should not be permitted to have military bases in Cambodia and Laos; he felt that an agreement could be worked out regarding the withdrawal of Viet Minh troops from Cambodia and Laos if such conditions were agreed to.[67]

In effect, Chou's proposal amounted to another attempt to preempt America's United Action initiatives. A settlement with the European powers would forestall any plans for allied military intervention. Chou understood the threat of intervention in Indochina to Chinese security, and he may even have exaggerated the immediate threat America posed to China. But he was determined to undermine United Action by striking at its heart. He understood that American containment strategy towards continental East Asia depended on the principle of collective deterrence.

The communists' concession appears to have been the result of several factors. They believed that if advances in negotiations were not forthcoming soon, Britain might abandon the conference. Eden himself had told the communists that the meetings of 8–10 June had threatened the disintegration of the conference.[68] The Chinese must have realized that intervention on the basis of United Action would thereby be one step closer to realization. The French were still keen on continued negotiations and therefore the prospects for settlement still existed. More important with respect to France was the coming to power of the more moderate government of Pierre Mendès-France. On 19 May, Eden reported that Chou had "said that there was a new French Government which really wanted peace," and that Chou's remark was "presumably an indication that the Communists think that they will find the new Government easier to deal with than the old."[69]

There was now less of a chance that the United Kingdom would give in to American pressure at the forthcoming Anglo-American discussions in Washington. Chou's diplomatic concession effectively undermined any opportunity that existed for the United Kingdom to agree to intervention before the end of the conference, and it renewed hope for a negotiated settlement. The Chinese foreign minister's proposals were not looked on favourably by the United States, which continued to hope for the possibility of future intervention.

Military conditions in northern Vietnam circumscribed the geographical location of allied intervention, but the basic premises of United Action were not altered. Although American officials were coming round to the conclusion that partition might be inevitable, they planned their military coalition for Southeast Asia on the basis that the conference might not reach a settlement or that settlement would lead to the loss of all of Vietnam. Dulles feared a partition "under conditions such that Communist takeover of all Vietnam looms ahead clearly."[70] The military situation now precluded allied intervention in the North, but the United States held out the possibility for intervention in the South. Moreover, military actions in the South had implications for action in the North as well. Dulles's strategy permitted the United States to move closer to the allied position regarding partition while still offering the possibility of United Action. The differences between the United States and Britain now centred on America's hopes for including Cambodia, Laos, and a partitioned Vietnam within the defence coalition for Southeast Asia and on Britain's position that unspecified action regarding Cambodia and Laos might be considered only if no agreement at Geneva was reached. If an agreement was reached that was acceptable to the British, then they would not want Cambodia or Laos in the defensive coalition. If only temporarily, Eden was prepared to accept Chou's proposals regarding the neutralization of those two states. As Sir Harold Caccia told American officials on 26 June, there was no profound philosophy behind these considerations, "but at Geneva it appeared that these areas would be neutralized behind a political line."[71]

During discussions with the British in June, the United States agreed to associate itself indirectly with an acceptable settlement at Geneva as part of a compromise solution to the Anglo-American deadlock. For Eden, this was an important concession that symbolized renewed American interest in the Geneva discussions.[72] This was only partially true, however, as the Americans never rejected the possibility that a form of allied military action might be required in the future: the American announcement that the United States would not upset the agreement by force if an agreement acceptable to it was negotiated did not commit it to not intervening in the longer term. Furthermore, its interpretation of minimum requirements for an acceptable settlement were more stringent than those laid down by its European allies. The United States could always argue that the conditions it had laid down for an acceptable agreement had been altered by communist actions. The hope for a unified anticommunist Vietnamese state remained an implicit objective of the Eisenhower administration's containment policy.

Despite differences regarding the composition of the defensive coalition for Southeast Asia, two important agreements were reached in Washington. The first was the decision to create an Anglo-American study group, which would coordinate the two countries' response to the outcome of the conference. The second agreement was more important in the short term, since it laid down minimum conditions for a settlement. The failure of United Action, France's determination to partition Vietnam, the virtual disintegration of the Vietnamese government, and Viet Minh military success set the context for the American decision. The Anglo-American text was delivered separately by the British and American ambassadors in Paris in late June. On 1 July, Dulles summarized the Anglo-American position to the National Security Council: "In substance, Laos and Cambodia would be left as free and independent states with the capability of maintaining their integrity." There was thus no guarantee of a neutral Cambodia and Laos. "Likewise, approximately half of Vietnam would remain non-Communist south of a line drawn approximately along the 18th parallel." He pointed out that complete agreement had not been reached at the discussions. The United States had hoped for an agreement saying that nothing less than this position would be acceptable; the British, however, "had merely wished to state a hope that the French wouldn't settle for anything less than this position." Dulles stated that the two countries had reached a compromise, but "we will continue to take a stiffer line than the British."[73]

The compromise position was the result of Anglo-American fears that the French might negotiate away important positions to the communists, and the fact that something was needed to bolster France's bargaining position. The implicit threat which the Europeans could now use in their negotiations was that if the communists did not agree to the conditions laid down by the United States and Britain, the West might dissociate itself from the conference. In which case, momentum for United Action could be regained.

In late June and early July there was some movement towards a settlement. The major differences between the communists and the West centred on the relationship between the two commissions designed to implement any agreement. The communists attempted to undermine any possibility of the West's using force within the structure of the agreement to achieve unification of Vietnam on its own terms. The communists were buying time and counting on elections to enhance their power in the country. They wanted to avoid any Western proposals giving an international commission military enforcement rights if "violations" in the armistice took place. There has been some speculation that the Viet Minh were in a much weaker military position in the spring of 1954 than was perceived at the time, and it is possible that the communist demands about the supervisory commission reflected this weakness. The communists wanted the supervisory structure to be as feeble as possible. They recommended that it should contain representatives from countries which had recognized the Viet Minh and that, on important issues where there was not unanimous agreement, it should refer to the joint commission. The joint commission itself was to consist of the representatives of the conference, who would then make a collective recommendation regarding the issue at hand.

The Western nations also recognized the weakness of their position. There was unanimous agreement that if elections were held, the Viet Minh would win. This was why any possibility of immediate elections leading to the formation of a coalition government in Vietnam was rejected. No Western diplomat argued that a solution could be found through genuine democracy. This was one aspect of the colonial and imperial stance of the Europeans and Americans at Geneva. The United States wanted the international commission to have access to force to implement its decisions. In addition, there was to be no communist representation on it. American officials were adamant that the international commission should not share responsibility for the implementation of the agreements with the joint commission. They wanted the joint commission to be subordinate to the international control commission. In theory, France and the United Kingdom agreed with these bargaining points. In practice, however, they were prepared to compromise on these positions in order to get a settlement based on the partition of Vietnam.

Progress in the negotiations was summarized by the Soviet deputy minister for foreign affairs, V.V. Kuznetsov, who was also ambassador to the People's Republic of China. At the twentieth restricted session on 2 July, Kuznetsov noted a "rapprochement" on two important issues: the interrelationship of the two commissions and the lack of need for the supervisory commission to have armed forces at its disposal. At that meeting the British had reserved their position on the relationship of the commissions, a declaration that must have angered the Americans.[74]

The Americans maintained their critical attitude towards the British and French negotiating stance at Geneva. In early July, Assistant Secretary Walter Robertson stated that the United Kingdom wanted a settlement "at any price." Dulles agreed with this assessment, saying that American terms for intervention were "thoroughly reasonable." To Robert Murphy, Dulles "expressed his disbelief" that the United States was really being kept informed of the secret negotiations between the French and Viet Minh; and he "expressed doubt that Mendès-France could be persuaded to adopt a strong line."[75]

The secretary of state relayed his dissatisfaction to the British foreign secretary on 7 July, telling Eden that the Europeans were not taking seriously enough the Anglo-American conditions for a satisfactory settlement at Geneva; whether or not he or Bedell Smith were in Geneva, the French would likely take a stance that did not meet the Anglo-American seven-point paper that had been drawn up in Washington. Dulles thus hinted that the United States might dissociate itself from both the Geneva Conference and negotiations with Britain regarding the Anglo-American Study Group: an American "high-level presence at Geneva might prove an embarrassment to all concerned,"[76] he noted. It was a warning that the United States might lift its previous commitment not to use force. The letter was aimed mainly at France, but the State Department hoped the British could put pressure on the French formally to accept the Anglo-American position. The next day a more direct approach was used. Dillon was instructed to explain to Mendès-France that there was "less danger of doing irreparable injury to Franco-American relations if we avoid getting into a position at Geneva which might require a disassociation under spectacular conditions which would be deeply resented by the French as an effort on our part to block at the last minute a peace which they ardently desire."[77]

The noncommunist Vietnamese delegation at Geneva was staunchly against any partition. Although, in the middle of the conference, Ngo Dinh Diem had replaced Buu Loc as prime minister of Vietnam, this did not affect their diplomacy at Geneva. The Vietnamese continued to criticize the French for making concessions to the communists. Johnson reported from Geneva on 3 July that the new foreign minister of Vietnam, Tran Van Do, "continues to view French actions as though colonial era still alive." On the tenth, Johnson was so concerned about the attitudes of the Vietnamese that he requested advice from the department about what to do if one or all of the associated states took a position "of open opposition to France," possibly even to the extent of leaving the conference. It is likely that American officials feared that the Vietnamese would declare their unilateral independence from the French Union or even come to a negotiated settlement with the Viet Minh.[78] The former action would have severely tested Franco-American relations, which were already on difficult footing; it might have forced the United States to make a decision between Vietnam and the European Defence Community. The latter action could have resulted in the loss of both.

These prospects induced a certain caution in American diplomacy towards France and the representatives from Vietnam. France had asked the United States to use its influence to prevent the Vietnamese from weakening the French position at Geneva; on the other hand, the Vietnamese were critical of French colonial policy and demanded greater American support for their position. The Vietnamese dislike for allied intervention without the granting of their sovereignty was one aspect of this national sentiment. Although U.S. policy was to make no guarantees to either side, the relative importance of the Vietnamese to the Americans was growing. Nevertheless, the high moral tone of a letter Dulles wrote to Diem would have meant little to most Vietnamese: "We know that struggle in Indochina is one for liberty against despotism and that you represent the spirit of resistance to a menace which threatens entire free world." More important for the future was Dulles's ominous emphasis on the transitional nature of any agreement reached at Geneva. The United States had agreed to negotiations at Geneva, he said, but "if as a result of such negotiations or of military operations there should now result any cease-fire line tending to divide Vietnam, we would be unwilling to consider it as final ... [We would] lend our best efforts to assist patriotic Vietnamese in building up strength in that part of Vietnam remaining outside Communist occupation." Although the conditions for intervention in North Vietnam had not been realized, Dulles continued, the recent Anglo-American conferences "made clear our strong opposition to any settlement which might be made on terms leading to permanent division"; both countries had agreed, and the French had been informed, that although the "temporary division" of Vietnam might be required to implement the regrouping of opposing military forces, the prospect of ultimate peaceful reunification could not be excluded.[79]

American tactics to save the situation in Indochina had now taken the form of pressure for a common minimum Anglo-American-French negotiating stance at Geneva. There was no longer enough time, before Mendès-France's deadline of 20 July, to organize a collective defence association for intervention, but the United States wanted to ensure that no agreement would be reached unless it was acceptable to all three allies. American officials still had faint hopes of stalemating the conference. On 10 July, Dulles sent a personal message to the French premier; in direct terms, he stated that Britain, France, and the United States did not seem to be prepared to "stand firmly" on the Anglo-American proposals for a settlement to the extent of breaking off negotiations and resuming the war.[80]

At this stage of the conference, Eisenhower suggested that Dulles go to France personally to discuss the matter with the French premier. These negotiations, which took place on 13–14 July, resulted in an agreed Franco-American position for future collaboration on Vietnam. The major concession which the French made to the United States related to the long-term defence of the associated states. The Franco-American position paper noted that the United States was prepared to establish a collective defensive organization "to preserve, against direct and indirect aggression, the integrity of the non-Communist areas of Southeast Asia following any settlement." The French had essentially agreed to give the United States a free hand in organizing for the defence of the region. The French agreed that it would be possible through negotiation to achieve a settlement that "does not impose on Laos, Cambodia or retained Vietnam any restrictions materially impairing their capacity to maintain stable non-Communist regimes; and especially restrictions impairing their right to maintain adequate forces for internal security, to import arms and to employ foreign advisers."[81] The agreement thus opened the way for the long-term American escalation of war in Vietnam.

At Geneva on 21 July a settlement was finally agreed. To Eden only a few days before, the prospects for success were only 50 per cent. Up to the last, United Action appeared as an unwanted but possible alternative. For the United States, the conference had presented an opportunity for collective action which never materialized. But American containment strategy on China's periphery had received only a temporary setback. The conference had accelerated the transition towards closer alignment with the Vietnamese. It had also diminished the power of French colonialism. The way was now paved for the United States to promote its own informal empire to help contain the Vietnamese communists. Intensification of the war and the broadening of conflict had only temporarily been averted at Geneva.

Despite the anguish associated with the negotiations at Geneva, the conference actually accomplished very little. Neither side viewed the agreements as permanent, and both sides viewed partition as a transitional stage towards reunification. The United States and Vietnam never signed the Geneva Accords, and elections scheduled for 1956 were never held. The communists had prevented the control commissions from retaining any substantial power of enforcement, and their Canadian, Indian, and Polish representatives spent most of their time disagreeing with one another. The Geneva Conference became a propaganda organ for the West, the communists, and the neutralists.

The conference was important in that it accelerated the decline of a traditional European power from the continent of Asia. British and French policies further demonstrated the weakened state of traditional colonial powers in the region. Despite this fact, the Europeans occupied an important role at the conference. They acted as the major check on America's risk-oriented policy directed at the Southeast Asian periphery. For this reason, America's New Look strategy, based on a collective deterrent and the wielding of atomic diplomacy, was not put to the test in Indochina in 1954.

8 Conclusion

Two factors were instrumental in defining the parameters of America's informal empire in East Asia after 1945: the bipolar structure of the international system and economic needs. Against the background of the global rivalry with the Soviet Union and the international dollar gap, U.S. policy attempted to consolidate pro-Western anticommunist governments in Vietnam and Korea. This objective was attained by providing economic and military aid to perceived "moderate" indigenous political groupings.

The United States was successful in developing South Korea as a partner in containing international communism. As the dominant power in Korea, America guided the direction of Korea's internal economic policies and its foreign policies. It was successful in preventing President Rhee from carrying out his unification schemes. Throughout the period covered, the United States maintained the balance of power in the bilateral relationship. However, the price of informal empire in Korea was constant frustration with Rhee and an agreement to expand the defensive perimeter to include the mainland through a Mutual Defense Treaty.

America's allies generally supported U.S. initiatives in Korea: they understood the value of their "special relationship" with the United States in the postwar bipolar world, and agreed to back Rhee's government. The American and allied response to the North Korean attempt to unify the country on communist lines represented an effort by the West to regain the initiative in the Cold War. Initial United Nations objectives were designed not only to roll back the borders of North Korean communism but to present a united challenge to the core of communist power, the Soviet Union. Chinese intervention in the winter of 1950–51 weakened Western solidarity somewhat, but the alliance was able to maintain a shaky unity. The passing of the aggressor resolution against China in February 1951 was symbolic of this unity. The U.S. strategy for ending the war also was reluctantly supported by its major allies. Despite reservations about America's belligerent attitude towards the Sino-Soviet alliance, British and Canadian diplomats publicly pledged their support to the United Nations Command's final negotiating terms of 25 May 1953. The Korean conflict had threatened the alliance with disunity, but the need to preserve allied unity was the deciding factor in allied diplomacy on the Northeast Asian periphery.

In Vietnam, America was increasing its influence among the anticommunist nationalists; but in this area of traditional Great Power influence, U.S. policymakers had to contend with the declining yet still substantial colonial power of the French. Various factors underlined the perceived need for the United States to support French power in Vietnam. These included America's defensive perimeter strategy and U.S. reliance on French troops to contain the Viet Minh. In strategic terms, the United States advocated the maintenance of the East Asian offshore perimeter and rejected any substantial commitment of forces to the continent. French Union troops would serve as an adequate proxy containment force until the State of Vietnam's indigenous military forces could be developed. There thus existed tensions between America's long-term strategy for Vietnam and its short-term policy of underwriting French rule in Indochina.

The nature of the bipolar system reinforced the need to rely on allies in the Cold War. The United States perceived itself to be in global competition for spheres of influence with the Soviet Union. One of these spheres was Southeast Asia. Since Tonkin was the gateway to the region, it was important to contain Soviet influence by supporting French military power in Vietnam. The strategic importance of the region's raw resources was augmented by the Korean War. Significantly, however, the United States was moving in the direction of an increased commitment to the anticommunist forces in Vietnam prior to the outbreak of the war.

French suspicion and the inability of Bao Dai to sustain a creditable national government also undermined American attempts to implement informal empire strategies in Vietnam. British officials were generally supportive of American measures to make the Vietnamese anticommunists more politically viable, though the British demonstrated a more realistic attitude about the possibilities of developing a pro-Western indigenous government in Vietnam. The United Kingdom was less inclined to support American policies that appeared in any way provocative to Communist China. Britain's preference for a defensive strategy for containing the Sino-Soviet threat manifested itself in its caution during the Korean War, in its policies for defending Southeast Asia, and its opposition to United Action.

America's anticolonial tendencies became stronger after 1952. Although Dean Acheson was willing to allocate a sphere of influence to the Commonwealth and France in Southeast Asia, Secretary Dulles was more critical of old-style colonialism in the region. He criticized Britain's defensive posture towards the People's Republic of China and remained sceptical of Britain's anticommunist credentials during the Indochina phase of the Geneva Conference. Like Dean Acheson, Dulles recognized the importance of maintaining allied support in this region of the international conflict. In Southeast Asia allied actions played an important role in restraining Dulles from implementing his provocative and risky containment strategy. America's allies were more reluctant to support U.S. strategy in Vietnam than they had been in Korea. This hampered the implementation of America's informal empire strategies for Vietnam.

Coercion has often been defined as the key element of imperialism. After 1945, the American empire in continental East Asia resorted to force but also to more subtle means of influence. America's informal empire rejected formal colonial rule and sought to displace European colonialism where it was seen to be detrimental to the long-term interests of the United States. The American empire after 1945 therefore cannot be viewed within a traditional framework of imperialism. It was informal in the sense that it sought to create indigenous elites with a stake in an alliance with the Western industrialized world. "Invitation" was an important aspect of this empire but not its predominant element. On the perimeter of the communist empire, Korea and Vietnam were to act as local Western proxies, to contain the outward expansion of the Soviet Union and China, and eventually to help retract communist power globally.

The economic underpinnings of Western containment strategies have formed another important dimension of this book. The United Kingdom's colonial interests in Malaya and Hong Kong were critical in determining Britain's response to the emergence of Communist China. They set the context for Britain's recognition strategy and its reluctance to support America's more risk-oriented containment policies in Northeast and Southeast Asia. Britain's economic difficulties after 1945, and especially those associated with rearmament after the Korean War, reinforced the trend towards caution in British policy and acted as a brake on British and allied strategies of containment for East Asia.

In the United States, the economic basis of informal empire lay in the dollar gap and America's need to reorient the trade of Japan, Western Europe, and the Third World in such a way as to lessen the demand for American dollars. American economic policies involving Korea and Japan, and attempts to tie Southeast Asia into the Western and Japanese nexus, represented trends in this direction. A strong Korea and Vietnam would bolster America's regional containment strategy *vis-à-vis* the communists and help Japan recover economically. The United States actively promoted the integration of the Japanese and Korean economies. Vietnam's importance to Japan stemmed largely from strategic considerations involving the preservation of Southeast Asia from communist control. Yet central to American preoccupations was not Japan but the need to contain Soviet and Chinese power in Asia. America's regional containment policies involving Japan emerged logically from these broader considerations.

There were limits to the Anglo-American special relationship in the postwar world. Bevin's conception of the special relationship in Asia was undermined by the onset of the Korean War and rearmament. The war prevented the United Kingdom and the Commonwealth from reaching an accommodation with the People's Republic of China. The United States was wary about underwriting the sterling area, and the Colombo Plan had a limited impact on drawing America into Southeast Asia, especially on the basis of Britain's defensive strategy. The impact of rearmament on Britain's economy reinforced Britain's weakness in Asia.

To a limited extent, the role of personalities was also important in defining the Anglo-American special relationship in this period. Secretary of State Dean Acheson was less critical of European colonial power in Southeast Asia than John Foster Dulles was. For his part, Anthony Eden was more reluctant than Bevin to pay the price for preserving good Anglo-American ties, and he came closer to advocating a third force policy than Bevin did. Over the period, there was a decline in the special relationship, and an important source of discord lay in East Asia. Britain's failure to support United Action, and its declining influence in world affairs, led the United States to rely more on the indigenous countries in the region. The Anglo-American partnership in Asia was a declining commodity after 1950.

The traditional relationships within the North Atlantic triangle also were in flux after 1945. Canada's economic ties with Britain and Europe were being replaced by increasing economic linkages with the United States. America had replaced Britain as Canada's major ally, and the dominant theme of Canadian foreign policy in the Cold War was the Canadian-American special relationship. But the United Kingdom continued to exert a considerable and subtle influence on Canadian foreign policy. The bipolar world left significant room for Britain in Canada's calculations, and the Canadian government recognized the importance of consolidating its special relationship with the United States in the broader context of the Atlantic alliance. In East Asia, Canada basically adopted Britain's defensive containment policy. Like British officials, Canadian policymakers in the Department of External Affairs were concerned about America's emotional response to communism and its lack of experience in international affairs. They felt that the U.S. willingness to use atomic diplomacy in East Asia threatened the cohesiveness of the Western alliance. The limits of the Anglo-Canadian strategy of restraint lay in these countries' very attempts to cultivate a special relationship. The need for America's continued involvement in world affairs, and the fear of a return to isolationist policies, kept many Western diplomats from pushing their policies of restraint very far.

The globalization of American foreign policy after 1945 pushed Canada into the world as well. Canadian involvement in the Korean War, its participation in the Colombo Plan, and its support of the "Bao Dai solution" in Indochina were all a function of attempts to maintain and direct its special relationship with the United States. Like the British, Canadian policymakers were often reluctant to follow the American lead. But in the longer term, dreams of Atlantic unity were to give way to increased reliance on the United States.

American containment policy in Asia during this period was not passive – it did not seek to preserve the status quo. Atomic diplomacy and increased pressure on China were the preferred methods of disrupting Sino-Soviet power. There was a counterrevolutionary aspect to U.S. containment strategies. The ultimate objective was the emergence of Western-oriented regimes in East Asia and the destruction of Soviet communism as a force in world politics. After 1949, and especially in the wake of the Korean conflict, the implementation of a more provocative containment strategy towards the East Asian periphery was viewed as a means of achieving these goals.

Notes

CHAPTER ONE

1 Gaddis, "The Emerging Post-Revisionist Synthesis," and Lundestad, *The American "Empire."*

2 Gaddis, "The Emerging Post-Revisionist Synthesis," 182.

3 Lundestad, *The American "Empire,"* 59.

4 The pioneering article was Robinson and Gallagher, "The Imperialism of Free Trade."

5 Lundestad, *The American "Empire,"* 55.

6 On this distinction and for an excellent survey of the history of empire until the nineteenth century, see Doyle, *Empires,* 13, 37–8, 44–7. Compare with Lundestad, *The American "Empire,"* 30.

7 Truman Library, Truman Papers, PSF, box 205, CIA memo, "Review of the World Situation," 16 September 1948.

8 Herring, "Franco-American Conflict in Indochina, 1950–1954."

9 Brands, *Bound to Empire,* ix.

10 Gaddis, *Strategies of Containment,* 21–2.

11 Charles Bohlen, as cited in Gaddis, *Strategies of Containment,* 57.

12 Gaddis, *Strategies of Containment,* chap. 2; Kennan, *Memoirs 1925–1950,* 359; Gaddis, *Strategies of Containment,* 39.

13 Schaller, *The American Occupation of Japan,* 83.

14 To conform with the period under study, this work has adopted the older Wade-Giles romanization system for Chinese names.

15 Kennan's early views and influence are described in Gaddis, *Strategies of Containment,* 47, and in Mayers, *George Kennan and the Dilemmas of U.S.*

Foreign Policy, 170–80; For Kennan's ideas about replacing the PRC, see PPS 39/1, 23 November 1948, in Etzold and Gaddis, *Containment,* 247–51. Foot analyses Dulles's use of atomic diplomacy during the Korean War in "Nuclear Coercion and the Ending of the Korean Conflict."

16 Etzold and Gaddis, *Containment,* 256.

17 Ibid., 264.

18 Ibid., 257, 260, 253.

19 Gaddis, *Strategies of Containment,* 56.

20 Cumings, "Preface," in his *Child of Conflict,* 15.

21 National Archives of Canada (NAC), RG25, acc. 90–91/008, box 179, 50068-40, telegram WA-103, 12 January 1948.

22 Truman Library, Truman Papers, PSF, box 205, "Review of the World Situation,"16 December 1948.

23 NAC, RG25, acc. 90–91/008, box 179, 50068-40, telegrams WA-798, 17 March 1948; and G.S. Patterson to the SSEA, no. 40, 16 September 1948.

24 See McGlothlen, "Acheson, Economics, and the American Commitment in Korea, 1947–1950."

25 Matray, *The Reluctant Crusade,* 173–4.

26 Department of State, *Foreign Relations of the United States (FRUS)* 1945, 6:557–8.

27 Hess, *The United States' Emergence as a Southeast Asian Power, 1940–1950,* 186.

28 *FRUS* 1946, 8:68.

29 Ibid., 1948, 6:45, 49.

30 Ibid., 28.

31 Truman Library, Acheson Papers, box 64, Memorandum of Conversation, 8 July 1949.

32 Public Record Office (PRO), FO371/76030, PUSC (53) Final, "Regional Co-operation in South-East Asia and the Far East," 20 August 1949; Hua Wu Yin, *Class and Communalism,* 90–1. See also Hinds, "Sterling and Imperial Policy, 1945–1951."

33 Hua Wu Yin, *Class and Communalism,* 94.

34 PRO, CAB 128, Cabinet Conclusions, 26 May 1949.

35 *FRUS* 1949, 7:84.

36 See, for example, Ovendale, *The English-speaking Alliance,* especially chap. 6; Watt, "Britain and the Cold War in the Far East."

37 PRO, FO371/76030, PUSC (32) Final, "The United Kingdom in South-East Asia and the Far East," 28 July 1949.

38 Ovendale, *The English-speaking Alliance,* 191–2.

39 Strang, *Home and Abroad,* 240; see also Moore, *Making the New Commonwealth,* 196.

40 Tarling, "The United Kingdom and the Origins of the Colombo Plan," 16.

41 Reynolds, "A 'Special Relationship'?" 7; Weiler, "British Labour and the Cold War," 65; and Smith and Zametica, "The Cold Warrior."

42 PRO, FO371/76030, PUSC (53) Final, 20 August 1949.

43 Adamthwaite, "Overstretched and Overstrung," 250.

44 See also Stairs, *The Diplomacy of Constraint*, which is appropriately subtitled *Canada, the Korean War, and the United States*; also Eayrs, *In Defence of Canada*, vols. 3–5, and Granatstein and Cuff, *American Dollars, Canadian Prosperity*.

45 NAC, RG2, B2, vol. 107, U-10-11, " 'Western Union' and an Atlantic Pact: A Survey of Recent Developments," 11 September 1948.

46 Ibid., RG25, acc. 89–90/029, box 70, file 323(s), "Influences Shaping the Policy of the United States towards the Soviet Union," 4 December 1947; ibid., RG25, vol. 3699, 5475-DC-40, James Gardiner to St Laurent, 9 February 1948.

47 Ibid., RG2, B2, vol. 68, D-2-5, 1943–50, 8 September 1947.

48 Ibid., RG2, Cabinet Conclusions, 30 June 1948.

49 Ibid., Cabinet Conclusions, 12 October 1948.

50 On this point, see also Evans and Frolic, *Reluctant Adversaries*, chaps. 2, 3, 5, and 6.

51 NAC, RG25, acc. 90–91/008, box 176, 50061–40, 10 February 1949. Ironically, Far Eastern issues were not discussed.

52 Ibid., box 178, 50067–40, Cabinet memo, 9 February 1949; RG25, vol. 3699, 5475-DG-3-40, Circular document A175, 8 November 1948.

CHAPTER TWO

1 Rotter, *The Path to Vietnam*, 163.

2 Department of State, *Foreign Relations of the United States* (*FRUS*) 1948, 6:1168–9. See also McGothlen, "Acheson," 36.

3 *FRUS* 1949, 7:978.

4 Ibid., 975.

5 National Archives, Washington (NA), lot 56, D151, box 14, file Top Secret 1949, 306, "U.S. Policy toward China and the Far East," Ogburn, 2 November 1949.

6 *FRUS* 1949, 7:976.

7 Truman Library, Acheson Papers, box 64, file July 1949, Memo of conversation, 11 July 1949. In September 1949 the JCS agreed to expand the force to 84,000 men.

8 Ibid., Truman Papers, PSF files, subject files, box 205, NSC Progress Report, 10 February 1950; ibid., Ohly Papers, box 115, Korea pt. 1, "U.S. Aid to Korea Since the Close of World War II," n.d.; *FRUS* 1950, 7:49.

9 *FRUS* 1949, 7:1005.

10 Ibid., 1075–6.

11 Ibid., 1084–5.

12 Ibid.

13 Ibid., 1950, 7:32. For the committee, see ibid., 10.

14 Ibid., 33.

15 Ibid., 37, 38.

16 NA, RG59, 895 B13, "Memorandum for the Record," 11 April 1950.

17 *FRUS* 1950, 7:49.

18 Cumings, *The Origins of the Korean War: The Roaring of the Cataract, 1947–1950*, 385.

19 Truman Library, Truman Papers, PSF, box 243, Korean War file, Acheson to Ross with enclosure, 20 January 1950.

20 NA, lot 58D, 258, box 4, file General – 5-Year Program Project, Merchant to Bruce, 16 February 1950.

21 McGlothlen, "Acheson," 46, 48.

22 Bullen, *Documents on British Policy Overseas*, ser. 2, 2:73.

23 Ibid.

24 Ibid., 54–63.

25 *FRUS* 1950, 3:1633.

26 Public Record Office (*PRO*), FO371/84544, CRO Y no. 93, 28 April 1950.

27 National Archives of Canada (NAC), RG25, 90–91/008, box 211, 50092-B-40, vol. 1, ICETP doc. 64.

28 Ibid., RG2, Cabinet document 130–50, 2 May 1950.

29 NAC, Pearson Papers, vol. 22, Meeting of Commonwealth Foreign Ministers, 1950, "Technical Assistance for Economic Development of Under-Developed Countries," n.d.

30 *FRUS*, 1950, 1:834.

31 NA, RG353, box 20, file 5.10, DDGWG 1950, doc. 19–26, DDG-19a, 11 September 1950.

32 Rotter, *The Path to Vietnam*, 163.

33 NA, RG25, box 20, file 5.10, DDGWG, 1950, doc. 19–26.

34 PRO, FO371/84493, FZ10114/3, "South-East Asia"; *FRUS* 1950, 3:1640.

35 PRO, FO371/75983, F/9106, Singapore to FO, 20 December 1949.

36 Ibid., Cabinet memo, CP(49) 244, 26 December 1949.

37 Porter, *Vietnam: A History in Documents*, 81.

38 Ibid.

39 PRO, FO371/83626, FF1051/2, "Indo-China"; and FF1051/7, Colombo to FO, no. 44, 13 January 1950.

40 Ibid., FF1051/9, Colombo to FO, no. 63, 17 January 1950.

41 Ibid., FO371/83626, FF1071/8, Colombo to FO, no. 47, 14 January 1950; FO371/84542, FZ1102/65, Inward CRO, Australia to UK, no. 95, 19 April 1950.

42 *FRUS* 1950, 6:692.

43 Ibid., 752–3, 747.

44 Ibid., 824.

45 Ibid., 825.

46 PRO, FO371/83608, FF1024/3, Browne to Lloyd, 11 May 1950.

47 *FRUS*, 1950, 6:768–9 (my emphasis).

48 Ibid., 783.

49 Ibid., 733.

50 Truman Library, Truman Papers, PSF, Intelligence files, box 257, ORE 92-49.

51 *FRUS* 1950, 6:810.

52 Ibid., 771.

53 NAC, RG25, 90–91/008, box 108, 50052-40, CRO Q, no. 126, 15 June 1948.

54 PRO, FO371/83626, FF1051/9, Colombo to FO, 17 January 1950; FO371/83607, FF1023/4, Paris to FO, no. 130, 11 April 1950.

55 PRO, FO371/83626, FF1051/8, no. 47.

56 Ibid., FO371/84493, FZ10114/11, n.d. [1950]; FO371/75976, F14115/G, 13 September 1949.

57 NAC, RG25, 90–91/008, box 109, 50052-40, London to SSEA, no. 447, 9 March 1950; PRO, FO371/83608, FF1024/2G, "Conversations," 7 March 1950.

58 PRO, CAB129, CP(50)114, 19May 1950.

59 Ibid., CP(50)115, 22 May 1950.

60 *FRUS* 1950, 6:717.

61 PRO, CAB128, Cabinet Conclusions, 7 February 1950.

62 NAC, Pearson Papers, vol. 22, Brief for Commonwealth Foreign Ministers, 1950, "Indo-China," 22 December 1949.

63 Ibid., RG25, 90–91/008, box 108, 50052-40, "Notes for Inclusion of Meeting of Heads of Divisions of October 25, 1949," 26 October 1949; Dispatch no. 930, Vanier to SSEA, 16 November 1949; Canadian Chiefs of Staff Committee Minutes (FOIA request), RG24, "Threat to Indo-China," 22 August 1950.

64 Ross, *In the Interests of Peace*, 39, Eayrs, *In Defence … Indochina*, 25.

65 NAC, RG2, B2, vol. 248, F5, Escott Reid to Pearson, February 21, 1950.

66 Eayrs, *In Defence … Indochina*, 17.

67 NAC, RG25 90–91/008, box 109, 50052–40, "Memorandum for the Minister, Relations with the Peking Government in China and with the Indo-Chinese States of Viet Nam, Cambodia and Laos," 9 June 1950; ibid., Cabinet Conclusions, 12 July 1950.

68 PRO, CAB129, CP(50)73, 20 April 1950.

69 Ibid.

70 NAC, St Laurent Papers, MG26L, vol. 233, China Recognition, Memo for PM, 24 November 1949.

71 Ibid., Pearson Papers, vol. 22, Commonwealth Foreign Ministers, 1950, pt. 2, "Survey of Present Strategic Situation," 31 December 1949.

72 Ibid., RG2, Cabinet Conclusions, 23 February 1950.

73 Ibid., RG2, Cabinet Memo, 55–50, 17 February 1950.

74 Ibid.

75 Ibid., Cabinet Conclusions, 10 March 1950. See also the Beecroft and Page articles in Evans and Frolic, *Reluctant Adversaries.*

76 NAC, RG25, acc. 1986–87/159, box 29, 5475-EJ-40, CRO telegram, 17 March 1950.

77 Ibid., 30 March 1950. For public opinion polls, see the Canadian Institute of Public Opinion, and Gallup, *Public Opinion Polls: Great Britain, 1937–1975.*

78 NAC, Wrong Papers, vol. 7, file 42, Pearson to Wrong, 24 March 1950; RG 25, 90–91/008, box 171, 50055–40, Canberra to Ottawa no. 5, 2 March 1950.

79 Simon, *Public Opinion,* 171.

80 NAC, RG25, 90–91/008, box 171, 50055–40, Pearson to Forde, Australian HC in Ottawa, 1 March 1950.

81 Tucker, "China's Place," 109–32. For a summary of the "Cohen-Tucker" thesis, see McMahon,"The Cold War in Asia."

82 PRO, FO800/517, Franks to Bevin, 8 March 1950; NAC, RG25, acc. 90-91/008, box 109, 50052–40, Bevin to UK ambassador in France, no. 266, 2 March 1950.

83 NAC, Wrong Papers, vol. 7, file 42, Pearson to St Laurent, 14 April 1950.

84 PRO, CAB129, CP(50)61, 3 April 1950; Martin, *Divided Counsel,* 140; NA, lot 58, D258, file FY 1953, Briefing Material, "Disposition of Former Chinese Airlines," 17 July 1951.

85 PRO, CAB128, Cabinet Conclusions, 24 April 1950.

86 Ibid., FO371, UF123/76, minute by P.C.H. Holmer, 16 May 1950.

87 *FRUS* 1950, 3:942; McLean, "American Nationalism, the China Myth and the Truman Doctrine."

88 Gaddis, "The American 'Wedge' Strategy, 1949–1955," 162.

89 PAC, RG2, Cabinet Conclusions, 14 June 1950.

90 PRO, FO371/88419, UP123/83, 11 May 1950.

91 Ibid., FO371/88419, UP123/79, memos by Hector McNeill and Ernest Davies, 2 and 14 June 1950, and FO to NY, no. 660, 15 June 1950.

92 NAC, RG25, acc. 1986–87/159, vol. 27, file 5475-EJ-40, Vanier to SSEA, 28 May 1950.

93 PRO, CAB129, CP(50)118, 26 May 1950.

94 Ibid., FO371, UP123/79, Washington to Foreign Office, 17 June 1950, no. 1696.

95 NAC, Wrong Papers, vol. 7, file 42, "Memo for the Prime Minister," 14 April 1950.

96 PRO, FO371, UP123/79, 17 June 1950, no. 1696.

CHAPTER THREE

1 Foot, "Anglo-American Relations," 57.

2 Stueck, "The Limits of Influence," 78.

3 Department of State, *Foreign Relations of the United States* (*FRUS*) 1950, 7:149–54.

4 Yasamee and Hamilton, *Documents on British Policy Overseas* (*DBPO*), ser. 2, 4:5.

5 Ibid., 8–9 n2.

6 *FRUS* 1950, 7:158.

7 Ibid., 1950, 1:241.

8 Ibid., 1950, 7:211.

9 Yasamee and Hamilton, *DBPO*, ser. 2, 4:7–9.

10 National Archives of Canada (NAC), RG2, Cabinet Conclusions, 27–28 June 1950; Stairs, *Diplomacy of Constraint*, 59.

11 O'Neill, *Australia*, 48–56.

12 Public Record Office (PRO), CAB128, Cabinet Conclusions, 27 June 1950.

13 Ibid.

14 *FRUS* 1950, 7:181.

15 Ibid., 313.

16 Ibid., 327.

17 NAC, RG2, Cabinet Conclusions, 12 July 1950.

18 *FRUS* 1950, 7:347.

19 Yasamee and Hamilton, *DBPO*, ser. 2, 4:64; NAC, RG2, B2, vol. 167, file K-10-C, WA 1521, Washington to SSEA, 12 July 1950.

20 Yasamee and Hamilton, *DBPO*, ser. 2, 4:68; NAC, RG25, 90–01/008, box 181, 50069-A-40, no. 474, 15 July 1950.

21 Canada, Department of National Defence, "Report" for year ending March 1952, 86.

22 NAC, RG25, 1990–91/008, 50069-A-40, Memorandum for the Minister," 18 July 1950.

23 Ibid., St Laurent Papers, MG26 L, vol. 234, file External Affairs Korea, 1950, CRO Q, no. 22, 25 July 1950.

24 Ibid., Pearson Papers, MG26 N1, vol. 35, "Memo for the Prime Minister," 26 July 1950.

25 Ibid., RG2, Cabinet Conclusions, 27 July 1950.

26 Ibid., Pearson Papers, vol. 35, Pearson to Wrong, 20 July 1950.

27 Truman Library, Acheson Papers, box 66, July 1950.

28 NAC St Laurent Papers, MG26 L, vol. 234, "Discussions with Mr. Acheson and Officials in Washington Saturday and Sunday, July 29th and 30th, 1950."See also Truman Library, Acheson Papers, Student Research file no. 32B, box 2, file 13, Memo of Conversation, 29 July 1950. Actual U.S. defence spending for FY 1951 came to $48.2 billion, a 257% increase over the original $13.5 billion. See Gaddis *Strategies*, 113.

29 Stairs, *Diplomacy of Constraint*, 89.

30 NAC, St Laurent Papers, MG26 L, External Affairs, Korea 1950, Attlee to St Laurent, 3 August 1950.

31 Ibid., RG2, Cabinet Conclusions, 7 August.

32 PRO, CAB128, Cabinet Conclusions, 4 September 1950; Reid, *Envoy to Nehru.*

33 PRO, CAB128, Cabinet Conclusions, 18 July 1950.

34 Stairs, *Diplomacy of Constraint,* 121–2.

35 *FRUS* 1950, 7:792.

36 Ibid., 823.

37 Ibid., 868–9.

38 NAC, RG2, B2, vol. 245, file C-20–5, 1950, 11 September 1950; 50069-A-40, dispatch no. 53, NY to ASSEA, 9 October 1950.

39 *FRUS* 1950, 7:929.

40 Ibid., 748.

41 Ibid., 749.

42 Ibid., 939.

43 Truman Library, Elsey Papers, Student Research File, Korean War, no. 32, box 1, file 9, "Substance of Statements made at Wake Island Conference."

44 Ibid.

45 Ibid.

46 Truman Library, Acheson Papers, Student Research File, no. 32B, box 2, file 15, addendum to Notes on Wake Island Conference.

47 Ibid., Elsey Papers, Student Research File, Korean War, no. 32, box 1, file 9, Rhee to MacArthur.

48 Ibid., Truman Papers, PSF, box 248, Daily Korean Summaries, September-October 1950.

49 *FRUS* 1950, 7:1005–6.

50 Ibid., 1017.

51 Ibid., 806.

52 Ibid., 1100.

53 Ibid., 1029, 1121.

54 Ibid.

55 Ibid., 1053.

56 Ibid., 1057, 1075.

57 Stairs, *Diplomacy of Constraint,* 135. For Bevin's buffer zone proposal, see Farrar, "Britain's Proposal"; NAC, RG2, Cabinet Conclusions, 22 November 1950. On hot pursuit, see Stueck, "The Limits of Influence," 91; and for an interpretation with a different emphasis than the one offered here, see Foot, *The Wrong War,* 91.

58 Truman Library, Acheson Papers, box 67, file August 1950, Memorandum of Conversation, 28 November 1950.

59 *FRUS* 1950, 3:1714, 1762.

60 NAC, RG2, Cabinet Conclusions, 9 December 1950.

61 *FRUS* 1950, 3:1728.

62 Ibid., 1765.

63 Ibid., 1771, 1772, 1785.

64 Ibid., 1763.

65 NAC, RG2, Cabinet Conclusions, 29 November 1950.

66 See Foot, *The Wrong War,* 124–30.

67 *FRUS* 1950, 7:459, 461, 481

68 NAC, RG25, acc. 1986–87/160, box 37, file 4457-B-40, 30 March 1951.

69 Dockrill, "The Foreign Office," 468.

70 *FRUS* 1950, 3:1720, 1709.

71 Ibid., 1721.

72 Ibid., 1770.

73 NAC, RG2, Cabinet Conclusions, 9 December 1950.

74 Ibid., 28–29 December 1950.

75 PRO, PREM8/1405, pt. 4, MOD to Tedder, 5 January 1951.

76 Yasamee and Hamilton, *DPRO,* set 2, 4:310–11. On this issue see also NAC, RG25, 50069-C-40.

77 Yasamee and Hamilton, *DBPO,* ser. 2, 4:310–11.

78 PRO, FO800/517, Strachey to Bevin, 2 January 1951.

79 Ibid., CAB128, Cabinet Conclusions, 18 December 1950.

80 NAC, RG2, Cabinet Conclusions, 28–29 December 1950.

81 Yasamee and Hamilton, *DBPO,* ser. 2, 4:301–02.

82 PRO, CAB128, Cabinet Conclusions, 22 January 1951.

83 Ibid., FO800/517, Dixon minute, 6 January 1951; Dockrill, "The Foreign Office," 468.

84 Foot, "Anglo-American Relations," 54.

85 PRO, CAB128, Cabinet Conclusions, 23 January 1951.

86 NAC, RG2, Cabinet Conclusions, 24 January 1951.

87 PRO, CAB128, Cabinet Conclusions, 25, 29 January 1951.

88 NAC, RG2, Cabinet Conclusions, 1 February 1951; PRO, CAB128, Cabinet Conclusions, 29 January 1951.

89 PRO, CAB128, Cabinet Conclusions, 29 January 1951; NAC, RG2, Cabinet Conclusions, 1 February 1951.

90 Foot, *The Wrong War,* 152.

91 *FRUS* 1950, 3:1770.

CHAPTER FOUR

1 Gaddis, "Was the Truman Doctrine a Turning Point?" 402.

2 Department of State, *Foreign Relations of the United States (FRUS)* 1951, 1:68.

3 Ibid., 1952–54, 2:145.

4 Ibid., 144.

5 Ibid., 1950, 7:202; 6:835.

6 Ibid., 1952–54, 1:144.

7 Etzold and Gaddis, *Containment,* 264.

8 *FRUS* 1951, 1:41.

9 Ibid., 1952–54, 12:246.

10 Truman Library, Truman Papers, PSF, Intelligence Files, box 253, National Intelligence Estimate, NIE-20, 20 March 1951.

11 *FRUS* 1952–54, 12:46.

12 Ibid., 1408.

13 Library of Congress, Declassified Documents Reference System, 1985, NSC 2664, memo dated 6 November 1953 of discussion at 169th meeting of the NSC, held 5 November 1953.

14 *FRUS* 1951, 6:333.

15 Ibid., 338, 337.

16 Ibid., 400.

17 Ibid., 333.

18 Truman Library, Truman Papers, PSF, Intelligence Files, box 253, NIE-35, 7 August 1951.

19 *FRUS* 1951, 6:875.

20 Ibid., 879.

21 *FRUS* 1952–54, 13:31.

22 Ibid., 264.

23 Ibid., 214.

24 Truman Library, Truman Papers, PSF, Intelligence Files, box 253, NIE-35–43, 3 March 1952.

25 *FRUS* 1952–54, 13:95–6; 294.

26 Ibid., 1951, 6:537.

27 Ibid., 1952–54, 13:120.

28 Ibid., 127.

29 National Archives (NA), lot 58D, 258, box 5, file FY 1953, Economic Programs.

30 Ibid.

31 Mutual Security Agency, *Mutual Security Program*, 30 June 1954, 29.

32 NA, lot 55D, 388, box 5, file Far East General, 1 April 1953.

33 *FRUS* 1951, 6:427, 450.

34 Ibid.

35 Ibid., 384–5, 426.

36 National Archives of Canada (NAC), RG25, acc. 1984–85/150, box 118, 9126–40, Reid to SSEA, 25 June, 1952.

37 Ibid., box 29, file 1846–40, Wallinger to Eden, 14 March 1953.

38 Public Record Office (PRO), FO371/106768, "Indo-China," n.d., but June–July 1953.

39 Ibid., CAB134/290, FE(O)C(50)45, 15 September 1950.

40 Ibid., FO371/101267, FZ1195/4, Scott, 30 January 1952.

41 Ibid.

42 Ibid.

43 Ibid., FO371/106768, "Indo-China."

44 Ibid.

45 Ibid., FO371/106768, FF1071/134G, 7 July 1953.

46 Ibid., FO371/106765, FF1071/18, n.d.

47 Ibid.

48 Ibid., CAB134/866, "Brief on Policy," March 1952.

49 Ibid.

50 Ibid., w, no. 80, 30 April 1952.

51 Ibid., FO371/101246, FZ1108/3, A.H.M. Hillis to Murray, 4 January 1952; CAB134/866, "Brief on Policy," March 1952.

52 Ibid., FO371/101246, Tahourdin to Graves, 3 October 1952.

53 Ibid., DO35/2721, Graves to Minister of Foreign Affairs, Saigon, 3 August 1951.

54 Ibid., FO371/101249, FZ11012/10, J. Thomson to A.W. Snelling, CRO, 9 September 1952.

55 Ross, *In the Interests of Peace*, 48. Ross makes the salient point that St Laurent was more enthusiastic about providing economic aid than underwriting French military operations.

56 Eayrs, *In Defence of Canada: Indochina Roots*, 27; (NAC), RG25, acc. 1991–92/109, box 121, 50273-40, Wilgress memo, September 1952; *FRUS* 1952–54, 13:321.

57 NAC, RG25, acc. 1991–92/109, box 121, 50273-40, 10 March 1953; 25 September 1952.

58 Ibid., 25 September 1952; RG25, acc. 1986–87/160, box 32, 4457-B-40, 21 February 1951.

59 Eayrs, In Defence of Canada: Indochina Roots, 30; Ross *In the Interests of Peace*, 64.

60 NAC, RG25, 90–91/008, box 110, 50052-40, DEA Summary; Canberra to Ottawa, 18 March 1953; and memo by Casey, "Record of Discussion with M. Letourneau at the Defence Department in Melbourne on Monday, 9th March, 1953."

61 PRO, FO371/99220, Makins, F1071/3, 3 January 1951.

62 Ibid., Scott, 28 December 1951; NAC, RG25, acc. 1990–91/008, box 177, 50062-40, Wilgress to SSEA, 18 December 1951.

63 *FRUS* 1951, 6:59; Radford, as cited in Gibbons, *The U.S. Government and the Vietnam War, Part I: 1945–1960*, 87.

64 *FRUS* 1952–54, 12:350.

65 NAC, RG25, acc. 1991–92/109, box 121, 50273-40, 11 May 1953.

66 *FRUS* 1952–54, 12:125–34, 132.

67 Ibid., 60.

68 PRO, FO371/101267, R.H. Scott, "Brief for Secretary of State," 16 February 1952.

69 *FRUS* 1952–54, 12:144.

70 Ibid., 232.

71 Ibid., 241.

72 Ibid., 1951, 6:34, 35, 51.

73 NAC, RG25, acc 1991–92/109, box 121, 50273-40, 1 December 1953.

74 *FRUS* 1952–54, 13:469, 479, 497.

75 Ibid., 526.

76 Ibid., 505.

77 Ibid., 507.

78 Ibid., 505.

79 PRO, FO371/106766, FF1071/72, 1 May 1953.

80 Ibid., FO371/106767, FF1071/13, "Foreign Affairs Debate," n.d. [early May 1953].

81 NAC, RG25, acc. 90–91/008, box 110, 50052-40, CRO telegram Y 168, 27 May 1953.

82 Ibid., Canadian Permanent Representative to the UN to SSEA, no. 283, 29 May 1953; Acting Secretary to UN, no. 255, 25 May 1953; Washington to USSEA, no. 1604, 14 August 1953.

83 PRO, FO371/106766, R.W. Selby of SEAD, quoting Churchill, 4 May 1953.

84 *FRUS* 1952–54, 5:1649.

85 Gibbons, *The U.S. Government and the Vietnam War*, 128.

86 *FRUS* 1952–54, 13:741; 780–9.

87 Ibid., 781–2.

88 Ibid., 747.

89 Ibid., 782.

90 See Immerman, *John Foster Dulles and the Diplomacy of the Cold War.*

CHAPTER FIVE

1 Truman Library, Truman Papers, PSF, box 253, "Effects of Operations in Korea on the Internal Situation in Communist China," NIE-32, 10 July 1951.

2 Library of Congress, Declassified Documents Reference System, DOS 1848, Meeting of NSC, 11 February 1953.

3 See, for example, Dingman, "Atomic Diplomacy," Foot, "Nuclear Coercion," and Keefer, "Eisenhower and the End of the Korean War."

4 Dingman, "Atomic Diplomacy," 79.

5 Truman Library, Truman Papers, PSF, box 220, Memorandum for the President, 25 January 1951.

6 Dingman, "Atomic Diplomacy," 69.

7 Ibid., 85, 87.

8 Discussion with Robert O'Neill, All Souls College, Oxford, May 1989.

9 Library of Congress, Declassified Documents Reference System, DOS000457, Discussion at 145th NSC Meeting, 20 May 1953.

10 On this point, see Foot, "Nuclear Coercion," 99–107.

11 Truman Library, Truman Papers, PSF, box 214, NSC48/5, Report to the NSC on US Objectives, Policies and Courses of Action in Asia, 17 May 1951.

12 Public Record Office (PRO), FO371/92064, F1022/29, R.H. Scott, 11 September 1951.

13 Ibid., F1022/25, CRO telegram Y534, 18 September 1951.

14 Department of External Affairs (DEA), Statements and Speeches, 21/24, 5 June 1951.

15 PRO, CAB134/291, FEOC, 12 February 1951.

16 Ibid., FE(O)(51)7, 3 February 1951.

17 Ibid., annex to COS(51)63, 10 February 1951.

18 Ibid.; see FE(O)(51)21, 4 June 1951, and FE(O)(51)31, Revise, 11 December 1951.

19 Ibid., CAB134/897, FEOC, 9 September 1952.

20 Ibid., CAB129, C(53)81, 2 March 1953.

21 DEA, Statements and Speeches, 51/24.

22 Barry, *Documents on Canadian External Relations* (*DCER*) (1952): 461, 311–12.

23 Truman Library, Truman Papers, PSF, box 214, Memo for the Executive Secretary, 2 October 1951; Foot, *The Wrong War*, 158.

24 Department of State, *Foreign Relations of the United States*, (*FRUS*) 1951, 7:1390.

25 Ibid., 1392–3.

26 Ibid., 1395.

27 PRO, CAB128, Cabinet Conclusions, 17 January 1952.

28 Ibid., FO371/99265, FC10338/14, George Toplas minute, 7 March 1952.

29 Ibid., 11 March 1952.

30 Ibid., FO371/99268, FC10345/21, 18 April 1952.

31 National Archives of Canada (NAC), RG25, acc. 1986–87/160, box 75, 5475-EJ-40, Holmes to Pearson, 21 May 1951.

32 *FRUS* 1952–54, 14:103.

33 NAC, RG25, acc. 91–92/109, box 186, 50393–40, 8 October 1952.

34 Ibid., RG25, acc. 90–91/008, box 171, 50055-B-40, PUSC(52)6, 31 March 1952.

35 PRO, FO371/99218, F1035/9G, 29 February 1952.

36 Foot, *The Wrong War*, 185–6.

37 PRO, PREM 11/111, annex 19, 24 November 1952.

38 Ibid., CAB128, Cabinet Conclusions, 16 December 1952.

39 Ibid., CAB128, Cabinet Conclusions, 4 December 1952; *FRUS* 1953–54, 15:663.

40 Ibid., 1952–54, 12:301–2.

41 PRO, CAB128, Cabinet Conclusions, 30 December 1952.

42 *FRUS* 1952–54, 14:133.

43 Ibid., 136.

44 Ibid., 177.

45 Library of Congress, Declassified Documents Reference System, 1985, NSC meeting, 5 November 1953.

46 *FRUS* 1952–54, 14:38, 170n2.

47 Ibid., 177.

48 DEA, Statements and Speeches, 53/7, 5–12 and 12 February 1953.

49 *DCER* 19 (1953):983.

50 Keefer, "Eisenhower and the End of the Korean War."

51 *FRUS* 1951, 7:1398.

52 National Archives (NA), RG59, lot 64D, 563, box 721, file "USSR, 1953."

53 Ibid., 10 March 1953.

54 Eisenhower Library, White House Central Files, Subject Series, box 65, Message to PSYWAR, 9 March 1953.

55 NA, RG59, lot 55D, 388, box 1, file Prisoners of War, 31 March 1953.

56 Eisenhower Library, White House Office, Special Assistant for National Security Affairs, NSC series, Administrative Subseries, box 5, Misc. 11, [CIA] memo, 8 April 1953. See also Alan Dulles' remarks to the NSC in Eisenhower Library, Ann Whitman file, NSC series, box 4.

57 *FRUS* 1952–54, 2:308.

58 Ibid., 307.

59 Ibid., 317.

60 Ibid., 272.

61 NA, RG218, 383.21 (3–19–45) sec. 128, 11 May 1953.

62 Eisenhower Library, NSC Staff Papers, Executive Secretary of NSC, Chronological File, box 1, Memorandum for General Robert Cutler, 7 May 1953.

63 Ibid., C.D. Jackson Records, 1953–54, box 6, 11 May 1953.

64 Library of Congress, Declassified Documents Quarterly, NSC49/2027, NSC Discussion, 6 May 1953.

65 Foot, *The Wrong War*, 209.

66 NAC, RG25, acc 1990–91/008, box 188, 50069-A-40, Wrong to SSEA, 28 May 1953.

67 Alcock, "Britain and the Korean War," 392.

68 NAC, RG25, acc. 190–01/008, box 188, 50069-A-40, Robertson to SSEA, 14 MAY 1953.

69 Ibid., Reid to SSEA, no. 94, 14 May 1953.

70 Ibid., Pearson to Wrong, 14 May 1953.

71 *FRUS* 1952–54, 15:1016, 1043.

72 Ibid., 1045.

73 PRO, PREM11/406, Eisenhower to Churchill, 23 May 1953.

74 NAC, RG25, acc. 1990–91/008, box 188, 50059-A-40, Canberra to Embassy in Ottawa, 26 May 1953.

75 Ibid., 27 May 1953.

76 Ibid., ASSEA to Washington, EX 950, 28 May 1953.

77 Eisenhower Library, Mark Clark Papers (on microfilm), box 11.

78 NAC, RG25 90–91/008, box 188, 50069-A-40, Washington to SSEA, WA-1325, 30 May 1953.

79 Ibid., Menzies to Casey, Australian High Commission in Washington to Australian High Commissioner in Ottawa, Misc. 30, 30 May 1953.

80 PRO, FO371/105497, FK1071/380, Gascoigne to FO, 3 June 1953.

81 *FRUS* 1951, 7:1387.

82 Truman Library, Truman Papers, Selected Records relating to the Korean War, Muccio to DOS, 17 July 1952.

83 NA, RG59, lot 55D, 388, box 1, file Korea, January through December 1953(2), Young to Robertson, 24 April 53.

84 Ibid., file South Korea, Attitude toward Armistice, May 1953.

85 NAC, RG25 1990–91/008, vol. 49, file 50069-A-40, Wrong to SSEA, 30 May 1953.

86 *FRUS* 1952–54, 15:1146; NAC, RG25, acc. 90–91/008, box 188, 50069-A-40, Tokyo to SSEA, no. 623, 6 June 1953; ibid., Washington to SSEA, WA-1713, 15 July 1953.

87 Macdonald, *U.S.–Korean Relations*, 250.

88 NA, 795B.5-MSP/4–2652, Strong to Dept and Enclosures.

89 Department of State, *Treaties and Other International Acts*, ser. 2593.

90 *FRUS* 1952–54, 15:1246–7.

91 Ibid., 1464.

92 Ibid., 1458.

93 Department of State, *Bulletin*, 6 July 1953, 4.

94 *FRUS* 1952–54, 15:1247.

95 Ibid., 1444.

96 NA, 795B.00(w), U.S. Ambassador, Seoul, to Assistant Chief of Staff, State, Navy, and Air, 30 October 1953; ibid., U.S. Ambassador, Seoul, to State, Navy, Air, and G2 Division, 27 November 1953. In 1952 Rhee had also criticized the U.S. for infringing on South Korea's economic sovereignty. It had been at Rhee's insistence that another clause was worked into the 1952 Economic Agreement which stated that the coordination of economic matters between the ROK and the UNC would be done "without infringing upon the sovereign rights of the Republic of Korea."

97 Ibid., U.S. Ambassador, Seoul, to State, Navy, Air, and G2, 18 December 1953.

CHAPTER SIX

1 See Fish, "After Stalin's Death"; and Young, "Churchill's Bid for Peace with Moscow," "Churchill, the Russians and the Western Alliance," and *The Foreign Policy of Churchill's Peacetime Administration*.

2 Great Britain, House of Commons, *Debates*, 5 March 1953.

3 Department of State, *Foreign Relations of the United States (FRUS)* 1952–54, 2:266.

4 Public Record Office (PRO), CAB129, C(51)1, 31 October 1951; CAB129, C(51)18, 15 November 1951, and C(51)1, 31 October 1951.

5 Ibid., CAB129, C(51)48, 17 December 1951.

6 Ibid., CAB129, C(52)141, 3 May 1952.

7 Great Britain, House of Commons, *Debates*, 2 March 1954.

8 PRO, PREM11/418, Colville to PM, 1 December 1953.

9 Ibid., FO371/111690, NS1051/1G, 23 December 1953.

10 Department of State, *Bulletin*, 11 August 1952, 229.

11 Ibid., 8 September 1952, 358.

12 Truman Library, Truman Papers, OF, box 1024, file 335-D, Bureau of the Budget, "Report to the President," 18 March 1952.

13 Department of State, *Bulletin*, 6 July 1953, 4.

14 Ibid., 8 September 1952, 361.

15 Ibid., 3 August, 1953, 144.

16 PRO, FO371/105530, FK1076/299, Allen to Graham, 21 October 1953.

17 NAC, RG25, acc. 1986–87/160, box 75, 5475-EJ-40, 15 May 1953.

18 Eisenhower Library, Ann Whitman, NSC series, box 4, NSC meeting, 4 June 1953.

19 *FRUS* 1952–54, 2:586–7.

20 Ibid., 583.

21 Ibid., 1952–54, 7:702, 690.

22 Royal Institute of International Affairs, *Documents on International Affairs*, 1953, 82–3.

23 PRO, FO371/105529, FK1076/297, *NCNA*, 16 September 1953.

24 For more on this theme, see Foot, "Nuclear Coercion," 107–8.

25 NAC, RG25, acc. 1990–91/008, box 189, 50069-A-40, Robertson to SSEA, 1 October 1953.

26 PRO, FO371/105532, FK1076/370, FO to Washington, 7 October 1953.

27 NAC, RG25, acc. 1990–91/008, box 189, 50069-A-40, vol. 57, SSEA to Washington, EX-765, 8 October 1953.

28 *FRUS* 1952–54, 7:678–9.

29 Ibid., 749–50.

30 Ibid., 769.

31 Ibid., 775.

32 PRO, CAB128, Cabinet Conclusions, 26 January 1954.

33 Ibid., PREM11/665, FO to Berlin, no. 40, 27 January 1954.

34 Ibid.

35 Ibid.

36 *FRUS* 1952–54, 7:790–1; 818.

37 Ibid., 847.

38 Ibid., 848.

39 Ibid., 1952–54, 8:1222.

40 Ibid., 1048.

41 Ibid., 1115.

42 Ibid., 1162.

43 PRO, CAB128, Cabinet Conclusions, 22 February 1954.

44 *FRUS* 1952–54, 15:1346.

45 PRO, FO371/105531, FK1071/344G, 18 September 1953.

46 Ibid., FO371/105527, FK1076/296, Graham to Salisbury, 26 August 1953.

47 Ibid., FO371/105528, FK1076/268, BBC Monitoring Report, 1 September 1953.

48 NAC, RG25, acc. 1990–91/008, box 190, 50069-A-40, 3 December 1953.

49 PRO, FO371/110546, FK1071/145, Y 120, 19 March 1954.

50 NAC, RG25, acc. 1990–91/008, box 191, 50069-A-40, Memo for the Minister, 27 April 1954; PRO, FO371/110556, FK1071/236, FO to Washington, no. 1556, 11 April 1954.

51 O'Neill, *Australia in the Korean War,* 386–7.

52 Eisenhower Library, Eisenhower Diary, box 6, Rhee to Eisenhower, 11 March 1954.

53 *FRUS* 1952–54, 16:264.

54 NAC, RG25, acc. 1990–91/008, box 191, 50069-A-40, 17 May 1954.

55 *FRUS* 1952–54, 16:240, 307.

56 Ibid., 292.

57 Ibid., 298, 333, 337.

58 NAC, RG25, acc. 1990–91/008, box 191, 50069-A-40, Canadian Delegation to SSEA, no. 80, 17 May 1954; *FRUS* 1952–54, 16:315–16.

59 *FRUS* 1952–54, 16:243.

CHAPTER SEVEN

1 Randle, *Geneva 1954,* ix; Billings-Yun, *Decision against War;* Marks, "The Real Hawk," 299.

2 Department of State, *Foreign Relations of the United States* (*FRUS*) 1952–54, 13:1166, 1173.

3 Ibid., 1234, 1240.

4 Ibid., 1217.

5 Ibid., 1229.

6 Ibid., 1173, 1222; Eisenhower Library, Dulles Papers, Subject Series, box 9, "Memorandum of Conversation," 26 April 1954.

7 *FRUS* 1952–54, 13:1411.

8 Ibid., 1505, 1508.

9 Ibid., 1420.

10 Ibid., 1535.

11 Ibid., 1259.
12 Eisenhower Library, Dulles Papers, Subject Series, box 9, "Memo for the Secretary's File," 5 April 1954.
13 *FRUS* 1952–54, 13:1256.
14 National Archives of Canada (NAC), RG25, acc. 1991–92/109, box 121, 50273-40, UK Geneva Conference Delegation to Washington, no. 126, 22 May 1954.
15 National Archives (NA), RG218, Admiral Radford Papers, box 10, file 091 Indochina (April 1954).
16 Public Record Office (PRO), FO371/112051, DF1071/202, Meeting with Dulles, n.d.
17 Ibid., DF1071/199, Allen minute, 10 April 1954.
18 Ibid., FO371/112053, DF1071/227, 10 April 1954.
19 Ibid., FO371/112051, DF1071/199, 10 April 1954.
20 Ibid., DF1071/202G, Confidential annex to COS(54), 42nd meeting, 10 April 1954.
21 NAC, RG25, acc. 1991–92/109, box 121, 50273-40, 12 April 1954.
22 Ibid., RG25, acc. 1990–91/008, box 110, 50052-40, "Memo for the Acting Minister," 29 April 1954.
23 Ibid., file 50055-B-40, no. 75, 15 May 1954; Eayrs, *Indochina Roots*, 42.
24 NAC, RG25, acc. 1990–91/008, box 110, 50055-B-40, no. 75, 15 May 1954.
25 Ibid., no. 28, 1 May 1954; see also Tang, *Britain's Encounter*, 118–25.
26 Eayrs, *Indochina Roots*, 46, 42; NAC, RG25, acc. 1990–91/008, box 110, 50052-40, WA-740, 28 April 1954, and WA-601, 7 April 1954. Canada's involvement in the conference is also discussed, without the benefit of primary documents, in Holmes, "Geneva: 1954."
27 PRO, FO371/112051, DF1071/186G, 6 April 1954.
28 Ibid., FO371/112053, DF1071/239, Reading, 20 April 1954.
29 Ibid., DF1071/229, 14 and 15 April 1954.
30 Ibid., FO371/112054, DF1071/256, 20 April 1954.
31 Ibid., FO371/112058, DF1071/396G, FO to MacDonald, 29 April 1954.
32 NA, RG218, JCS Geographic File, 1954–56, 092 Asia (6–25-48) sec. 53, JCS 1992/262, 6 January 1954.
33 Ibid., RG 218, Admiral Radford Papers, box 10, file 091, Indo-China, February–April 1954, 13 April 1954.
34 PRO, FO371/112064, DF1071/517, 12 May 1954.
35 Ibid., FO371/112059, DF1071/434, 27 April 1954.
36 NAC, RG25, acc. 1990–91/008, box 110, 50052-40, WA-740, April 28, 1954.
37 *FRUS* 1952–54, 13:1485
38 Ibid., 1648.
39 Ibid., 12:522.
40 PRO, FO371/112067, DF1071/579, 12 May 1954.

41 *FRUS* 1952–54, 13:1535.

42 Ibid., 1527–8.

43 Ibid., 1446–7.

44 Ibid., 1528.

45 Ibid., 16:872–3.

46 Ibid., 13:1613.

47 Ibid., 1610.

48 Ibid., 1480.

49 Ibid., 1610, 1600.

50 Ibid., 1677.

51 Ibid., 1619.

52 PRO, FO371/112052, DF1071/218, 16 April 1954; FO371/112065, DF1071/538, 15 May 1954.

53 Ibid., FO371/112058, DF1071/417G, 4 May 1954.

54 Ibid., FO371/112063, DF1071/505G, 11 May 1954.

55 NAC, RG25, acc. 1990–91/008, box 111, 50052-40, no. 77, 16 May 1954.

56 PRO, FO371/112067, DF1071/561G, 17 May 1954; Kirkpatrick minute, 18 May 1954.

57 *FRUS* 1952–54, 13:1590, 159.

58 Ibid., 16:1054–6.

59 Ibid., 1083.

60 PRO, FO371/112070, DF1071/659, 15 June 1954. The Thai letter noted that the conflict in Indochina constituted a threat to Thailand and asked the Security Council to send a Peace Observation Commission to Thailand. The request constituted part of the American strategy for legitimizing United Action, and a draft resolution of 18 June regarding the sending of observers was vetoed by the Soviet Union. In early July, Thailand sent another letter to the secretary general of the United Nations, but the discussions at Geneva and the eventual partition agreement precluded further action.

61 *FRUS* 1952–54, 16:1118.

62 Ibid., 13:1689, 1711, 1716; 16:1056.

63 Ibid., 13:1665, 1746.

64 Eisenhower Library, Collins Papers, box 24, Briefing Book on Vietnam (3), McClintock to Smith, 12 August 1954.

65 *FRUS* 1952–54, 13:1953–4.

66 Eisenhower Library, Ann Whitman file, Legislative Meetings series, box 1, 1954(3), Memorandum for the Record, 23 June 1954.

67 PRO, FO371/112073, DF1071/719G, Eden to Foreign Office, 16 June 1954.

68 Ibid., DF1071/732, 18 June 1954.

69 Ibid., DF1071/741, 19 June 1954.

70 *FRUS* 1952–54, 16:1172.

71 Ibid., 12:576.

72 NAC, RG25, acc. 1991–92/109, box 121, 50273–40, vol. 4, CRO telegram Y 266, 30 June 1954.

73 *FRUS* 1952–54, 13:1758n5.

74 Ibid., 16:1273.

75 Ibid., 1281.

76 Ibid., 1294.

77 Ibid., 1310.

78 Ibid., 1277, 1324. See also 1275, 1325.

79 Ibid., 1326.

80 Ibid., 1330–1.

81 Ibid., 1363–4.

Bibliography

PRIMARY SOURCES

Archival Collections

DWIGHT D. EISENHOWER LIBRARY, ABILENE, KANSAS
Mark Clark Papers
J. Lawton Collins Papers
John Foster Dulles Papers
Dwight D. Eisenhower Papers
C.D. Jackson Records
White House Central Files
White House Office

NATIONAL ARCHIVES, WASHINGTON
Diplomatic Branch, RG 59
Military Branch, RG 218
Arthur Radford Papers

NATIONAL ARCHIVES OF CANADA, OTTAWA
Department of External Affairs, RG 25.
Department of National Defence, RG 24.
Privy Council Office, RG 2
Brooke Claxton Papers
Lester Pearson Papers

Escott Reid Papers
Louis St Laurent Papers
Hume Wrong Papers

PUBLIC RECORD OFFICE, LONDON
Cabinet, CAB 128, 129, 131, 134
Chiefs of Staff, DEFE 4,5
Dominions Office, DO 35
Foreign Office, FO 371
Prime Minister's Office, PREM 11
Clement Attlee Papers
Ernest Bevin Papers
Winston Churchill Papers
Anthony Eden Papers

HARRY S. TRUMAN LIBRARY, INDEPENDENCE, MISSOURI
Dean Acheson Papers
George Elsey Papers
Paul Hoffman Papers
Albert Huntington Papers
Edgar Johnson Papers
John Melby Papers
John Ohly Papers
Theodore Tannenwald Papers
Harry S. Truman Papers

Oral Histories

Becker, Nathan. Truman Library
Bond, Niles. Truman Library
Bowie, Robert. Eisenhower Library
Briggs, Ellis. Eisenhower Library
Clark, Mark. Eisenhower Library
Danielian, N.R.. Eisenhower Library
Draper, William. Eisenhower Library
Fitzgerald, Dennis. Eisenhower Library
Folsom, Marion. Eisenhower Library
Gray, Gordon. Eisenhower Library
Halaby, Najeeb. Eisenhower Library
Hanes, John. Eisenhower Library
Lacy, William. Eisenhower Library
Lightner, E. Allen. Truman library

Muccio, John. Truman Library
Tannenwald, Theodore. Truman Library
Wood, C. Tyler. Truman Library

Published Primary Sources

BRITAIN
Bullen, Roger, ed. *Documents on British Policy Overseas*, series 2, vol. 2. London:
    HMSO, 1988.
Yasamee, Heather, and K.J. Hamilton. *Documents on British Policy Overseas*, series
    2, vol. 4. London: HMSO, 1991.
House of Commons. *Debates*.
Royal Institute of International Affairs. *Documents on International Affairs*.

CANADA
Department of External Affairs. Statements and Speeches.
Department of National Defence. Reports.
Barry, Don, ed. *Documents on Canadian External Relations*, vols. 18–19, 1952–53.
    Ottawa: Government Printing Office, 1990, 1991.
Mackenzie, Hector. *Documents on Canadian External Relations*, vol. 14, 1948.
    Ottawa: Government Printing Office, 1994.
House of Commons. *Debates*.

UNITED STATES
Library of Congress. Declassified Documents Reference System. Research
    Publications. Retrospective Collection. Woodbridge, Connecticut.
Department of Defense. *United States: Vietnam Relations, 1945–1967.*
Department of State. *Foreign Relations of the United States 1945–1954.*
– *Bulletin.*
– *Treaties and Other International Acts.*
Mutual Security Agency, *Mutual Security Program.*

SECONDARY SOURCES

Acheson, Dean. *Present at the Creation: My Years in the State Department.* New York:
    Norton, 1969.
Adamthwaite, Anthony. "Overstretched and Overstrung: Eden, the Foreign
    Office and the Making of Policy, 1951–5." *International Affairs* 64 (spring
    1988): 241–58.
Alcock, Christian. "Britain and the Korean War, 1950–1953." PHD thesis,
    University of Manchester, 1986.
Ambrose, Stephen. *Eisenhower, the President.* London: Allen & Unwin, 1984.

Anderson, David L. *Trapped by Success: The Eisenhower Administration and Vietnam.* New York: Columbia University Press, 1991.

Aronsen, Lawrence. "The Northern Frontier: United States Trade and Investment in Canada, 1945–1953." PH D thesis, University of Toronto, 1980.

Baldwin, Frank. *Without Parallel: The American-Korean Relationship since 1945.* New York: Pantheon, 1975.

Bartlett, C.J. *The Long Retreat: A Short History of British Defence Policy.* London: Macmillan, 1972.

Beecroft, S.J. "Walking The Tightrope: Canadian China Policy, 1948–1957." PH D thesis, University of Cambridge, 1986.

Bernstein, Barton. "New Light on the Korean War." *International History Review* 3 (April 1981): 256–77.

Billings-Yun, Melanie. *Decision against War: Eisenhower and Dien Bien Phu, 1954.* New York: Columbia University Press, 1988.

Blum, Robert. *Drawing the Line: The Origin of the American Containment Policy in East Asia.* New York: Norton, 1982.

Boardman, Robert. *Britain and the People's Republic of China, 1949–1974.* London: Macmillan, 1976.

Borden, William. *The Pacific Alliance: United States Foreign Economic Policy and Japanese Trade Recovery, 1947–1954.* Madison: University of Wisconsin Press, 1984.

Borg, Dorothy, and Waldo Heinrichs, eds. *Uncertain Years: Chinese-American Relations, 1947–1950.* New York: Columbia University Press, 1980.

Brands, Henry. *Bound to Empire.* New York: Oxford University Press, 1992.

– *Cold Warriors: Eisenhower's Generation and American Foreign Policy.* New York: Columbia University Press, 1988.

– "The Dwight D. Eisenhower Administration, Syngman Rhee and the 'Other' Geneva Conference of 1954." *Pacific Historical Review* 56 (February 1987): 59–85.

Brinkley, Douglas, ed. *Dean Acheson and the Making of U.S. Foreign Policy.* New York: St Martin's Press, 1993.

Bullock, Alan. *Ernest Bevin: Foreign Secretary 1945–1951.* London: Heinemann, 1983.

Cable, James. *The Geneva Conference of 1954 on Indochina.* London: Macmillan, 1986.

Calingaert, Daniel. "Nuclear Weapons and the Korean War." *Journal of Strategic Studies* 11 (June 1988): 177–202.

Cameron, Allan. *Viet-Nam Crisis: A Documentary History, 1940–1956.* Ithaca: Cornell University Press, 1971.

Canadian Institute of Public Opinion. Polls and Special Releases.

Carlton, David. *Anthony Eden.* London: Allen & Unwin, 1986.

Chauvel, Jean. *Commentaire: D'Alger à Berne (1944–1952)*. Paris, 1972.

Chen, Jian. "China's Changing Aims during the Korean War." *Journal of American–East Asian Relations* 1 (Spring 1992): 8–41.

Cohen, Warren. *America's Response to China*. New York: Wiley, 1980.

– "Conversations with Chinese Friends: Zhou Enlai's Associates Reflect on Chinese-American Relations in the 1940s and the Korean War." *Diplomatic History* 11 (summer 1987): 283–9.

– ed. *New Frontiers in American-East Asian Relations: Essays Presented to Dorothy Borg*. New York: Columbia University Press, 1983.

Cohen, Warren, and Akira Iriye, eds. *The Great Powers in East Asia*. New York: Columbia University Press, 1990.

Colville, John. *The Fringes of Power: 10 Downing Street Diaries, 1939–1955*. London: Hodder and Stoughton, 1985.

Condit, Kenneth. *The Joint Chiefs of Staff and National Policy*. Vol. 2, *1947–1949*. Washington: Michael Glazier, 1979.

Cotton James, and Ian Neary, eds. *The Korean War in History*. Manchester: Manchester University Press, 1989.

Cumings, Bruce. *The Origins of the Korean War: Liberation and the Emergence of Separate Regimes*. Princeton: Princeton University Press, 1981.

– *The Origins of the Korean War: The Roaring of the Cataract 1947–1950*. Princeton: Princeton University Press, 1990.

– ed. *Child of Conflict: The Korean-American Relationship, 1943–1953*. Seattle: University of Washington Press, 1983.

Dallos, Jacques. *La guerre d'Indochine, 1945–1954*. Paris: Editions du Seuil, 1987.

Darwin, John. *Britain and Decolonisation*. London: Macmillan, 1988.

Deighton, Anne, ed. *Britain and the First Cold War*. New York: St Martin's Press, 1990.

Devillers, Philippe, and Jean Lacouture. *End of a War: Indochina 1954*. New York: Praeger, 1969.

Dilks, David. "'The Great Dominion': Churchill's Farewell Visits to Canada, 1952 and 1954." *Canadian Journal of History* 23 (April 1988): 49–72.

Dingman, Roger. "Atomic Diplomacy during the Korean War." *International Security* 13 (winter 1988–89): 50–91.

– "The Dagger and the Gift: The Impact of the Korean War on Japan." *Journal of American–East Asian Relations* 2 (spring 1993): 29–55.

– "John Foster Dulles and the Creation of the South-East Asia Treaty Organization in 1954." *International History Review* 11 (August 1989): 457–77.

– "Truman, Attlee and the Korean War Crisis." *The East Asian Crisis, 1945–1951*. London, 1982.

Dockrill, Michael. *British Defence since 1945*. Oxford: Blackwell, 1988.

- "The Foreign Office, Anglo-American Relations and the Korean War, June 1950–June 1951." *International Affairs* 62 (summer 1986): 459–76.

Doyle, Michael. *Empires.* Ithaca: Cornell University Press, 1986.

Duus, Peter, Ramon Myers, and Mark R. Peattie, eds. *The Japanese Informal Empire in China 1895–1937.* Princeton: Princeton University Press, 1989.

Eayrs, James. *In Defence of Canada: Growing Up Allied.* Toronto: University of Toronto Press, 1980.

- *In Defence of Canada: Indochina Roots of Complicity.* Toronto: University of Toronto Press, 1983.

Eden, Anthony. *Full Circle.* London: Cassell, 1960.

Eisenhower, Dwight. *The White House Years: Mandate for Change, 1953–1956.* New York: Doubleday, 1962.

Elgy, Georgette. *Histoire de la quatrième république: La république des contradictions, 1951–1954.* Paris: Fayard, 1965.

English, John. *Shadow of Heaven: The Life of Lester Pearson: 1897–1948.* Toronto: Lester and Orpen Dennys, 1989.

- *The Worldly Years: The Life of Lester Pearson, 1949–1972.* Toronto: Knopf, 1992.

Etzold, Thomas, and John Gaddis. *Containment: Documents on American Policy and Strategy, 1945–1950.* New York: Columbia University Press, 1978.

Evans, Paul, and Michael Frolic, eds. *Reluctant Adversaries: Canada and the People's Republic of China.* Toronto: University of Toronto Press, 1991.

Fall, Bernard, ed. *Ho Chi Minh on Revolution: Selected Writings, 1920–66.* New York: Praeger, 1967.

- *The Two Vietnams.* New York: Praeger, 1967.

Farrar, Peter. "Britain's Proposal for a Buffer Zone South of the Yalu in November 1950: Was It a Neglected Opportunity to End the Fighting in Korea?" *Journal of Contemporary History* 18 (April 1983): 327–51.

Ferrell, Robert. *The Eisenhower Diaries.* New York: Norton, 1981.

Fifield, Russell. *The Diplomacy of Southeast Asia 1945–1958.* New York: Harper, 1958.

Fish, Steven. "After Stalin's Death: The Anglo-American Debate over a New Cold War." *Diplomatic History* 10 (fall 1986): 333–55.

Foot, Rosemary. "Anglo-American Relations in the Korean Crisis: The British Effort to Avert an Expanded War, December 1950–January 1951." *Diplomatic History* 10 (winter 1986): 43–57.

- "Nuclear Coercion and the Ending of the Korean Conflict." *International Security* 13 (winter 1988–89): 92–112.

- *A Substitute for Victory: The Politics of Peacemaking at the Korean Armistice Talks.* Ithaca: Cornell University Press, 1990.

- *The Wrong War: American Policy and the Dimensions of the Korean Conflict, 1950–1953.* Ithaca: Cornell University Press, 1985.

Gaddis, John Lewis. "The American 'Wedge' Strategy, 1949–1955." In *Sino-American Relations, 1945–1955*, ed. Harry Harding and Yuan Ming. Wilmington: Scholarly Resources, 1989.

– "The Emerging Post-Revisionist Synthesis on the Origins of the Cold War." *Diplomatic History* 7 (summer 1983): 171–90.

– *The Long Peace: Inquiries into the History of the Cold War.* New York: Oxford University Press, 1987.

– *Strategies of Containment: A Critical Appraisal of Post-War American National Security Policy.* New York: Oxford University Press, 1982.

– "Was the Truman Doctrine a Turning Point?" *Foreign Affairs* 52 (January 1974): 386–402.

Galan, Meroslav. "Canada-Korean Relations 1947–55: The Continentalization of Canadian Foreign Policy." PH D thesis, McGill University, 1981.

Gallichio, Marc. *The Cold War Begins in Asia.* New York: Columbia University Press, 1988.

Gallup, George H. *The Gallup International Public Opinion Polls: Great Britain, 1937–1975.* New York: Random House, 1976.

Gardner, Lloyd. *Approaching Vietnam.* New York: Norton, 1988.

George, Alexander, and Richard Smoke. *Deterrence in American Foreign Policy: Theory and Practice.* New York: Columbia University Press, 1974.

Gibbons, William. *The U.S. Government and the Vietnam War: Executive and Legislative Roles and Relations 1945–1960.* Princeton: Princeton University Press, 1986.

Gilbert, Martin. *Winston Churchill Never Despair. 1945–1965.* London: Heinemann, 1988.

Goncharov, Sergei, John Lewis, and Xue Litai. *Uncertain Partners: Stalin, Mao and the Korean War.* Stanford: Stanford University Press, 1993.

Gopal, Sarvepalli. *Jawaharlal Nehru: A Biography 1947–1956.* London: Jonathan Cape, 1979.

Granatstein, Jack, and Robert Cuff. *American Dollars, Canadian Prosperity.* Toronto: Samuel Stevens, 1978.

Grasso, June. *Harry Truman's Two-China Policy, 1948–1950.* New York: M.E. Sharpe, 1987.

Griffith, Robert. "Dwight D. Eisenhower and the Corporate Commonwealth." *American Historical Review* 87 (February 1982): 87–122.

Guerrier, Steven. "NSC-68 and the Truman Rearmament 1950–1953." PH D thesis, University of Michigan, 1988.

Guhin, Michael. *John Foster Dulles.* New York: Columbia University Press, 1972.

Halliday, Jon, and Bruce Cumings. *Korea: The Unknown War.* London: Viking, 1988.

Hammer, Ellen. *The Struggle for Indochina, 1940–1955.* Stanford: Stanford University Press, 1966.

Harding, Harry, and Yuan Ming, eds. *Sino-American Relations, 1945–1955.* Wilmington: Scholarly Resources, 1989.

Hayasaki, Yasuhiro. "British Policy towards Japan's Re-entry into International Society: 1952–57." M PHIL thesis, University of Oxford, 1990.

Hermes, Walter. *Truce Tent and Fighting Front.* Washington: U.S. Government Printing Office, 1966.

Herring, George. *America's Longest War: The United States and Vietnam, 1950–1975.* New York: Temple University Press, 1979.

– "Franco-American Conflict in Indochina, 1950–1954." In *Dien Bien Phu and the Crisis of Franco-American Relations, 1954–1955*, ed. Lawrence Kaplan and Mark Rubin. Wilmington: Scholarly Resources 1989.

– "The Truman Administration and the Restoration of French Sovereignty in Indochina." *Diplomatic History* 1 (spring 1977): 97–117.

Herring, George, and Richard Immerman. "Eisenhower, Dulles and Dienbienphu: 'The Day We Didn't Go to War' Revisited." *Journal of American History* 71 (September 1984): 343–63.

Hess, Gary. "The First American commitment in Indochina: The Acceptance of the 'Bao Dai Solution,' 1950." *Diplomatic History* 2 (fall, 1978): 331–50.

– *The United States' Emergence as a Southeast Asian Power, 1940–1950.* New York: Columbia University Press, 1987.

Hinds, A.E. "Sterling and Imperial Policy, 1945–1951." *Journal of Imperial and Commonwealth History* 15 (January 1987): 148–69.

Ho Chi Minh. *On Revolution.* New York: Praeger, 1967.

Holland, Robert. *European Decolonization, 1918–1981.* London: Macmillan, 1981.

Holmes, John. "Geneva: 1954." *International Journal* (summer 1967): 457–83.

– *The Shaping of Peace: Canada and the World Order 1943–1957.* Toronto: University of Toronto Press, 1982.

Hua Wu Yin. *Class and Communualism in Malaysia.* London: Zed Books, 1983.

Immerman, Richard, ed. *John Foster Dulles and the Diplomacy of the Cold War.* Princeton: Princeton University Press, 1990.

– "The United States and the Geneva Conference of 1954: A New Look." *Diplomatic History* 14 (winter 1990): 43–66.

Iriye, Akira. *The Cold War in Asia.* New Jersey: Prentice-Hall, 1974.

Irving, R.E.M. *The First Indochina War.* London: C. Helm, 1975.

James, Robert. *Anthony Eden.* London: Weidenfeld and Nicolson, 1986.

Jeffrey, Robin, ed. *Asia: The Winning of Independence.* London: Macmillan, 1981.

Jervis, Robert. "The Impact of the Korean War on the Cold War." *Journal of Conflict Resolution* 24 (December 1980): 563–92.

Johnson, Gregory. "North Pacific Triangle? The Impact of the Far East on Canada and Its Relations with the United States and Great Britain, 1937–1948." PH D thesis, York University, 1989.

The Joint Chiefs of Staff and the War in Vietnam: History of the Indochina Incident, 1940–1954. Vol. 1. Wilmington: Michael Glazier, 1982.

Kahin, George. *Intervention.* New York: Knopf, 1986.

Kaplan, Lawrence, and Mark Rubin, eds. *Dien Bien Phu and the Crisis of Franco-American Relations, 1954–1955: A Joint Reassessment of a Critical Decade.* Wilmington: Scholarly Resources, 1989.

Kaufman, Burton. *The Korean War: Challenges in Crisis, Credibility and Command.* Philadelphia: Temple University Press, 1986.

Keefer, Edward. "President Dwight D. Eisenhower and the End of the Korean War." *Diplomatic History* 10 (summer 1986): 267–89.

Kennan, George. *Memoirs 1925–1950,* London: Hutchinson, 1968.

Koh, B.C. "The War's Impact on the Korean Peninsula." *Journal of American–East Asian Relations* 2 (spring 1993): 57–76.

Kolko, Gabriel. *Vietnam: Anatomy of War.* New York: Pantheon, 1986.

Kolko, Joyce, and Gabriel Kolko. *The Limits of Power: The World and United States Foreign Policy, 1945–1954.* New York: Harper and Row, 1972.

Lacouture, Jean. *Ho Chi Minh: A Political Biography.* London: Allen Lane, 1968.

Lacy, Michael, ed. *The Truman Presidency.* New York: Cambridge University Press, 1989.

LaFeber, Walter. *The American Age.* New York: Norton, 1989.

– "NATO and the Korean War: A Context." *Diplomatic History* 13 (fall 1989): 461–77.

Leffler, Melvyn. "The American Conception of National Security and the Beginnings of the Cold War, 1945–1948." *American Historical Review* 89 (April 1984): 346–81.

Levant, Victor. *Quiet Complicity: Canadian Involvement in the Vietnam War.* Toronto: Between the Lines, 1986.

Levering, Ralph. *The Public and American Foreign Policy, 1918–1978.* New York: William Morrow, 1978.

Liao, Dong. "Chester A. Ronning and Canada-China Relations (1945–1954)." MA thesis, University of Regina, 1983.

Lockhart, Gregg. *Nation in Arms: The Origins of the People's Army of Vietnam.* London: Allen & Unwin, 1989.

Louis, William Roger. *Imperialism: The Robinson and Gallagher Controversy.* New York: New Viewpoints, 1976.

Louis, William Roger, and Hedley Bull, eds. *The Special Relationship: Anglo-American Relations since 1945.* Oxford: Oxford University Press, 1986.

Lowe, Peter. *The Origins of the Korean War.* London: Longman, 1986.

Lundestad, Geir. *The American 'Empire.'* London: Norwegian University Press, 1990.

Lyons, Gene. *Military Policy and Economic Aid: The Korean Case, 1950–1953.* Columbus: Ohio State University Press, 1960.

McCormick, Thomas. *America's Half-Century: United States Foreign Policy in the Cold War.* Baltimore: Johns Hopkins University Press, 1989.

MacDonald, Callum. *Korea: The War Before Vietnam.* London: Free Press, 1986.

Macdonald, Donald Stone. *U.S. Korean Relations from Liberation to Self-Reliance: The Twenty Year Record.* Boulder: Westview Press, 1992.

McGlothlen, Ronald. "Acheson, Economics, and the American Commitment in Korea, 1947–1950." *Pacific Historical Review* 57 (August 1989): 23–54.

McLean, David. "American Nationalism, the China Myth, and the Truman Doctrine: The Question of Accommodation with Peking, 1949–1950." *Diplomatic History* 10 (winter 1986): 25–42.

McMahon, Robert. "The Cold War in Asia: Toward a New Synthesis?" *Diplomatic History* 12 (summer 1988): 307–27.

– *Colonialism and the Cold War: The United States and the Struggle for Indonesian Independence, 1945–1949.* Ithaca: Cornell University Press, 1981.

Mao Tse-tung. *Selected Works.* Vols. 4,5. Peking: Foreign Languages Press, 1971, 1977.

Marks, Frederick. "The Real Hawk at Dienbienphu: Dulles or Eisenhower?" *Pacific Historical Review* 59 (August 1990): 297–322.

Martin, Edwin. *Divided Counsel.* Lexington, Ky: University Press of Kentucky, 1986.

Matray, James. *The Reluctant Crusade.* Honolulu: University of Hawaii Press, 1985.

Mayers, David. *Cracking the Monolith: U.S. Policy against the Sino-Soviet Alliance, 1949–1955.* Baton Rouge: University of Louisiana Press, 1986.

– *George Kennan and the Dilemmas of U.S. Foreign Policy.* New York: Oxford University Press, 1988.

Melanson, Richard, and David Meyers, eds. *Reevaluating Eisenhower: American Foreign Policy in the Fifties.* Urbana: University of Illinois Press, 1987.

Merrill, Denis. "Indo-American Relations, 1947–50: A Missed Opportunity in Asia." *Diplomatic History* 11 (summer 1987): 203–26.

Millett, Allan, and Peter Maslowski. *For the Common Defense: A Military History of the United States of America.* New York: Free Press, 1984.

Mommsen, Wolfgang, and Jürgen Osterhammel, eds. *Imperialism and After.* London: Allen & Unwin, 1986.

Moore, R.J. *Making the New Commonwealth.* Oxford: Oxford University Press, 1987.

Morgan, Kenneth. *Labour in Power.* Oxford: Clarendon Press, 1984.

Muirhead, Bruce. "Canadian Trade Policy, 1949–57: The Failure of the Anglo-European Option." PH D thesis, York University, 1986.

Munro, John, and Alex Inglis, eds. *Mike: The Memoirs of the Right Honourable Lester Pearson.* Vol. 2, *1948–1957.* Toronto: University of Toronto Press, 1973.

Nagai, Yonosuke, and Akira Iriye, eds. *The Origins of the Cold War in Asia.* New York: Columbia University Press, 1977.

Nelson, Anna. "President Truman and the Evolution of the National Security Council." *Journal of American History* 72 (September 1985): 360–78.

O'Neill, Robert. *Australia in the Korean War, 1950–1953, Strategy and Diplomacy.* Canberra: Australian Government Publication Service, 1981.

Ovendale, Ritchie. *The English-speaking Alliance: Britain, the United States, the Dominions and the Cold War, 1945–1951.* London: Allen & Unwin, 1985.

– ed. *The Foreign Policy of the British Labour Governments, 1945–51,* Leicester: Leicester University Press, 1984.

Pemberton, Gregory. "Australia the United States and the Indochina Crisis of 1954." *Diplomatic History* 13 (winter 1989): 45–66.

Poole, Walter. *The Joint Chiefs of Staff and National Policy.* Vol. 4, *1950–1952.* Wilmington: Michael Glazier, 1979.

Porter, Brian. *Britain and the Rise of Communist China: A Study of British Attitudes, 1945–1954.* London: Oxford University Press, 1967.

Porter, Garath. *Vietnam: A History in Documents.* New York: New American Library, 1981.

Randle, Robert. *Geneva, 1954: The Settlement of the Indochinese War.* Princeton: Princeton University Press, 1969.

Reeve, W.D. *The Republic of Korea.* London: Oxford University Press, 1963.

Reid, Escott. *Envoy to Nehru.* London: Oxford University Press, 1981.

Reynolds, David. "A 'Special Relationship'? America, Britain and the International Order since the Second World War." *International Affairs* 62 (winter 1985–86): 1–20.

Robinson, Ronald, and John Gallagher. "The Imperialism of Free Trade." *Economic History Review* 6, no. 1 (August 1953): 1–15.

Rosecrance, R.N. *Defense of the Realm.* New York: Columbia University Press, 1968.

Ross, Douglas. *In the Interests of Peace: Canada and Vietnam, 1954–1973.* Toronto: University of Toronto Press, 1984.

Rotter, Andrew. *The Path to Vietnam: Origins of American Commitment to Southeast Asia.* Ithaca: Cornell University Press, 1987.

– "The Triangular Route to Vietnam: The United States, Great Britain, and Southeast Asia, 1945–1950." *International History Review* 6 (August 1984): 404–23.

Schaller, Michael. *The American Occupation of Japan: The Origins of the Cold War in Asia.* New York: Oxford University Press, 1985.

Shai, Aron. "Imperialism Imprisoned: The Closure of British Firms in the People's Republic of China." *English Historical Review* 103 (January 1989): 88–109.

Schnabel, James. *The Joint Chiefs of Staff and National Policy.* Vol. 1, *1945–1947.* Wilmington: Michael Glazier, 1979.

Schnabel, James, and Robert Watson. *The Joint Chiefs of Staff and National Policy.* Vol. 3, *The Korean War.* Wilmington: Michael Glazier, 1979.

Short, Anthony. *The Origins of the Vietnam War.* London: Longman, 1989.

Shuckburgh, Evelyn. *Descent to Suez: Diaries 1951–56.* London: Weidenfeld and Nicolson, 1986.

Simon, Rita James. *Public Opinion in America: 1936–1970.* Chicago: Rand McNally, 1974.

Smith, Denis. *Diplomacy of Fear: Canada and the Cold War, 1941–1948.* Toronto: University of Toronto Press, 1988.

Smith, Raymond, and John Zametica. "The Cold Warrior: Clement Attlee Reconsidered, 1945–1947." *International Affairs* 61 (spring 1985): 237–52.

Stairs, Denis. *The Diplomacy of Constraint: Canada, the Korean War and the United States.* Toronto: University of Toronto Press, 1974.

Strang, Lord. *Home and Abroad.* London: André Deutsch, 1956.

Stueck, William. "The Korean War as International History." *Diplomatic History* 10 (fall 1986): 291–309.

– "The Limits of Influence: British Policy and American Expansion of the War in Korea." *Pacific Historical Review* 55 (February 1986): 65–95

– *The Road to Confrontation: American Policy towards China and Korea, 1947–1950.* Chapel Hill: University of North Carolina Press, 1981.

– "The Soviet Union and the Origins of the Korean War." *World Politics* 4 (July 1976): 622–35.

Suh, Dae-Sook. *Kim Il Sung.* New York: Columbia University Press, 1988.

Tang, James Tuck-Hong. *Britain's Encounter with Revolutionary China, 1949–1954.* New York: St Martin's Press, 1992.

Tarling, Nicholas. "The United Kingdom and the Origins of the Colombo Plan." *Journal of Commonwealth and Comparative Politics*, March 1986, 3–34.

Thomson, Dale. *Louis St Laurent: Canadian.* New York: St Martin's Press, 1968.

Thorne, Christopher. *Allies of a Kind: The United States, Britain, and the War against Japan, 1941–1945.* New York: Oxford University Press, 1981.

Truman, Harry. *Memoirs: Years of Trial and Hope.* New York: Doubleday, 1956.

Truscott, Peter. "The Korean War in British Foreign and Domestic Policy, 1950–1952." D PHIL thesis, University of Oxford, 1986.

Tucker, Nancy. "China's Place." In *Dean Acheson and the Making of U.S. Foreign Policy*, ed. Douglas Brinkley. New York: St Martin's Press, 1993.

– *Patterns in the Dust: Chinese-American Relations and the Recognition Controversy, 1949–1950.* New York: Columbia University Press, 1983.

Warner, Geoffrey. "The Anglo-American Relationship." *Diplomatic History* 13 (fall 1989): 479–99.

– "The United States and Vietnam 1945–1965, Parts 1–2," *International Affairs* 48 (July–October 1972): 379–94; 593–615.

Watson, Robert. *The Joint Chiefs of Staff and National Policy.* Vol. 5, *1953–1954.* Wilmington: Michael Glazier, 1986.

Watt, D.C. "Britain and the Cold War in the Far East." In *The Origins of the Cold War in Asia*, ed. Yonosuke Nagai and Akira Iriye, New York: Columbia University Press, 1977.

Weathersby, Kathryn. "The Soviet Role in the Early Phase of the Korean War: New Documentary Evidence." *Journal of American–East Asian Relations* 2 (winter 1993): 425–58.

Weiler, Peter. "British Labour and the Cold War: The Foreign Policy of the Labour Governments, 1945–1951." *Journal of British Studies* 26 (January 1987): 54–82.

Wells, Samuel. "The Origins of Massive Retaliation." *Political Science Quarterly* 96 (spring 1981): 31–52.

– "Sounding the Toscin: NSC 68 and the Soviet Threat." *International Security* 4 (fall 1979): 116–58.

West, Philip. "Confronting the West: China as David and Goliath in the Korean War." *Journal of American–East Asian Relations* 2 (spring 1993): 5–28.

Whiting, Allen. *China Crosses the Yalu: The Decision to Enter the Korean War.* Stanford: Stanford University Press, 1960.

Wolf, David. "To Secure a Convenience: Britain Recognized China – 1950." *Journal of Contemporary History* 18 (April 1983): 299–326.

Young, John. "Churchill's Bid for Peace with Moscow, 1954." *History* 73 (October 1988): 425–48.

– "Churchill, the Russians and the Western Alliance: The Three-Power Conference at Bermuda, December 1953." *English Historical Review* 101 (October 1986): 889–912.

– *The Foreign Policy of Churchill's Peacetime Administration, 1951–1955.* Leicester: Leicester University Press, 1988.

Zhang, Shuguang. "'Preparedness Eliminates Mishaps': The CCP's Security Concerns in 1949–1950 and the Origins of the Sino-American Confrontation." *Journal of American–East Asian Relations* 2 (spring 1992): 42–72.

Index